THE MATERIAL GEOGRAPHIES OF THE BELT AND ROAD INITIATIVE

Infrastructures and Political Ecologies on the New Silk Road

Edited by
Elia Apostolopoulou, Han Cheng,
Jonathan Silver and Alan Wiig

First published in Great Britain in 2026 by

Bristol University Press
University of Bristol
1–9 Old Park Hill
Bristol
BS2 8BB
UK
t: +44 (0)117 374 6645
e: bup-info@bristol.ac.uk

Details of international sales and distribution partners are available at bristoluniversitypress.co.uk

© Editorial selection and editorial matter © Elia Apostolopoulou, Han Cheng, Jonathan Silver and Alan Wiig 2026. Individual chapters © their respective authors 2026

DOI: 10.51952/9781529240665

The digital PDF and ePub versions of this title are available open access and distributed under the terms of the Creative Commons Attribution-NonCommercial-NoDerivatives 4.0 International licence (https://creativecommons.org/licenses/by-nc-nd/4.0/) which permits reproduction and distribution for non-commercial use without further permission provided the original work is attributed.

British Library Cataloguing in Publication Data
A catalogue record for this book is available from the British Library

ISBN 978-1-5292-4064-1 paperback
ISBN 978-1-5292-4065-8 ePub
ISBN 978-1-5292-4066-5 OA PDF

The right of Elia Apostolopoulou, Han Cheng, Jonathan Silver and Alan Wiig to be identified as editors of this work has been asserted by them in accordance with the Copyright, Designs and Patents Act 1988.

All rights reserved: no part of this publication may be reproduced, stored in a retrieval system, or transmitted in any form or by any means, electronic, mechanical, photocopying, recording, or otherwise without the prior permission of Bristol University Press.

Every reasonable effort has been made to obtain permission to reproduce copyrighted material. If, however, anyone knows of an oversight, please contact the publisher.

The statements and opinions contained within this publication are solely those of the editors and contributors and not of the University of Bristol or Bristol University Press. The University of Bristol and Bristol University Press disclaim responsibility for any injury to persons or property resulting from any material published in this publication.

Bristol University Press works to counter discrimination on grounds of gender, race, disability, age and sexuality.

Cover design: Hayes Design and Advertising
Front cover image: Elia Apostolopoulou

Contents

List of Figures and Tables	v
Notes on the Contributors	vii
Acknowledgements	vii
Introduction: The World Transformed – Grounding the Belt and Road Initiative	1
Elia Apostolopoulou, Han Cheng, Jonathan Silver and Alan Wiig	
1 The Contested Coal-Fired Power in the Belt and Road Initiative: Indonesia as a Case Study *Bowen Gu*	29
2 Dynamics of Grassroots Collectivism in Thailand's Special Economic Zones: Cases of Natural Resource Conflicts within the Belt and Road Initiative *Ratchada Arpornsilp*	44
3 Railways of Hope, Railways of Conflict: Governance of the Domestic Environmental Impacts of a Belt and Road Project *Xiaofeng Liu*	59
4 A Debt to Whom? The Nature Questions in Sino-Sri Lankan Development Narratives *Orlando Woods, Kanchana Ruwanpura, Loritta Chan and Barnabas Mah*	76
5 Waiting, Acceleration, Stabilization: Polychronic Temporalities as Drivers of a Large-Scale Chinese Green Technology Project in Thuringia, Eastern Germany *Hannes Langguth*	93
6 Silk Road on Ice: Extractivism, Climate Change and Resistances *Ksenija Hanaček*	113
7 Donor Competition, Local Agency and Contingency: Jakarta-Bandung High-Speed Railway in Indonesia *Caixia Mao*	129

8	A Postcolonial Belt and Road Initiative? Dependency, Development and Geopolitics in China-Latin America Relations *Simone Vegliò*	146
9	The Elusive Rainbow at the End of the Belt and Road: Chinese Investment, Finance and Trade Controversies in Southern Africa *Patrick Bond*	161
10	Beyond the Logistical Monolith: Multiplicity and Differentiation Along the Adriatic Corridor *Francesca Governa, Leonardo Ramondetti, Astrid Safina, Angelo Sampieri and Alberto Valz Gris*	182
11	Capitalizing on the Logistical Future: Discounting Uncertainty in the Georgian Belt and Road Initiative *Evelina Gambino*	198
12	Infrastructure-Led Development, Urban Transformation and Inequality in China's Belt and Road Initiative: A Marxist Postcolonial Geographies Analysis *Elia Apostolopoulou*	214

Afterword: The Material Futures of the Belt and Road Initiative 237
Elia Apostolopoulou, Han Cheng, Jonathan Silver and Alan Wiig

Index 249

List of Figures and Tables

Figures

0.1	Gates to the Allama Iqbal Industrial City Special Economic Zone in Pakistan, under construction	2
0.2	How the BRI is restructuring the planet	6
0.3	'The beginning of hope', Piraeus Port, Athens, Greece	18
0.4	Piraeus COSCO container terminal	18
0.5	A COSCO container on the Northern Corridor in Kenya	19
0.6	Underneath the BRI-financed Orange Line in Lahore	19
0.7	A wall on the boardwalk reads 'No to the mega-port', Chancay, Peru	20
0.8	Tangier, Morocco, a new waterfront development	21
0.9	The Export-Import Bank of China-funded standard gauge railway in Kenya	21
0.10	Valencia port (Spain), next to Las Arenas beach – COSCO Shipping operates one of the port terminals	22
2.1	Locations of SEZ areas and Bun Rueang wetland in Chiang Rai province	47
2.2	Locations of SEZ areas and targeted land for appropriation in Nongkhai province	48
3.1	Map of the China-Laos railway	60
3.2	A slogan on the wall at the China-Laos railway	66
4.1	A view of the Colombo Port City under construction, looking north from Galle Face Green	78
5.1	Construction noticeboard for Erfurter-Kreuz industrial site in Arnstadt-Ichtershausen. In the background is the construction site of the new gigafactory for manufacturing electric vehicle battery cells by the Chinese corporation CATL	98
5.2	Drone image showing the construction site of the new gigafactory for manufacturing electric vehicle battery cells by the Chinese corporation CATL in the Erfurter-Kreuz industrial park. In the background are other industries and the town of Arnstadt, Thuringia	100

6.1	Icebreaker *Xue Long* in the middle of the Arctic Ocean	117
10.1	Adriatic Corridor	184
10.2	Trieste Port, Dock 5, May 2022	189
10.3	Container stocking in Aspropyrgos, June 2022	191
11.1	Anaklia Port building site, 2018	199
11.2	Map of Georgia's key transit infrastructure	201
11.3	The abandoned port territory from Lela's window	204
11.4	The abandoned port territory, April 2023	209
12.1	Piraeus port, Lipasmata redevelopment area, Athens, Greece	215
A.1	Tangier, Morocco – a new waterfront development	245

Tables

1.1	Overview of CFPPs in the case studies	32
1.2	Timeline of legal mobilization against Teluk Sepang power plant in Bengkulu	34
A.1	Interviewees	109
7.1	The final bidding proposals by China (KCIC) and Japan for the Jakarta-Bandung HSR	133

Notes on the Contributors

Elia Apostolopoulou is Associate Professor at the Centre for Environmental Policy at Imperial College London. A human geographer and political ecologist, her research examines how infrastructure, urban investments, and neoliberal policies reshape spaces, natures and livelihoods, with a focus on grassroots struggles for justice. She has held positions at the Universities of Cambridge and Oxford and at the Autonomous University of Barcelona and she was a visiting scholar at the City University of New York (CUNY) and LMU Munich. Elia has published three more books and has received major international fellowships, including Marie Skłodowska-Curie, Carson and Ramón y Cajal, and funding from the European Union, UK Research and Innovation, the British Academy and the Royal Geographical Society. Since 2020, she has been an editor for *Dialogues in Human Geography*.

Ratchada Arpornsilp is PhD candidate in the Resources, Environment and Development Research Group at the Crawford School of Public Policy, Australian National University. She was a Thai Fulbright Hubert H. Humphrey Fellow for 2017–18 at the International Program, College of Agriculture and Life Sciences, Cornell University. She has over 12 years of professional experience with international NGOs and public agencies working in regional development programmes across Asia and the Pacific region. Her research interests are in the field of environmental politics, particularly at the interface of natural resource conflicts and grassroots activism, in light of large-scale development projects.

Patrick Bond is University of Johannesburg Distinguished Professor of Sociology and Director of the Centre for Social Change. His best-known book is *Elite Transition*, and he authored the democratic government's first White Paper, on Reconstruction and Development, in President Mandela's office in 1994. He is involved in many local and international labour, environmental and social movement networks.

Loritta Chan is a researcher with a focus on young people's livelihoods, cities and the environment. She holds a PhD in Human Geography from the University of Edinburgh, where her dissertation project was centred on the lives of children from waste picker families in Delhi. Loritta was a Postdoctoral Fellow at the University of Edinburgh on a project on inclusive cities that was co-produced together with young people in India and Brazil. More recently, she was a Postdoctoral Fellow at the University of Hong Kong, where she focused on water and sustainable cities.

Han Cheng is Visiting Senior Research Fellow at the Lise Meitner Research Group titled 'China in the Global System of Science' at the Max Planck Institute for the History of Science, Berlin. His research examines the shifting geographical imagination and spatial politics of knowledge production in relation to China's global expansion. Han received his PhD from the University of Cambridge and previously held positions in Beijing and Singapore. He is Editor of *Dialogues in Human Geography* and an editorial board member for *Political Geography* and *The People's Map of Global China* and *Global China Pulse*.

Evelina Gambino is Margaret Tyler Research Fellow in Geography at Girton College, University of Cambridge. Her research is concerned with a situated analysis of global logistics. Through ethnographic work around connectivity infrastructures in Georgia and the South Caucasus, Evelina's research maps the ways in which planetary projects of circulation, such as the Belt and Road Initiative, are translated into local contexts. In dialogue with feminist critiques of capitalism, her analysis highlights the different kinds of work that this translation entails.

Francesca Governa is Professor of Economic and Political Geography at the Department of Urban Studies and Planning at Politecnico and Università di Torino, Italy. From 2020 to 2023 she served as Scientific Coordinator of the Marie Skłodowska-Curie action SURGE – Sinofinancialization and urban change in Addis Ababa and Nairobi. During this time, she also acted as Principal Investigator for the Rescaling the Belt and Road Initiative: Urbanisation Processes, Innovation Patterns and Global Investments in Urban China project, funded by MUR – Italian Ministry of Research. Currently, she leads two research projects on the financialization of urban megaprojects in Milan, Italy, funded by the Politecnico di Torino and MUR. She has published extensively in both national and international journals and books about urban China, global infrastructure and urbanization processes, and critical urban theory.

Bowen Gu is Postdoctoral Research Fellow in the Global Development Policy Center at Boston University. Her research concerns the political ecology of coal and transition minerals in China and 'Global China', and explores the intersection of environmental governance, energy transition and climate justice. Bowen holds a PhD in Environmental Science and Technology from the Institute of Environmental Science and Technology at the Autonomous University of Barcelona (ICTA-UAB), where she has also been a member of the Global Atlas of Environmental Justice team.

Ksenija Hanaček is a political ecologist and a postdoctoral fellow in Global Development Studies at the University of Helsinki and the Institute of Environmental Science and Technology at the Autonomous University of Barcelona (ICTA-UAB). Her research focuses on environmental conflicts caused by extractive, industrial and infrastructural projects in the Arctic region. Her current research examines the Belt and Road Initiative expansion to the Arctic ('Polar Silk Road'), climate coloniality, green extractivism, nuclear supply chain and environmental justice struggles in post-Soviet spaces.

Hannes Langguth is an urban researcher in the German Research Foundation (DFG)-funded research training group 'Urban Future-Making' at HafenCity University Hamburg. His work lies at the intersection of critical urban theory, urban ethnography and urban planning and governance. His current research addresses the planning and governance of large-scale green transition projects and their (trans)local urban effects.

Xiaofeng Liu is Assistant Professor in the Urban Governance and Design Thrust at the Hong Kong University of Science and Technology (Guangzhou). She obtained a PhD in Geography from the University of Hong Kong with a thesis on the environmental politics of China's Green Belt and Road Initiative. Her research interests include political geography, environmental politics and governance, infrastructure, the Belt and Road Initiative and digital transformation. Her research contributes to the understanding of the processes and consequences of a rising and globalizing China.

Barnabas Mah is Research Assistant at the Urban Institute, Singapore Management University. His research interests are diverse and include urban heritage and place-making, urban and environmental history, and public housing and transportation in Singapore and Southeast Asia. He holds a BA (Hons) in Urban Studies from Yale-NUS College, Singapore.

Caixia Mao is PhD candidate in Urban Planning at Columbia University. Her current research investigates the politics of transnational railway projects funded by China and Japan in Indonesia by looking at the Jakarta-Bandung high-speed railway project and the Jakarta mass rapid transit project. Besides infrastructure research, she has conducted research on sustainability governance and worked as a policy researcher prior to starting her PhD. She has published in a variety of journals, including: *Technological Forecasting and Social Change*; *The Pacific Review*; *Resources, Conservation and Recycling*; and the *Journal of International Development*. She has native-level proficiency in both Chinese and Japanese.

Leonardo Ramondetti is Post-doctoral Researcher at the Interuniversity Department of Regional and Urban Studies and Planning, Università di Torino, Italy. His field of research is urban design theory and planning culture, with a particular interest in infrastructure-led urbanizations. He is the author of *The Enriched Field: Urbanising the Central Plains of China* (2022), and is Principal Investigator for the 'HyperSCAPES: Extreme infrastructure projects and new forms of urbanity in the Anthropocene' project, funded by the Italian Ministry of Research (FIS 2023), which investigates the spatial, environmental and socioeconomic impact of large-scale infrastructure projects in Southern Europe, Central China and South America.

Kanchana Ruwanpura is Professor at the University of Gothenburg, Sweden, and an Honorary Fellow at the University of Edinburgh, Scotland. With a PhD from the University of Cambridge, England, she has published extensively on feminist, labour and ethnic politics. She is the author of *Garments without Guilt?* (2022) and co-editor of the *Routledge Handbook of Contemporary Sri Lanka*. Her work has been funded by the European Research Council, the British Academy Global Challenges Research Fund, the Economic and Social Research Council, the Natural Environment Research Council, and the Arts and Humanities Research Council. She currently holds a fellowship supported by the Bromanska Foundation, and she was a fellow of the Humboldt Foundation, National University of Singapore-Asia Research Institute, Singapore, and Institute for Advanced Study, Nantes, France.

Astrid Safina is Post-doctoral Researcher at Sapienza University of Rome. She was a post-doctoral researcher at Politecnico di Torino, a visiting scholar at South China University of Technology and a junior research assistant at Universidad Central de Venezuela. Her research collocates at the intersection of Chinese urbanization processes, infrastructural studies and global urbanism. Her most recent work includes the 'Rescaling the Belt and Road Initiative' project, looking at the complexities of infrastructural and logistical spaces in Europe.

Angelo Sampieri is Associate Professor of Urban Planning at the Interuniversity Department of Regional and Urban Studies and Planning, Politecnico di Torino, Italy. His research deals with theories, cultures and techniques of contemporary urban planning and design with particular attention paid to the relationships with infrastructure and landscape. On these issues, he participated in research in Europe and China, and wrote articles and edited volumes. Since 2017 he has been member of the China Room Research Group, within which he participated in design and research activities on urbanization processes in contemporary China. Until 2024 he worked on the 'Rescaling the Belt and Road Initiative: Urbanization Processes, Innovation Models and Global Investments' project, focusing on the variety of urbanization patterns produced by contemporary global infrastructure networks.

Jonathan Silver is Deputy Director and Senior Research Fellow at the Urban Institute, University of Sheffield. He is author of the MIT Press-released *The Infrastructural South: Techno-Environments of the Third Wave of Urbanization*, which builds on long-term investigations of infrastructure across diverse urban contexts. He leads the European Research Council-funded GlobalCORRIDOR project, which investigates the role of new infrastructure corridors in shaping the urbanization process and inequality in a series of global regions.

Alberto Valz Gris is an urban geographer and Post-doctoral Researcher at the Interuniversity Department of Regional and Urban Studies and Planning, Politecnico di Torino, Italy. His research is concerned with the intersection of urbanization processes, natural resource extraction and global infrastructure. His recent projects have explored the dynamics of natural resource extraction and the layered histories of infrastructural development, drawing on fieldwork in different contexts, such as the boom of lithium extraction in the Atacama, Argentina and Chile, and the urban outcomes of port expansion in Piraeus, Greece, and Genova, Italy.

Simone Vegliò is Project Researcher at Malmö University. He holds a PhD in Geography from King's College London, and his research is situated at the intersection of urban geography and political geography. His current work interrogates the implementation of 'global infrastructure' in South America's River Plate basin. By focusing on commercial ports as critical infrastructures serving the basin's agribusiness structure, he investigates the socio-spatial and environmental impacts of infrastructure investments, specifically evaluating China's role in the region. His previous research analysed neo-extractive and logistical operations in the southern area of Dock Sud, Buenos Aires, assessing the socio-material consequences on the urban environment. Earlier, he explored Latin America's urbanization from a historical and 'postcolonial' perspective.

Alan Wiig is Associate Professor in the Department of Geography at the University of Florida. His research critiques the new digital divides emerging alongside smart city and artificial intelligence projects, the anti-democratic politics of large-scale urban revitalization efforts, and the spatial strategies through which transnational logistics corridors are remaking city regions. Alan's work has been published in journals including: *Cambridge Journal of Regions, Economy, and Society*; *City: Analysis of Urban Trends, Theory, Policy, Action*; *Environment and Planning C: Politics and Space*; *Journal of Urban Technology*; *Regional Studies*; and *Urban Geography*. He is co-editor of another Bristol University Press volume, *Infrastructuring Urban Futures: The Politics of Remaking Cities* (2023).

Orlando Woods is Professor of Geography at the College of Integrative Studies, Singapore Management University, where he also serves as Director of the SMU Urban Institute. His research interests span cities, infrastructure and digital transformation in South and Southeast Asia. Orlando holds a BA (first-class honours) and a PhD in Geography from University College London and the National University of Singapore, respectively.

Acknowledgements

This book is made Open Access through the 'University of Sheffield Institutional Open Access Fund'.

Jonathan Silver would like to acknowledge this work was funded by the European Research Council (ERC) under the European Union's Horizon 2020 research and innovation programme as part of the GlobalCORRIDOR project (grant agreement ID: 947779).

Elia Apostolopoulou would like to acknowledge funding from a Cambridge Humanities Research Grant (CHRG) and a Global Sustainability Fellowship (CISL, University of Cambridge).

Introduction: The World Transformed – Grounding the Belt and Road Initiative

Elia Apostolopoulou, Han Cheng, Jonathan Silver and Alan Wiig

The new geography of the Belt and Road Initiative

As China's Belt and Road Initiative (BRI) moves into a second decade, it has become a highly visible and at times contentious international cooperation and economic strategy intersecting and influencing planetary presents and futures. Announced in 2013 by Chinese President Xi Jinping, the BRI has been heralded as the single largest infrastructure project since the post-World War II Marshall Plan, with a scope and scale perhaps unprecedented in modern history (Ferdinand, 2016). The BRI's origins are often attributed to two overlapping interpretations.

The first interpretation is based on an economic logic, in which the Government of the People's Republic of China responded to the 2008 global financial crisis with a state-funded economic stimulus package (Tooze, 2018) that supported the large-scale reorganization of accumulation regimes (Jiang, 2015) and led to the exporting of China's so-called construction boom in the post-2008 period. This response to the financial crisis also coincided with China's existing and ongoing major regional development initiatives, such as the Great Western Development beginning in 1999, the Northeast Area Revitalization since 2003 and the Rise of Central China since 2006 (Liu and Liu, 2017). The construction boom from these earlier projects resulted in major oversupply and excess productive capacity in industrial sectors (Furlong, 2022), and the gradual decline in demand, also linked to the post-2008 financial crash in the European Union and the United States, eventually led to a contraction of China's exports. In light of these developments, the BRI has been understood as a major 'spatial fix' to capital's overaccumulation crisis in China (Harvey, 2016; Summers, 2016; Zhang, 2017; Clarke, 2018; Apostolopoulou, 2021a) due to its potential

Figure 0.1: Gates to the Allama Iqbal Industrial City Special Economic Zone in Pakistan, under construction

Source: Photograph by Jonathan Silver

to revitalize economic growth by facilitating geographical expansion and spatial reorganization.

The second interpretation is based on a geopolitical logic that sees the BRI as China's strategic attempt at (re)aligning global markets and international relations away from the dominance of the United States and its power in shaping the contemporary global order over the past few decades This sits alongside a *longue durée* perspective in which the BRI is understood beyond immediate China–US relations but as part of a wider shift to global economic geography away from centuries anchored in the North Atlantic and toward the Pacific Ocean. In a geopolitical reading, the BRI can be understood primarily as a scramble over network centrality (that is, across logistics, production and telecommunication networks) that some have called the Second Cold War (Schindler et al, 2023) in which Chinese-financed transnational projects signal the rise of a new world power.

This edited volume outlines a material understanding of the BRI, drawing from these broader narratives and underlying logics while focusing on the making and living of the massive new projects that constitute the planning and delivery of this strategy.[1] Our intention is to foreground where in space – and for whom – the experiences, interactions and impacts of BRI investments, plans and operations are found. The contributions set out across the chapters of this book focus on these material dimensions of the BRI, demonstrating how grand economic and political interpretations become grounded in particular social and environmental realities. This exploration is centred around two main foci: the *political-ecological* and *infrastructural* conditions being produced. The BRI is mobilized through substantial financial commitments, with projected plans requiring up to USD 8 trillion (Hurley et al, 2018) in investment and its geographic scope involving 140 countries (Hillman, 2020) and a dizzying assortment of corporate and state actors.

After over a decade of operation, the BRI has significantly influenced the (re)making of many spaces and places. The massive investments associated with BRI projects continue to expand across ever-growing territories of logistical circulation, while diverse new construction activities proceed rapidly. From Kenya to Nepal, Jamaica to Kazakhstan, the BRI is often the dominant factor in investment inflows, leading to localized, material transformation. Debates about shifting geopolitical and economic power shaping global futures often underscore how policy makers, politicians and the public approach, debate and respond to the BRI. However, with this volume, we put specific focus on how the changes being unleashed are already being felt and experienced in many parts of the world. This book turns its gaze toward this world transformed.

The BRI as territorial restructuring

Despite the notion of creating a continuous surface, as implied by the term 'belt', the movement of capital, goods and people instigated through the BRI occurs primarily across corridors, within and between key urban nodes, with strategically located flagship projects in selected cities even as these projects move across extended territories of operation, including rural hinterlands. As evidenced by the BRI's vision document (Chinese Government, 2015), the allocation of investments (Derudder et al, 2018) and a significant body of academic, policy and journalistic analysis, the BRI has become a global catalyst of extensive material transformation. It inscribes new connections linking regions and reconfiguring existing cities into trade, financial and tourist hubs and producing entirely new cities (Apostolopoulou, 2021b; Apostolopoulou et al, 2024). The BRI introduces novel combinations of large-scale infrastructure alongside industrial projects (Blanchard et al, 2017) and significant investments across multiple economic sectors. This encompasses railways, roads, waterways, airports, ports, industrial parks, manufacturing zones, special economic zones (SEZs) and fibre-optic telecommunication networks as well as initiatives such as smart cities, greenfield investments, real estate developments, agribusinesses and commercial projects.

We find it useful to highlight *three types of BRI-led territorial restructuring* that convey why we pay close attention to how social and environmental geographies are being transformed. First, the BRI has been organized in direct relation to the Sino-centric regional and global production networks in which investments in the built environment and infrastructure are directly territorially connected and integrated into China's economy. This has proceeded through the BRI's six international economic corridors: the New Eurasian Land Bridge and the China-Mongolia-Russia, China-Central Asia-Western Asia, China-Indochina Peninsula, China-Pakistan and Bangladesh-China-India-Myanmar corridors and their various offshoots. For instance, the China-Mongolia-Russia Economic Corridor connects the Chinese city of Tianjin, across massive hinterlands and rural areas, with Mongolian cities, such as Choyr and Darkah, and Russian cities, such as Ulan-Ude (Vorobyev et al, 2018). The China-Pakistan Economic Corridor (CPEC) is intended to open up new economic connections for western China by providing direct access to the Indian Ocean (Malik et al, 2021). In doing so, it generates new flows, interdependencies and relational forms of urban and rural growth. Xinjiang's economic fate is now arguably entwined with the Baluchistan port city of Gwadar, which is heralded as Pakistan's 'Dubai' (Al-Shammari, 2017) and is being transformed through billions of US dollars of BRI investment. Through these investments, hopes for 'economic revival for Pakistan and prosperity in the western region of China' are manifested via new infrastructural connections (Perveen and Khalil, 2015, p 353). Additionally, the direct connectivity created by these corridors are generating new cross-border urban and rural spaces, such as the Muse Border Economic Zone in Myanmar and its connected Chinese city of Ruili (Song et al, 2020) as part of the China-Myanmar Economic Corridor. Studies focused on this type of BRI-led restructuring of territory highlight the ways in which economic growth both inside and outside China becomes entwined and intensified through BRI investments, connecting to longer (both modern and ancient) shared histories (for example, Safina et al, 2023). And these direct territorial restructurings are also taking place far beyond China's borders. For instance, the city of Duisburg, Germany, has rapidly transformed into one of the central logistics hubs in Europe (Pascha, 2021) through its connection to Chongqing, southwest China, via the Chongqing-Xinjiang-EU transcontinental railway corridor.

Second, we draw attention to territories that do not have direct land connections with China, but are integral to logistical network expansions on which the BRI vision and plan are established, encompassing regions including sub-Saharan Africa, the Caribbean and Latin America. These investments are often part of large-scale, cross-border infrastructure corridors financed through various Chinese state-owned enterprises that incorporate urban-rural restructuring as part of the systemic restructuring of logistical networks. Studies of these projects emphasize the critical role of coastal zones in the BRI, which are connected through various oceanic routes that comprise the Maritime Silk Road and a new global network of ports aligned to the BRI. For instance, the Lamu Port-South Sudan-Ethiopia Transport Corridor project (LAPSSET), anchored in Kenya, aims to integrate the hinterlands of East Africa into enhanced economic relations both in the region and facing out towards the Indian Ocean. LAPSSET finds its start (or end) points in port cities and expansion of port facilities in Lamu (Wan et al, 2021) that criss-cross and transform rural territories. The selective connectivity of these spaces generates political ecological and infrastructural conditions that shape conflicting patterns of regional transformation, urbanization, geopolitical formations, geo-economic divisions of labour, structures of social and political life (Graham and Marvin, 2022; Salamanca and Silver, 2022) and new forms of social-environmental inequality and uneven development, producing 'exclusions, deprivations, disruptions, vulnerabilities, and dispossessions for large population segments' in hinterland areas (Brenner, 2019, p 379).

Third, and finally, BRI projects have spilled out into various different initiatives, investments and projections with planetary ambitions across diverse spaces, scales and locations that offer a further form of territorial restructuring. This includes a Digital (Seone, 2020), a Polar (Woon, 2020) and a Space Silk Road (Filijović, 2020). These ambitions by China are also generating shifting political ecologies and infrastructural conditions. While these unfolding projects might not fit into the direct and extended forms of territorial restructuring highlighted earlier, the new patterns, dynamics and spaces being produced are important in how we think about the BRI's material geographies. For instance, the Digital Silk Road involves infrastructural investment across multiple locations, but also broader restructuring of digital space across sectors such as finance, surveillance and big data management through new forms of digitization and a global vision for dominance over ICT sectors and associated manufacturing (Chang, 2023). Such projects often overlap, associate with and build off the other forms of investment being promoted through BRI-led territorial restructuring.

How the BRI is territorially restructuring the planet

In thinking through the implications of these three types of BRI-led territorial restructuring, we want to emphasize that a China-centric focus alone is insufficient to account for the transformations occurring across multiple spaces, scales and places. While the BRI is of course Chinese-led, in its broader objectives, through financial mechanisms such as loans from the Export-Import Bank of China and construction companies such as the China Road and Bridge Corporation, this represents only part of the

Figure 0.2: How the BRI is restructuring the planet

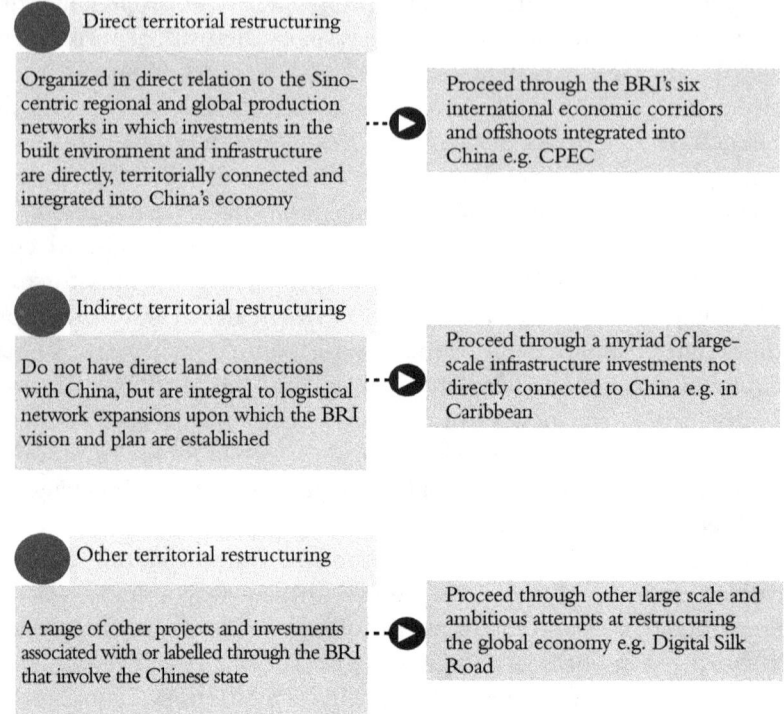

Source: Diagram by the editors

landscape when analysing the transformation of social and environmental geographies discussed in this volume. In many cases, the BRI is financing and mobilizing long-standing ambitions of national governments rather than initiating an entirely new set of economic and spatial strategies. The LAPSSET project, for example, restructured the port city of Lamu and some of Kenya's 'secondary' cities, such as Isiolo, as well as regional hinterlands (Bremner, 2013; Elliott, 2020). However, as studies have demonstrated, much of the spatial planning for LAPSSET has previously been bound up in the Kenyan Vision 2030 plan (Aalders et al, 2021) even if it becomes mobilized through Chinese logistical objectives, finance and expertise.

This does not imply that the BRI has a minor impact on national and regional scale politics, power dynamics and associated geopolitical relations. Rather, it underscores the importance of understanding the interplay between previously existing national or regional territorial plans and policies, diverse national, local, private and state interests, and Chinese-led interests and BRI projects. This also suggests that a close reading of the longer histories of these plans, extending back to the colonial and early and later independence eras in Kenya's case, can help analyse the ever-shifting and evolving geographies and unequal power relations of projects such as LAPSSET (Kimari and Ernstson, 2020). In this context, the BRI is best understood as a contextual and contingent cross-scale geography, the product of complex interrelations between people, places, socionatures, ideas, practices and processes that produce BRI's multiple social and environmental spaces (Cheng and Apostolopoulou, 2023).

The need for a grounded approach to the BRI

The BRI has given rise to a burgeoning literature that has expanded across varied disciplines, topics and geographical boundaries. BRI scholarship has focused on geopolitical (Blanchard et al, 2017), geo-economic (Lee et al, 2018; Sum, 2019), geo-cultural (Winter, 2016) and political economy (Summers, 2016) analyses, BRI's critical genealogies (Sidaway et al, 2020), its role in globalization patterns, environmental (Ahmad et al, 2018; Hughes, 2019; Teo et al, 2019) and energy aspects, and finance (Lai et al, 2020) and debt implications (Hurley et al, 2018; Jones and Harmeiri, 2020). Despite its relevance and breadth, BRI studies have tended to prioritize the macroeconomic and geopolitical factors (Sidaway et al, 2020) over the ways in which its territorial restructuring transforms space and place, with social and environmental implications. This is partly explained by the time it takes for many of these large projects to be planned, constructed and operated. Nonetheless, a growing number of scholars drawing on various fields, including geography, urban studies, political economy and political ecology, have moved beyond seeing the BRI as a static and top-down, state-centric strategy originated in Beijing. They emphasize, as we have, the need to conceptualize the BRI as a flexible (Alff, 2020), relational process with uncertain outcomes subject to the spatial embeddedness of each project and local political and fiscal conditions (Han and Webber, 2020). This has led to calls in the past few years to explore the initiative 'from the ground' (de LT Oliveira et al, 2020; Murton and Lord, 2020) and pay attention to the intertwined policies, discourses and projects involved in its unfolding.

A grounded approach offers important insights that point to the spaces and places being transformed through BRI projects and the way society and environments are profoundly impacted. This includes empirical investigations on: land speculations and the uneven and gendered vulnerabilities for marginalized groups, such as women or migrant labourers, living and working in places where BRI projects are materialized (Beazley and Lassoie, 2017); exclusions of vulnerable populations from infrastructure construction (Dwyer, 2020); processes of accumulation and dispossession related to the privatization of strategic infrastructure (Neilson 2019); and the intensification of labour precarity, worsening of working conditions and violation of worker's rights. It extends to critically assessing the creation of logistical zones across urban spaces (Gambino, 2019), the rapid emergence of free enterprise zones, manufacturing areas and commercial projects that alter space and the geographies of everyday lives, and the role of BRI projects in reshaping parts of towns and cities into industrial enclaves and transit corridors. In this edited volume, we contribute to, consolidate and map future directions in this scholarship focused on the material transformations that reverberate throughout the making and operating of the BRI.

Critical approaches to the material transformations of the BRI

The underpinning approach to examining the material transformations of the BRI and the structure of this volume is rooted in two closely interrelated bodies of scholarship: political ecology (Perrault et al, 2015) and infrastructure studies (Graham and Marvin, 2001). These complementary and overlapping approaches draw on multidisciplinary perspectives and debates across geography, anthropology, urban studies and science-technology-society studies, among others. As editors and contributors to this volume on the BRI, we have built our work on the multifaceted and, importantly, grounded lens that these conceptual approaches open up to critical scholarship.

Political ecology foregrounds questions about how environment-society relations are being reshaped through the BRI, highlighting the dynamics and processes through which massive new investments impact humans and non-human natures in multiple ways. It serves as a critical analytical tool crucial for discerning the material transformations driven by China's BRI. By focusing on the relations between political economy, politics and socio-natural transformation, a political ecology approach makes visible the manifold impacts of BRI projects on diverse ecosystems, landscapes, resource systems and livelihoods. In other words, it offers a comprehensive view into how BRI-driven investments, operations, flows and extractions interact with and reshape ecosystems and places, triggering environmental and spatial change, injustice, land use reconfigurations and socioeconomic disruptions. Political ecology theories often explore the metabolism of environmental flows (Swyngedouw, 2006; Smith, 2010), demonstrating how large-scale projects may generate new socio-natural circulations across territories and produce effects at multiple scales. These effects can range from the national scale (for example, new financial flows into specific cities or hinterlands) down to households (for example, the environmental harms caused by displacement). By doing so, political ecology can support an interdisciplinary analysis of the effects and contested nature of BRI-driven material transformations on the contours of everyday lives, places and socionatures. For instance, Harlan (2020) uses political ecology to question the 'green development' agenda within the BRI by analysing investments in low-carbon infrastructure and technologies. Joniak-Lüthi (2020) examines the political ecological complexity of road maintenance in the Sino-Inner Asian borderlands. Likewise, Beazley and Lassoie (2017) explore the impact of expanding rural road networks on social and ecological systems in the Nepalese Himalaya. Seeing both urban and rural places impacted by the BRI through a 'metabolic lens' broadens the epistemology of social-environmental change and the objects of geographical and political ecology research to encompass, for example, port infrastructure, the built environment, marine ecosystems, policies, laws, livelihoods and struggles.

Infrastructure studies centre on the pivotal role of these networks within the BRI and across various scales, spanning from local to global. Infrastructure encompasses a vast assortment of networks, including energy grids, urban provision systems, transportation and logistics systems, telecommunication technologies and more (Wiig et al, 2023). Infrastructure functions as the underlying foundation for the circulation of people, goods and information. This circulation, in turn, not only sustains but also produces and maintains the fabric of everyday life, underscoring the interconnectedness between material transformation, relations between humans and non-human natures, and the built environment across contemporary societies. Moreover, drawing on infrastructure studies, we can see these systems, networks and the spaces they occupy (Carse, 2016) as the foundation of the BRI's social, economic and geopolitical power. While often remaining 'black boxed' (Star, 1999), infrastructure has recently emerged as a key object of study, foregrounding the production of both global economic flows and the local dimensions of everyday lives (Graham and McFarlane, 2014) through these combined social and technical constellations. For instance, Lesutis (2021) examines how BRI projects in Kenya, particularly new railways, shape and reflect state practices of infrastructural territorialization that reconstitute racial and socioeconomic inequalities. In Lamu, Kenya, Alden et al (2021) highlight how the port expansion connected to the BRI-financed LAPSSET project was predicated on the displacement of local people, including farming and fishing communities, as rural land was transformed into global urban and logistical space. Stories of infrastructural-led displacement related to the BRI also feature prominently in studies within cities, such as the Orange Line metro in Lahore (Tassadiq, 2022), and on roads and railway projects between cities and across rural hinterlands (Enns and Bersaglio, 2020). Infrastructure studies can help to make visible the ways in which BRI projects create new forms of injustice as large-scale projects cut across urban and rural spaces, demanding the displacement of existing communities, exclude people from premium enclave spaces, such as new economic zones, and disrupt existing infrastructure services, such as water or energy, during construction and operation.

Crucially, while the construction of new BRI infrastructure projects may promise enhanced global connections, it also often disrupts and undermines existing relations, disproportionately impacting the most vulnerable by alienating them from previously familiar spaces. Such transformations echo broader analyses of private real estate or logistical enclaves (Appel, 2012), with emerging infrastructures acting as securitized symbols that escalate growing inequality and governmental neglect of public infrastructure. States and companies across the Global South and North are increasingly prioritizing the optimal operation of global supply networks over social reproduction infrastructures, almost inevitably subjugating democratic principles and the wellbeing of human and non-human lives to the imperative of seamless capital circulation (Chua et al, 2018; Ziadah, 2018), exemplified by the heightened exploitation of workers, socionatures and communities along trade routes and shipping corridors (Mezzadra and Neilson, 2019; Apostolopoulou, 2021b; Danyluk, 2021). As Apostolopoulou and Pizarro (2025) have shown in their work on the Chancay mega-port and logistics centre in Peru, from the perspective of state territorial and spatial planning, these megaprojects reflect increasing foreign involvement in local affairs, shaping development policies while failing to address the needs of marginalized communities. From the standpoint of local communities and the most vulnerable, they register as the entrenchment of state abandonment, marginalization and exclusion. Unlike public infrastructures that evoke a sense of abandonment due to malfunctioning, these contested infrastructures evoke despair, fear and loss due to their functioning and the potential ways they will shape new, currently unknown, futures that exacerbate infrastructural violence with detrimental consequences for both local livelihoods and ecosystems (see Apostolopoulou and Pizarro, 2025; see also Apostolopoulou, 2024).

Drawing on infrastructure and political ecology studies, we can begin to see how the materialization of the BRI through various projects draws attention to complex socio-technical processes (Murton and Lord, 2020) that are simultaneously social, ecological and relational (Star, 1999). These processes mediate lives and socionatures, reconfiguring the production of non-human nature and space, as well as the geographies of everyday life (Lefebvre, 1970; Graham and McFarlane, 2015). New and reinforced vulnerabilities become visible as the BRI materially transforms the fabric of societies (Joniak-Lüthi, 2020) and environments. The projects being materialized through the BRI act as enabling mechanisms, involving a constellation of material relations and flows that facilitate specific social and material activities (Larkin, 2013; Bosworth, 2022). Examining BRI projects through the lens of the contradictory forces and unequal power dynamics that influence their creation and daily experience enables us to determine under what circumstances they can have detrimental or beneficial effects, and for whom, as infrastructure studies scholarship has long considered

(Graham and Marvin, 2001; Mmanca and Silver, 2022). In this sense, BRI projects constitute sites where state actions intersect with the global economy and development processes (Ferguson, 2010) and are integral to daily life, influencing the systemic conditions of possibility under which people can act (Harvey, 2018).

In foregrounding the social and environmental (re)orderings that are manifested and experienced in the materialization of BRI projects, we can also begin to see how the provision, maintenance and transformation of these territorial restructurings are contested and politicized, enabling and embodying various forms of state and corporate violence (Datta and Ahmed, 2020). Rodgers and O'Neill (2012, pp 401–3), drawing on Mann's concept of infrastructural power and Graham's notion of infrastructural warfare, use the term infrastructural violence to describe how 'processes of marginalisation, discrimination and exclusion' are often operated and sustained by infrastructure, drawing attention to how 'the workings of infrastructure can be substantially deleterious'. The concept of infrastructural violence uncovers the political economy behind the socio-spatial production of suffering by providing a concrete way to discuss who is responsible for harm and spark action toward achieving infrastructural justice (Enns and Sneyd, 2020). As Datta and Ahmed (2020) argue, infrastructural violence is often located in geopolitical and ecological conflicts and in disaster and crisis contexts (Rodgers and O'Neill, 2012), and is entwined with the structural violence of neoliberal urbanization (Graham and Marvin, 2001). In their work on Nepal, Apostolopoulou and Pant (2022) demonstrate, for example, how BRI projects have become vehicles towards 'Naya Nepal', a new infrastructural myth emerging from the ruins of the past as the ultimate path to achieving a long due rural-to-urban transition. However, this transition exacerbates decades of infrastructural violence and precarity, suppressing people's struggles against the unequal geographies of BRI-driven material transformation. Throughout the chapters in this book, we ask the reader to hold this idea of infrastructural violence in mind and to think about it in a wider sense of both the social and environmental harms being produced and the ways in which BRI projects produce injustice and inequality. Many of the contributions directly or indirectly address such forces and experiences, providing a critical focus for grounded studies of the BRI that move beyond geo-economic and geopolitical readings.

The book's underpinning in political ecology and infrastructure studies means centring open-ended ideas of inequality and violence at the core of understanding the material transformations driven by BRI projects. This framing shifts attention to a range of possible injustices, including the loss of livelihoods and homes, violations of workers' rights, shifting labour conditions, land acquisitions, environmental degradation, intensification of social segregation, spatial fragmentation, territorial stigmatization and discrimination, displacement, dispossession, and gentrification, as well as the loss, privatization and enclosure of public space, the unequal impacts of techno-social differentiation and the suppression of local struggles and rights to the city, nature and the commons. This approach broadens the analysis of contestation surrounding BRI projects, which has been relatively limited in the first decade of its operations, reflecting a broader gap in integrating social and environmental struggles. In this regard, infrastructural violence and injustice are inextricably linked to environmental injustice, simultaneously affecting socionatures, places and livelihoods and uniting struggles for social, environmental and spatial justice. This also underscores the vital role of conflict in the unfolding of the BRI on the ground, emphasizing the variations, disruptions, uncertainties and anticipations that shape its outcomes.

By bringing infrastructure and political ecology studies into productive dialogue, we aim to draw attention to the range of issues outlined so far. The geographical extent and material fixity of BRI projects (Li, 2018) exacerbate social and environmental challenges faced by communities. The duration and impact of these projects underscore the urgency of addressing the social and environmental consequences that arise from them. This, we contend, is why a grounded, material analysis of BRI projects that places at its epicentre the way marginalized communities experience infrastructural and political ecological conditions is vital for developing a critical research agenda over a decade into the BRI.

Developing a critical research agenda

This edited volume provides an agenda-setting analysis that is also policy-relevant and socially-environmentally significant, highlighting the novel ways in which the BRI reconfigures the patterns of global inequality. Through a geographically expansive understanding of the BRI, the volume unravels the distinct and diverse ways BRI projects remake lives, natures and places across the Global South and North through transforming infrastructures and political ecologies. Moreover, the volume offers an analysis that moves beyond a binary understanding of the BRI that currently prevails in extant scholarship, which tends to either exaggerate the grandiose nature of the BRI (Hillman, 2020) and Chinese exceptionalism (Zhang, 2013) or undermine the BRI as a cohesive, geopolitically driven grand strategy (Jones and Zeng, 2019) and present it as a fragmented initiative driven solely by project-specific characteristics (Cheng and Apostolopoulou, 2023). By analysing the BRI as a materially grounded field of practice (Oakes, 2021), we hope to advance an extroverted perspective of place (Massey, 1994) that aspires to the planetary (Brenner and Schmid, 2015) through the intensive study of the concrete and the particular to understand a large-scale, multi-scalar process through its fragments and sedimented effects (Katz, 2021), confronting the challenge of theorizing from anywhere (Robinson, 2011). That way, we argue for a focus on the BRI that needs not imply a one-dimensional interpretation of China or stand in opposition to Global China scholarship that perceives China as a method (Shin et al, 2022). Instead, we hope to reflect a theorization of the BRI as an exemplar of a broader process of infrastructure-led development that is rapidly becoming hegemonic worldwide, as evidenced by initiatives like the European Union's EUR 300 billion European Union Global Gateway, the USD 600 billion Partnership for Global Infrastructure and Investment, and the newly born India-Middle East-Europe Economic Corridor.

The political ecologies and infrastructures of the BRI

The BRI has emerged as a transformative force reshaping landscapes and livelihoods across continents. As this global infrastructure project unfolds, it redraws territorial, urban and economic geographies and its political, environmental and social implications come to the fore, generating diverse narratives, conflicts and challenges. The contributors in this volume focus on diverse case studies spanning the Global South and North and offering critical insights into the complex dynamics at play. From the contested coal-fired power projects in Indonesia to the grassroots environmentalism in Thailand's SEZs, and from the environmental politics of the China-Laos railway to the nature of Sino-Sri Lankan development narratives, the chapters illuminate the intricate intersections of infrastructure, power, ecology, geopolitics, sustainability agendas and development within the broader framework of the BRI.

In particular, in her chapter, **Bowen Gu** closely examines the contested coal-fired power in the BRI using Indonesia as a case study. Chinese companies and financiers have played an important role in supporting the development of coal-fired power plants (CFPPs) in Indonesia in the past decade. These projects have met increasing resistance from local communities and civil society due to land disputes, air and water pollution, biodiversity loss and health impacts. Based on a systematic mapping and comparative analysis of social mobilizations and community resistance against CFPPs with Chinese investment in Indonesia in the Global Atlas of Environmental Justice, as well as in-depth interviews, the chapter focuses on the community-level environmental, health and socioeconomic impact of CFPPs in BRI projects and the power relations that led to local grassroot struggles.

Also grounded in the Southeast Asian context, **Ratchada Arpornsilp**'s chapter discusses the dynamics of grassroots environmentalism in the case of natural resource conflicts in Thailand's SEZs. In Thailand, the military-installed government directed the establishment of SEZs in ten border provinces in 2014 under regional economic connectivity collaborations that constitute the components of the BRI. The ambiguous and contested process of acquiring public or communal lands for SEZs has been conducted without the informed engagement and consent of local stakeholders, who previously accessed these lands and resources to sustain their livelihoods. Combining the analytical framings of political ecology and social movement theory, Arpornsilp explores, with a focus on the border of Thailand and Laos, how SEZs as well as land and natural resource conflicts stimulate grassroots anti-dispossession responses and local collective actions vis-à-vis the state counter-movements.

Xiaofeng Liu takes us to another case in the region by studying the environmental politics of the China-Laos railway, especially its China section (Yuxi-Mohan railway) in China's Yunnan province. Using materials collected from the field, including government documents and interviews with railway companies and local governments and communities, she argues that as a much-anticipated project, the Yuxi-Mohan railway also generates conflicts at the intersection of local development, national mission, international connectivity and geopolitics. Local conflicts concerning environment and resources, often concealed behind grand narratives, can be attributed to contradictions across scales, namely clashes between local planning, national ecological redlines and international pressure, as well as asymmetric relations of different stakeholders. Her research contributes to theoretical discussion on environmental politics of infrastructure and offers practical implications for improving the sustainability of transnational infrastructure projects.

In the South Asian context, **Orlando Woods, Kanchana Ruwanpura, Loritta Chan** and **Barnabas Mah** raise the nature question in Sino-Sri Lankan development narratives. The authors place the question of nature within the narrative of Sri Lanka's debt crisis specifically, and its postwar political economy more generally. In doing so, they move the debt discourse beyond its normative financial associations and consider the plurality of 'debts' that infrastructure megaprojects like those of the BRI can give rise to. They argue that Chinese lending does not have prohibitive interest rates, but it has come without the proper due diligence afforded by technical feasibility studies, financial viability studies or environmental impact assessments. By taking this approach, the authors intend to bring the 'debt-trap' narrative into conversation with recent scholarly work on the social and environmental consequences of BRI-associated infrastructure projects in Sri Lanka. Hence, they explore both the ecological ramifications of indebtedness, but also the role of nature in providing a way out in the form of debt-for-nature swaps. By doing so, they seek to move the question of debt to whom beyond its normative geo-economic and geopolitical associations by considering the natural world as both the subject and object of 'debt'.

This volume also examines the political ecologies of the BRI in the Global North. **Hannes Langguth**'s chapter focuses on the deployment of a large-scale Chinese green technology project in Eastern Germany. Driven by the European Union's green transition, formerly bypassed regions in Europe are increasingly becoming the focus for large-scale green energy projects, of which a significant part is driven by Chinese outbound investment. Drawing on empirical material related to a recently established Chinese gigafactory for electric vehicle battery cells and associated energy, research and logistics infrastructure in Eastern Germany, Langguth's chapter illustrates how state-level governments become key drivers in the deployment of the project, while marginalizing local actors in the process. Thus, this chapter highlights the role of host-state actors and place-specific histories and power structures, which significantly shape the localization of China's global infrastructure expansion.

Moreover, **Ksenija Hanaček**'s chapter conceptualizes the Polar Silk Road corridor as a continuation of colonialism of the Arctic region through foreign investment, infrastructure expansion, extractivism and climate change – all of which serve the Polar Corridor development. It does so by analysing several resistances to climate emergency, oil, liquified natural gas and mining projects as well as massive nuclear maritime infrastructure developments. The main argument underlined in this chapter is that climate-ecological disruptions inform colonial past and present as well as contested visions for the Arctic future by Indigenous peoples and local communities. As the Polar Silk Road extends its reach into the Arctic, the discourse on climate coloniality and resistance gains prominence, offering new perspectives on the planetary implications of transnational infrastructure projects.

With regards to transnational infrastructure initiatives in Asia, **Caixia Mao** applies the concept of infrastructure assemblage in Chinese and Japanese initiatives, focusing on the railway projects in Indonesia. Through case studies such as the Jakarta-Bandung High Speed Railway by China and the Jakarta-Surabaya medium-speed railway by Japan, Mao analyses the political economic drivers for state and non-state Chinese and Japanese actors in launching the BRI and the Partnership for Quality Infrastructure (PQI). By elucidating the interaction between Chinese and Japanese actors and local stakeholders in Indonesia, the chapter enriches theoretical discussions surrounding the BRI and PQI, offering insights into the complexities of infrastructure development within diverse sociopolitical contexts. Moreover, it contributes to an inter-Asian comparative lens on transnational infrastructure initiatives in the BRI context, facilitating a deeper understanding of the dynamics shaping regional connectivity and development strategies.

Simone Vegliò's chapter proposes a theoretical and geopolitical discussion of the BRI from the vantage point of Latin America. Over the past few years, a proliferation of bilateral agreements between China and Latin American nations has been promoting the construction of mega infrastructure projects. While several Latin American governments and institutions are portraying these projects as new material articulations that can trigger the socioeconomic development of the region, a process of substantial 're-primarization' of its national economies is nonetheless evident. On the one hand, this kind of 'infrastructure-led development' appears just to reinforce Latin America's position as a global exporter of primary resources, which has largely characterized its economy since the colonial period. From this perspective, there seems not to be a significant change, but rather a reiteration – or even a solidification – of the 'dependency' relations that have historically produced Latin America within the global space; yet, at the same time, it is hard to deny the radical novelty of having China as a new actor in search for geo-economic and geopolitical hegemony from a position of substantial power outside the 'traditional' North. By discussing the most recent projects, debates and issues of the BRI's action in Latin America, the chapter provides a 'postcolonial' analysis on the topic.

Patrick Bond draws our attention to the BRI in Africa by discussing Chinese investment, finance and trade controversies in Southern Africa. Bond argues that Chinese engagements in Southern Africa exhibit under-developmental and super-exploitative characteristics, rooted in Chinese capitalist crisis conditions. By conceptualizing the BRI as a spatial fix for overaccumulated capital, Bond sheds light on the extreme manifestations of global uneven development in the region. Through a critical examination of Chinese investments and trade relations, the chapter contributes to a nuanced understanding of the socioeconomic dynamics shaping BRI engagements in Africa.

There are also two chapters focusing on the BRI's implications for Europe. **Francesca Governa, Leonardo Ramondetti, Astrid Safina, Angelo Sampieri and Alberto Valz Gris** examine how the intersection of the BRI with pre-existing development trajectories in Southern Europe is generating diverse spatial configurations and socioeconomic conditions, challenging the perceived uniformity of this infrastructure-led development programme. This is particularly evident along the Adriatic Corridor, where trade between the ports of Piraeus and Trieste is rapidly growing thanks to the Maritime Silk Road. Although this corridor is a logistical continuum, these two terminals differ significantly. Beyond any comparative approach, this chapter illustrates the varied approaches the BRI adopts with the national contexts, the diverse development strategies it pursues and the varying degrees of formal participation by China. The authors invite reflection on two critical issues: first, how the BRI navigates and adapts to diverse contexts in order to ensure the smooth circulation of goods and investments; and, second, how the interplay of different local political, economic and social conditions results in the fragmentation of the BRI into multiple and differentiated geographies.

Evelina Gambino traces the attempted development of Anaklia, a village on the Georgian Black Sea coast, into a major logistical hub seen as vital for Georgia's transformation into a transit corridor, an element of the BRI that would forge new connections between Europe and Asia. The project came to a halt in 2019, however. In the wake of this failure, this chapter analyses the creation of Anaklia as a future-oriented logistical space. Competition between different corridors is at the heart of the BRI, and each physical infrastructure depends on a complex entanglement of (im)material infrastructures – concessions, contracts, synchronization of data and practices – to become operative. Developmental promises attached to logistics are thus resting on shaky and often unpredictable grounds. Drawing on feminist analyses of the economy and its multifaceted reproduction, this chapter delves into the different forms of labour – manual, affective and administrative – necessary to turn the uncertainty and unevenness of competition-based global systems into a certain prediction of Georgia's logistical future.

Last but not least, **Elia Apostolopoulou**'s chapter brings together various themes discussed so far by offering a comparative account that crosses the North and South. It explores the links between infrastructure-led development, urban transformation and inequality in the BRI. Here, the BRI is theorized as a spatial fix to the overaccumulation problems of Chinese capitalism, and particular attention is paid to the role of urbanization. By drawing on postcolonial geographies, the chapter offers a relational analysis of divergent trajectories of socio-spatial urban change driven by BRI projects in Athens, Colombo and London. The key argument is that urban transformation driven by the BRI signals the emergence of a new form of infrastructure-led authoritarian neoliberal urbanism. This engenders both new urban formations and new urban politics that, despite variegated expressions across different contexts, are reconfiguring urban space and are transforming the social geography of each city by creating, facilitating or exacerbating spatial fragmentation and social segregation.

Overall, by bridging various traditions of geographical, development, urban, and science-technology-society studies, as well as political ecology research, this edited volume aims to provide a cohesive and critical analysis of the multifaceted impacts of BRI projects on space, livelihoods and ecosystems. Through this interdisciplinary approach, it seeks to uncover the interconnectedness of these impacts, shedding light on the material

Figure 0.3: 'The beginning of hope', Piraeus Port, Athens, Greece

Source: Photograph by Elia Apostolopoulou

Figure 0.4: Piraeus COSCO container terminal

Source: Photograph by Elia Apostolopoulou

realities and the sociopolitical, economic and environmental dynamics at play. Spanning four continents and encompassing diverse regional, national and urban contexts, the edited volume provides a comprehensive geographical breadth necessary for theorizing a global initiative like the BRI. Through its rigorous examination, the volume aims to unravel both existing and emerging

Figure 0.5: A COSCO container on the Northern Corridor in Kenya

Source: Photograph by Jonathan Silver

Figure 0.6: Underneath the BRI-financed Orange Line in Lahore

Source: Photograph by Jonathan Silver

Figure 0.7: A wall on the boardwalk reads 'No to the mega-port', Chancay, Peru

Source: Photograph by Alejandra Pizarro. Previously published in E. Apostolopoulou and A. Pizarro (2024) Contesting the anticipated infrastructural city: a grounded analysis of Silk Road urbanization in the multipurpose port terminal in Chancay, Peru, *Annals of the American Association of Geographers*, 115(1), 223–41. doi: 10.1080/24694452.2024.2415718. Available under creative commons license CC BY-NC-ND 4.0.

forms of injustice engendered by the BRI, ranging from dispossession and displacement to issues of race, class, gender discrimination, violations of workers' rights and unequal access to space and nature. Grounded in empirical research, it strives to centre those often marginalized in mainstream scholarship and policy making, bringing their voices and experiences to the forefront. Importantly, by recognizing the pivotal role of people's struggles in shaping the outcomes of infrastructure projects, the volume delves into the intricacies of daily negotiations, improvisations and resistance against the impacts of contentious projects. Our inspiration is to use this analysis as a critical tool for deciphering 21st-century infrastructure-led development and unpacking the implications of what some have termed the era of extreme infrastructure (Hildyard and Sol, 2017), as well as for exploring the potential of emerging global-local alliances to pave the way for radically different futures.

Figure 0.8: Tangier, Morocco, a new waterfront development

Source: Photograph taken by Elia Apostolopoulou

Figure 0.9: The Export-Import Bank of China-funded standard gauge railway in Kenya

Source: Photograph taken by Jonathan Silver

Figure 0.10: Valencia port (Spain), next to Las Arenas beach – COSCO Shipping operates one of the port terminals

Source: Photograph taken by Elia Apostolopoulou

Note
[1] We would like to highlight that the title of the book (*Material Geographies*) is inspired by the historical materialism approach.

References

Aalders, J.T., Bachmann, J., Knutsson, P. and Musembi Kilaka, B. (2021) The making and unmaking of a megaproject: contesting temporalities along the LAPSSET corridor in Kenya, *Antipode*, 53(5), 1273–93.

Ahmad, F., Draz, M.U., Su, L., Ozturk, I. and Rauf, A. (2018) Tourism and environmental pollution: evidence from the one belt one road provinces of Western China, *Sustainability*, 10(10), art 3520. doi: 10.3390/su10103520

Alden, C., Chichava, S., Jiang, L., Murg, B. and Lim, G. (2021) China-driven port development: lessons from Kenya and Malaysia, *Africa Portal*. Available at: www.africaportal.org/publications/china-driven-port-development-lessons-kenya-and-malaysia/

Alff, H. (2020) Belts and roads every-and nowhere: conceptualizing infrastructural corridorization in the Indian Ocean, *Environment and Planning C: Politics and Space*, 38(5), 815–19.

Al-Shammari, T. (2017) Dubai and Gwadar: the silent economic war in the Gulf of Oman, *Open Democracy*, 14 August. Available at: www.opendemocracy.net/en/north-africa-west-asia/dubai-and-gwadar-silent-economic-war-in-gulf-of-oman/

Apostolopoulou, E. (2021a) A novel geographical research agenda on Silk Road urbanisation, *The Geographical Journal*, 187(4), 386–93.

Apostolopoulou, E. (2021b) Tracing the links between infrastructure-led development, urban transformation, and inequality in China's Belt and Road Initiative, *Antipode*, 53(3), 831–58.

Apostolopoulou, E. (2024) The dragon's head or Athens' sacrifice zone? Spatiotemporal disjuncture, logistical disruptions, and urban infrastructural justice in Piraeus port, Greece, *Urban Geography*. doi: 10.1080/02723638.2024.2433968

Apostolopoulou, E. and Pant, H. (2022) 'Silk Road here we come': infrastructural myths, post-disaster politics, and the shifting urban geographies of Nepal, *Political Geography*, 98, art 102704. doi: 10.1016/j.polgeo.2022.102704

Apostolopoulou, E. and Pizarro, A. (2025) Contesting the anticipated infrastructural city: a grounded analysis of Silk Road urbanization in the multipurpose port terminal in Chancay, Peru, *Annals of the American Association of Geographers*, 115(1), 223–41.

Apostolopoulou, E., Cheng, H., Silver, J. and Wiig, A. (2024) Cities on the new silk road: the global urban geographies of China's Belt and Road Initiative, *Urban Geography*, 45(6), 1095–114.

Appel, H.C. (2012) Walls and white elephants: oil extraction, responsibility, and infrastructural violence in Equatorial Guinea, *Ethnography*, 13(4), 439–65.

Beazley, R. and Lassoie, J.P. (2017) *Himalayan Mobilities: An Exploration of the Impact of Expanding Rural Road Networks on Social and Ecological Systems in the Nepalese Himalaya*, Springer International.

Blanchard, J-M.F. and Flint, C. (2017) The geopolitics of China's maritime Silk Road initiative, *Geopolitics*, 22, 223–45.

Bosworth, K. (2022) What is 'affective infrastructure'? *Dialogues in Human Geography*, 13(1), 54–72.

Bremner, L. (2013) Towards a minor global architecture at Lamu, Kenya, *Social Dynamics*, 39(3), 397–413.

Brenner, N. (2019) *New Urban Spaces: Urban Theory and the Scale Question*, Oxford University Press.

Brenner, N. and Schmid, C. (2015) Towards a new epistemology of the urban? *City*, 19(2–3), 151–82.

Carse, A. (2016) Keyword: infrastructure: how a humble French engineering term shaped the modern world, in P. Harvey, J. Casper and A. Morita (eds) *Infrastructures and Social Complexity*, Routledge, pp 45–57.

Chang, Y.Y. (2023) China beyond China, establishing a digital order with Chinese characteristics: China's growing discursive power and the Digital Silk Road, *Politics & Policy*, 51(2), 283–321.

Cheng, H. and Apostolopoulou, E. (2023) Locating the Belt and Road Initiative's spatial trilectics, *Geography Compass*, 17(4), e12683. doi: 10.1111/gec3.12683

Chinese Government (2015) Belt and Road Initiative Vision document. Available at: https://reconasia-production.s3.amazonaws.com/media/filer_public/e0/22/e0228017-7463-46fc-9094-0465a6f1ca23/vision_and_actions_on_jointly_building_silk_road_economic_belt_and_21st-century_maritime_silk_road.pdf

Chua, C., Danyluk, M., Cowen, D. and Khalili, L. (2018) Introduction: turbulent circulation: building a critical engagement with logistics, *Environment and Planning D: Society and Space*, 36(4), 617–29.

Clarke, M. (2018) The Belt and Road Initiative: exploring Beijing's motivations and challenges for its New Silk Road, *Strategic Analysis*, 42(2), 84–102.

Danyluk, M. (2021) Supply-chain urbanism: constructing and contesting the logistics city, *Annals of the American Association of Geographers*, 111(7), 2149–64.

Datta, A. and Ahmed, N. (2020) Intimate infrastructures: the rubrics of gendered safety and urban violence in Kerala, India, *Geoforum*, 110. doi: 10.1016/j.geoforum.2020.01.016

de LT Oliveira, G., Murton, G., Rippa, A., Harlan, T. and Yang, Y. (2020) China's Belt and Road Initiative: views from the ground, *Political Geography*, 82, art 102225. doi: 10.1016/j.polgeo.2020.102225

Derudder, B., Romain, J., Xingjian, L. and Kunaka, C. (2018) *Connectivity Along Overland Corridors of the Belt and Road Initiative*, World Bank Group. [See also: www.merics.org/en/bri-tracker/interactive-map]

Dwyer, M.B. (2020) 'They will not automatically benefit': the politics of infrastructure development in Laos's Northern Economic Corridor, *Political Geography*, 78, art 102118. doi: 10.1016/j.polgeo.2019.102118

Elliott, H. (2020) Town-making at the gateway to Kenya's 'new frontier', in J. Lind, D. Okenwa and I. Scoones (eds) *Land, Investment and Politics: Reconfiguring Eastern Africa's Pastoral Drylands*, James Currey, pp 43–54.

Enns, C. and Bersaglio, B. (2020) On the coloniality of 'new' mega-infrastructure projects in East Africa, *Antipode*, 52(1), 101–23.

Enns, C. and Sneyd, A. (2020) More-than-human infrastructural violence and infrastructural justice: a case study of the Chad–Cameroon pipeline project, *Annals of the American Association of Geographers*, 111(2), 481–97.

Ferdinand, P. (2016) Westward ho-the China dream and 'one belt, one road': Chinese foreign policy under Xi Jinping, *International Affairs*, 92(4), 941–57.

Ferguson, J. (2010) The uses of neoliberalism, *Antipode*, 41, 166–84.

Filijović, M. (2020) The Silk Road leads to the Moon: China's outer space strategy and its future development, *The Review of International Affairs*, 71(1178), 5–26.

Furlong, K. (2022) Geographies of infrastructure III: infrastructure with Chinese characteristics, *Progress in Human Geography*, 46(3), 915–25.

Gambino, E. (2019) The Georgian logistics revolution: questioning seamlessness across the New Silk Road, *Work Organisation, Labour & Globalisation*, 13(1), 190–206.

Graham, S. and McFarlane, C. (eds) (2015) *Infrastructural Lives: Urban Infrastructure in Context*, Routledge.

Graham, S. and Marvin, S. (2001) *Splintering Urbanism: Networked Infrastructures, Technological Mobilities and the Urban Condition*, Routledge.

Graham, S. and Marvin, S. (2022) Splintering urbanism at 20 and the 'infrastructural turn', *Journal of Urban Technology*, 29(1), 169–75.

Han, X. and Webber, M. (2020) From Chinese dam building in Africa to the Belt and Road Initiative: assembling infrastructure projects and their linkages, *Political Geography*, 77, art 102102. doi: 10.1016/j.polgeo.2019.102102

Harlan, T. (2021) Green development or greenwashing? A political ecology perspective on China's green Belt and Road, *Eurasian Geography and Economics*, 62(2), 202–26.

Harvey, D. (2016) *The Ways of the World*, Oxford University Press.

Harvey, P. (2018) Infrastructures in and out of time: the promise of roads in contemporary Peru, in N. Anand, A. Gupta and H. Appel (eds) *The Promise of Infrastructure*, Duke University Press, pp 80–101.

Hildyard, N. and Sol, X. (2017) *How Infrastructure is Shaping the World: A Critical Introduction to Infrastructure Mega-Corridors*. Counter Balance.

Hillman, J.E. (2020) *The Emperor's New Road: China and the Project of the Century*, Yale University Press.

Hughes, A.C. (2019) Understanding and minimizing environmental impacts of the Belt and Road Initiative, *Conservation Biology*, 33(4), 883–94.

Hurley, J., Morris, S. and Portelance, G. (2018) *Examining the Debt Implications of the Belt and Road Initiative from a Policy Perspective*, Center for Global Development. Available at: www.cgdev.org/publication/examining-debt-implications-belt-and-road-initiative-a-policy-perspective

Jiang, Y. (2015) Vulgarisation of Keynesianism in China's response to the global financial crisis, *Review of International Political Economy*, 22(2), 360–90.

Jones, L. and Zeng, J. (2019) Understanding China's 'Belt and Road Initiative': beyond 'grand strategy' to a state transformation analysis, *Third World Quarterly*, 40(8), 1415–39.

Jones, L. and Hameiri, S. (2020) *Debunking the Myth of 'Debt-Trap Diplomacy'*, Chatham House.

Joniak-Lüthi, A. (2020) A road, a disappearing river and fragile connectivity in Sino-Inner Asian borderlands, *Political Geography*, 78, art 102122. doi: 10.1016/j.polgeo.2019.102122

Katz, C. (2021) Splanetary urbanization, *International Journal of Urban and Regional Research*, 45(4), 597–611.

Kimari, W. and Ernstson, H. (2020) Imperial remains and imperial invitations: centering race within the contemporary large-scale infrastructures of east Africa, *Antipode*, 52(3), 825–46.

Lai, K.P.Y., Lin, S. and Sidaway, J.D. (2020) Financing the Belt and Road Initiative (BRI): research agendas beyond the 'debt-trap' discourse, *Eurasian Geography and Economics*, 61(2), 109–24.

Larkin, B. (2013) The politics and poetics of infrastructure, *Annual Review of Anthropology*, 42(1), 327–43.

Lee, S.O., Wainwright, J. and Glassman, J. (2018) Geopolitical economy and the production of territory: the case of US–China geopolitical-economic competition in Asia, *Environment and Planning A: Economy and Space*, 50(2), 416–36.

Lefebvre, H. (1970) *La révolution urbaine*, Gallimard.

Lesutis, G. (2021) Infrastructural territorialisations: mega-infrastructures and the (re) making of Kenya, *Political Geography*, 90, art 102459. doi: 10.1016/j.polgeo.2021.102459

Li, T.M. (2018) After the land grab: infrastructural violence and the 'mafia system' in Indonesia's oil palm plantation zones, *Geoforum*, 96, 328–37.

Liu, H. and Liu, W. (2017) Study on relationship between the Belt and Road Initiative and regional development strategies of China (in Chinese), *Bulletin of Chinese Academy of Sciences*, 32(4), 340–7.

Malik, A., Parks, B., Russell, B., Lin, J., Walsh, K., Solomon, K. et al (2021) *Banking on the Belt and Road: Insights from a New Global Dataset of 13,247 Chinese Development Projects*, AidData.

Massey, D. (1994) *Space, Place and Gender*, University of Minnesota Press.

Mezzadra, S. and Neilson, B. (2019) *The Politics of Operations: Excavating Contemporary Capitalism*, Duke University Press.

Murton, G. and Lord, A. (2020) Trans-Himalayan power corridors: infrastructural politics and China's Belt and Road Initiative in Nepal, *Political Geography*, 77, art 102100. doi: 10.1016/j.polgeo.2019.102100

Neilson, B. (2019) Precarious in Piraeus: on the making of labour insecurity in a port concession, *Globalizations*, 16, 559–74.

Oakes, T. (2021) The Belt and Road as method: geopolitics, technopolitics and power through an infrastructure lens, *Asia Pacific Viewpoint*, 62, 281–5.

Pascha, W. (2021) *Duisburg and Its Port, Endpoint of China's Silk Road: Opportunities and Risks (Report No 2021-1)*, Ordnungspolitische Diskurse.

Perreault, T.A., Bridge, G. and McCarthy, J. (eds) (2015) *The Routledge Handbook of Political Ecology*, Routledge.

Perveen, S. and Khalil, J. (2015) Gwadar-Kashgar economic corridor: challenges and imperatives for Pakistan and China, *Journal of Political Studies*, 22, 351–66.

Robinson, J. (2011) Cities in a world of cities: the comparative gesture, *International Journal of Urban and Regional Research*, 35(1), 1–23.

Rodgers, D. and O'Neill, B. (2012) Infrastructural violence: introduction to the special issue, *Ethnography*, 13(4), 401–12.

Safina, A., Ramondetti, L. and Governa, F. (2023) Rescaling the Belt and Road Initiative in urban China: the local complexities of a global project, *Area Development and Policy Geopolitics*, advance online publication. doi: 10.1080/23792949.2023.2174888

Salamanca, O.J. and Silver, J. (2022) In the excess of splintering urbanism: the racialised political economy of infrastructure, *Journal of Urban Technology*, 29, 117–25.

Schindler, S., Alami, I., DiCarlo, J., Jepson, N., Rolf, S., Bayırbağ, M.K. et al (2023) The Second Cold War: US-China competition for centrality in infrastructure, digital, production, and finance networks, *Geopolitics*, advance online publication. doi: 10.1080/14650045.2023.2253432

Seone, M.F.V. (2020) Alibaba's discourse for the digital Silk Road: the electronic World Trade Platform and 'inclusive globalization', *Chinese Journal of Communication*, 13(1), 68–83.

Shin, H.B., Zhao, Y. and Koh, S.Y. (2022) The urbanising dynamics of global China: speculation, articulation, and translation in global capitalism, *Urban Geography*, 43(10), 1457–68.

Sidaway, J.D., Rowedder, S.C., Woon, C.Y., Lin, W. and Pholsena, V. (2020) Politics and spaces of China's Belt and Road Initiative, *Environment and Planning C*, 38(5), 795–802.

Smith, N. (2010) *Uneven Development: Nature, Capital, and the Production of Space*, University of Georgia Press.

Song, T., Chahine, T. and Sun, M. (2020) Ruili, China: the China–Myanmar nexus hub at the crossroads, *Cities*, 104, art 102766. doi: 10.1016/j.cities.2020.102766

Star, S.L. (1999) The ethnography of infrastructure, *American Behavioral Scientist*, 43(3), 377–91.

Sum, N.L. (2019) The intertwined geopolitics and geoeconomics of hopes/fears: China's triple economic bubbles and the 'One Belt One Road' imaginary, *Territory, Politics, Governance*, 7(4), 528–52.

Summers, T. (2016) China's 'New Silk Roads': sub-national regions and networks of global political economy, *Third World Quarterly*, 37(9), 1628–43.

Swyngedouw, E. (2006) Circulations and metabolisms: (hybrid) natures and (cyborg) cities, *Science as Culture*, 15(2), 105–21.

Tassadiq, F. (2022) Producing dispossessed and humanitarian subjects: land acquisition and compensation policies in Lahore, Pakistan, *PoLAR: Political and Legal Anthropology Review*, 45(2), 240–56.

Teo, H.C., Lechner, A.M., Walton, G.W., Chan, F.K.S., Cheshmezangi, A., Tan-Mullins, M. et al (2019) Environmental impacts of infrastructure development under the Belt and Road initiative, *Environments*, 6(6), 72. doi: 10.3390/environments6060072

Tooze, A. (2018) *Crashed: How a Decade of Financial Crises Changed the World*, Allen Lane.

Vorobyev, N.V., Emelyanova, N.V. and Rykov, P.V. (2018) The urbanization and development of urban agglomerations in Siberia and North China in the context of the new Silk Road, *Problems of Economic Transition*, 60(8–9), 597–613.

Wan, C., Zhao, Y., Zhang, D. and Yip, T.L. (2021) Identifying important ports in maritime container shipping networks along the Maritime Silk Road, *Ocean & Coastal Management*, 211, art 105738. doi: 10.1016/j.ocecoaman.2021.105738

Wiig, A., Ward, K., Enright, T., Hodson, M., Pearsall, H. and Silver, J. (eds) (2023) *Infrastructuring Urban Futures: The Politics of Remaking Cities*, Policy Press.

Winter, T. (2016) One belt, one road, one heritage: cultural diplomacy and the Silk Road, *The Diplomat*, 29, 1–5.

Woon, C.Y. (2020) Framing the 'Polar Silk Road' (冰上丝绸之路): critical geopolitics, Chinese scholars and the (re)positionings of China's Arctic interests, *Political Geography*, 78, art 102141. doi: 10.1016/j.polgeo.2019.102141

Zhang, F. (2013) The rise of Chinese exceptionalism in international relations, *European Journal of International Relations*, 19(2), 305–28.

Zhang, X. (2017) Chinese capitalism and the maritime silk road: a world-systems perspective, *Geopolitics*, 22(2), 310–31.

Ziadah, R. (2018) Constructing a logistics space: perspectives from the Gulf Cooperation Council, *Environment and Planning D: Society and Space*, 36(4), 666–82.

1

The Contested Coal-Fired Power in the Belt and Road Initiative: Indonesia as a Case Study

Bowen Gu

Introduction

Since the 'Going Out' strategy in the 2000s, which encouraged Chinese corporations to invest abroad, and the launch of the Belt and Road Initiative (BRI) in 2013, China has increasingly extended its domestic coal value chain beyond its border. According to a study published in 2019, Chinese investment accounts for more than a quarter of the 399 gigawatts of coal-fired power plants (CFPPs) under development outside China (Shearer and Buckley, 2019). While President Xi Jinping announced China's commitment to stop overseas coal-fired power financing at the United Nations General Assembly in September 2021 (Ministry of Foreign Affairs of the People's Republic of China, 2021), the projects that have been planned and constructed and those that are in operation will continue to impact local communities, Indigenous people and the climate prospects.

Energy infrastructure projects are a product of social relations. From coal investment to coal exit, from fossil fuel divestment to renewable energy deployment, energy transition is not only techno-economic but also deeply social and political (Temper et al, 2020; Sovacool et al, 2022). This calls for a multidisciplinary political ecology approach to investigate and understand the role of social movements in the energy transition process. Indonesia, the world's fourth-largest democracy by population and the top recipient country of Chinese coal finance, makes an appealing case study country to critically examine Chinese investment in the coal-fired power sector from a political ecology lens.

In an earlier study, I conducted a country-wide analysis of socio-environmental conflicts over CFPPs in Indonesia with Chinese investment (Gu, 2024). This was based on a comparative political ecology analysis of 25 case studies in the Global Atlas of Environmental Justice (EJAtlas), the world's largest online database of environmental movements, co-created with scholarly and activist knowledge (Temper et al, 2015; Scheidel et al, 2018; Martínez-Alier, 2023). The study demonstrates how various forms of politics from below and local power structures shape BRI energy infrastructure investment and the top-down vision of 'green BRI' in practice. This chapter builds on this work and presents in more detail four case studies that exemplify how different types of CFPPs under the BRI – namely, general, mine-mouth and captive plants – are perceived and contested by local communities and civil society organizations. In addition to secondary sources, this chapter draws insights from interviews with local and international actors.

The concept of languages of valuation in ecological economics provides an important analytical lens to examine socio-environmental conflicts (Martínez-Alier, 2009; Zografos, 2023). It builds on the argument for value incommensurability that holds that not all values can be commensurable and measured in the same unit, especially the same monetary unit (Martínez-Alier et al, 1998). This calls for taking into consideration the plurality of languages of valuation in understanding and resolving socio-environmental conflicts. Neyra (2025), for example, uses this concept to illustrate how a mining company's governance approach favours monetary claims, which leads to loss of traditional values and division among local communities near Las Bambas copper mine. In this chapter, the four CFPP case studies further demonstrate that languages of valuation by local communities and civil society may differ or clash with the monetary reductionism approach adopted by the project developers and financiers. Despite the potential for electrification and the opportunity for economic income brought about by coal-fuelled energy infrastructure development, these cases demonstrate the unevenly distributed impacts of these CFPP projects and the multidimensional deprivation of marginalized communities, such as traditional fisherfolk and Indigenous people, in their access to clean air, water, land, health and traditional values embedded in their livelihoods.

Overview of Chinese investment in CFPPs in Indonesia

Coal has been an important source of both domestic electricity access and export in Indonesia, fuelling the country's growth to become the largest economy in Southeast Asia in the past decade and still accounting for more than 60 per cent of the country's electricity mix (IEA, 2021; World Bank, 2023). China's increasing overseas investment in CFPPs coincides with Indonesia's domestic energy infrastructure boom in the past decades, including three large-scale electricity infrastructure programmes based predominantly on coal-fired power (Tritto, 2021). These include fast-track programmes FTP-1 (2005) and FTP-2 (2010), launched by former president Susilo Bambang Yudhoyono, and the 35,000 megawatt (MW) project launched by President Joko Widodo in 2015, which superseded the previous fast-track programmes (Ordonez et al, 2021).

Indonesia's state-owned utility company, PT PLN, plays a monopoly role in the electricity market and controls the country's energy generation, transmission and distribution. Since the launch of FTP-2, Indonesia has increased its reliance on independent power producers, which renders opportunities for domestic and international companies to build and operate CFPPs through signing power purchase agreements with PLN. Against this background, Chinese companies started entering the Indonesia market in the 2000s as engineering, procurement and construction contractors, and over the years increasingly took up more ownership of projects in the form of equity investment and joint ventures (Liu et al, 2022a). Despite being a relative latecomer, compared to Japan and Korea, China has secured a major role in Indonesia's energy infrastructure boom, accounting for almost 30 per cent of Indonesia's total coal power capacity (Liu et al, 2022b).

Three major types of CFPPs have emerged among those with Chinese investment: general CFPPs, which are mostly located along the coast; mine-mouth CFPPs; and off-grid captive CFPPs that are part of an industrial complex that includes aluminium smelters and nickel industrial parks (Gu, 2024). In the following section, case studies representing different types of CFPP are presented to illustrate various forms of Chinese stakeholder involvement in Indonesia's energy infrastructure, which is inextricably intertwined with extractive industries, including coal and nickel.

Case studies

The four case studies in this section have been selected to represent the diverse geography and the three types of CFPPs. The cases are: two general CFPPs, one located on the coast of Sumatra and one on the coast of Java; one mine-mouth CFPP in South Sumatra; and one captive CFPP complex that is part of a nickel industrial park in North Maluku. Table 1.1 provides an overview of these four cases and the role Chinese companies and financiers play for each one, based on aggregated data from the EJAtlas (2024).

Teluk Sepang power plant, Bengkulu

The Teluk Sepang Power Plant, located on Baai Island in Teluk Sepang, Bengkulu, is a 200 MW CFPP that is part of Indonesia's 35,000 MW

Table 1.1: Overview of CFPPs in the case studies

Power plant	Type	Location	Capacity (MW)	Chinese company	Chinese financier
Teluk Sepang power plant	General	Bengkulu	200	PowerChina	ICBC (Industrial and Commercial Bank of China), Export-Import Bank of China
Celukan Bawang power plant	General	Bali	380	China Huadian	China Development Bank
Sumsel-8 power plant (Bangko Tengah)	Mine-mouth	South Sumatra	1,200	China Huadian (55%)	Export-Import Bank of China
Weda Bay Industrial Park captive plants	Captive	North Maluku	3,400	Tsingshan Holding Group, Zhenshi Holding Group, Zhejiang Huajun Investment Co, Ltd, Zhejiang Huayou Cobalt Co, Ltd	-

Source: EJAtlas (2024)

programme, an infrastructure programme launched by President Joko Widodo in 2015 to boost Indonesia's electricity generation (EJAtlas, 2023a). In November 2015, the state-owned Power Construction Corporation of China (PowerChina) secured the power purchase agreement with PLN (Global Energy Monitor, 2024a). A joint venture, PT Tenaga Listrik Bengkulu, was formed between PowerChina and PT Intraco Penta to oversee the construction and operation of the plant under the Build-Own-Operate-Transfer model. The construction began in October 2016 (Global Energy Monitor, 2024a).

Compared to many other CFPP projects with Chinese investment, the scale of the Bengkulu plant is relatively small, making it seemingly inconspicuous. However, a story made its way to *The Jakarta Post* in February 2020, revealing that local residents of Baai Island had protested in response to the death of sea turtles after the first trial of the power plant (The Jakarta Post, 2020). By February 2020, the deaths of 28 turtles had been confirmed, although local authorities disputed that the turtles had died of polluted power plant water. Shortly after this incident, in response to the news that President Jokowi would be in the region for the inauguration of the plant in February 2020, local communities, fisherfolk and environmental group Koalisi Langit Biru (meaning Blue Sky Coalition) put up a 2 metre by 12 metre banner at the Teluk Sepang bay area near the Bengkulu plant that said: 'Jokowi, PLTU Membunuh Laut Kami' (Jokowi, coal-fired power plant kills our sea). While the President ultimately cancelled his trip for unknown reasons, the local communities' struggles continued.

It was reported that the opposition towards the plant had already started before the construction began, when the Indonesian grassroots NGO WALHI raised concerns in August 2016 (EJAtlas, 2023a). On the first day of construction in 2016, hundreds of local people (mostly fisherfolk) blocked the road leading to the plant. A petition was also sent to the governor of Bengkulu. In August 2018, several residents of Teluk Sepang protested in the streets, demanding a renewable energy alternative and urging the government to support the farmers whose land had been flooded due to the damming of a local stream by the construction team in early 2018, which allegedly led to the loss of 15 ha of agricultural land and crops (EJAtlas, 2023a). Also of particular concern for these protesters were the potential effects of air pollution on the environment and people's health.

In June 2019, local residents, including smallholder fishermen and farmers, with the support of environmental groups Kanopi Hijau (meaning Green Canopy) and, again, Koalisi Langit Biru, filed a lawsuit at the Bengkulu State Administrative Court against the Teluk Sepang power plant, seeking revocation of its environmental permit (Malinda, 2021). The lawsuit was ruled in favour of the power plant operators in December 2019, after 20 trial sessions. Despite the opposition from local communities and civil society organizations, the Bengkulu power plant went into operation in July 2020 (EJAtlas, 2023a). In the meantime, the subsequent appeal at a higher court, as well as a cassation and judicial review at the Supreme Court (see Table 1.2), ended in failure. When filing the case for judicial review at the Bengkulu State Administrative Court, a theatrical action, with civil society organizations and students participating, was performed in front of the court to show opposition against the CFPP.

Celukan Bawang power plant, Bali

Bali is widely known as a tourist destination. In November 2022, it hosted the G20 conference, where the Indonesian Just Energy Transition Partnership agreement was signed in support of Indonesia's just energy transition. However, few of those visiting Bali would have known about the 426 MW CFPP located at Celukan Bawang village in Buleleng District on the northern side of the island. Built by PT General Energy Bali, which is owned by China Huadian Engineering (51 per cent), Merryline International Pte

Table 1.2: Timeline of legal mobilization against Teluk Sepang power plant in Bengkulu

Filing date	Level of court	Reason
June 2019	Bengkulu State Administrative Court	Request to revoke the plant's environmental permit due to discrepancies in the environmental impact assessment (AMDAL), including inaccurate information about public acceptance and inadequate planning for earthquake and tsunami
April 2020	Medan Administrative High Court	To appeal the decision made at the Bengkulu State Administrative Court
July 2020	Bengkulu State Administrative Court	To submit a memorandum of cassation to the Supreme Court
September 2021	Supreme Court	To request judicial review because the judge had made a mistake in the decision to reject the citizens' lawsuit from the first instance and in the following appeal, and did not see that the plaintiffs were victims who had a legal standing

Source: EJAtlas (2024)

Ltd, and PT General Energy Indonesia, the Celukan Bawang power plant has been supplying 40 per cent of Bali's electricity since 2015 (EJAtlas, 2023b).

Local communities have been fighting against the socio-environmental impacts of the Celukan Bawang power plant and its expansion plan for years. One of the protests took place only three months before the G20 Summit in 2022; this was in response to a barge loaded with over nine tonnes of coal to be used by the power plant being stranded near the shore of Celukan Bawang village in August 2022 (EJAtlas, 2023b). Ten local fishermen launched a protest outside the governor's office and urged the officials to take action over the coal spill in the coastal waters of Buleleng.

The villagers' opposition to the CFPP was supported by both local and international NGOs, including Greenpeace. In January 2018, three community members, supported by Greenpeace and Bali Legal Aid Foundation, initiated a legal action to stop the expansion of the plant. The case is known as *Wijana, Sufarlan, Astawa & Greenpeace Indonesia v Governor of Bali* (Wardana, 2022). The community members were concerned with the potential impacts on their livelihoods, while Greenpeace was concerned with the climate and environmental impacts. The lawsuit was rejected by the Denpasar State Administrative Court on procedural grounds as the court considered that the plaintiffs did not have legal standing because they did not suffer any loss (Global Energy Monitor, 2024b). Like the Bengkulu case, the dismissal at the lower court was upheld by the Surabaya High Court and the Supreme Court. Despite the failure in court, the controversy of the power plant came to the attention of the new governor of Bali at the time, Wayan Koster, who requested that the Celukan Bawang power plant be converted from coal to a more sustainable fuel, or at least to gas (EJAtlas, 2023b).

Mobilization has also been expressed in artistic forms, including the Summer Festival 2.0 music festival in August 2019, which was organized by Greenpeace and took place near the Celukan Bawang CFPP. The Indonesian musicians participating in the concert later released an album titled *Senandung Energi Bumi* (Harmony of the Earth). In addition, the Greenpeace Rainbow Warrior ship staged a solidarity campaign near the coast of Celukan Bawang, with banners in Bhasa bearing slogans such as 'End Coal' and 'Tolak PLTU Batubara' (Reject coal-fired power plant; EJAtlas, 2023b).

Sumsel-8 (Bangko Tengah) power plant, South Sumatra

Sumsel-8 power plant, also known as SS-8 or Bangko Tengah power plant, is a mine-mouth CFPP that is part of Indonesia's 35,000 MW programme (EJAtlas, 2023d). Mine-mouth CFPPs make use of the coal – mostly lignite with lower calorific value – from mining sites near the plant to reduce the transportation costs; this feature has been used to promote domestic consumption of coal in Indonesia (Gu, 2024). With a capacity of 1,320 MW, Sumsel-8 is the largest mine-mouth power plant in Indonesia and Southeast Asia. It is located at Tanjung Lalang village in Muara Enim Regency, South Sumatra province, 2 km from the Bangko Tengah coal mine. The plant was developed by PT Huadian Bukit Asam Power (PT HBAP), a joint venture consortium formed by Indonesian state coal miner PT Bukit Asam Tbk (PTBA, 45 per cent) and China Huadian (55 per cent).

The Sumsel-8 power plant is a national strategic project and expected to connect with PLN's substation at Muara Enim through a newly constructed 45 km extra-high voltage (500 kV) transmission network built by the HBAP consortium. It was reported that the transmission line passes through community-owned (ulayat) land, and the construction allegedly caused conflicts between the communities and the mining company PTBA (EJAtlas, 2023d). According to the grassroots NGO AEER, the ulayat land was claimed unilaterally by the oil palm plantation company PT Sawindo Bumi Permai (PT SBP) in the 1990s, and the plantation land, amounting to approximately 10,000 ha, owned by PT SBP was then sold and acquired by PTBA in 2014 for coal mining (Harahap et al, 2021). The villagers, through village heads and Indigenous community leaders, objected and protested the acquisition process and then formed the Tanjung Agung Bersatu Community Forum to carry out actions to close the access road to oil palm plantations owned by PT SBP. The actions lasted for nine months, until two community members were arrested and criminalized in violation of article 2 of Emergency Law No 12 of 1951, related to the possession of sharp weapons (EJAtlas, 2023d). It was also reported that the villagers refused the company's negotiation offers, including monetary compensation and the offer to construct infrastructure facilities at Tanjung Agung village; instead, they insisted on the return of the customary land to the village (EJAtlas, 2023d).

In early 2021, AEER sent a letter expressing environmental and social concerns about the Sumsel-8 power plant project to the main financier, the Export-Import Bank of China, and the lead company in charge of the project, China Huadian Corporation, as well as the Chinese embassy in Jakarta. While the Export-Import Bank of China (and the other Chinese institutions mentioned earlier) did not respond directly to AEER's letter, the bank's chairwoman indicated in an interview in March 2022 that it would no longer finance new overseas coal power projects and would remain committed to supporting emission reduction upgrades for completed projects (EJAtlas, 2023d).

Coal-fuelled Indonesia Weda Bay Industrial Park, North Maluku

The Indonesia Weda Bay Industrial Park (IWIP) is a mega-nickel integrated mining and smelting project and also the 'first vertical, from mine mouth to finished products, integrated Electric Vehicle battery and stainless-steel industry complex in the world' (IWIP, nd). It is located in Weda, Central Halmahera Regency, North Maluku. The IWIP is one of Indonesia's strategic projects, designed to expand its domestic nickel processing capacity after the country banned unprocessed ore exports. It is a joint venture between three Chinese companies: Tsingshan Group (with a 40 per cent shareholding through its subsidiary, Perlus Technology), Huayou Group (30 per cent) and Zhenshi Group (30 per cent; EJAtlas, 2023c).

The construction of the industrial park started in 2018, including the planned development of ferronickel, cobalt and battery production, as well as captive power plants to fuel the energy-intensive smelters (EJAtlas, 2023c). It has been estimated that the total coal-fired power capacity operating or under development at Weda Bay is at least 3,400 MW, while the off-grid nature of the captive power plant and the lack of transparency makes it difficult to estimate the exact capacity of the CFPP both in operation and under development (Global Energy Monitor, 2024c).

IWIP is located in one of the least populous islands in Indonesia, Halmahera Island, which is mostly covered with forests and mountains and is home to approximately 28 ethnic groups (Climate Rights International, 2024). Over the years, the Indonesian government has been trying to resettle the Indigenous group in the region outside the forest, forcing them to adopt conventional settled lifestyles instead of their traditional nomadic lifestyle. One of these groups is called the O Hongana Manyawa (also referred to as Tobelo Dalam), which means 'forest people'. They are one of the five last remaining nomadic Indigenous peoples in Indonesia and categorized as endangered according to Aliansi Masyarakat Adat Nusantara (Indigenous Peoples' Alliance of Nusantara), the main representative organization for Indonesia's Indigenous peoples (EJAtlas, 2023c). According to an interview with Tupa, one of the members of the six remaining tribes that are still practising the traditional nomadic lifestyle in the forest, the 'trees are gone and replaced with the big road, where giant machines go in and out making noise and driving the animals away' (EJAtlas, 2023c). For the few last remaining tribe members in the forest, the forest is not only a place to inhabit and find sources of food, but 'also a home and "the bridge" that connects them with the spiritual world' (EJAtlas, 2023c). Moreover, the reclamation of nickel ore storage areas by IWIP in the Karkar area has affected the fishing activities that used to take place in the same area.

The villagers of Lelilef Sawai, Lelilef Waibulan, and Gemaf have complained about respiratory problems due to air pollution from captive CFPPs that use low-calorie coal. Local residents have also had their access to clean water restricted, with the Ake Sake River dammed and diverted for the construction of one of the IWIP smelters, while other rivers such as Seslewe Sini and Kobe have been polluted. The increase in logging and the damming and diversion of the Ake Sake River have led to deforestation and reduced water absorption capacity, contributing to the flood that took place in August 2020, which inundated the villages and roads, including the IWIP area.

Some local residents had no choice but to sell their land to the companies, and the bid price from the companies was low (for example, IDR 8,000–9,000 – equivalent to around half a euro – per square metre) based on regional regulations. While the majority of residents sold their land, a few refused to do so. In 2019, protests occurred by the relatives of O Hongana Manyawa band living in Akejira forest. Another protest took place in July 2020, with 450 South Wasile residents walking for two days to Kao Rahai, where PT Weda Bay Nickel was opening a new nickel mining area, and blocking roads with tents, to halt mining activities. In addition, there were protests from students and civil society organizations in Ternate, a major city in North Maluku. On 23 October 2019, another demonstration was held by Aliansi Masyarakat Ake Jira Halmahera (the Ake Jira Halmahera Community Alliance) in front of the Ternate mayor's office. The crowd carried banners saying, in Bhasa, 'Selamatkan Ake Jira' (Save Ake Jira).

Despite complaints and protests, the operation of IWIP and the construction of new CFPPs have continued. Allegedly, residents of Tobelo Dalam who lived in Ake Jira left their original residential area (EJAtlas, 2023c).

Lessons for BRI governance: embodied energy justice and blue justice

While China committed to no more overseas coal financing in 2021, the legacy of both built and planned CFPPs will persist. Resonating with Rogelja's (2020) analysis in the Balkan context, the inertia from CFPP projects remains long after they are built and paid off. While studies have begun to look at post-mining landscapes in Indonesia, the socio-environmental injustice legacies of CFPPs, some of which are still under construction, tend to become silenced and invisible behind the facade of the so-called 'just transition' agendas. The four case studies presented here have made such legacies of environmental pollution and dispossession visible.

The concept of 'embodied energy justice', introduced by Healy et al (2019, p 230), aims to 'reframe considerations of energy justice to explicitly consider hidden and distant injustices, upstream or downstream, arising from the extraction, processing, transportation and disposal of energy sources'. It provides an important framework for capturing transboundary, direct and indirect, as well as visible and hidden, socio-environmental impacts of energy infrastructure and to connect local struggles with broader national and global politics. In the context of CFPPs with Chinese investment and entangled in the local sociopolitical dynamics in Indonesia, embodied energy justice serves as a useful lens for analysis. As exemplified in the four case studies, the impacts of CFPPs extend beyond the infrastructure site and immediate neighbourhoods, reaching communities involved in coal mining, marine areas where coal is transported and rivers affected by interception. This illustrates the concept of 'embodied injustice' within the coal-fuelled value chain. These dynamics occur in the context of rising coal consumption in China, Indonesia and globally (IEA, 2023).

In addition to visible and measurable impacts, the loss of incommensurable values, such as traditional forms of fishing and Indigenous livelihoods, have been conveyed through socio-environmental conflicts, often resulting in failed lawsuits. Despite corporate efforts to compensate through corporate social responsibility initiatives, the loss of livelihoods, traditions and cultural values that are incommensurable can hardly be recovered or reimbursed. In some cases, monetary compensation is rejected by communities, underscoring the inadequacy of financial remedies in addressing these losses. This resonates with studies in regions with legacies of colonial influence, where local responses to foreign investments need to be understood from the context of local histories and Indigenous cultures (Neyra, 2025).

Social mobilizations embody the 'hope' for a future that can be changed or transformed. The findings of this study resonate with scholars who argue that Chinese investment abroad is significantly influenced by local sociopolitical contexts, which can limit the impact of local resistance against CFPPs (Oliveira et al, 2020; Rogelja, 2020; Apostolopoulou, 2021; Pavlićević and Talmacs, 2022; Tritto and Camba, 2022). The weak environmental governance system and the lack of redress mechanisms in the host country, in this case Indonesia, contribute to a gap between the 'green BRI' vision and the realities on the ground. This gap is further exacerbated by the increasing entanglements between transition mineral extraction and energy infrastructure, as seen in the IWIP case and other emerging coal-fuelled nickel industrial parks in Indonesia.

This chapter sheds light on the grounded perspectives of the BRI through the lens of grassroots socio-environmental conflicts involving communities and civil society. In the absence of 'green BRI' governance on the ground, the socio-environmental conflicts under analysis exemplify 'resistance as governance' or local people's 'self-governance' to preserve their culture and livelihoods (Gobby et al, 2021; Apostolopoulou and Pant, 2022). They demonstrate the valuation languages and value systems of local communities and civil society, which encompass traditional forms of knowledge and livelihoods as well as incommensurable values that are often overlooked in economic compensation and corporate social responsibility.

Frictions are sometimes unavoidable during the planning and construction of energy infrastructure projects. In Indonesia, projects financed and supported by other countries, such as Japan and Korea, have also received various forms of opposition. However, Chinese stakeholders have been less communicative and responsive when confronted with such frictions. This highlights the need for more transparent communication and engagement with local communities to resolve conflicts and maintain the reputation of project financiers and engineering companies.

Revealing grassroots perceptions and resistances helps us understand why and how grassroots opposition to energy infrastructures empowers marginalized voices. It also underscores the need for research and policy efforts that take such perspectives into consideration, instead of viewing communities as passive recipients of an energy infrastructure boom influenced by Global China. Public participation and feedback from bottom-up mobilizations could potentially provide risk warning signals for Chinese companies investing in overseas CFPPs, helping to reduce operational risks and prevent or alleviate socio-environmental conflicts.

The connection with international networks and broader alliances that bridge local livelihood and environmental concerns with the global climate crisis helps support local struggles amid domestic political constraints and global capital influence. However, local communities in Indonesia, especially fisherfolk, have been shouldering a large proportion of the resistance against injustices stemming from CFPPs. This calls for more studies on the impact of Chinese investment on marine socioecological systems and coastal livelihoods from a 'blue justice' perspective, in addition to terrestrial and more visible effects.

References

Apostolopoulou, E. (2021) Tracing the links between infrastructure-led development, urban transformation, and inequality in China's Belt and Road Initiative, *Antipode*, 53(3), 831–58.

Apostolopoulou, E. and Pant, H. (2022) 'Silk Road here we come': infrastructural myths, post-disaster politics, and the shifting urban geographies of Nepal, *Political Geography*, 98, art 102704. doi: 10.1016/j.polgeo.2022.102704

Climate Rights International (2024) Nickel Unearthed: The Human and Climate Costs of Indonesia's Nickel Industry. Available at: https://cri.org/wp-content/uploads/2024/01/NICKEL_UNEARTHED.pdf

EJAtlas (2023a) Bengkulu coal-fired power plant, Indonesia. Available at: https://ejatlas.org/conflict/bengkulu-coal-fired-power-plant-bengkulu-province-indonesia

EJAtlas (2023b) Celukan Bawang coal power station, North Bali, Indonesia. Available at: https://ejatlas.org/conflict/celukan-bawang-coal-power-station-north-bali-indonesia

EJAtlas (2023c) Indonesia Weda Bay Industrial Park (IWIP), North Maluku, Indonesia. Available at: https://ejatlas.org/conflict/indonesia-weda-bay-industrial-park-iwip-north-maluku-indonesia

EJAtlas (2023d) Sumsel-8 coal-fired power plant, South Sumatra, Indonesia. Available at: https://ejatlas.org/conflict/sumsel-8-coal-fired-power-plant-south-sumatra-indonesia

EJAtlas (2024) Global Atlas of Environmental Justice. Available at: https://ejatlas.org

Global Energy Monitor (2024a) Bengkulu coal-fired power plant. Available at: www.gem.wiki/Bengkulu_power_station

Global Energy Monitor (2024b) Celukan Bawang power station. Available at: www.gem.wiki/Celukan_Bawang_power_station

Global Energy Monitor (2024c) Weda Bay power station. Available at: www.gem.wiki/Weda_Bay_power_station

Gobby, J., Temper, L., Burke, M. and von Ellenrieder, N. (2021) Resistance as governance: transformative strategies forged on the frontlines of extractivism in Canada, *The Extractive Industries and Society*, preprint. doi: 10.1016/j.exis.2021.100919

Gu, B. (2024) Black gold and green BRI–a grounded analysis of Chinese investment in coal-fired power plants in Indonesia, *The Extractive Industries and Society*, 17, art 101411. doi: 10.1016/j.exis.2024.101411

Harahap, W., Ginting, P., Distincta, H., Rushdi, M. and Burmansyah, E. (2021) Low *Carbon Development of South Sumatra Has the Potential to Be Hampered By Low Quality Coal Investment* [Batu Bara Kualitas Rendah Berpotensi Menghambat Pembangunan Rendah Karbon Sumatera Selatan], AEER. Available at: www.aeer.or.id/en/south-sumatera-low-carbon-development-to-be-hampered-by-low-quality-coal-investment/

Healy, N., Stephens, J.C. and Malin, S.A. (2019) Embodied energy injustices: unveiling and politicizing the transboundary harms of fossil fuel extractivism and fossil fuel supply chains, *Energy Research & Social Science*, 48, 219–34.

IEA (2021) *Coal 2021: Analysis and Forecast to 2024*, IEA. Available at: www.iea.org/reports/coal-2021

IEA (2023) Global coal demand set to remain at record levels in 2023, IEA, 27 July. Available at: www.iea.org/news/global-coal-demand-set-to-remain-at-record-levels-in-2023

IWIP (nd) About Indonesia Weda Bay Industrial Park, IWIP. Available at: https://iwip.co.id/en/about-iwip/

Liu, C., Hale, T. and Urpelainen, J. (2022a) Explaining the energy mix in China's electricity projects under the Belt and Road Initiative, *Environmental Politics*, advance online publication. doi: 10.1080/09644016.2022.2087355

Liu, C., Hale, T. and Urpelainen, J. (2022b) *Supply and Demand for Clean Power in the Belt and Road: Comparing the Political Economy of Pakistan and Indonesia*, Climate Works Foundation, ISEP and Blavatnik School of Government.

Malinda, R. (2021) The legal battle of a town in Indonesia against coal-fired power plant, Climate Tracker. Available at: https://climatetracker.org/legal-battle-coal-power-plant-indonesia/

Martinez-Alier, J. (2009) Social metabolism, ecological distribution conflicts, and languages of valuation, *Capitalism Nature Socialism*, 20(1), 58–87.

Martínez-Alier, J. (2023) *Land, Water, Air and Freedom: The Making of World Movements for Environmental Justice*, Edward Elgar.

Martinez-Alier, J., Munda, G. and O'Neill, J. (1998) Weak comparability of values as a foundation for ecological economics, *Ecological Economics*, 26(3), 277–86.

Ministry of Foreign Affairs of the People's Republic of China (2021) Xi Jinping attends the General Debate of the 76th Session of the United Nations General Assembly and delivers an important speech. Available at: www.fmprc.gov.cn/mfa_eng/wjb_663304/zzjg_663340/gjs_665170/gjsxw_665172/202109/t20210923_9580159.html

Neyra, R. (2025) Colonial governance in the mining sector: Las Bambas' RSC and the conflicts with the communities, *Capitalism Nature Socialism*, 36(1), 64–83.

Oliveira, G. de L.T., Murton, T., Rippa, A., Harlan, T. and Yang, Y. (2020) China's Belt and Road Initiative: views from the ground, *Political Geography*, 82, art 102225. doi: 10.1016/j.polgeo.2020.102225

Ordonez, J.A., Jakob, M., Steckel, J.C. and Fünfgeld, A. (2021) Coal, power and coal-powered politics in Indonesia, *Environmental Science and Policy*, 123, 44–57.

Pavlićević, D. and Talmacs, N. (2022) Answering the 'China question': local responses to Global China, in D. Pavlićević and N. Talmacs (eds) *The China Question: Contestations and Adaptations*, Springer Nature, pp 1–20.

Rogelja, I. (2020) Concrete and coal: China's infrastructural assemblages in the Balkans, *Political Geography*, 81, art 102220. doi: 10.1016/j.polgeo.2020.102220

Scheidel, A., Temper, A., Demaria, F. and Martínez-Alier, J. (2018) Ecological distribution conflicts as forces for sustainability: an overview and conceptual framework, *Sustainability Science*, 13(3), 585–98.

Shearer, C. and Buckley, T. (2019) China at a Crossroads: Continued Support for Coal Power Erodes Country's Clean Energy Leadership, Institute for Energy Economics and Financial Analysis.

Sovacool, B.K., Hess, D.J., Cantoni, R., Lee, D., Brisbois, M.C., Walnum, H.J. et al (2022) Conflicted transitions: exploring the actors, tactics, and outcomes of social opposition against energy infrastructure, *Global Environmental Change*, 73, art 102473. doi: 10.1016/j.gloenvcha.2022.102473

Temper, L., del Bene, D. and Martínez-Alier, J. (2015) Mapping the frontiers and front lines of global environmental justice: the EJAtlas, *Journal of Political Ecology*, 22(1), 255–78.

Temper, L., Avila, S., Del Bene, D., Gobby, J., Kosoy, N., Le Billon, P. et al (2020) Movements shaping climate futures: a systematic mapping of protests against fossil fuel and low-carbon energy projects, *Environmental Research Letters*, 15(12). doi: 10.1088/1748-9326/abc197

The Jakarta Post (2020) Residents reject Bengkulu power plant after turtles die, *The Jakarta Post*, 6 February. Available at: www.thejakartapost.com/news/2020/02/06/residents-reject-bengkulu-power-plant-after-turtles-die.html

Tritto, A. (2021) China's Belt and Road Initiative: from perceptions to realities in Indonesia's coal power sector, *Energy Strategy Reviews*, 34, art 100624. doi: 10.1016/j.esr.2021.100624

Tritto, A. and Camba, A. (2022) State-facilitated industrial parks in the Belt and Road Initiative: towards a framework for understanding the localization of the Chinese development model, *World Development Perspectives*, 28, art 100465. doi: 10.1016/j.wdp.2022.100465

Wardana, A. (2022) Governing through courts? A gloomy picture of climate litigation in Indonesia, *Völkerrechtsblog*. Available at: https://voelkerrechtsblog.org/governing-through-courts/

World Bank (2023) GDP growth (annual %) – Indonesia. Available at: https://data.worldbank.org/indicator/NY.GDP.MKTP.KD.ZG?locations=ID

Zografos, C. (2023) Languages of valuation, in S. Villamayor-Tomas and R. Muradian (eds) *The Barcelona School of Ecological Economics and Political Ecology: A Companion in Honour of Joan Martínez-Alier*, Springer, pp 47–58.

2

Dynamics of Grassroots Collectivism in Thailand's Special Economic Zones: Cases of Natural Resource Conflicts within the Belt and Road Initiative

Ratchada Arpornsilp

Introduction

Special economic zones (SEZs) have rapidly expanded as a spatial model and engine to promote industrial economic growth and development across the world. The first free trade zone was established in 1959, and the World Bank recorded over 4,300 operating SEZs by 2015, with almost 50 per cent located in Asia and the Pacific (Competitive Industries and Innovation Program, 2017). In the Greater Mekong Subregion (GMS), the promotion of SEZs is based also on the logic of regional integration and connectivity. They function as nodes of 'complementarity' to shared resources and competencies within the broad geography of economic corridors (Asian Development Bank, 2018). For Thailand, the previous military government directed the establishment of SEZs in ten target border provinces in 2014 under the collaborative frameworks of the Association of Southeast Asian Nations (ASEAN) Economic Community, the Greater Mekong Subregion Economic Cooperation Programme, and the Ayeywady-Chao Phraya-Mekong Economic Cooperation Strategy (National Economic and Social Development Council, 2019). These regional frameworks are central to the China-ASEAN Free Trade Area, which functions as a major corridor for the China's Belt and Road Initiative (BRI; Geopolitical Monitor, 2017).

In Thailand, the ambiguous and contested process of transitioning and repurposing public or communal lands for SEZs often proceeds without the informed engagement of local stakeholders whose existing livelihoods depend on accesses to these resources. Combining the analytical framing of political ecology with an emphasis on social movements and environmental justice literature, I explore why and how land and natural resource conflicts in SEZ development stimulate or reinvigorate grassroots collective actions that presumably were curtailed under the previous military-led regime in Thailand. Employing a nested case study approach with situated ethnographic and participatory methodologies, I investigate grassroots movements in the Chiang Khong SEZ in Chiang Rai province of northern Thailand. This is perceived as 'a critical case' because, in contrast to other provinces, the Subcommittee on Land Acquisition and Management under the Thai National Committee on SEZ policy has abandoned the use of state-owned land for SEZs in Chiang Rai province (National Economic and Social Development Council, 2019). I also supplement this primary case with contrasting analysis from the Nongkhai SEZ located at the northeastern border of Thailand and Lao People's Democratic Republic (Lao PDR).

Through a political ecology lens, this chapter compares findings from the cases of the Bun Rueang wetland protection in Chiang Khong SEZ and the Chaiya community forest dispossession in Nongkhai SEZ to make three broad arguments. First, I show that even though SEZs are usually framed around economic benefits, their fundamental motivation is territorial control and consolidation of state authority to enhance state formation (Ong, 2006; Moberg, 2017). Second, the cases illustrate that grassroots resistance can emerge in Thailand's authoritarian setting, although actions and outcomes may be very different. Third, I affirm that frontier landscapes and borderlands are key sites for state formation (Lamb, 2014; Mahanty, 2018; Chettri and Eilenberg, 2021). In this context, border SEZs provide important insights on state authority and territorialization, and how rural resistance to enclosures of commons can operate within Thailand's authoritarian politics.

Development context of selected SEZ cases

Increased Mekong regional connectivity through the BRI and the ASEAN Community is the development backdrop for the Chiang Khong and Nongkhai SEZ cases. The Asian Development Bank-driven regionalization efforts, known as the Greater Mekong Subregion initiative, overlaid the Economic Quadrangle that has facilitated extensive border trade between northern Thailand, Lao PDR, Myanmar and Yunnan province in China (Asian Development Bank, 2018). Since the 13th century, these areas have been connected through trade routes, regional exchanges and relationships between various chiefdoms and kingdoms (Sari, 2018). However, during colonialism and as national boundaries solidified in the 1890s, the Thai state and French colonial administration mapped and demarcated control at the territorial borders between Siam and Indochina along the Mekong River. They also seized cross-border trade benefits from local rulers and disrupted traditional interaction patterns (Walker, 2008). Further alienation and border delineations occurred during the Cold War period. The reopening of national borders and the transition from battlefield to marketplace, driven by the GMS regional integration scheme, has reshaped mainland Southeast Asia's border landscape.

Chiang Khong SEZ in Chiang Rai provincial development context

At the northern border province of Chiang Rai, the districts of Mae Sai, Chiang Saen and (my focal area) Chiang Khong have been included in the regionalization efforts since the early 1990s. The Chiang Rai SEZ project was part of this shift to greater connectivity in the post-Cold War era. Since 2006, the Thai government has planned to model Chiang Khong as the pilot for border industrial estate development (Kuaycharoen et al, 2021). The SEZ Policy Committee targeted Chiang Rai SEZ as a 'hub for tourism, agricultural products and food production, [and] international logistics and [a] multi-modal goods transportation center'. As shown in Figure 2.1, this large SEZ spans 21 sub-districts in three border districts, covering an area around 13 per cent of the total province. Chiang Rai SEZ sits within the GMS' North-South Economic Corridor, connecting with Southern China in Yunnan. On land, Chiang Rai SEZ is connected to neighbouring countries with the R3A Highway through Chiang Khong and the R3B Highway through Mae Sai. Chiang Saen and Chiang Khong are also connected through the Mekong riverway (Department of Provincial Administration, 2017).

Contemporary SEZs like Chiang Rai have accelerated more broadly in Thailand under the current authoritarian administration (Kuaycharoen et al, 2021). The Master Plan of Chiang Rai SEZ Development envisions distinct roles for each target locality within the SEZ. To fulfil this vision, the government incrementally disbursed up to THB 5,503 million (USD 184.28 million) between 2016 and 2019 to build basic infrastructure and facilities for SEZ development in Chiang Rai province (National Economic and Social Development Council, 2016). An additional budget of THB 2,139 million (USD 70 million) was allocated specifically for Chiang Khong Intermodal Facility, which was completed in early 2021 (National Economic and Social Development Council, 2021a).

At the centre of these developments, Chiang Khong SEZ included an approximate 480 ha of Bun Rueang wetland forest. Officially, this wetland is registered as public utility land that has been communally accessible

Figure 2.1: Locations of SEZ areas and Bun Rueang wetland in Chiang Rai province

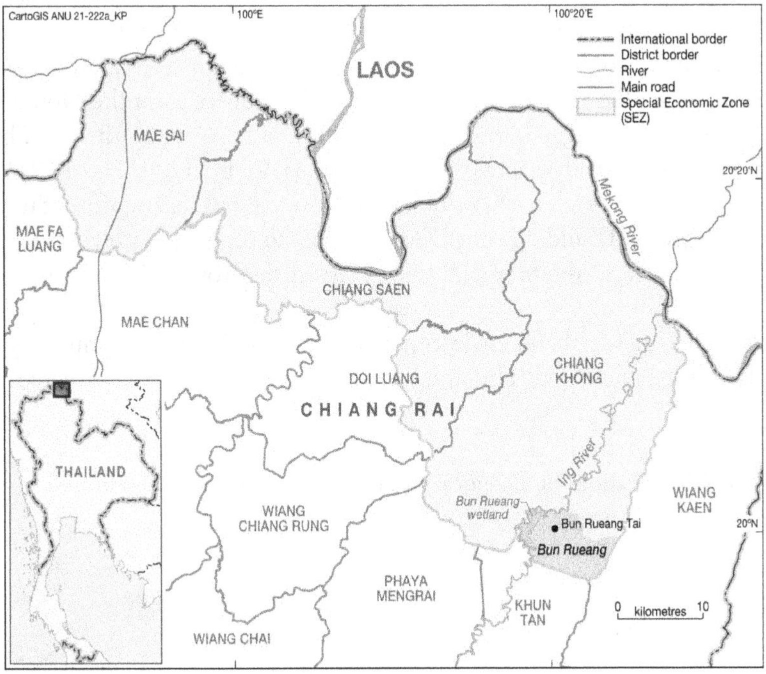

Source: Provided by CartoGIS, The Australian National University

to the local community members. The concerns over land and natural resource conversion led to grassroots mobilization supported by local groups, academics and civil society organizations. The movement disrupted state land conversion and eventually resulted in a withdrawal of the government's proposition to use public lands for private lease in Chiang Rai province. Contrary to other SEZs, the Chiang Rai SEZ investment acquires lands through Board of Investment schemes and private deals (National Economic and Social Development Council, 2021b).

Nongkhai SEZ development context

In the north-eastern province of Thailand, Nongkhai has been strategically important to regional integration. Nongkhai is situated along the North-South Economic Corridor within the GMS initiative and incorporated into the China-Indochina Peninsula Economic Corridor. In effect, since 2010, this corridor has been the backbone of the China-ASEAN Free Trade Area to promote trade, logistics, tourism and transport among South China, Indochina peninsular, Malaysia and Singapore (Gu and Li, 2008;

Kuaycharoen et al, 2021) and is a major corridor integrated into China's BRI (Geopolitical Monitor, 2017). Nongkhai province is therefore targeted to facilitate connectivity within the GMS and with other ASEAN countries.

In 2015, National Council for Peace and Order (NCPO) Order no 17/2558 and SEZ Policy Committee Announcement no 2/2558 on land provision for SEZ specified Mueang and Sa Krai districts for the Nongkhai SEZ (see Figure 2.2). Both districts are located adjacent to the 1st Thai-Lao Friendship Bridge across the Mekong to Vientiane in Lao PDR. In 2016, the NCPO issued Order no 3/2559 on the legal exemption of urban planning law and building control law in SEZs to support its previous Order by removing legal requirements stipulated in the Town Planning Act BE 2518 (1975).

In effect, the social and environmental safeguards previously stipulated in the laws were attenuated. This process paved the way for the transition of rural

Figure 2.2: Locations of SEZ areas and targeted land for appropriation in Nongkhai province

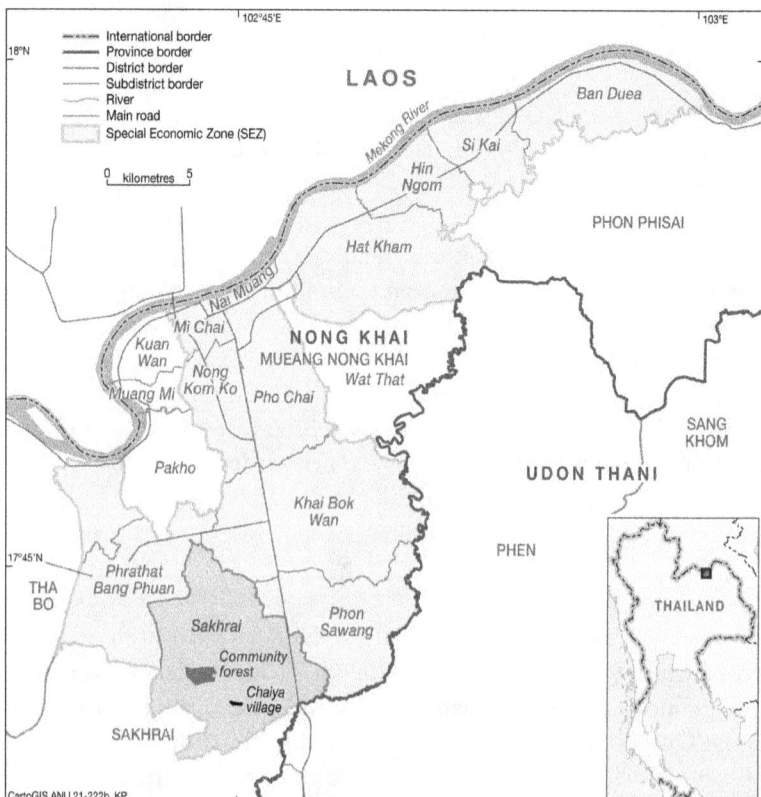

Source: Provided by CartoGIS, The Australian National University

and/or agricultural areas into industrial or development areas without the need to go through full-fledged public consultation and hearings, including on environmental and health impact assessment. In this regard, Chaiya public land, which used to be in the green zone within the abolished town plan, was re-demarcated into the purple zone for SEZ development. The Nongkhai SEZ policy statement emphasized the potential for connecting with several SEZs under the Vientiane Industrial and Trade Area and linkages with the Chinese market (National Economic and Social Development, 2021a).

The investment for Nongkhai SEZ development has focused predominantly on hard infrastructure construction for transportation, border checkpoint, waterworks, electricity and other utilities, and urban planning. From the beginning, the government has discharged a budget estimated at least USD 584 million to execute Nongkhai SEZ establishment plan, justifying these efforts to improve infrastructures as a way to facilitate business development and attract investment into the target areas. Providing long-term leasehold concessions for public land is another component of the SEZ initiative to incentivize the private sector.

The public land acquisition saw conflicts with local people. The areas identified in the NCPO Order for Nongkhai SEZ included 115 ha of public utility land for cattle grazing located in Chaiya village in Sa Krai district. This land had been managed as a community forest and officially registered with the Royal Forest Department since 2009. The NCPO's directive and ensuing land conversion processes for the SEZ revoked the Chaiya public land status (*Nangsue Samkhan Tii Luang* or *NorSorLor* in Thai) and transferred it into state property (*Ratchaphatsadu*) land in early 2016. Such process aimed to accumulate and prepare public lands for private and government uses under SEZ initiatives, yet they resulted in the dispossession of communal and public use rights over the forest resources of local people.

State-making through SEZ territorialization

SEZ development, particularly in the context of regional integration, exemplifies state efforts to control people and resources in the borderland. States tend to justify SEZs in terms of their potential to drive markets and national growth through increased investment and trade (Carter and Harding, 2010). In this process, states also gain new ways to exercise authority, discipline subjects and strengthen sovereignty in the name of globalized economic integration (Ong, 2000). Border SEZs have particular importance for state formation (Hayter et al, 2003), since they often call for novel institutional interactions and tactics to support state territoriality (Sassen, 1996; Ong, 2006).

In this way, SEZs enable states to tighten sovereign control of territory and to govern social relations in border frontiers that may have historically been at the margins of state authority (Ong, 2000; Sidaway et al, 2005). A key instrument used in this process is the application of zoning to create liberalized exclusive border enclaves (Kleibert, 2018). SEZ lands are typically obtained through coercive expropriation by the state (Levien, 2018). Often, state actors then assist elite capitalists to accumulate these lands and natural resources cheaply (Ong, 2006; Glassman, 2010; Laungaramsri, 2014).

In Thailand's authoritarian context, the coercive seizure of land and resources for SEZs has become more common and concerning. The two case studies described earlier illustrate the significance for Thai state formation. The military coup of 2014 saw the formalization of the national SEZ 'mega development plan', which had been stalled due to public criticism (Laungaramsri, 2014; Manorom, 2018; Kuaycharoen et al, 2021). Under the constrained civic space that followed, the military-installed NCPO enforced Article 44 of Interim Constitution 2014 to issue a specific Order for SEZ establishment. The legal enforcement mechanisms of military government curtailed public participation in SEZ decision-making processes and suppressed opposition.

The constriction of rights and consent processes that is common in SEZs was also visible in Thailand. States use a diverse set of instruments, institutions and tactics to enforce land acquisition (Nevins and Peluso, 2008; Hall et al, 2015; Mahanty, 2018). These include subtle coercion and threat, surveillance, direct and indirect policing over staged consent-seeking efforts (Peluso and Watts, 2001; Peluso and Vandergeest, 2011). Under Thailand's military government, the civic space to criticize the state agenda became even more restricted. Existing state-adjacent institutions at the village level became state agents to fulfil legal requirements and procedures for public land transfer and private leases. These new and unique instruments enabled the Thai government to progress the development of SEZs in the two case studies and elsewhere.

In both case studies, the authoritarian approach to accumulate communally managed public lands for SEZs was a highly centralized process with little space for disagreement at the localized levels of state bureaucracy. Both SEZ cases presented here illustrate an intense coercion by central authorities over local officials regarding the SEZ directive. As the Thai state strengthened its chain of bureaucratic authority from the centre to the village, it removed several district chiefs and provincial governors from their positions. Furthermore, local state agencies, such as Nongkhai Provincial Forestry Center, which opposed SEZ development on what was formerly the Chaiya community forest, were excluded from consultations and SEZ preparations. Spaces for deviation within state bureaucracies was tightened by the centre to enforce compliance among officials.

State territorialization for SEZs can simultaneously attempt to subdue communities through logics that emphasize economic growth and the public good (Levien, 2018). In rural Thailand, these manifest through state promises of modernity, waged employment and infrastructure development. Implementing agencies, such as the Treasury Department and provincial SEZ-related bodies, often adopt persuasion tactics that highlight future economic and material benefits. As seen in the Nongkhai SEZ, villagers, especially those living close to the public forest, expected the SEZ project to bring infrastructure improvements, such as paved roads and stable electricity, to their neighbourhoods. The SEZ project spoke to villagers' aspirations for these basic public services and the expectation of casual work needed to clear and level forest-lands. The cases show that where SEZ developments tap into the material desires of local people, they can elicit local support and progress territorialization.

The dispossession of public land for SEZ development constructs a land broker state, which assists capitalists to overcome barriers and mitigate costs of land accumulation (Levien, 2012; 2018). The question is why investors, rather than procuring land through market exchange, need the state to facilitate public land access (Levien, 2012; Jenkins et al, 2014). The adoption of a 'land brokering' role by states, where states work to reallocate public lands (Parwez, 2016), addresses situations of unclear tenure (Levien, 2012) while maximizing the scope for profits from frontier commons (Manorom, 2018; Kuaycharoen et al, 2021). This argument assumes a neat alignment of state and elite private interests. However, the Nongkhai SEZ case, which saw community forests reappropriated as state property, reveals an important discrepancy between state and investor interests. Despite a substantial reduction in land rental fees, the government's third tender for the SEZ concession project in September 2022 received no bids from any prospective investors (Prachachat, 2022). This shows the fragilities of land broker states in the Thai context, in spite of state narratives regarding economic development. In this case, the state's accumulation of public forest-land only materialized in non-productive and speculative purposes where the land is left unmanaged and open to exploitation.

This section has laid out the role of border SEZs in state territorialization and state formation, as well as associated frictions. In both of the cases presented in this chapter, the SEZ vision was unable to fulfil the economic benefits or profits promised to investors. Yet, they did advance state-making in various ways. At the same time, state-driven dispossession precipitated tensions with villagers, who lost resource access and governance rights. Interactions around the SEZs then became a 'shifting operational assemblage' (Ong, 2006, p 99) that involved a web of opposed but related actors (Campbell, 2018). The two Thai cases also show that SEZ state territorialization is a complex process that produces differentiated results and local responses, which I discuss next.

Grassroots movements against the SEZs

Even though Thailand was under authoritarian military rule at the time of this research, grassroots resistance to state-driven territorial SEZs emerged at Chiang Khong. This is because of the dynamic, non-linear and triangulated relations between the state, villagers and civil society organizations in Thailand (Sangkhamanee, 2021), which were also visible in both case studies. These factors complicate state-society relations in SEZ projects and challenge the view of state and society as distinct entities (Sato, 2014).

Counter-movements against territorialization here reflect power struggles over the control of land and resources (Vandergeest and Roth, 2017). At my study sites, these struggles could leverage state fragmentation in order to contest the state's territorial control and land enclosures. Such fragmentation exists even within authoritarian settings, which enabled community organizers to mobilize around this space. While some scholars see village and sub-district government as part of a centralized Thai state (Mala, 2016), I found that the interactions between the state-endorsed village committee and grassroots movement actors can be spaces of friction and incongruity. As seen in Chiang Khong, the village chief and committee did not take a neutral position, but instead allied themselves with the grassroots movement against state territorialization. Strong social pressures and ties among local state and grassroots movement actors can be the decisive factor for state fragmentation.

These local politics can be critical to the success and endurance of social movements within authoritarian contexts. In my two case studies, intra- and inter-village power struggles could create and mobilize intra-state fragmentation because of the mixed identities and affiliations of the village committees – they were made up of both village representatives and local bureaucrats. This is consistent with prior evidence that most significant state fragmentation in Thailand occurs through the multiple and shifting identities at the village level (Pankaew et al, 2018). Such struggles allow grassroots bodies to advocate to local officials the multiple values of communal resources that they use, while problematizing the dispossession of public land.

A second crucial factor in successful resistance was the formation of an informal community body. This can be an important means to challenge and reconfigure power asymmetries by mobilizing social pressure against state actions (McCarthy and Zald, 2015). In the Chiang Khong case, the structure of the resistance body, the Bun Rueang Wetland Conservation Group (BRWCG), mimicked state territorial strategy – for example, by setting up a community forest committee – to secure land tenure from below (Kramp et al, 2022). The BRWCG consisted of local elite returnees who had nostalgic visions of communal rural livelihoods. These individuals helped to coordinate the movement and to gain influence in promoting customary rights in negotiations with the state. By imitating the governance and committee structure of state-promoted community forest regime, the BRWCG was able to gain a degree of legitimacy in negotiating with the state where it aimed to protect and govern the customary use of wetland common resources. The BRWCG deployed state community forest narratives and management practices to retain community voice in negotiations with the state. Through BRWCG facilitation, the communal resource utilization rules were ultimately formalized.

In contrast, Chaiya villagers in the Nongkhai SEZ case lacked clear local leadership. The villagers expressed the view that Chaiya community forest management and protection were the responsibility of official village leaders, as this was an initiative of the government. The village committee was set up to follow the state orders. These contrasting experiences show that a local body can counter state SEZ efforts in order to build a momentum towards reterritorialization. This occurs when there is leadership and shared community goals in relation to resource governance. The capacity of communities to exploit internal frictions within the state at a local level, even in a repressive political context, is crucial (Kenney-Lazar et al, 2018).

Another way in which communities gained political ground was by formulating counter-narratives to those promulgated by the state (Wolford and Keene 2015). As a tool of activism, narratives are imbued with power and engage with politics around environmental actions and resource claims (Lueg et al, 2020). The Chiang Khong SEZ case demonstrated the adoption and internalization of environmentalist narratives that transformed the villagers' identity to wetland protectors. Resistance against the dispossession of Bun Rueang wetland forest framed the movement narrative away from opposing SEZ sentiments and resonated more with the opposition to use wetland for SEZ on the grounds of riparian ecology protection. Avoiding outright confrontation with the national SEZ policy agenda was a strategic move to mitigate antagonistic counter-resistance from the Provincial Governor's Office. On the other hand, the Chaiya village committee framed the anti-dispossession movement as opposing SEZ and village development, disrupting public prosperity. In this case, when the state narrative was dominant, the political opportunity to create alternative discourse that could solidify mobilization became limited and weakened over time. Grassroots movements only gained leverage through narratives framing legitimate identity and the local people's agenda.

This analysis shows how the narrative of an effective grassroots movement emphasizes unity and communalism (Wolford and Keene, 2015). This in turn draws from an existing collective identity and communal belonging in relation to place and commons governance. A sense of ownership in the Chiang Khong case was strengthened through the process of generating knowledge on wetland ecology that aligned local people's experiences and relationship to nature with their political struggle (Rocheleau,

2015). As the environmentalist narrative was continually reproduced in village deliberations, daily conversations and interactions, the movement subtly reframed villagers' perceptions, identity and relationship with the wetland forest. Moreover, at the landscape level of the Ing River basin, the destruction of one wetland would affect other wetlands in the same watershed. This served to strengthen watershed-level community ties. The basin-wide ecological discourse thus had the effect of consolidating local-watershed unity. On this basis, the People's Council of Ing River Basin and its civil society alliance worked in solidarity with the Bun Rueang wetland conservation movement (Wajjwalku, 2019). They contributed to collaborative activities that shared local ecological knowledge and that were also central to collective identity-making.

These cases show how the emergence and durability of grassroots activism are contingent on several factors. State-endorsed village committees can be a space of friction where local representatives are pressured by the state, but also enlisted by movement actors. The adoption of state environmentalist narratives and community forest governance institutions in the Chiang Khong case helped to build alliances and gain legitimacy. Here, counter-narratives that emphasized local ecological knowledge, land use mapping and zoning (Li, 2007) enabled local groups to undermine the SEZ project. These narratives also extended to everyday practices and reshaped collective local identity, while legitimizing claims to the commons. Conversely, such tactics can confine grassroots actors to a form of environmentality (Agrawal, 2005), where other use rights may ultimately be restricted. In the Nongkhai case, there was a history of state capture of village institutions for rural development projects, which crippled the possibility for organized resistance. In these two cases, the state-society dynamics within the local context of SEZ land and natural resource territorialization have significantly shaped the configurations of movements and their impacts.

Conclusion

Using a political ecology lens, this chapter has highlighted relationships between social movements and state formation in the SEZ development context. The natural resource contentions around SEZ development unfolded within state-led efforts to exert spatial control over land, resources and people. Border SEZ development, illustrated in both cases as intensified by the BRI, functions as a state formation technology to territorialize resource commons at spatial frontiers. The variegated responses to SEZ territorialization reflected the different historical trajectories and particularities of state-society-commons relationships and interactions, which lead to differing results. Such contestation over land has been critical throughout SEZ development efforts in Thailand.

The contrasting cases here show that some forms of grassroots movements can thrive and sustain within the Thai authoritarian state and resist integration into regional economic connectivity. The cases demonstrate that the enabling conditions for grassroots collectivism include: (1) the local state frictions caused by strong social ties and pressures, (2) the formation of an informal community body and (3) the use of counter-narratives to those promulgated by the state. The grassroots movements and civil society alliance to counter state territorialization or reclaim commons against SEZ development must, in various capacities and actions, negotiate with the authorities' demands. Their relationships are complex and embedded in the exchanges of control and mutual interests. The resistance must be explicit in its intent of not dismantling the authoritarian government and power which delimit the linkage between grassroots movements and broad-based democratization. Although the mobilization expands democratic and inclusive space in local development visions, additional cross-case investigations are needed to validate the extent of resisting state territorialization under SEZ policy to counter authoritarian power at the larger scale.

References

Agrawal, A. (2005) Environmentality: community, intimate government, and the making of environmental subjects in Kumaon, India, *Current Anthropology*, 46(2), 161–90.

Asian Development Bank (2018) *The Role of Special Economic Zones in Improving Effectiveness of Greater Mekong Subregion Economic Corridors*, Asian Development Bank.

Campbell, S. (2018) *Border Capitalism, Disrupted: Precarity and Struggle in a Southeast Asian Industrial Zone*, Cornell University Press.

Carter, C. and Harding, A. (eds) (2010) *Special Economic Zones in Asian Market Economies*, Routledge.

Chettri, M. and Eilenberg, M. (2021) Introduction: enclave development and socio-spatial transformations in Asian borderlands, in M. Chettri and M. Eilenberg (eds) *Development Zones in Asian Borderlands*, Amsterdam University Press, pp 11–32.

Competitive Industries and Innovation Program (2017) *Special Economic Zones: An Operational Review of Their Impacts*, The World Bank.

Department of Provincial Administration (2017) *Master Plan on Chiang Rai Special Economic Zone Development: Chiang Khong Gate to the Future*.

Geopolitical Monitor (2017) Fact sheet: Kunming-Singapore High Speed Rail Network. Available at: www.geopoliticalmonitor.com/fact-sheet-kunming-singapore-high-speed-rail-network

Glassman, J. (2010) *Bounding the Mekong: The Asian Development Bank, China, and Thailand*, University of Hawaii Press.

Gu, X. and Li, M. (2008) *Nanning-Singapore Corridor: A New Vision in China-ASEAN Cooperation*, RSIS Commentaries. Available at: www.rsis.edu.sg/wp-content/uploads/2014/07/CO08114.pdf

Hall, R., Edelman, M., Borras, S.M., Jr, Scoones, I., White, B. and Wolford, W. (2015) Resistance, acquiescence or incorporation? An introduction to land grabbing and political reactions 'from below', *The Journal of Peasant Studies*, 42(3–4), 467–88.

Hayter, R., Barnes, T.J. and Bradshaw, M.J. (2003) Relocating resource peripheries to the core of economic geography's theorizing: rationale and agenda, *Area*, 35(1), 15–23.

Jenkins, R., Kennedy, L. and Mukhopadhyay, P. (2014) Introduction: power, protest, and India's special economic zones, in R. Jenkins, L. Kennedy and P. Mukhopadhyay (eds) *Power, Policy and Protest: The Politics of India's Special Economic Zones*, Oxford University Press, pp 1–38.

Kenney-Lazar, M., Suhardiman, D. and Dwyer, M.B. (2018) State spaces of resistance: industrial tree plantations and the struggle for land in Laos, *Antipode*, 50(5), 1290–310.

Kleibert, J.M. (2018) Exclusive development(s): special economic zones and enclave urbanism in the Philippines, *Critical Sociology*, 44(3), 471–85.

Kramp, J., Suhardiman, D. and Keovilignavong, O. (2022) (Un)making the upland: resettlement, rubber and land use planning in Namai village, Laos, *The Journal of Peasant Studies*, 49(1), 78–100.

Kuaycharoen, P., Longcharoen, L., Chotiwan, P., Sukin, K. and Lao Independent Researchers (2021) *Special Economic Zones and Land Dispossession in the Mekong Region*, Land Watch Thai.

Lamb, V. (2014) Making governance 'good': the production of scale in the environmental impact assessment and governance of the Salween River, *Conservation and Society*, 12(4), 386–97.

Laungaramsri, P. (2014) Commodifying sovereignty: special economic zone and the neoliberalization of the Lao frontier, *Journal of Lao Studies*, 3(1) 29–56.

Levien, M. (2012) The land question: special economic zones and the political economy of dispossession in India, *The Journal of Peasant Studies*, 39(3–4), 933–69.

Levien, M. (2018) *Dispossession without Development: Land Grabs in Neoliberal India*, Oxford University Press.

Li, T. (2007) Rendering technical? in *The Will to Improve: Governmentality, Development, and the Practice of Politics*, Duke University Press, pp 123–55.

Lueg, K., Bager Starbaek, A. and Lundholt, M.W. (2020) What counter-narratives are: dimensions and levels of a theory of middle range, in K. Lueg and M. Wolff Lundholt (eds) *Routledge Handbook of Counter-Narratives*, Routledge.

Mahanty, S. (2018) Contingent sovereignty: cross-border rentals in the Cambodia-Vietnam borderland, *Annuals of the American Association of Geographers*, 108(3), 829–44.

Mala, T. (2016) The existence of Kam-nan and Poo-yai-ban in the contexts of local decentralization [การคงอยู่ของกำนันผู้ใหญ่บ้านในบริบทของการกระจายอำนาจสู่ท้องถิ่น], *Valaya Alongkorn Rajabhat University Research and Development Journal*, 11(1), 305–17.

Manorom, K. (2018) *Social Equity and Land Governance in Northeastern and Northern Special Economic Zones in Thailand* [ความเป็นธรรมทางสังคมและธรรมาภิบาลที่ดินในเขตเศรษฐกิจพิเศษในภาคอีสานและภาคเหนือประเทศไทย], Coordinating Center for Thailand's University Network on Border Studies.

McCarthy, J. and Zald, M. (2015) Social movement organizations, in J. Goodwin and J.M. Jasper (eds) *The Social Movements Reader: Cases and Concepts*, Blackwell Publishing, pp 159–74.

Moberg, L. (2017) *The Political Economy of Special Economic Zones: Concentrating Economic Development*, Routledge.

National Economic and Social Development Council (2019) *Special Economic Zones Development Budget: Central Budget and Strategic Budget for SEZ Development Integration Plan for Fiscal Year 2015–2019* [งบประมาณเขตพัฒนาเศรษฐกิจพิเศษ – งบกลาง และ งบประมาณในลักษณะบูรณาการเชิงยุทธศาสตร์ แผนงานบูรณาการพัฒนาพื้นที่เขตเศรษฐกิจพิเศษ ปีงบประมาณ พ.ศ. 2558 – 2560].

National Economic and Social Development Council (2021a) NESDC organized the first SEZ Development Policy Committee through VDO conference, Office of National Economic and Social Development Council.

National Economic and Social Development Council (2021b) *Special Economic Zones (SEZs) Development Progress*, Progress report, Office of National Economic and Social Development Council.

Nevins, J. and Peluso, N.L. (2008) Introduction, in *Taking Southeast Asia to Market: Commodities, Nature, and People in the Neoliberal Age*, Cornell University Press, pp 1–24.

Ong, A. (2000) Graduated sovereignty in South-East Asia, *Theory, Culture & Society*, 17(4), 55–75.

Ong, A. (2006) *Neoliberalism as Exception: Mutations in Citizenship and Sovereignty*, Duke University Press.

Pankaew, A., Choeisiri, P. and Taksapaibool, K. (2018) Developmental scheme for Village Committee Organization as an instrument for implementing 'Pracharat Policy on the basis of the Philosophy of Sufficiency Economy', *Journal of Politics and Governance*, 8(2), 1–15.

Parwez, S. (2016) A study on special economic zone implicated land acquisition and utilisation, *International Journal of Development and Conflict*, 6, 136–53.

Peluso, N.L. and Watts, M. (2001) *Violent Environments*, Cornell University Press.

Peluso, N.L. and Vandergeest, P. (2011) Political ecologies of war and forests: counterinsurgencies and the making of national natures, *Annals of the Association of American Geographers*, 101(3), 587–608.

Prachachat (2022) Nongkhai SEZ plans for logistics distribution hub after the 3rd SEZ bid failed [หนองคายซงดึงฮับกระจายสินค้าหลังประมูลเขตเศรษฐกิจ 700 ไร่ ล่ม 3 รอบ]. Available at: www.prachachat.net/local-economy/news-1062998

Rocheleau, D.E. (2015) Roots, rhizomes, networks and territories: reimagining pattern and power in political ecologies, in R.L. Bryant (ed) *The International Handbook of Political Ecology*, Edward Elgar, pp 70–88.

Sangkhamanee, J. (2021) State, NGOs, and villagers: how the Thai environmental movement fell silent, in P. Jobin, M. Ing-sho Ho and H.-H. Michael Hsiao (eds) *Environmental Movements and Politics of the Asian Anthropocene*, ISEAS–Yusof Ishak Institute Singapore, pp 233–60.

Sari, B.R. (2018) Transnational migration and diaspora in Thailand border areas of Mae Sai and Chiang Khong: an introduction, in B.R. Sari (ed) *Borders and Beyond: Transnational Migration and Diaspora in Northern Thailand Border Areas with Myanmar and Laos*, Yayasan Pustaka Obor Indonesia, pp 7–24.

Sassen, S. (1996) *Losing Control? Sovereignty in an Age of Globalization*, Columbia University Press.

Sato, J. (2014) Resource politics and state-society relations: why are certain states more inclusive than others? *Comparative Studies in Society and History*, 56(3), 745–73.

Sidaway, J.D., Grundy-Warr, C. and Park, B.-G. (2005) Asian sovereigntyscapes, *Political Geography*, 24(7), 779–83.

Vandergeest, P. and Roth, R. (2017) A Southeast Asian political ecology, in P. Hirsch (ed) *Routledge Handbook of the Environment in Southeast Asia*, Routledge, pp 82–98.

Wajjwalku, S. (2019) Civil society and water governance in Northern Thailand: local NGOs and management of Mekong's tributaries in Chiang Rai, in K. Otsuka (ed) *Interactive Approaches to Water Governance in Asia*, Springer, pp 123–54.

Walker, A. (2008) Borders in motion on the upper Mekong: Siam and France in the 1890s, in Y. Goudineau and M. Lorrillard (eds) *New Research on Laos*, Ecole francaise d'Extreme-Orient, pp 183–201.

Wolford, W. and Keene, S. (2015) Social movements, in T. Perreault, G. Bridge and J. McCarthy (eds) *The Routledge Handbook of Political Ecology*, Routledge, pp 573–84.

3

Railways of Hope, Railways of Conflict: Governance of the Domestic Environmental Impacts of a Belt and Road Project

Xiaofeng Liu

Introduction

This chapter contributes to debates on the environmental impacts and governance of infrastructure development by focusing on the domestic consequences of the China-Laos railway, a transboundary railway project under China's Belt and Road Initiative (BRI). Against the backdrop of a global 'infrastructural turn' (Dodson, 2017), governments frequently promise that infrastructure development will deliver growth, prosperity and modernity; however, this is often controversial regarding the social and ecological consequences and, thus, intensely political (Flyvbjerg, 2007; Brunn, 2011). The material and political life cycle of infrastructure highlights the intricate manner in which it supports relations among people, objects and institutions, with interconnected costs and benefits. The infrastructure projects under the umbrella of the BRI exhibit these complexities as well, and they have provoked significant debates regarding environmental and social impacts (Hughes et al, 2020; Liu et al, 2022).

Meanwhile, China is promoting 'ecological civilization', or 'ecocivilization', as its environmental ideology (Geall et al, 2018; Chung et al, 2021). This envisions a sustainable society in which ecology and natural resources are protected 'without compromising economic growth' (Pow, 2018, p 865). Under the umbrella of ecocivilization, the government has increasingly championed measures to clean up the environment and prevent potential negative environmental damage. For instance, China has explored a redline paradigm (Lü et al, 2013; Bai et al, 2016) to restrict the boundaries of development and protect the ecological environment, including eco-environmental conservation redlines (ECRLs), arable land minimums (ALMs) and urban growth boundaries. Furthermore, the Chinese government and state-owned media have promoted these redline schemes as providing valuable Chinese experience to share with BRI partners (Zhang, 2021). How these environmental endeavours interact with the undertaking under the BRI has received limited exploration.

The China-Laos railway, a flagship BRI infrastructure project, offers a salient case for exploring the interaction between the BRI undertaking and domestic environmental dynamics. Inaugurated on 3 December 2021, the railway runs from Kunming, the capital of China's Yunnan province, to Vientiane, the capital of Laos (Figure 3.1). Designed to reach a speed

Figure 3.1: Map of the China-Laos railway

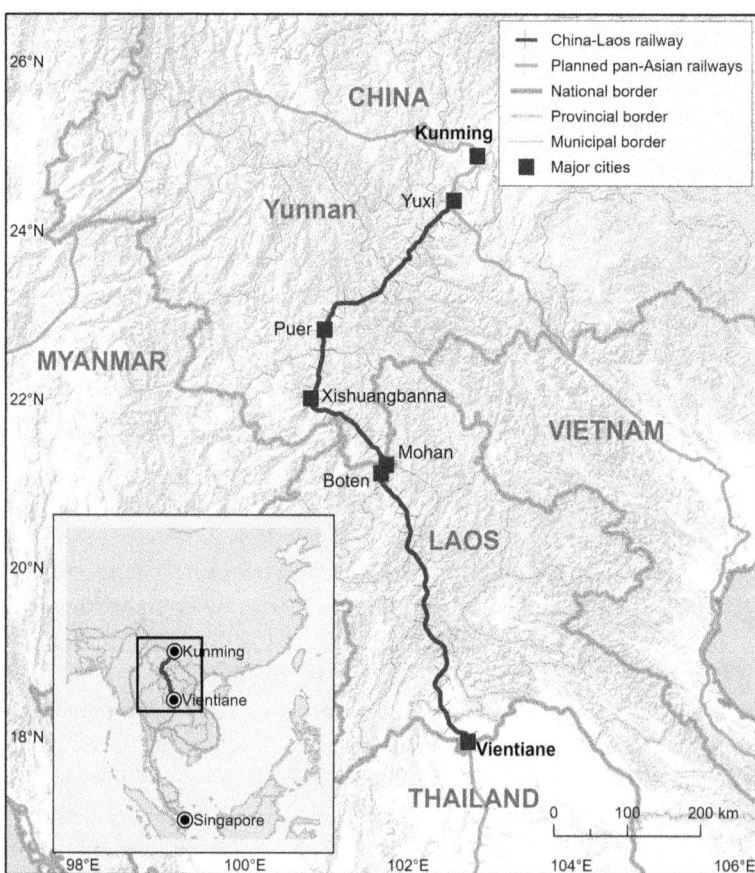

Source: Author

of 160 km per hour, the China-Laos railway reduces the travel time from Vientiane to Kunming from two or three days to just ten hours. China wrapped it as a 'gift' for the celebration of the Lao 46th anniversary of the Lao People's Democratic Republic and the 60th anniversary of Laos-China diplomatic relations. The transboundary railway crosses the border between Mohan, China, and Boten, Laos, and the rail line is divided into two separate parts in China and Laos. The China segment, Yuxi-Mohan railway (YMR) spans 507 km, surpassing the 422 km of the Laos section. It operates as an exclusively owned subsidiary of China Railway Kunming Group, an affiliate of the China State Railway Group. The construction responsibilities for the sections and stations integral to the YMR were allocated to more than 20 contracting firms.

Scholars have analysed the multifaceted ramifications of the railway on the Laos side, encompassing economic, environmental and societal aspects (Chen, 2020; DiCarlo, 2021). These inquiries have unveiled disputes involving railway enterprises, local communities and governmental bodies, primarily revolving around issues related to land acquisition and labour rights. However, limited scholarly attention has been directed towards its Chinese section, namely the YMR. This is an important gap as the domestic and international environmental consequences of the BRI are often interlinked (Klinger, 2020). Relevant research can, therefore, elucidate the nexus between China's global infrastructure initiatives and resultant local environmental and social implications on the domestic frontier.

To address this gap, this chapter asks the questions: How do China's BRI activities interact with its domestic environmental governance? And what problems emerge in the process? To answer these questions, I focus on two cases that show the environmental and social impacts of the YMR: land occupation and water shortage in villages near the railway. The analysis that follows relies on both second-hand archives and first-hand materials collected in fieldwork conducted in March and April 2021 along the YMR in Yunnan province. In the regions that the railway crosses, from Kunming to Yuxi and Xishuangbanna, interviews, informal communications and group discussions were conducted with around 40 informants, including government officials, railway company managers and local residents. A multitude of textual resources, including both physical copies and digital materials, were gathered at various stages, before, during and after fieldwork. These were sourced from local libraries, local government websites and various media outlets.

Environmental governance failure, scale and the political ecology of the BRI

The links between development and the environment are inherently political (Hecht, 1985) and often also geopolitical (McMichael, 2009). Political ecologists interpret these politics by uncovering the unequal distribution of costs and benefits of environmental change among actors and the differential power dynamics that generate social and environmental consequences (Robbins, 2019). Recent infrastructure-led development projects, including the BRI, though wrapped in discourses of social benefit and sustainability, often bear environmental consequences across multiple scales (Hughes et al, 2020), with tensions continuously unfolding around projects, such as coal plants (Springer et al, 2021), hydropower projects (Neal, 2021) and transportation projects (Wang et al, 2020). A political ecology perspective helps reveal the politics of how green is defined and implemented, and with what uneven effects in the BRI's environmental governance (Harlan, 2021).

Environmental governance refers to 'the set of regulatory processes, mechanisms, and organizations through which political actors influence environmental actions and outcomes' (Lemos et al, 2006, p 298). Political ecologists scrutinize the actors, scales and impacts of environmental governance policies and projects (O'Brien, 2010; McCarthy, 2017), viewing the environment as politically constructed rather than an objective entity (Walker, 2007; Rangan et al, 2009). For instance, the scarcity of resources and the need to adjust ecological zones are often discursively constructed by capital and the state for specific development purposes (Adger et al, 2001).

Despite efforts to manage environments to achieve 'good governance' (Rothstein, 2012), 'governance failure' (Bakker et al, 2008) frequently occurs in practice. The concept of governance failure signifies that the adoption of governance paradigms does not necessarily address perceived policy gaps (Arnouts et al, 2009). Therefore, the concept is often linked with the notions of 'capability' and 'capability set' (Robeyns, 2005), which indicate the ability to mobilize resources to achieve certain objectives. Peters (2015) identifies two types of governance failure: one concerning systematic government direction and polity legitimacy, and the other related to addressing social and economic problems within specific domains. Aligning with the second category, Bakker et al (2008) use the concept to indicate deficiencies in water supply, particularly in reaching economically disadvantaged households despite pro-poor policies. Following a similar trajectory, this chapter considers the second type of governance failure, specifically the incapacity to solve specific problems related to the YMR's environmental impacts.

A pivotal inquiry concerning governance failure pertains to its causes. Providing a universal framework, Howlett et al (2014) consider two orders or levels of governance failure: the mismatch of problem context and governance mode, and the mismatch between governance capacity and governance mode. Different types of 'governance mode' are characterized by varying relations between the government and other actors or by solutions to the governed objects. Governance failure occurs when a given governance mode proves operationally incapable of addressing a specific problem or when governmental capabilities fall short of achieving an optimal resolution. Scholars have identified several factors to explain governance failure in water supply, including the government's governance culture, constraints of land use planning and policies, business models with cost recovery requirements, tariff-related economic incentives and lack of effective social participation (Bakker et al, 2008; Rugemalila et al, 2015). Moreover, an increase in actors involved in environmental governance may lead to problems in policy arrangements, including actor overload, power struggles, conflicting discourses and unclear rules, which can cause governance failure (Arnouts and Arts, 2009).

This chapter conceptualizes the problems related to the YMR's environmental governance through the lens of 'governance failure'. From the political ecology perspective, the definition of capacity or incapacity of environmental governance can be viewed as constructed and contested by various actors. Specifically, the chapter examines the inability of local governance entities, particularly governments and companies along the YMR, to address water shortages and land use issues caused by the railway's construction. In addition, the chapter seeks to understand the problems' spatial features by incorporating the concept of 'scale' to consider what Arnouts and Arts (2009) depict as the vertical and horizontal dimensions of governance involving diverse policy levels and actors.

The concept of scale is a widely used theoretical framework in political ecology and environmental studies, valued for its ability to discern spatial attributes and interactions among diverse actors (Rangan and Kull, 2009). Scale is now commonly conceived as a socially produced arena fraught with power relationships (Smith, 2010 [1984]). It is considered both materially and discursively (Chung et al, 2016) and both practically and analytically (Moore, 2008). As environmental issues often transcend geographical borders and scales, the quest to pinpoint an 'optimal scale for effective governance' (Newig et al, 2017, p 477) poses a significant challenge in addressing environmental problems. Focusing on social and ecological interactions across scales (Sayre, 2005), political ecologists ask how particular scales make ecology political (Rangan and Kull, 2009). They seek to unveil the processes through which various political actors define and reconfigure the scale of environmental problems and governance measures. Governance failure may emerge within the processes.

The BRI has been conceptualized as a multifaceted amalgamation of state-driven spatial strategies operating across multiple scales (Apostolopoulou, 2021; Chen, 2023). Regarding the environmental governance of BRI infrastructure projects, scholars have traced China's domestic official governance arrangements, the engagement of international actors and non-state actors and the encounter of Chinese governance with BRI local political and social configurations. First, China's domestic governance structures significantly influence the greening of the BRI (Zhang, 2022), such as partnerships under the BRI International Green Development Coalition, an official Green BRI partnership platform affiliated with China's Ministry of Ecology and Environment (MEE; Geng et al, 2022). Second, although state leadership remains a key feature of the BRI capital exports and environmental governance, non-state actors (Loh, 2021), including state-owned enterprises and policy banks, possess substantial commercial and managerial autonomy, leading to variegated outcomes (Shi et al, 2021; Liu et al, 2024). Moreover, international actors and civil society groups also shape China's BRI policies and impact the environmental governance of projects under the BRI (Hale et al, 2020; Gong and Lewis, 2023; Liu et al, 2023). Third, the environmental governance of BRI projects is influenced by the political and social contexts of host countries, and the implementation of environmental and social safeguards often depends on host countries' capacities, local contestations and geopolitical contexts (Suhardiman et al, 2021; Apostolopoulou and Pant, 2022). In the collusion of Chinese actors and host countries' domestic actors, Carrai (2021) identified an 'adaptive governance' mode in projects like the Ethiopia-Djibouti railway, reflecting China's inclination to abstain from imposing specific governance frameworks on host countries to uphold its core foreign policy principles of sovereignty and non-interference. Nonetheless, this approach may inadvertently bolster poor governance norms and compromise the environmental and social efficacy of BRI projects. For instance, in the Laos section of the China-Laos railway, affected local communities are often marginalized in localized governance (Dwyer, 2020).

While studies have extensively examined the environmental and social consequences of BRI projects beyond China's borders, the effects of this international scheme on China's domestic environment and society have remained relatively under-explored. However, the BRI is not merely about China 'going out', but also concerns 'how transnational and global interests, imaginations, institutions, and politics shape things that are happening inside China' (Lee, 2022, p 328). This perspective underscores the interconnectedness of China's BRI pursuits with its domestic clean-up objectives (Klinger, 2020) and emphasizes the need to consider the BRI's consequences both domestically and internationally (Franceschini et al, 2022). By looking into the impacts of a BRI transboundary project on China's domestic environment and society, this research contributes to ongoing debates in infrastructure and BRI studies by bridging China's domestic and extraterritorial politics to analyse the implementation and consequences if BRI infrastructure projects. Through a framework combining governance failure and scale, this chapter also contributes to studies on the political ecology of the BRI by shedding light on debates on cross-scale conflicts arising from infrastructure's environmental governance.

Railways of hope and a symbol of China–Laos friendship

Chinese central and regional authorities have accorded significant emphasis to the China-Laos railway. Within official discourses, the railway is portrayed as a 'project of hope' promising to usher in affluence for both Laos and China. The Laotian government, situated within one of the world's most underdeveloped nations, and with a rudimentary 4 km railway predating this project, is relying on the new railway to transition from a landlocked state into a land-linked hub. The railway presents an opportunity to enhance connectivity and augment the export of goods to China from Laos. Its logistical significance is poised to expand with the integration of additional rail lines into the Southeast Asian network. Ultimately, China seeks to establish railway connections with Southeast Asia, extending from Thailand to Malaysia and reaching as far as Singapore (Lampton et al, 2020). The project is the first railway that extends China's railway network into other countries using the full suite of Chinese technologies and standards under the BRI (Schindler et al, 2021). Therefore, the prospective success of this project holds the potential to bolster the trust of partner nations in China. It may function as an exemplary project facilitating the groundwork for the strategic development of further railway networks in the long term (Lampton et al, 2020).

The railway offers economic growth visions for local governments and communities in the region, as well. The southern part of Yunnan, a less developed, mountainous province bordering Vietnam, Laos, and Myanmar barely had railways in operation predating the YMR. Meanwhile, the province has aimed to be a pivot of China's opening-up to South and Southeast Asia. Although three branches of the railway leading to Southeast Asia are in planning, the China-Laos railway is the only one that can be completed in the short term. Thus, the YMR has been regarded as the only foreseeable opportunity for Yunnan to seize. A government official explained in an interview that not only does YMR aim to connect with Laos, but it also has the potential to be extended to Myanmar due to the short distance between Mohan and China-Myanmar border towns.

In their 14th five-year planning, several local governments along the railway envisioned their roles as being logistical pivots on the completion of the project and supporting facilities. In an interview, one government officer pictured their planning with a logistical industrial park near the railway station. With the railway and supporting logistical infrastructure, the officer highlighted that they aim to turn their town into a transport hub for the distribution of tropical fruits and commodities from Southeast Asia to markets in Kunming and other parts of China. The officer believed the railway will facilitate the local government's brand building. Moreover, the project is welcomed by

Figure 3.2: A slogan on the wall at the China-Laos railway

Source: Photograph by the author

some communities near the railway. In interviews, several villagers expressed their expectations of generating income by vending local products or small commodities near the stations to cater to tourists traveling by railways.

Moreover, official reports publicize the railway as a 'green ecological corridor' (Liu, 2021), underscoring the careful ecological planning in the railway's design, which was completed by the China Railway Eryuan Engineering Group, a subsidiary of China State Railway Group. The design manual detailed restrictions and measures to control and treat pollution, land occupation, deforestation, biodiversity loss and other problems. For instance, for wastewater management and water source protection, the design manual instructed the discharge standard as the highest class of GB 8978-1996, China's integrated wastewater discharge standard detailing the maximum allowable concentration of 69 categories of water pollutants.

Despite the high standards set out in specifications, environmental and social disputes frequently arise in implementation. Major problems include water cut-offs, pollution and land cover change. Chief stakeholders include central and local government authorities, the railway owner (China Railway Kunming Group), construction companies and local communities, who hold disparate environmental concerns and pursue divergent goals. Governance failures frequently arise in efforts to tackle the environmental and social problems associated with large-scale infrastructure projects. The following sections examine these failures through two case studies related to the YMR: land occupation and water shortages.

Land use adjustment for railway occupation

One major impact of railway development is land occupation, which not only causes environmental problems, such as deforestation and habitat loss, but can also lead to social conflicts due to resettlement and compensation. These impacts are prominent and have been widely researched (Rogers et al, 2019; Apostolopoulou, 2021; DiCarlo, 2021). For the YMR case, this chapter pays attention to the land use adjustment following the railway's land occupation, which has received less examination. The aim here is to unveil the failure to adjust land use for railway construction at the local scale under the oversight of national environmental protection institutions, notably the redline schemes.

In order to build 'ecocivilization', the Chinese government has explored redline frameworks, such as ALM and ECRL, to delimit the boundaries of development (Lü et al, 2013). These are operated and supervised by the Ministry of Land Resources (MLR, now the Ministry of Natural Resources) and the Ministry of Ecology and Environment. Under the restrictions of these schemes, approval procedures for construction land use can be highly complex and time-consuming. 'Pre-approval land use' (*xianxing yongdi*) thus has been allowed for imperative projects, such as large-scale infrastructure and post-disaster reconstruction. This enables formal procedures for land use approval to be deferred for subsequent completion. The YMR exemplifies this approach. The MLR permitted the pre-approval land use for the YMR specifying that in order to bolster the economic and social development of Yunnan Province and expedite the construction process, in recognition of the practical complexities inherent to the project's implementation and the constricted timeframe, it was decided to pre-approve 210.4728 ha of land.

Due to the high priority of the railway project, the central government granted a pre-approval land use quota to the project, which however is not the end of the story. The responsibility to acquire the necessary land, including the land that was pre-approved, was delegated to local governments, who must also align land use within the parameters of national land and environmental protection redline schemes. For instance, redline mechanisms such as ALM and ECRL require the preservation of arable land and ecological zones, respectively. If land is acquired for construction purposes, there is a principle of supplementing or reclaiming an equal amount of land as that occupied, known as the balance between occupation and supplement (*zhanbu pingheng*). Local governments, specifically departments of natural resources, bear the responsibility for supplementing arable and ecological areas in their jurisdictions. Furthermore, auxiliary infrastructure for the railway, such as roads to the railway station and station squares, requires additional land that is not included in the YMR's design. Moreover, driven by a desire to capitalize on the railway's potential for economic growth, local governments plan to construct more supporting facilities, such as logistic industrial zones. All these infrastructures necessitate government allocation and supplementation of land resources. A government official complained in interviews that they had to supplement 2,000 ha of arable land, including land occupied by the YMR. To achieve this balance, the transformation of forests into arable land is a common approach for supplementing the occupied land, albeit at the expense of further environmental degradation.

In this manner, governance failure in addressing nature resource and environmental issues stems from local governments' financial and bureaucratic limitations. One potential solution to avoid reclaiming forests for land supplementation is to purchase land quotas from nearby prefectures that have sufficient arable land or ecological areas. Nevertheless, most of the prefectures along the YMR are underdeveloped and have limited fiscal budgets, making it financially challenging to procure land from other entities. Additionally, lack of involvement of local governments at the stage of the railway route design has further exacerbated land-related challenges. According to a local official who I interviewed, local authorities were not consulted during the planning of the railway route. Although the main rail route itself is designed away from critical areas and redlines, the designers don't usually take into account the location of auxiliary infrastructure, such as station squares and auxiliary roads, which sometimes inevitably intersect with those redline areas.

Overall, despite national redline schemes aimed at sustaining natural environments, local governments' efforts to address the YMR's land occupation have caused further ecological loss and environmental deterioration. Since the release of the ecological protection redline guidance in 2018, all provinces have commenced to demarcate their ecological zones to establish baselines for the development and restrictions of different types of ecological areas, including forests. Consequently, transformations from forest to arable land will no longer be feasible. Moreover, compensations for other types of land, such as forests and grasslands, may also become necessary, particularly considering that the ecological protection redline will be an all-around scheme. How local governments will propose new counter-measures to address the problems imposed by national- and even international-scale projects remains unclear. What is evident is that environmental governance failure can still easily occur given the limited capacity of local governments to resolve issues related to higher-level schemes.

Water transfer project for water shortage

Another case is related to the environmental and social repercussions for neighbouring local communities, which showcase more complicated governance failure. In 2016, during the commencement of one of the YMR's lengthiest tunnel projects, two construction companies inadvertently disrupted the water supply system for several villages in proximity to the railway. These communities have been living on crops and livestock for generations. The railway construction, situated a few kilometres from the villages, caused a decline in surface water levels, resulting in the cessation of water availability for both the irrigation of rice crops and drinking water for the villages' inhabitants and livestock.

Construction companies hold environmental responsibility delegated by the railway owner. However, these companies limit the spatial scope of their responsibility within their construction sections, particularly the space delimited by the redline of the project's land use map approved by the MLR. Typically, this demarcated area lies approximately 8 m to 20 m adjacent to the railway track. The initial intention of project redlines was to delineate the limits of project development, aiming to safeguard the ecological space beyond this boundary from construction-related harm. However, in this case, companies utilized the redline as justification to limit the extent of their responsibilities within its confines. The water cut-offs were evidently situated beyond the designated redline, leading the companies to refuse accountability for them.

Local government authorities held responsibility for monitoring and addressing environmental problems within their administrative units. Nevertheless, the local government fell short of expectations to solve local communities' problems either by enforcing the duties of the construction companies or by addressing the issues directly, a circumstance that this chapter characterizes as a manifestation of governance failure. The failure can be attributed to factors such as lack of financial capacity, asymmetric power hierarchies and higher-level pressures.

One potential resolution to this issue entailed the implementation of a water transfer project, which required substantial financial resources. The local government lacked the necessary financial resources and capacity to initiate such a project. According to local government officials in interviews, they resorted to utilizing drought relief funds to temporarily provide water for the affected villages. These funds were originally designated for local authorities to offset agricultural losses resulting from extreme weather and natural disasters. While there is a degree of flexibility in reallocating funds for similar purposes, the available resources fell short of meeting the financial requirements for a permanent water transfer project.

Another factor contributing to the local government's failure to resolve the issue stems from its inability to compel the railway companies to assume responsibility, owing to an asymmetric bureaucratic relation. China Railway Group, the parent company of the railway's owner, was established in 2013 as a market-oriented reform entity, a restructuring effort stemming from the former Ministry of Railways, a powerful ministry responsible for overseeing nearly all aspects of China's railway systems. Although the Ministry of Railways no longer exists, the railway companies still retain considerable control over the railway system, effectively preserving the hierarchical administrative structure. The lineage of construction companies is more intricate. Parent organizations of these firms, namely China Railway Engineering Group and China Railway Construction Corporation, derived from the Ministry of Railways' Engineering Bureau and the People's Liberation Army's Railway Corps. In interviews, representatives of the local authorities and communities commonly referred to these companies as the 'railway bosses' (*tielaoda*), contending that these entities are unresponsive to their concerns due to their elevated bureaucratic stature. Consequently, local authorities possess limited leverage in negotiations with these entities, and certainly they are not able to make them solve a problem they don't regard as their responsibility.

Furthermore, the expeditious construction process required by the central government and railway owner afforded railway companies minimal time to engage in negotiations with local governments and communities to address environmental and social challenges, particularly those demanding a more protracted duration for resolution. Given the specific deadline in December 2021, when the Chinese central government committed to presenting the transboundary railway as a gift for Laos National Day, construction progress took precedence. This resulted in limited time for stakeholders to engage in negotiations and develop more refined plans. Moreover, the construction firms utilized these narratives to deflect inquiries and negotiations from the local government and to excuse their poor performance.

The governance for the water shortage problem was stranded at the local scale with insufficient financial capacities, asymmetric power relations between local government and railway companies, and lack of engagement of local communities. Facing the failure, local communities struggled to upscale the issue, seeking higher-level support to solve the local governance failure. After a few rounds of petitioning (*shangfang*) by villagers to provincial branches of the Public Complaints and Proposals Administration, the villagers' voices attracted higher-level attention and incorporated more actors beyond railway companies and local authorities. With the involvement of provincial units, a construction management bureau was established for a water transfer project, which was finally completed in 2020 to divert water from a reservoir to the villages. In this sense, governance failure is often trapped in the specific scale of governance, necessitating a process of rescaling to extricate it from the predicament.

Conclusion

The tension between infrastructure development and environmental protection is a long-standing debate, exacerbated in recent decades by global infrastructure initiatives like the BRI. By adopting a governance failure framework, this study examines the impacts of a BRI transboundary infrastructure project on China's domestic environment and society, using the environmental governance of the YMR as a case study, to shed light on effects emerging beyond the capacities of governance entities. In the governance of the YMR's water and land impacts, top-down measures posed by national-scale schemes, such as redline systems, unintentionally engendered conflicts in the definition and implementation of governance responsibilities of local governments and companies, and governance failures arose with limited financial capacity, imbalanced power dynamics and inadequate local consultation faced by local-scale governance entities. The findings highlight the necessity of institutional coordination across scales and actors to fix environmental and social problems stemming from infrastructure development.

This chapter contributes to studies on the political ecology of the BRI in two ways. First, it sheds light on the often-overlooked domestic consequences of China's BRI pursuits, providing insight into how the governance of these environmental and social repercussions clashes with China's domestic efforts to protect nature. Second, it offers insights for theorizing the failures in governing infrastructure's environmental and social impacts by revealing cross-scale, multistakeholder conflicts in demarcating and fulfilling governance responsibilities.

References

Adger, W.N., Benjaminsen, T.A., Brown, K. and Svarstad, H. (2001) Advancing a political ecology of global environmental discourses, *Development and Change*, 32(4), 681–715.

Apostolopoulou, E. (2021) Tracing the links between infrastructure-led development, urban transformation, and inequality in China's Belt and Road Initiative, *Antipode*, 53(3), 831–58.

Apostolopoulou, E. and Pant, H. (2022) 'Silk Road here we come': infrastructural myths, post-disaster politics, and the shifting urban geographies of Nepal, *Political Geography*, 98, art 102704. doi: 10.1016/j.polgeo.2022.102704

Arnouts, R. and Arts, B. (2009) Environmental governance failure: the 'dark side' of an essentially optimistic concept, in B. Arts, A. Lagendijk and H. van Houtum (eds) *The Disoriented State: Shifts in Governmentality, Territoriality and Governance*, Springer, pp 201–28.

Bai, Y., Jiang, B., Wang, M., Li, H., Alatalo, J.M. and Huang, S. (2016) New ecological redline policy (ERP) to secure ecosystem services in China, *Land Use Policy*, 55, 348–51.

Bakker, K., Kooy, M., Shofiani, N.E. and Martijn, E.-J. (2008) Governance failure: rethinking the institutional dimensions of urban water supply to poor households, *World Development*, 36(10), 1891–915.

Brunn, S.D. (2011) *Engineering Earth: The Impacts of Megaengineering Projects*, Springer Science & Business Media.

Carrai, M.A. (2021) Adaptive governance along Chinese-financed BRI railroad megaprojects in East Africa, *World Development*, 141, art 105388. doi: 10.1016/j.worlddev.2020.105388

Chen, A.L.Q. (2023) The Belt and Road Initiative as a variegated agglomeration of multi-scalar state spatial strategies, *Territory, Politics, Governance*, 11(3), 478–501.

Chen, W.K. (2020) Sovereign debt in the making: financial entanglements and labor politics along the Belt and Road in Laos, *Economic Geography*, 96(4), 295–314.

Chung, C.K.L. and Xu, J. (2016) Scale as both material and discursive: a view through China's rescaling of urban planning system for environmental governance, *Environment & Planning C: Government & Policy*, 34(8), 1404–24.

Chung, C.K.L. and Xu, J. (2021) Scalar politics of urban sustainability: governing the Chinese city in the era of ecological civilisation, *Transactions of the Institute of British Geographers*, 46(3), 689–703.

DiCarlo, J. (2021) *Mind the Gap: Grounding Development Finance and Safeguards through Land Compensation on the Laos-China Belt and Road Corridor*, Global Development Policy Center.

Dodson, J. (2017) The global infrastructure turn and urban practice, *Urban Policy and Research*, 35(1), 87–92.

Dwyer, M.B. (2020) 'They will not automatically benefit': the politics of infrastructure development in Laos's Northern Economic Corridor, *Political Geography*, 78, art 102118. doi: 10.1016/j.polgeo.2019.102118

Flyvbjerg, B. (2007) Policy and planning for large-infrastructure projects: problems, causes, cures, *Environment and Planning B: Planning and Design*, 34(4), 578–97.

Franceschini, I. and Loubere, N. (2022) *Global China as Method*, Cambridge University Press.

Geall, S. and Ely, A. (2018) Narratives and pathways towards an ecological civilization in contemporary China, The China Quarterly, 236, 1175–96.

Geng, Q. and Lo, K. (2022) China's Green Belt and Road Initiative: transnational environmental governance and causal pathways of orchestration, *Environmental Politics*, 32(7), 1163–85.

Gong, W. and Lewis, J.I. (2023) The role of international engagement in greening China's Belt and Road Initiative, *Environmental Politics*, 32(7) 1208–30.

Hale, T., Liu, C. and Urpelainen, J. (2020) *Belt and Road Decision-Making in China and Recipient Countries: How and to What Extent Does Sustainability Matter?* ISEP & BSG Report, ISEP, BSG and ClimateWorks Foundation.

Harlan, T. (2021) Green development or greenwashing? A political ecology perspective on China's Green Belt and Road, *Eurasian Geography and Economics*, 62(2), 202–26.

Hecht, S.B. (1985) Environment, development and politics: capital accumulation and the livestock sector in Eastern Amazonia, *World Development*, 13(6), 663–84.

Howlett, M. and Ramesh, M. (2014) The two orders of governance failure: design mismatches and policy capacity issues in modern governance, *Policy and Society*, 33(4), 317–27.

Hughes, A.C., Lechner, A.M., Chitov, A., Horstmann, A., Hinsley, A., Tritto, A. et al (2020) Horizon scan of the Belt and Road Initiative, *Trends in Ecology & Evolution*, 35(7), 583–93.

Klinger, J.M. (2020) Environment, development, and security politics in the production of Belt and Road spaces, *Territory Politics Governance*, 8(5), 657–75.

Lampton, D.M., Ho, S. and Kuik, C.C. (2020) *Rivers of Iron: Railroads and Chinese Power in Southeast Asia*, University of California Press.

Lee, C.K. (2022) Global China at 20: why, how and so what? *The China Quarterly*, 250, 313–31.

Lemos, M.C. and Agrawal, A. (2006) Environmental governance, *Annual Review of Environment and Resources*, 31, 297–325.

Liu, L. (2021) Green road to Vientiane, *China News*. Available at: www.yn.chinanews.com.cn/news/2021/1206/65977.html

Liu, X. and Bennett, M.M. (2022) The geopolitics of knowledge communities: situating Chinese and foreign studies of the Green Belt and Road Initiative, *Geoforum*, 128, 168–80.

Liu, X. and Bennett, M.M. (2023) Going out and going green: NGOs in the environmental governance of Global China, *Eurasian Geography and Economics*, 1–26. doi: 10.1080/15387216.2023.2279549

Liu, X. and Bennett, M.M. (2024) Governing the extraterritorial: global environmentalities of China's Green Belt and Road Initiative, *Annals of the American Association of Geographers*, 114(1), 236–54.

Loh, D.M.H. (2021) The 'Chinese Dream' and the 'Belt and Road Initiative': narratives, practices, and sub-state actors, *International Relations of the Asia-Pacific*, 21(2), 167–99.

Lü, Y., Ma, Z., Zhang, L., Fu, B. and Gao, G. (2013) Redlines for the greening of China, *Environmental Science & Policy*, 33, 346–53.

McCarthy, J. (2017) Political ecology, in *International Encyclopedia of Geography*, Elsevier Science, pp 228–33.

McMichael, P. (2009) Contemporary contradictions of the global development project: geopolitics, global ecology and the 'development climate', *Third World Quarterly*, 30(1), 247–62.

Moore, A. (2008) Rethinking scale as a geographical category: from analysis to practice, *Progress in Human Geography*, 32(2), 203–25.

Neal, T. (2021) *The Environmental Implications of China-Africa Resource-Financed Infrastructure Agreements: Lessons Learned from Ghana's Sinohydro Agreement*, Nicholas Institute for Environmental Policy Solutions, Duke University.

Newig, J. and Moss, T. (2017) Scale in environmental governance: moving from concepts and cases to consolidation, *Journal of Environmental Policy & Planning*, 19(5), 473–9.

O'Brien, K. (2010) Responding to environmental change: a new age for human geography? *Progress in Human Geography*, 35(4), 542–9.

Peters, B. G. (2015) State failure, governance failure and policy failure: exploring the linkages, *Public Policy and Administration*, 30(3–4), 261–76.

Pow, C. (2018) Building a harmonious society through greening: ecological civilization and aesthetic governmentality in China, *Annals of the American Association of Geographers*, 108(3), 864–83.

Rangan, H. and Kull, C.A. (2009) What makes ecology 'political'? Rethinking 'scale' in political ecology, *Progress in Human Geography*, 33(1), 28–45.

Robbins, P. (2019) *Political Ecology: A Critical Introduction*, John Wiley & Sons.

Robeyns, I. (2005) The capability approach: a theoretical survey, *Journal of Human Development*, 6(1), 93–117.

Rogers, S. and Wilmsen, B. (2019) Towards a critical geography of resettlement, *Progress in Human Geography*, 44(2), 256–75.

Rothstein, B. (2012) Good governance, in D. Levi-Faur (ed) *The Oxford Handbook of Governance*, Oxford University Press, pp 143–54.

Rugemalila, R. and Gibbs, L. (2015) Urban water governance failure and local strategies for overcoming water shortages in Dar es Salaam, Tanzania, *Environment and Planning C: Government and Policy*, 33(2), 412–27.

Sayre, N.F. (2005) Ecological and geographical scale: parallels and potential for integration, *Progress in Human Geography*, 29(3), 276–90.

Schindler, S., DiCarlo, J. and Paudel, D. (2021) The new cold war and the rise of the 21st-century infrastructure state, *Transactions of the Institute of British Geographers*, 47(2), 331–46.

Shi, W. and Ye, M. (2021) Chinese capital goes global: the Belt and Road Initiative and beyond, *Journal of East Asian Studies*, 21(2), 173–92.

Smith, N. (2010 [1984]) *Uneven Development: Nature, Capital, and the Production of Space*, Verso.

Springer, C.H., Evans, S. and Teng, F. (2021) An empirical analysis of the environmental performance of China's overseas coal plants, *Environmental Research Letters*, 16(2), art 054062. doi: 10.1088/1748-9326/abf287

Suhardiman, D., DiCarlo, J., Keovilignavong, O., Rigg, J. and Nicol, A. (2021) (Re)constructing state power and livelihoods through the Laos-China Railway project, *Geoforum*, 124, 79–88.

Walker, P.A. (2007) Political ecology: where is the politics? *Progress in Human Geography*, 31(3), 363–9.

Wang, X., Wong, Y.D., Yuen, K.F. and Li, K.X. (2020) Environmental governance of transportation infrastructure under Belt and Road Initiative: a unified framework, *Transportation Research Part A: Policy and Practice*, 139, 189–99.

Zhang, H. (2021) China to promote ecological 'red line' program to countries along BRI, *Global Times*, 13 October. Available at: www.globaltimes.cn/page/202110/1236246.shtml

Zhang, M. (2022) The Belt and Road Initiative's environmental champion–villain paradox: how new governance mechanisms pave the way for a green Belt and Road, *China: An International Journal*, 20(2), 50–68.

4

A Debt to Whom? The Nature Questions in Sino-Sri Lankan Development Narratives

Orlando Woods, Kanchana Ruwanpura, Loritta Chan and Barnabas Mah

Introduction

Depending on who you talk to, 9 July 2022 marked either the zenith of Sri Lankan democracy or the nadir of Sri Lankan nepotism. The official residence of incumbent President Gotabaya Rajapaksa was stormed by hundreds of protestors, many of them reportedly travelling from across the country to force political change. Years of economic mismanagement, compounded by the COVID-19 pandemic, forced Sri Lanka to default on its sovereign debt in April 2022. Soon after, inflation approached 70 per cent, and daily essentials – food, fuel and medicine – were strictly rationed. Amid these social, economic and political catastrophes, many questions were asked. Arguably the most resonant among both domestic and international observers was how the country had gotten into this position in the first place. The discourse of debt is central to many of the answers, especially the Chinese 'debt-trap diplomacy' associated with the many infrastructural megaprojects that various public and private sector Chinese entities have spearheaded in the postwar years as part of its region-building Belt and Road Initiative (BRI; Lai et al, 2020). This dominant narrative is reproduced by both media and academic circles. The Hambantota International Port project, located on the southern tip of the island, about 240 km away from Colombo, for instance, attracted more than USD 2 billion in Chinese investment, triggering claims that China was luring 'Sri Lanka into taking loans it could not pay back, as a strategy to take over the port' (Wooley et al, 2023). More generally, over the past decade or so, they contend that most infrastructural megaprojects have been funded by China in return for significant control and even ownership over both infrastructural and territorial assets. In turn, the concern is that Sri Lanka's political autonomy, national sovereignty and economic independence are compromised (Abi-Habib, 2018; Prasso, 2018; Wooley et al, 2023).

We contend, however, that temperance is needed. A growing chorus of scholars and public commentators, locally and internationally, have highlighted the exaggerated and often misleading assumptions that underpin the debt-trap discourse (for example, Brautigam and Rithmire, 2021; Gunawardena et al, 2023; Nicholas and Illanperuma, 2023). Specifically, Moramudali and Panduwawala (2022) observe that Sri Lanka's debt troubles can be traced back to the mid-2000s when the country became dependent on international commercial debt (or international sovereign bonds – ISBs) and export credits to finance its deficits. While it is undeniable that China has grown to become Sri Lanka's largest bilateral creditor over the past two decades, it still accounts for slightly less than 20 per cent of public external debt (Moramudali and Panduwawala, 2022). Rather, Sri Lanka's reliance on ISBs has played a considerably more important role in the country's recent default. By 2019, ISBs accounted for USD 15 billion (or 40 per cent of government external debt) and carried the highest effective interest rates of 6 to 7 per cent compared to 3 to 4 per cent for Chinese lending (Moramudali and Panduwawala, 2022). In response to these data points, Nicholas and Nicholas (2023, p 1132) assert that 'Sri Lanka certainly fell into a debt trap – but it is an ISB debt trap, not a Chinese one', while adding that the more fundamental reason for Sri Lanka's debt crisis could be the result of a failure by the administration to transition the economy to a more diversified export-oriented manufacturing base. The narrative of debt traps conceals the lack of due diligence by the International Monetary Fund and instead emphasizes the complex geopolitics that downplays predatory financial lending (Chandrasekhar et al, 2023; Kelegama 2024).

We are sympathetic to these critiques, although we are also of the view that infrastructure lending needs to be scrutinized and critiqued. In this spirit, we seek to expand the debate by placing the question of nature within the narrative of Sri Lanka's debt crisis specifically and its postwar political economy more generally. In doing so, we aim to move the debt discourse beyond its normative financial associations and consider the plurality of 'debts' that infrastructural megaprojects like those of the BRI can give rise to. Rather than assume China's role in Sri Lanka's political economy to be 'predatory', we instead embrace the balance provided by Sarvananthan's (2023) assertion that it might better be described as 'quasi-predatory'. That is, while Chinese lending does not have prohibitive interest rates, it has come without the proper due diligence afforded by technical feasibility studies, financial viability studies and environmental impact assessments. By taking this approach, we intend to bring the 'debt-trap' narrative into conversation with recent scholarly work on the social and environmental consequences of BRI-associated infrastructure projects in Sri Lanka. Work by Chan et al (2019), Radicati (2020), Ranawana (2023) and Woods (2022) has highlighted the ecological distress, biodiversity loss and degradation of coastal systems and the commons brought about by projects such as the Hambantota International Port and Port City Colombo. Moreover, recent work has considered how the climate crisis exacerbates the socio-environmental complexities triggered by Sri Lankan debt (Jayaram, 2022). Hence, we explore both the ecological ramifications of indebtedness and the role of nature in providing a way out in the form of debt-for-nature swaps. By doing so, we seek to move the question of *debt to whom* beyond its normative geo-economic and geopolitical associations by considering the natural world as both the subject *and* object of 'debt'.

Three sections follow. The first traces the history of Chinese involvement in Sri Lanka and how such involvement occurred in parallel with several domestic political shifts. The second explores the question of 'a debt to whom' by considering some of the scholarly literature on debt and focusing on the question of whether Port City Colombo (shown in Figure 4.1) can be considered a form of ecological debt. The third explores how debt-for-nature swaps might help us consider how a sense of ecological agency can help reframe the discourse of debt in, and debt and, Sri Lanka.

Figure 4.1: A view of the Colombo Port City under construction, looking north from Galle Face Green

The political economy of Sino-Sri Lankan entanglements

The political end of Sri Lanka's decades-long civil war in 2009 marked an era of relative sociopolitical stability and investment from multiple foreign actors. Of these, China has been the largest investor in Sri Lankan infrastructural megaprojects, with Sri Lanka's postwar epoch dovetailing approximately with the formalization of China's region-building BRI in 2013. The Sino-Sri Lankan development narrative is, therefore, one of aligned interests: Sri Lanka needed to rebuild its infrastructure, economy and reputation on the world stage after decades of destabilizing violence, while China needed a willing recipient of its loans and construction ambitions. Since 2014, this narrative has materialized as various projects – ranging from highways to monuments and ports – of which Port City Colombo provides a point of empirical focus. Garnering worldwide attention given China's involvement and investment of USD 1.4 billion, second only to the investment in the Hambantota International Port project, the original idea for the Port City Colombo can be traced back to 2004, a time of relative peace in Sri Lanka, when a long-standing ceasefire was in place. The first official proposal was the government-initiated Western Region Megapolis Regional Structure Plan, released in July 2004, aiming to attract foreign investment and spur economic growth by expanding Colombo's central business district through reclamation of 145 ha. However, with the political transition after the 2004 parliamentary election heralding the beginnings of the decade-long Mahinda Rajapaksa era, along with the massive costs associated with the project and the enduring effects of civil war, the project was put on hold.

It was resurrected in April 2011, when the China Communications Construction Company (CCCC) – a publicly traded company with links to the Chinese state through its fully owned subsidiary China Harbour Engineering Company (CHEC) – submitted an unsolicited proposal for the development of a new 'Colombo Port City Project' (Gunawansa, 2018). This proposal increased the amount of reclaimed land to 233 ha and was envisaged to be financed entirely as a foreign direct investment (Central Engineering Consultancy Bureau – CECB, 2015). The CCCC and Sri Lanka Ports Authority signed a memorandum of understanding in September 2012, and after two years of negotiations, a concession agreement was signed on 16 September 2014 between the Ministry of Highways, Ports and Shipping and the newly incorporated CHEC Port City Colombo, marking the formal initiation of the project and solidifying China's crucial involvement (Gunawansa, 2018). In 2014, the Port City Colombo project officially commenced construction, under an agreement where the CCCC would reclaim a total of 233 ha of land and retain ownership of 88 ha on a 99-year lease and 20 ha on a freehold basis, with the other 125 ha belonging to the government of Sri Lanka (Chowdhury, 2015a). In a ceremony held on 17 September 2014, the Port City Colombo project was launched by Chinese President Xi Jinping and Sri Lankan President Mahinda Rajapaksa, where President Xi described Sri Lanka as an 'all-weather' friend (The Economic Times, 2014). However, the project soon encountered a disruptive phase when the political landscape of Sri Lanka shifted following the 2015 Sri Lankan presidential election.

Before the 2015 election, President Mahinda Rajapaksa had passed the controversial Eighteenth Amendment to the Constitution of Sri Lanka in 2010, abolishing the two-term presidential re-election limit and allowing the President to seek re-election any number of times (Sultana, 2010). In November 2014, amid speculations of an early presidential election due to the fading popularity of the government, President Rajapaksa sought clarification from the Supreme Court and was permitted to stand in the presidential election for an unprecedented third time (Aneez and Sirilal, 2014). Despite protests surrounding the impartiality of the Supreme Court following the impeachment of the former Chief Justice the year prior, President Rajapaksa called for the presidential election on 20 November 2014 and announced that he would seek re-election (Bastian and Harris, 2014). The day following the sudden announcement, the general secretary of the ruling Sri Lanka Freedom Party, Maithripala Sirisena, quit the cabinet and defected to the opposition to run against the incumbent President Mahinda Rajapaksa (DW, 2014). As part of Sirisena's campaign, he argued that the Rajapaksa family had 'captured the country's economy, wealth, administration and the management of the political party' and accused President Rajapaksa of moving the country 'towards a dictatorship' (DW, 2014). In his election manifesto, Sirisena specifically highlighted the rampant corruption of Rajapaksa's administration and the dangers of foreign debt, warning that 'the country and its properties would be forfeited as mortgages' (Sirisena, 2014). He further pledged to 'prevent the appropriation by foreign states or companies of strategic locations that endanger the economic security of Sri Lanka', naming Port City Colombo (Sirisena, 2014).

In what was generally seen as a major upset, Maithripala Sirisena won the 2015 presidential election, and he subsequently appointed Ranil Wickremesinghe as prime minister (BBC, 2015). Following through on the promise to reassess the financial terms and environmental impacts of the Port City Colombo project, on 30 January 2015 the newly formed Sirisena government appointed an Evaluation Committee to review the project (CECB, 2015). Citing 'environmental regulatory violations by the project developer' (Sivaram, 2017), the cabinet suspended work on the project in March 2015 without consulting the project company, casting a shadow over the project's future (Samarawickrama, 2014; Revi, 2021). With the suspension of the project, the CCCC reported estimated initial losses of USD 380,000 per day, citing damage to segments of the development that were already built, and noted the impact of the suspension on the thousands of direct and indirect employees working on the project (China. org.cn, 2015). By February 2016, these compensation claims had grown to USD 143 million for the delay of the project (Aneez and Sirilal, 2016b). The Sirisena administration was under tremendous pressure from China to restart the project to preserve Chinese confidence in Sri Lanka, and it also faced enormous domestic pressure to halt the project on environmental grounds and due to national security fears that the project would provide China a strategic foothold in the Indian Ocean (Pattanaik, 2015).

Following the conclusion of a supplementary environmental impact assessment (SEIA) commissioned by the Evaluation Committee, an updated agreement was signed between the Government of Sri Lanka, the Urban Development Authority of Sri Lanka and the Project Company in August 2016, approximately 16 months after the project was suspended (Gunawansa, 2018). Under the new agreement, the Project Company withdrew its compensation claim and surrendered its contractual right to the 20 ha of freehold land. In return, the Port City Colombo project would recommence and be expanded to 269 ha to be more commercially viable, and the Project Company would retain a total of 110 ha on a 99-year lease basis (Aneez and Sirilal, 2016a). The Port City Colombo project recommenced smoothly in 2016, and more than 60 per cent of the land reclamation was completed by the end of 2017 (CHEC Port City Colombo (Private) Limited, 2017b). Just as the project began to make headway, Sri Lanka became embroiled in a constitutional crisis beginning on 26 October 2018 and lasting several weeks. In an unconstitutional move, President Maithripala Sirisena abruptly appointed former President Mahinda Rajapaksa as the new prime minister, before dismissing Prime Minister Ranil Wickremesinghe, plunging the country into political turmoil (BBC, 2018). Eventually, Wickremesinghe was reinstated as prime minister after the Supreme Court ruled against the dissolution of Parliament (Daily Mirror, 2018).

Gotabaya Rajapaksa was elected as president in 2019, and he appointed his elder brother and former President Mahinda Rajapaksa as prime minister (Abi-Habib, 2020). Following the onset of the COVID-19 pandemic shortly afterwards, Sri Lanka began to face its worst-ever economic crisis, spurred on by unprecedented levels of inflation and depletion of its reserves (Schultz, 2022). Amid all of this, the Colombo Port City Economic Commission Bill was introduced in April 2021, aiming to establish a special economic zone and providing Colombo Port City Commission with extensive powers to govern and regulate economic, trade and investment matters (Colombo Telegraph, 2021). Critics argued that the bill would transform Port City into an offshore tax haven and money laundering hub, while also allowing foreign influence to overshadow local governance and pollute the commons

(Moorthy, 2021; Kelegama, 2024). At a time when international media accused China of taking advantage of the COVID-19 pandemic to influence politics in countries like Sri Lanka (Tewari, 2021), some critics even argued that the draft bill had been written by the CHEC (Mendis, 2021). Further claims of Chinese interference surfaced in September 2023, when Port City Colombo held a roadshow in the United Arab Emirates to market the project as an investment prospect. At the event, former UK Prime Minister and newly appointed Foreign Secretary David Cameron was invited as a guest of honour, giving a keynote speech that praised the governance and distinct financial system of the Port City Colombo project as visionary (Daily FT, 2023). Cameron positioned Sri Lanka as the centre of a region with massive growth potential and cited a report that claimed Port City Colombo would generate over 200,000 jobs in Sri Lanka. Subsequently, it was claimed that the report was commissioned directly by the CHEC (Mason, 2023).

A debt to whom? The nature question in focus

While the political economy of the Port City Colombo project reveals a clear picture of incremental indebtedness to China amid political turmoil, our concern here is the other forms of 'debt' that have been accrued throughout the project's development. In doing so, we contribute to the vibrant yet niche literature on alternative forms of debt incurred through infrastructure development. In a publication by the Debt Observatory in Globalisation on mega-infrastructures and mechanisms of indebtedness, the authors argue that mega-infrastructure projects often entail the creation of 'other debts', such as ecological and gender debt. Not only do projects like the BRI carry social and environmental implications, such as unsustainable extraction of natural resources, ecological damage, devastation of the commons and impacts on livelihoods, but the construction of these infrastructure projects also involves an unequal distribution of resources, time, jobs and responsibilities between men and women (Lindberg and Biddulph, 2021; Ruwanpura and Ferdoush, 2023). Considering the social and environmental implications of Port City Colombo encourages us to consider how these mega-infrastructure projects reorder spaces, territories and gendered livelihoods, creating indebtedness and imbalances beyond monetary and economic terms. In other words, critically, we contend that debt, as well as a financial concept, is also a political, social, ecological and gendered construct. The question, then, is: what forms of more-than-monetary debt are created by the Port City Colombo project, and how might they be reconciled, or overcome, in the future?

Central to the Port City Colombo project is the controversy over the extensive reclamation of land from the sea, which has raised widespread environmental concerns due to potential impacts on marine life, coastline erosion, water quality and coastal communities (see also Ruwanpura et al,

2020; Ranawana, 2023). Following initial plans for a breakwater project at the location of Port City Colombo, the Sri Lanka Ports Authority commissioned an environment impact assessment (EIA) for a reclamation area of 200 ha, to be conducted by the University of Moratuwa (CECB, 2015). This first EIA report was made available for public comment (as required under Section 16 Sub-section 2(b) of the Coast Conservation Act No 57 of 1981) in April 2011 (CECB, 2015). In light of a new unsolicited proposal submitted by the CCCC, which proposed a reclamation area of 233 ha instead of the original 200 ha, the University of Moratuwa prepared an addendum report to the EIA and submitted it in September 2013 to the Department of Coast Conservation and Coastal Resource Management for approval (CECB, 2015). The addendum was accepted and a permit was provided for the reclamation, dredging and construction of the breakwaters required, although the 2013 addendum to the EIA was not open for public review and comment (CECB, 2015). The CCCC-led Port City Colombo project began construction in 2014, backed by the 2011 EIA and 2013 addendum, although the EIA report was initially meant for an earlier proposal of the project. The absence of a proper EIA corresponding specifically to the new proposal was a key reason for the subsequent suspension of the project in 2015 (Chowdhury, 2015b).

In 2015, following the formation of the new government, several NGOs publicly criticized the Port City Colombo project, citing environmental concerns and arguing that the project would have a profound impact on the coastal and marine environments (Gunawansa, 2018). The main criticisms were that the EIA process was not comprehensive enough and lacked depth and field research and that the 2013 addendum was never made publicly available for review (Jayawardane, 2015). Additionally, it was noted that the EIA and the addendum did not address issues regarding the availability of sand for extraction and transportation, which is key to the land reclamation component of the project and a major lapse (Fernando, 2015). Two NGOs began legal proceedings against Port City Colombo in 2015. One was the All Ceylon Fisher Folk Trade Union of Sri Lanka, which alleged that the sea erosion and loss of marine life due to the land reclamation and dredging would affect their livelihood; the other was the Centre for Environmental Justice, which challenged the validity of the EIA (Gunawansa, 2018; Ranawana, 2023). As part of the negotiations for the recommencement of the Port City Colombo project, an SEIA was commissioned by the Evaluation Committee. In response to the specific criticism of the EIA, the SEIA addressed sand mining in specific areas and suggested a compensation of LKR 500 million for fishermen affected by the mining activities (Sivaram, 2017). The SEIA also claimed that studies 'clearly establish that Port City will not cause coastal erosion' (CECB, 2015). Accounting for accidental damage, monitoring, mitigation and compensation costs, the SEIA concluded that the total environmental costs of the Port City Colombo project in monetary terms would be approximately USD 10 million, which should be weighed against the total foreign direct investment of USD 1.4 billion (Gunawansa, 2018).

While the SEIA addressed specific shortcomings of the earlier EIA, it also faced severe criticism. Opponents argued that the SEIA lacked specificity and transparency (Hundlani and Kannangara, 2020). Professor Naazima Kamardeen of the University of Colombo criticized the fact that most of the environmental impacts and mitigation methods mentioned in the SEIA report were based on desk research and that previous feasibility reports were simply referenced (cited in Fernando, 2019). She also argued that a significant portion of the SEIA praised the development benefits of the project but did not duly consider all possible alternatives, including the no-action alternative. Following the release of the SEIA, continued protests by NGOs and hunger strikes by local fishing communities, led by the All Ceylon Fisher Folk Trade Union, resulted in the dredging of sand being pushed further offshore in 2016 (Prasso, 2018). Although officials from Port City Colombo have produced statistics showing that fish catches have increased and that the livelihoods of fishing communities have improved, local fishermen have stated otherwise and claimed that there has been a decline in fish stocks of up to a 20 per cent, significantly impacting the livelihood of the coastal community (Prasso, 2018). To the credit of the Project Company, between 2016 and 2019 it completed the fishermen's livelihood support programme as laid out in the SEIA, spending more than LKR 500 million to the benefit of more than 9,000 families in the area (Daily FT, 2019). After the release of the SEIA, Port City Colombo commissioned a long-term Sustainability Master Plan to set development standards that will control pollution, waste control, biodiversity and overall environmental sustainability in the newly built segment (Hundlani and Kannangara, 2020). Notwithstanding, the project has continued to face criticism from environmental activists, local fishing communities and local women for neglecting ecological, spatial and gendered impacts. That local women are front-facing the People's Movement Against the Port City illustrates how gendered the impacts are on fishing communities (Fernando, 2019; Ruwanpura et al, 2020; Lindberg and Biddulph 2021).

These developments yield multiple insights into the nature question in Sino-Sri Lankan development narratives. Foremost is the idea that nature is something to be conquered or vanquished in return for material growth. Nature may be passive, but it also provides an effective force that can galvanize communities in response to its desecration. Taking a step back, we can see how large-scale infrastructure projects often, and easily, incur a debt to nature. It is the collateral damage of rapid developmentalism. In the same vein, so too does it hold a potency of value that can be leveraged in manifold ways. One way, discussed earlier, is as a rallying call for resource-dependent, and thus dispossessed, communities, who can use it to assert political authority. Another way, discussed next, is as a financial tool through which debt can be exchanged for the protection of natural ecosystems. In doing so, debt-for-nature swaps reveal the latent value of ecological futurity that countries like Sri Lanka are supposed to harness, but the uneven developmentalism needs attentiveness on our part.

Debt-for-nature swaps and the promises of ecological futurity

In recent years, debt-for-nature or debt-for-climate solutions have garnered attention as a silver bullet to tackle both debt and climate crises that many developing nations face. Debt swaps involve a conditional debt reduction whereby the freed-up investment is redirected towards environmental action plans, such as conservation programmes and climate adaptation initiatives. In recent years, countries such as Barbados, Ecuador and Seychelles have engaged in these debt swaps in exchange for 'blue bonds' dedicated to marine conservation. Seychelles, for example, signed a deal in 2017 where USD 22 million of its national debt was reneged in exchange for a promise to create 13 new marine protected areas where fishing and oil exploration would be banned or severely restricted (Iveson, 2023a). As one of the first countries to engage in a debt-for-nature swap for ocean conservation, the deal saw considerable success. Seychelles could write off part of its debt, and it could also progress from protecting 0.04 of its national waters to protecting to 30 per cent (Gerretsen, 2020).

As it restructures its debt, Sri Lanka is actively required to consider debt-for-nature swaps (Costa, 2023; Mudugamuwa, 2023). While the deliberations are still ongoing, the restructured amount purportedly under consideration is USD 1 billion (Ahmed, 2023). With this swap, these debts could be used to invest in sustainable growth, such as renewables to reduce the import of fossil fuels and agriculture to improve food production, as well as nature-based tourism (Steele, 2022). With high interest rates and high existing debt levels, which can limit investments, including climate-related investments, swapping debt for nature is an alluring win-win solution to tackle both debt and climate crises. With China as one of the largest bilateral creditors, debt-for-nature conversions allegedly play a significant role in addressing the global debt and climate crises. Although China has not engaged in any debt-for-nature swaps yet, with their booming investments in the green bond market and their pledge to be carbon-neutral by 2060, China is actively considering these swaps in their 2030 policy toolkit (Simmons et al, 2021).

However, this proposal is not without limitations. In practice, debt-for-nature swaps involve high transaction costs, as well as heavy administrative and reporting responsibilities. According to a report by the International

Monetary Fund, grants specifically for climate projects or goals are more efficient than debt-for-nature swaps, as they have more targeted goals, are less complex and entail fewer transaction and reporting costs. In early debt-for-nature swaps during the 1980s and 1990s, lack of transparency was another issue, as well as the exclusion of Indigenous communities and civil society organizations. In some cases, a focus on marine conservation led to the privatization of fishing rights, ecotourism and advancing blue carbon trading, jeopardizing the rights and livelihoods of local fishing communities as the commons are intruded upon (Standing, 2022). This can also be a consequence of greenwashing, whereby environmental, social and governance-related finance solutions become a politicized and tokenized tick-box exercise enveloping the commons (Standing, 2022; Chandrasekhar, 2023). From an economic standpoint, the value involved in these swaps is a fraction of the total accrued debt, thus not a means to restore debt sustainability. While in the short-term debt swaps can help mobilize additional resources for climate projects, in the long-term the impact on a country's fiscal situation remains minimal (Fresnillo, 2023; Iveson, 2023b). Instead of debt swaps, critics have emphasized reforms in the global financial system as a more sustainable long-term solution. This might include international trade regimes, international cooperation in addressing sovereign debt and addressing the rampant financialization that corrupts capitalism as we know it (see also Standing, 2017). To swap debt for nature negates the deeper-rooted colonial legacies and inequalities within the international economic architecture that has kept developing countries in a state of debt-based dependence for decades (Kaboub, 2023). As proposed in 2022 by Prime Minister of Barbados Mia Amor Mottley in the Bridgetown Initiative, rather than focus on fiscal policy and financial regulations, which Watson and Argueta (2023) describe as internal 'consistency makers' that influence financial flows and regimes, it is better to create an inclusive and equitable international financial architecture that considers the nexus issues of debt, climate and colonial legacies in our global economic system.

Conclusion

In conclusion, Sri Lanka's debt crisis, and addressing questions around debt to whom, requires us to move beyond narrow conceptualizations of debt as limited to instruments (dept-for-nature swaps, for instance) promoted by the hegemonic global economic order. It requires us to acknowledge that China's forays in the Global South were not shaped by altruism because of a misplaced claim that it is socialist or communist, but rather by geopolitical and geo-economic interests. China's entry into the global finance terrain may have offered the impetus for Bretton Woods institutions to compete in providing funds to large infrastructural projects. However, China's lending to a corrupt political regime in Sri Lanka and the risky loans provided by international finance capital (that is, ISBs) to this same government are equally culpable of allowing corruption within the country to continue unabated.

In this regard, Sri Lanka's debt crisis epitomizes how the widespread practice of funding corrupt regimes has persisted, underlining how colonial and neocolonial dynamics are perpetuated by both ISB creditors and Chinese lending. The neoliberal logic of finance capitalism and its consequences demand close scrutiny in Sri Lanka, as they do across the globe, as a global debt crisis continues to unfold. What Standing (2017), calls the corruption of capitalism compels us to examine not only the financial mechanisms at play but also the possibilities for 'commoning' financial debt – a process that often obscures community and local responses to the ecological destruction caused by large infrastructure projects, such as the Port City in Sri Lanka. Sri Lanka's debt, then, extends beyond the various numbers floating around. The overdevelopment embraced by a corrupt political regime for a decade and a half requires us to keep harping on the debt to nature, the debt to dispossessed communities and the debt to ecological systems to better appreciate both Sino-Sri Lankan narratives around BRI-funded developmentalism and the broader corrupt underpinnings of financialized capitalism in the 21st century.

References

Abi-Habib, M. (2018) How China got Sri Lanka to cough up a port, *The New York Times*, 25 June. Available at: www.nytimes.com/2018/06/25/world/asia/china-sri-lanka-port.html

Abi-Habib, M. (2020) Sri Lanka election hands Rajapaksa family a bigger slice of control, *The New York Times*, 6 August. Available at: www.nytimes.com/2020/08/06/world/asia/sri-lanka-elections-rajapaksa.html

Ahmed, O. (2023) How debt-for-nature swaps can help create a more resilient South Asia, *The Hindu*, 22 May. Available at: www.thehindu.com/sci-tech/energy-and-environment/how–debt-for-nature-swaps-can-help-create-a-more-resilient-south-asia/article66879949.ece

Aneez, S. and Sirilal, R. (2014) Sri Lanka's Supreme Court okays president's third term, *Reuters*, 11 November. Available at: www.reuters.com/article/uk-sri-lanka-politics-court-idUKKCN0IV1GS20141111/

Aneez, S. and Sirilal, R. (2016a) Sri Lanka blocks sale of freehold land in $1.4 bln Chinese deal, *Reuters*, 13 August. Available at: www.reuters.com/article/uk-sri-lanka-china-portcity-idAFKCN10N1XX/

Aneez, S. and Sirilal, R. (2016b) Sri Lanka says Chinese firm drops claim over Colombo Port City's delay, *Reuters*, 2 August. Available at: www.reuters.com/article/sri-lanka-china-portcity-idUSL3N1AJ2Q3/

Bastian, D. and Harris, G. (2014) Sri Lanka's president to seek unprecedented third term, *The New York Times*, 20 November. Available at: www.nytimes.com/2014/11/21/world/asia/sri-lanka-president-mahinda-rajapaksa-to-seek-third-term.html

BBC (2015) Sri Lanka's Rajapaksa suffers shock election defeat, 9 January. Available at: www.bbc.com/news/world-asia-30738671

BBC (2018) Sri Lanka crisis: Supreme Court suspends dissolution of parliament, 13 November. Available at: www.bbc.com/news/world-asia-46196979

Brautigam, D. and Rithmire, M. (2021) The Chinese 'debt trap' is a myth, *The Atlantic*, 6 February. Available at: www.theatlantic.com/international/archive/2021/02/china-debt-trap-diplomacy/617953/

CECB (Central Engineering Consultancy Bureau) (2015) *Supplementary Environmental Impact Assessment Report: Proposed Colombo Port City Development Project*, Central Engineering Consultancy Bureau.

Chan, L., Ruwanpura, K.N. and Brown, B. (2019) Environmental neglect: other casualties of post-war infrastructure development, *Geoforum*, 105, 63–6.

Chandrasekhar, C.P. (2023) Swapping debt for nature: does Ecuador show the way? *Economic & Political Weekly*, 58(37), 10–12.

Chandrasekhar, C.P., Ghosh, J. and Das, D. (2023) *Paying with Austerity: The Debt Crisis and Restructuring in Sri Lanka*, Working Paper No 590, Political Economy Research Institute, University of Massachusetts Amherst.

CHEC Port City Colombo (Private) Limited (2017) The Port City project: where things stand now. Available at: www.portcitycolombo.lk/press/2017/12/12/the-port-city-project-where-things-stand-now.html

China.org.cn (2015) Chinese firm hit by Sri Lanka suspended port city project, 11 March. Available at: www.china.org.cn/business/2015-03/11/content_35027822.htm

Chowdhury, D.R. (2015a) Shock for Chinese backers as billion-dollar Sri Lanka project runs into a political mess, *South China Morning Post*, 20 March. Available at: www.scmp.com/news/asia/diplomacy/article/1742272/shock-chinese-backers-billion-dollar-sri-lanka-project-runs

Chowdhury, D.R. (2015b) Sri Lanka clears the decks for controversial Chinese project, *South China Morning Post*, 11 December. Available at: www.scmp.com/business/global-economy/article/1889625/colombo-clears-decks-port-city-project

Colombo Telegraph (2021) Port City Bill red flags: experts warn of economic zone will be black money tax haven, parallel govt in Lanka, 9 April. Available at: www.colombotelegraph.com/index.php/port-city-bill-red-flags-experts-warn-of-economic-zone-will-be-black-money-tax-haven-parallel-govt-in-lanka/

Costa, M. (2023) Sri Lanka becomes latest country to consider debt-for-nature swaps, *Green Central Banking*. Available at: https://greencentralbanking.com/2023/05/05/sri-lanka-debt-for-nature-swaps/

Daily FT (2019) Port City completes Rs. 500m livelihood support program, 9 July. Available at: www.ft.lk/News/Port-City-completes-Rs-500-m-livelihood-support-program/56-681570

Daily FT (2023) Colombo Port City to become a major economic hub in the region – Former British PM David Cameron, 9 October. Available at: www.ft.lk/business/Colombo-Port-City-to-become-a-major-economic-hub-in-the-region-Former-British-PM-David-Cameron/34-753826

Daily Mirror (2018) SC order: resounding victory for people's franchise, 13 November. Available at: www.dailymirror.lk/breaking-news/SC-order-Resounding-victory-for-people-s-franchise/108-158306

DW (2014) Rajapaksa rival emerges, 21 November. Available at: www.dw.com/en/sri-lankas-rajapaksa-facing-electoral-rebellion/a-18078912.

Fernando, E.C. (2015) To sink or swim with Colombo Port City? *The Sunday Times*, 5 April. Available at: www.sundaytimes.lk/150405/news/to-sink-or-swim-with-colombo-port-city-143604.html

Fernando, N. (2019) Top academic claims fundamental flaws in Port City's EIA process, *Daily Mirror*, 16 September. Available at: www.dailymirror.lk/business__main/Top-academic-claims-fundamental-flaws-in-Port-Citys-EIA-process/245-174545

Fresnillo, I. (2023) Miracle or mirage? Are debt swaps really a silver bullet? *European Network on Debt and Development*. Available at: https://assets.nationbuilder.com/eurodad/pages/3225/attachments/original/1701693052/debt-swaps-report-final-dec04.pdf?1701693052

Gerretsen, I. (2020) The deal that saved Seychelles' troubled waters, *BBC*. Available at: www.bbc.com/future/article/20200803-the-deal-that-saved-seychelles-troubled-waters

Gunawansa, A. (2018) Creation of new urban land by reclaiming the sea in Colombo Port City, Sri Lanka, in *Strengthening Environmental Reviews in Urban Development*, Urban Legal Case Studies Vol 6, United Nations Human Settlements Programme (UN-Habitat), pp 98–119.

Gunawardena, D., Kadirgamar, N. and Kadirgamar, A. (2023) The IMF trap: debt, austerity, and inequality in Sri Lanka's historic crisis, *Phenomenal World*. Available at: www.phenomenalworld.org/analysis/the-imf-trap/

Hundlani, D. and Kannangara, P. (2020) The Belt and Road in Sri Lanka: beyond the debt trap discussion, *The Diplomat*, 7 May. Available at: https://thediplomat.com/2020/05/the-belt-and-road-in-sri-lanka-beyond-the-debt-trap-discussion/

Iveson, M. (2023a) *Policy Briefs: 'Debt-for-Renewables' Swaps: How to Address Climate, Debt and Energy Sector Vulnerabilities in Sri Lanka*, Lakshman Kadirgamar Institute of International Relations and Strategic Studies.

Iveson, M. (2023b) Can Sri Lanka afford to go green? *The Diplomat*, 2 October. Available at: https://thediplomat.com/2023/10/can-sri-lanka-afford-to-go-green/

Jayaram, D. (2022) Unravelling the environmental dimensions of the Sri Lankan crisis, *Climate Diplomacy*, 31 August. Available at: https://climate-diplomacy.org/magazine/environment/unravelling-environmental-dimensions-sri-lankan-crisis

Jayawardane, D. (2015) Critical analyses of Colombo Port City project, *Daily Mirror*, 16 February. Available at: www.dailymirror.lk/63749/critical-analyses-of-colombo-port-city-project

Kaboub, F. (2023) Decolonising the global economic architecture: the prerequisite for a just transition, *The Bretton Woods Project*, 13 December. Available at: www.brettonwoodsproject.org/2023/12/decolonising-the-global-economic-architecture-the-prerequisite-for-a-just-transition/

Kelegama, T. (2024) Sri Lanka in 2022 and 2023: things fall apart – can Sri Lanka hold on? *Asian Survey*, 64(22), 353–64.

Lai, K.P.Y., Lin, S. and Sidaway, J.D. (2020) Financing the Belt and Road Initiative (BRI): research agendas beyond the 'debt-trap' discourse, *Eurasian Geography and Economics*, 61(2), 109–24.

Lindberg, J. and Biddulph, R. (2021) China's Belt-and-Road Initiative: the need for livelihood inclusive stories, *Geoforum*, 121, 138–41.

Mason, R. (2023) Fresh China questions for Cameron as video shows him praising port project, *The Guardian*, 24 November. Available at: www.theguardian.com/politics/2023/nov/24/fresh-china-questions-for-david-cameron-video-port-project

Mendis, D.L. (2021) Colombo Port City Economic Commission Bill 2021, *The Island*, 19 April. Available at: https://island.lk/colombo-port-city-economic-commission-bill-2021/

Moorthy, N.S. (2021) Why new Bill makes Colombo Port City a 'Chinese province' in Sri Lanka, *Observer Research Foundation*, 22 April. Available at: www.orfonline.org/expert-speak/why-new-bill-makes-colombo-port-city-a-chinese-province-in-sri-lanka/

Moramudali, U. and Panduwawala, T. (2022) Evolution of Chinese Lending to Sri Lanka Since the mid-2000s – Separating Myth from Reality, China Africa Research Initiative Briefing Paper No 8, School of Advanced International Studies, Johns Hopkins University.

Mudugamiwa, M. (2023) Debt-for-nature swap: govt. in early stages of forming framework, *The Morning*. Available at: www.themorning.lk/articles/C7wLCNoG2Yf9B0DtqoT0

Nicholas, B. and Illanperuma, S. (2023) The real cause of Sri Lanka's debt trap, *The Diplomat*, 2 March. Available at: https://thediplomat.com/2023/03/the-real-cause-of-sri-lankas-debt-trap/

Nicholas, H. and Nicholas, B. (2023) An alternative view of Sri Lanka's debt crisis, *Development and Change*, 54(5): 1114–35.

Pattanaik, S. (2015) Controversy over Chinese investment in Sri Lanka, *East Asia Forum*, 5 June. Available at: www.eastasiaforum.org/2015/06/05/controversy-over-chinese-investment-in-sri-lanka/

Prasso, S. (2018) A Chinese company reshaping the world leaves a troubled trail, *Bloomberg*, 19 September. Available at: www.bloomberg.com/news/features/2018-09-19/a-chinese-company-reshaping-the-world-leaves-a-troubled-trail

Radicati, A. (2020) The unstable coastline: navigating dispossession and belonging in Colombo, *Antipode*, 52(2), 542–61.

Ranawana, A.M. (2023) Rage against the Port City: Southern theologies mobilising for climate justice, *Politics*, 43(2), 236–49.

Revi, V. (2021) Colombo Port City project: controversial since its inception, *Observer Research Foundation*, 28 December. Available at: www.orfonline.org/expert-speak/colombo-port-city-project/

Ruwanpura, K.N. and Ferdoush, A. (2023) Gendering the BRI: a viewpoint, *Gender, Place and Culture*, advance online publication. doi: 10.1080/0966369X.2023.2234660

Ruwanpura, K.N., Brown, B. and Chan, L. (2020) (Dis)connecting Colombo: situating the megapolis in postwar Sri Lanka, *The Professional Geographer*, 72(1), 165–79.

Samarawickrama, C.P. (2014) Colombo Port City will be scrapped: Ranil, *Daily Mirror*, 16 December. Available at: www.dailymirror.lk/59031/colombo-port-city-will-be-scrapped-ranil

Sarvananthan, M. (2023) Chinese lending to Sri Lanka: a factual cum 'reality' check, *Daily FT*, 17 February. Available at: www.ft.lk/columns/Chinese-lending-to-Sri-Lanka-A-factual-cum-reality-check/4-745392

Schultz, K. (2022) A powerful dynasty bankrupted Sri Lanka in just 30 months, *Bloomberg*, 27 April. Available at: www.bloomberg.com/news/features/2022-04-27/the-powerful-rajapaksa-dynasty-bankrupted-sri-lanka-in-just-30-months

Simmons, B., Ray, R., Yang, H. and Gallagher, K.P. (2021) China can help solve the debt and environmental crises, *Science*, 371(6528), 468–70.

Sirisena, M. (2014) *A Compassionate Maithri Governance: A Stable Country*, New Democratic Front. Available at: https://groundviews.org/wp-content/uploads/2014/12/MS-2015.pdf

Sivaram, K. (2017) *'Locked-In' to China: The Colombo Port City Project*, Center for Democracy, Development, and the Rule of Law, Stanford University. Available at: https://cddrl.fsi.stanford.edu/lad/publication/locked-china-colombo-port-city-project

Standing, A. (2022) Debt-for-nature swaps and the oceans: the Belize blue bond, *Coalition for Fair Fisheries Arrangements*. Available at: www.cffacape.org/publications-blog/debt-for-nature-swaps-and-the-oceans-the-belize-blue-bond

Standing, A. (2022) Sovereign ESG bonds in the global south: 10 questions for those concerned about debt and climate justice, *European Network on Debt and Development*. Available at: https://assets.nationbuilder.com/eurodad/pages/3227/attachments/original/1701795920/ESG_Brief_V3.pdf?1701795920

Standing, G. (2017) *The Corruption of Capitalism*, Biteback Publishing.

Steele, P. (2022) The looming global debt crisis: lessons from Sri Lanka, *Green Economy Coalition*. Available at: www.greeneconomycoalition.org/news-and-resources/the-looming-global-debt-crisis-lessons-from-sri-lanka

Sultana, G. (2010) *18th Amendment: Making a Mockery of Democracy in Sri Lanka*, Manohar Parrikar Institute for Defence Studies and Analyses.

Tewari, S. (2021) Sri Lanka: COVID increases China influence in India's backyard, *BBC*, 21 May. Available at: www.bbc.com/news/world-asia-57167091

The Economic Times (2014) Chinese President Xi Jinping launches $1.4 billion Sri Lanka port city, 17 September. Available at: https://economictimes.indiatimes.com/news/international/business/chinese-president-xi-jinping-launches-1-4-billion-sri-lanka-port-city/articleshow/42716772.cms

Watson, C. and Argueta, B. (2023) Putting climate-resilient development at the heart of Article 2.1c to further its equitable implementation, *Overseas Development Institute*, 1 December. Available at: https://odi.org/en/insights/putting-climate-resilient-development-at-the-heart-of-article-21c-to-further-its-equitable-implementation/

Woods, O. (2022) Infrastructure's (supra)sacralizing effects: contesting littoral spaces of fishing, faith, and futurity along Sri Lanka's western coastline, *Annals of the American Association of Geographers*, 112(8), 2344–59.

Wooley, A. Zhang, S., Fedorochko, R. and Patterson, S. (2023) *Harbouring Global Ambitions: China's Ports Footprint and Implications for Future Overseas Naval Bases*, Aid Data at William & Mary.

5

Waiting, Acceleration, Stabilization: Polychronic Temporalities as Drivers of a Large-Scale Chinese Green Technology Project in Thuringia, Eastern Germany

Hannes Langguth

Introduction

The successful implementation of the European Union's green transition relies heavily on large-scale green technology projects and associated infrastructure. These materialize as, for example, offshore and onshore wind farms, solar photovoltaic and solar thermal technologies, green hydrogen and hydropower plants, as well as large-scale gigafactories for the manufacturing and recycling of electric vehicle (EV) battery cells. The latter, in recent years, have expanded rapidly across Europe, with research, technologies and significant portions of the global supply chain dominated by East Asian, particularly Chinese, corporations (Brown, 2022). Although the constraints of the global COVID-19 pandemic caused an abrupt decline in China's outbound investment to Europe in 2020, Chinese investments in the European EV industry have since recovered swiftly and now form the cornerstone of China's economic engagement in Europe (Kratz et al, 2023).

The proliferation of large-scale green technology and infrastructure projects across Europe, as exemplified by Chinese investments in Europe's EV sector, reflects what scholars in urban studies frame as global 'infrastructure turn', encompassing both its material and social implications (Graham and McFarlane, 2015; Dodson, 2017; Addie et al, 2020; Shatkin, 2022). While their conceptual and methodological approaches dwell on various disciplinary roots, they mobilize infrastructure as a productive lens for the study of urban dynamics and its (trans)local effects. Approaches range from political-economic inquiries into governments' attempts of reconfiguring global flows of people, goods and capital across territories and scales (Easterling, 2014; Wiig and Silver, 2019; Schindler and Kanai, 2021; Schindler et al, 2022) to more place-sensitive explorations on questions of how infrastructures enable and constrain everyday urban practices and how social relations (re)produce urban infrastructural systems (Simone, 2004; Graham and McFarlane, 2015; Lawhon et al, 2018). Both strands have recently developed a growing interest in studying China's global infrastructure expansion, particularly focusing on its Belt and Road Initiative (BRI; Wiig and Silver, 2019; Apostolopoulou, 2021; Oakes, 2021; Zheng et al, 2021; Shin et al, 2022; Apostolopoulou et al, 2023). By conceptualizing associated large-scale projects and infrastructure as place-specific outcomes or intermediaries of globally interconnected flows, interests and politics, scholars offer critical insights into how the material and social geographies of the BRI are interconnected, disrupted, fragmented and/or bypassed worldwide (Graham, 2010; Young and Keil, 2010; Sawyer et al, 2021).

However, contemporary infrastructure scholarship on the BRI focuses predominantly on the role of space and spatiality, often neglecting infrastructures' inherent temporal aspects. Aside from a few contributions in critical urban and infrastructure studies (Besedovsky et al, 2019; Elsner et al, 2019; Walker, 2021; Addie, 2024; Addie et al, 2024; Biglieri and Keil, 2024; DiCarlo, 2024) urban research exhibits a persistent tendency to overlook the significance of time and temporalities in envisioning, planning, transforming or governing BRI-related projects and infrastructure. As Massey (1992) emphasizes, spatiality and temporality are intricately intertwined, forming an integral part of how the urban materializes. Spatial developments are deeply embedded in temporal processes of planning, construction and maintenance while also being shaped by unexpected events and interruptions. They are informed by individual and collective experiences from the past to improve how we live in the future, and at the same time they constitute new path-dependent futures. Following this, the deployment of large-scale projects and infrastructure can be understood as a 'constant state of becoming' that is composed of overlapping time frames, cycles and rhythms, such as those related to political decision-making, material flows or financialization.

This chapter develops a temporal-relational approach to examine the heterogeneous imaginations, motifs and interests behind the deployment of a large-scale Chinese green technology project in Eastern Germany. The empirical focus lies on the strategic coupling, planning and implementation processes related to a new gigafactory for the manufacturing of EV battery cells and associated research, energy and logistics infrastructure, located on the outskirts of the small town of Arnstadt-Ichtershausen, Thuringia. Promoted as a green flagship initiative, the investment is framed by local policy makers as a long-awaited catalyst for economic development and regional competitiveness. At the same time, the project integrates the region into global networks of China's EV supply chain, transforming it into a new (geo)political arena where global-local interdependencies are continually rearticulated, entrenched and negotiated across multiple scales and time frames.

By understanding time as socially constructed and experienced diversely (Elias, 1992; Nowotny, 1992), while also acknowledging its changing conceptions across political and economic systems (Barak, 2013), this chapter views time not merely as a pre-existing backdrop to the project's deployment, but as actively shaping *and* shaped by its implementation processes. This forms the conceptual ground for a qualitative analysis building on 14 expert interviews conducted between March 2023 and June 2024. The interviewees were planning, policy and administration professionals, spanning from local municipalities and districts to state authorities and ministries to external planning agencies and Chinese corporations. The interviews were supplemented by ethnographic explorations and participatory observations (both analogue and digital) during a range of planning-related information events, town council meetings and site visits, and by analysis of textual sources such as urban development plans, architectural layouts, expert reports, approval documents, newspaper articles, local official gazettes and social media posts.

The chapter offers three conceptual lenses to convey the temporal dynamics at work: *waiting*, *acceleration* and *stabilization*. These temporalities relate to the place-specific policy and planning practices, documents and histories as well as the political and economic elites' ongoing imaginaries and speculative manoeuvres in accessing new markets. They are not limited solely to the project duration itself, but also extend far beyond it, illustrating how the region's sociopolitical development significantly influenced the deployment of the Chinese gigafactory project. I argue that the interplay of the temporal dynamics – which I refer to as 'polychronism' – creates the foundational condition for successful project implementation. Concurrently, it is precisely this polychronic interplay that fosters various forms of speculative development while reinforcing relations between dominance and dependence within the region and beyond. The findings indicate that the Thuringian federal state government has mainly shaped the project's implementation by mobilizing the diverse temporalities to govern recurring modes of uncertainty over various periods of time while also strengthening its position in shaping the future of the region. Parallel, unequal power dynamics, particularly exacerbating the marginalization of local actors in decision-making processes, have gradually been solidified over time. The chapter thus provides a temporal-relational analysis framework that integrates the diverse temporalities involved in the project's deployment, alongside a grounded examination of (trans)local histories and power structures.

Time, temporalities and infrastructure

Enhancing the focus on time-infrastructure relations within critical urban infrastructure scholarship necessitates an examination of what Nowotny (1992) defines as 'social time'. This entails a transition from the predominance of 'natural time', including clock time or astronomical time, towards acknowledging time as socially constructed and experienced diversely (Giddens, 1987; Elias, 1992; Nowotny, 1994). In other words, time is embedded in social, political and economic systems that define a multitude of differing conceptions of time (Barak, 2013). This means that time cannot be perceived as a mere backdrop to daily life; rather, it actively shapes everyday experiences *and* is itself shaped by human practices on the ground.

The multifaceted nature of time is underscored by the notion of 'pluritemporalism' (Nowotny, 1992, p 424), which encompasses the simultaneity of natural and social time, as well as of different social temporalities and various geographies of time (Barak, 2013; Ogle, 2013). Following this, the plural form of temporalities particularly emphasizes the diversity of temporal experiences as well as the variety of constructions in and through which these experiences are embedded. Besedovsky et al (2019, p 581) even conceptualize temporalities *as* infrastructure to develop an analytic lens 'to elucidate the ways in which political, social, and economic conditions shape and exert authority over the everyday urban'. Thus, temporalities not only exhibit diversity but also possess a political dimension, influencing and perpetuating social inequalities. Understanding the ordering effects of temporalities requires considering both the power structures that shape the production of temporalities and the power effects that result through their ordering at different urban scales and in varying modalities. For instance, scholars in postcolonial studies illuminate the global dominance of Western time (Fabian, 2002; Barak, 2013) and the imposition of temporal norms by nation states, impacting citizens' daily lives through the varying rhythms of political time, juridical time or bureaucratic time across different scales (Auyero, 2012; Raco, et al, 2018; Baumann, 2019).

In line with recent initiatives (Besedovsky et al, 2019; Addie et al, 2024), I argue that examining urban infrastructure developments, such as those within the context of BRI, through the lens of temporalities facilitates the examination of complex time-infrastructure relations. This approach, in turn, unveils the (trans)local politics and practices that shape these developments. Following this, the engagement with the temporal, particularly in the context of large-scale Chinese green technology projects, bears the potential to not only identify the key drivers and manifold interests underpinning these projects, but also uncover the inherent rhythms of the projects' deployment and their structuring effects on – for example, Sino-German cooperation and broader implementation practices on-site. It highlights the complex political, social and ecological challenges underlying green transition efforts in response to the urgency of the climate crisis (Bond, 2019; Elsner et al, 2019; Walker, 2021). Moreover, in terms of infrastructural aspirations, a temporally attuned approach also unpacks the mediatory role between societal pasts, presents and futures (Edwards, 2003) that is inherent to the deployment of large-scale projects and infrastructure, including the contradictory implications of 'infrastructure-based futuring' (Coutard, 2024; see also Enright, 2022). Moreover, delving into the temporal aspects of the projects' investments would also offer a more profound understanding of the growing disparity between short-term profit generation and long-term impacts on socio-ecological environments (Grafe and Hilbrandt, 2019; Silver, 2021; DiCarlo, 2024). Before examining the diverse structuring effects of identified temporalities, I provide a brief overview of my case study in the next section, including its development trajectory, key stakeholders and sociopolitical context.

The case of Arnstadt-Ichtershausen in Thuringia, Eastern Germany

On 18 October 2019, the groundbreaking ceremony took place for the first Chinese gigafactory for manufacturing EV battery cells in Europe (the site is shown in Figure 5.1). It was held in the western part of the 439 ha Erfurter-Kreuz industrial park, located on the northern outskirts of Arnstadt, a town of 28,000 inhabitants, 40 km southwest of Thuringia's state capital, Erfurt. However, the actual construction site was situated within the administrative boundaries of the neighbouring municipality of Ichtershausen, which was therefore the responsible local authority. It was part of the 8,000-strong municipal association of Amt Wachsenburg. With an initial cost of USD 1.8 billion, which later rose to over EUR 2 billion, the new gigafactory was built in just three years and, to date, constitutes the largest single investment in the history of the federal state of Thuringia. The facility was initially announced as a three-stage expansion project with a total manufacturing capacity of 60 gigawatt hours (GWh) per year. However, as reported in 2023, the facility was able to reach up to 14 GWh, which is equivalent to an annual output of 20 million cells, or the powering of around 350,000 mid-range EVs with a 40 kilowatt hour (kWh) battery (Waldersee, 2023). At the end of 2023, following an inaugural test phase, the site operated at a capacity of 8 GWh.

Figure 5.1: Construction noticeboard for Erfurter-Kreuz industrial site in Arnstadt-Ichtershausen. In the background is the construction site of the new gigafactory for manufacturing electric vehicle battery cells by the Chinese corporation CATL.

Source: Photograph by Marcus Glahn, 2024. Reproduced with permission.

The investor behind the gigafactory is Contemporary Amperex Technology Thuringia GmbH. Founded in 2018, it is a wholly owned subsidiary of the Chinese EV battery cell world market leader CATL (Contemporary Amperex Technology Co Limited), headquartered in Ningde, Fujian province. Established in 2011, CATL is relatively young compared to major competitors such as South Korea's LG Chem and Samsung SDI. Its rapid rise can be attributed largely to various political and financial measures implemented by the Chinese government. Between 2009 and 2018, the Chinese government invested more than EUR 50 billion to support its domestic EV industry and plans to allocate an additional EUR 40 billion by 2028 to solidify this trajectory both domestically and internationally (Huang and Rathi, 2018). In addition to government subsidies for EVs, CATL's rapid ascent was aided by the temporary state-mandated exclusion of South Korean competitors from the Chinese market in 2016 and 2017. This facilitated the signing of numerous contracts, initially with Chinese car manufacturers such as FAW and Dongfeng, followed by multi-billion-euro agreements with Hyundai, Toyota, PSA Peugeot Citroën, Mercedes-Benz Group, Volkswagen and BMW. The latter three were a decisive factor in CATL's choice of location (AR13, 2024), as the new gigafactory site was in relative proximity to BMW's operational EV manufacturing sites in

Dingolfingen and Regensburg (both in Bavaria) and Volkswagen's plant in Salzgitter (Lower Saxony).

The implementation of the CATL gigafactory included additional office buildings, research facilities and infrastructural developments across the wider region. In 2019, CATL purchased the vacant SolarWorld factory and office complex to establish its European headquarters and a bonded warehouse for the tax-free storage of commodities and battery cell modules (AR13, 2024). Furthermore, CATL co-partnered in the newly founded Battery Innovation and Technology Center together with the Fraunhofer Institute for Ceramic Technologies and Systems. The research centre was subsidized by the Thuringian state government with EUR 13.5 million (AR03, 2023). In 2021, plans were announced for the construction of a new Rail Logistics Center in collaboration with DB (Deutsche Bahn) Cargo to manage complex logistics demands. Initially, the repurposing of Arnstadt's former freight station was proposed for this purpose; however, the project was cancelled in January 2023 (AR09, 2023). At the time of writing, CATL utilizes the freight station of the former Opel car manufacturing plant in nearby Eisenach to handle essential imports and exports of raw materials, components and battery cells. Additionally, CATL rents warehouses in Erfurt-Vieselbach and Magdeburg-Sülzetal in Saxony-Anhalt.

A key institution in CATL's developments in Arnstadt-Ichtershausen and the wider region throughout the entire duration of the project's deployment is the State Development Corporation of Thuringia. As an independent, privately operated development agency, it acts directly on behalf of the Thuringian Ministry of Economic Affairs, Science and Digital Society. The corporation actively pursued CATL's investment through multiple trips to Ningde and by organizing a series of high-level meetings between the Thuringian minister of economic affairs and CATL's executive board (AR02, 2023). After a year of confidential negotiations, CATL's investment was officially announced in July 2018 during the fifth German-Chinese intergovernmental consultations (TMWWDG, 2023). The strong negotiating position of the State Development Corporation of Thuringia was closely tied to its planning authority and ownership of the relevant land (AR06, 2023). As a result, the corporation was able to swiftly provide CATL with a fully prepared 34 ha site in the Erfurter-Kreuz industrial expansion area (the construction is shown in Figure 5.2), including ready-made access to transport infrastructure and utilities such as water, wastewater treatment facilities, gas and electricity (AR03, 2023).

However, attracting CATL as a significant investor to Arnstadt-Ichtershausen was part of broader and long-term initiatives around the Erfurter-Kreuz industrial park that have been quite paradigmatic for the general socioeconomic development of Eastern Germany. Following the extensive restructuring of landownership and institutional reforms in the wake

Figure 5.2: Drone image showing the construction site of the new gigafactory for manufacturing electric vehicle battery cells by the Chinese corporation CATL in the Erfurter-Kreuz industrial park. In the background are other industries and the town of Arnstadt, Thuringia.

Source: Photography by Marcus Glahn, 2024. Reproduced with permission.

of Germany's political reunification in 1989/90, the new East German federal states were promised investments to modernize and enhance the environmental standards of the German Democratic Republic's former key industries. Instead, the anticipated economic effects failed to materialize and the transfer of a 'ready-made state' (Rose and Haerpfer, 1997) from West to East Germany led to radical deindustrialization, resulting in soaring unemployment rates and significant outmigration, particularly among younger populations. Low birth rates in the following years exacerbated population decline, plunging many regions into a downward spiral of socioeconomic deterioration, urban shrinkage and infrastructural decay (Lang, 2012).

Against this backdrop, the Thuringian state government and the newly founded Development Corporation Thuringia sought to attract new investments, focusing particularly on large-scale industries with high structural and supraregional significance. These consisted predominantly of new manufacturing facilities operating as extended workbenches for mainly West German corporations, resulting in cheap labour and outward-oriented value flows. In parallel, the developments contributed to the enduring presence of large-scale built infrastructures that persist well beyond the erratic, short-term cycles of economic upheaval and profit-making, leaving the region constantly at risk of being burdened with under-utilized and vacant infrastructure (Carse and Kneas, 2019). Consequently, from the mid-2000s onwards, the region has become increasingly reliant on the ongoing influx of new investments to continuously maintain its local economy and infrastructure (AR06, 2023). CATL's investment in the EV sector must be understood both as a continuation of these dependencies and as an attempt to reorient and modernize industrial production towards green technologies.

Entangled temporalities driving the deployment of CATL's gigafactory

Three temporal dynamics were at work in the deployment of CATL's EV battery cell gigafactory and associated research and logistics infrastructure in Eastern Germany: *waiting, acceleration* and *stabilization*. These temporalities were linked to the place-specific policy and planning practices, documents and histories, the political and economic elites' imaginaries on particular future development paths and the speculative manoeuvres of Chinese investors and German car manufacturers targeting the access to emerging EV markets. Although the three temporal dynamics varied across scale and temporal spans, it was their simultaneous coexistence and interaction, which I refer to as a polychronic interplay of temporalities, that shaped the foundational conditions necessary for the project's successful implementation. At the same time, it was this 'polychronism' that has perpetuated various modes of dominance and dependence within the region and beyond.

Waiting

The first temporality spanned a period of more than two decades and refers to decisions made in the late 1990s to develop long-term strategies aimed at countering deindustrialization, outmigration and shrinkage during the post-reunification period in Eastern Germany. At the time, the State Development Corporation of Thuringia purchased large plots of land and prepared them with infrastructure for the future deployment of particularly large-scale industrial projects. To achieve this, exceptionally large plots of land were retained in local development plans and held back repeatedly over an extended period. This resulted in a form of strategic waiting, characterized by a deliberate period of active assessment and an international search for powerful 'flagship' investors, intended to bring innovative capacity and strong development prospects 'at the right time'.

The urban development plan for the Erfurter-Kreuz industrial park, along with statements from local planning authorities, indicate that the establishment of a supraregional flagship investor at the current site of CATL's gigafactory had been envisaged since the early 2000s. To this end, exceptionally large plots of land were held back for years (AR06, 2023). The possibility of this occurring can be traced back to decisions made during the post-reunification era of the 1990s. As public funding dwindled and municipal responsibilities were reduced, the municipalities of Arnstadt and Ichtershausen began selling industrial sites to the State Development Corporation of Thuringia (AR06, 2023). In doing so, they handed over responsibility for the development of these areas, thereby weakening their negotiating power over future investment conditions. However, this arrangement provided a significant advantage for the location in Thuringia over potential sites in other German federal states, where equivalent state-level development corporations typically did not own land and acted solely as intermediaries between investors, municipalities and landowners. As a result, the State Development Corporation of Thuringia was able to deliberately reserve a substantial 70 ha site in the western expansion zone of the industrial park for large-scale new projects. Several inquiries were received from smaller investors, but these were rejected and the decision was made not to subdivide the zone (AR06, 2023). Instead, over the years, the state has actively sought large investments capable of combining strong international appeal with cutting-edge technology (AR03, 2023).

The decision to withhold land to bring a flagship project of considerable scale to the region triggered compulsive development for both the state and local governments in the following decades. Particularly in light of the ongoing transition in the domestic automotive sector towards e-mobility, the Thuringian state felt compelled to realize plans aimed at creating a decisive pull factor for other firms focused on green technologies. In this context, attempts were made to attract transnational corporations, including use of artificial intelligence to analyse stock market prices and identify firms in the global market that might be considering expansion (AR03, 2023). This was also the case with CATL, which had no plans to invest in Germany. Instead, they had already decided in favour of a new 100 GWh manufacturing site in Hungary before the State Development Corporation of Thuringia intervened and persuaded CATL to invest.

To attract CATL's investment to be localized in Arnstadt-Ichtershausen, and thus redirect the firm from its initial plans, the state made significant concessions. Central to this was the commitment to assist CATL in collaborating with leading German corporations to enhance automation in manufacturing, thereby establishing a more cost-effective workflow with reduced labour requirements that would later be transferred to other CATL manufacturing sites worldwide. In agreement with the electricity grid operators, electricity costs for CATL were negotiated down from EUR 0.18 per kWh – the already discounted price for energy-intensive industries in Germany – to EUR 0.04 per kWh (AR03, 2023). Moreover, a close partnership with all relevant planning and policy institutions was established, which, through regular taskforce meetings, discussed the key developments and thus immediately linked CATL and its partnering with a growing network of local policy, administration and planning professionals.

The strategic and long-term waiting, coupled with the search for suitable investors, characterized the first temporal dynamic of the project's deployment. While the decision to transfer landownership in the late 1990s benefited the state government by preparing contiguous sites for large-scale projects, it significantly curtailed the agency and political participation of local municipalities. Furthermore, the state's efforts to attract CATL's gigafactory as a prominent flagship project also resulted in a departure from traditional role allocations. State-level officials acknowledged in interviews that, driven by self-interest and the desire for success, they delved much deeper into the negotiation and planning processes than they typically would have (AR03, 2023; AR05, 2023). Thus, the strategy of withholding, coupled with meticulous searching, diminished the scope of action for local planning, administration and policy professionals – a situation that had solidified until 2017 to 2018, the years of CATL's project announcement.

Acceleration

A second temporal dynamic highlights a relatively short period between 2018 and 2023 marked by an accelerated array of speculative practices and decision-making. It was stimulated by the political advocacy of the Thuringian state government to tackle the transition challenges of the Eastern German automotive industry. This was fuelled by CATL's recurring public announcements of large but unverified manufacturing capacities during initial stages of the project's implementation, combined with the unconditioned will of both the investor and the federal state government to be the first to implement an EV battery cell gigafactory in Europe, and beat competition from other global battery cell manufacturers and regions (AR03, 2023). Following this, a 'pioneering spirit' emerged that has kept a broad spectrum of collaborators, local authorities and the public in a perpetual state of excitement and uncertainty, while also amplifying the individual and collective risk-taking among the involved parties.

Despite CATL promptly acquiring a 34 ha site and publicly affirming a three-phase 60 GWh expansion plan, as of 2022, the company was yet to provide a precise commitment regarding the manufacturing volumes to be expected on-site (AR09, 2023; AR13, 2024). Instead, during the planning and approval procedures for the Rail Logistics Center, CATL revealed that this information could not be provided and no precise commitment could be made. CATL's speed-oriented urban redevelopment with a lack in guaranteeing development goals, which has been described elsewhere as characteristic of Chinese speed urbanism (Chien and Woodworth, 2018), collided with the German planning context and led to the Rail Logistics Center's cancellation in early 2023. The project turned out to be a speculative manoeuvre for DB Cargo, as the firm had already invested a single-digit million-euro prepayment sum into the project's development (AR09, 2023).

In 2019, CATL's plans, promoted widely by the state government, garnered the attention of numerous other speculative investments and initiatives, and this continued in subsequent years. Right after the project was announced, the Thuringian tourism industry started to plan for an increasing number of Chinese tourists to come. This led to a fast-tracked initiative to launch information brochures and guidance systems in Chinese characters, such as at the Leuchtenburg Kahla, one of the region's most important sights, located close to Arnstadt (AR03, 2023). Local officials confirmed that they even sent employees of the town's tourism office to training programmes focusing on the peculiarities of an as-yet untapped Chinese tourism market (AR04, 2023). Simultaneously, the local real estate market was affected. International investors, including some Chinese investors, acquired numerous apartments in the town of Arnstadt as well as entire multifamily houses and vacant hotels in several villages within the broader region (AR04, 2023). The local real estate market underwent a huge transformation in only two years, which quickly drove up property prices. Between 2021 and 2023, the listing prices for apartments in Arnstadt increased by 47 per cent, and then fell by 38 per cent at the beginning of 2024 (Immowelt, 2025). Shortly before, CATL had announced the cancellation of the initially planned three-stage 60 GWh expansion of the gigafactory, combined with the temporary furlough of a significant portion of its workforce; at the same time, it started construction of a new 100 GWh manufacturing site in Debrecen, Hungary (MDR, 2023).

Nevertheless, CATL's speculative and publicly reiterated plans for Arnstadt-Ichtershausen radiated a pivotal signal to business partners and granted the firm increased liability. Shortly after the groundbreaking ceremony for the gigafactory in 2019, CATL signed new contracts with German car manufacturers, notably with BMW. The agreement involved an increase in the order volume of battery cells – initially set at EUR 4 billion – to EUR 7.3 billion, along with an extension of the collaboration until 2031 (Schaal, 2019). This underscores the role of car manufacturers, who not only influenced CATL's decision to establish its presence in Germany but have also been pursuing a speed-oriented implementation of the gigafactory to position themselves as forerunners in the emerging European EV market (AR013, 2024).

The temporal lens of acceleration highlights that speed becomes a crucial means of attracting multilateral investment, enhancing transnational connectivity (Schindler and Kanai, 2021) and fostering economic centrality. Simultaneously, new and perceived economic opportunities arrive with 'multiple and risky attempts to forge new global-local relations through these networks without any assurance of success' (Wiig and Silver, 2019, p 921). Following this, the rapid influx of global capital triggers new speculative and risk-taking actions by other multilevel state and non-state actors, leading to various modes of uncertainty and forms of speculative urbanism (Leitner and Sheppard, 2023), such as a new under-utilized gargantuan gigafactory complex, a cancelled logistics terminal at the vacant local freight station and overvalued property prices and development trends in the broader region.

Stabilization

The third temporal dynamic refers to recurring intervals and has been a steady motif in Eastern Germany since the post-socialist era of the 1990s. It is characterized by the imperative stabilization of future development paths in periods of structural upheavals and related economic uncertainties. This relates to the political and economic elites' fixation on particularly large-scale transnational investments in outstanding technology and industry projects paired with grand narratives about future prosperity. Thus, a future that is not only 'flourishing' but also 'predictable' is presented, which reuses familiar development paths and at the same time neglects alternative imaginaries from below.

Grand narratives of the future that anticipate large-scale and, in particular, 'innovative' industry and technology projects with international impact and scope have been a recurring motif in the history of Eastern Germany. This applies, for instance, to the attempt of various regions in Saxony-Anhalt, Saxony and Thuringia to shape futurity around photovoltaic solar cell manufacturing in the early 2000s, which were politically designated as future 'solar valleys', only to be dismantled a mere ten years later following acquisition by East Asian firms (Dunford et al, 2012). Yet, at the core of these initiatives and their narratives lies the motif of seeking supraregional recognition, visibility and connectivity (AR02, 2023; AR06, 2023).

Another iterative moment of economic stabilization through politically motivated gestures towards future-oriented technologies was constituted by the CATL investment. This became apparent at the groundbreaking ceremony in 2019, when Wolfgang Tiefensee, Thuringia's minister of economic affairs, looked ahead and spoke of a 'gigantic investment that will push the Free State of Thuringia towards [being] the future world-leading and value-creating location for EV battery technology in the heart of Europe' (TMIL, 2019). Fuelled by CATL's extensive involvement in Thuringia and a series of recently announced investment projects – such as Intel's new EUR 30 billion semiconductor facilities in Magdeburg, Saxony-Anhalt – narratives of the future were extended, proclaiming that 'Eastern Germany is finally in the fast lane'. Against this backdrop, a competitive dynamic has emerged among Eastern German states in showcasing innovative flagship projects. CATL's case exemplifies intense rivalry, with each entity keeping its strategies closely guarded in pursuit of individual success (AR03, 2023).

In addition, greenwashing narratives of CATL's gigafactory were of great importance to political and economic elites. Contrary to CATL's interests, who were trying to pursue a fast-tracked and pragmatic manufacturing set-up, the state government, in tandem with car manufactures, wanted to create an image that would radiate far beyond the region and thus support the goal of purchasing a 'greenest' possible end product (AR03, 2023; AR01, 2023). Therefore, they pushed the supply of renewable energies, which resulted in the installation of Germany's largest rooftop solar park. It was the state government that ensured that this anticipated image of a 'green industry' remained valid. Contrary to the EV battery valley rhetoric, certain segments preferred not to be localized next to CATL's site. Instead, they have been redirected to other, more 'hidden and polluted industrial parks' (AR03, 2023), as has been evident in the investment in EV battery recycling by the Korean firms SungEel HiTec and Samsung C&T in Gera-Cretzschwitz, Thuringia.

The rhythmic interplay of structural upheaval and grand narratives around 'innovative' and 'green' flagship projects becomes a key temporality in anticipating new developments and thus creating centrality and stabilizing economic development in Eastern Germany. However, despite their recurring fixation on grand gestures around CATL's gigafactory, political and economic elites have been shifting away more and more from actual demands at the local level, thus gradually excluding local planning, administration and policy professionals. Instead, the latter are faced with a lack of transparency and participation while managing the manifold on-ground implications that arise from the project's development. This includes, for instance, environmental safety risks or increased truck traffic and the unexpected expansion of municipal roads at the expense of the local municipalities (AR01, 2023; AR05, 2023 AR10-11, 2023). Such 'eat or die' mentality comes with an increasing state paternalism, which further drives the contentious fronts between state-level and local authorities.

Conclusion

This chapter interrogates the role of time and temporalities in the deployment of a large-scale green technology project in Eastern Germany to unveil its heterogeneous imaginations, motifs and interests. With an empirical focus on Chinese outbound investment in a new EV battery cell gigafacory and associated research, energy and logistics infrastructure in the small town of Arnstadt-Ichtershausen in Thuringia, I offer three conceptual lenses to convey the temporal dynamics at work: *waiting*, *acceleration* and *stabilization*. I argue that the coexistence and interplay of the identified temporalities structured the conditions for anticipating and successfully implementing the large-scale project, thus enhancing the region's transnational connectivity and economic centrality. Concurrently, it was this 'polychronism' of the identified temporal registers that reinforced multi-scalar relations of dominance and dependence. This mainly refers to the hardening of local institutions' exclusion from decision-making processes and power networks.

The investigation through the temporal lens prompts me to conclude that my empirical material deviates from existing propositions in at least two significant aspects. First, contrary to the widespread perception of China approaching global activities as an orchestrated strategy of 'economic statecraft' (Easterling, 2014) with distinct Chinese characteristics, it was primarily the host-state actors that structurally prepared, actively shaped and persuasively attracted the project's implementation. Fuelled by competition with other states, the Thuringian state government and its development corporation were the driving force behind the long-term waiting and search for the right investors, the short-term acceleration of multilateral investments and the rhythmic stabilization through recurring narratives on the region's future based on large-scale industrial projects with innovative character. By mobilizing the entangled temporalities, they steered an infrastructure-based future for the region (Coutard, 2024), at the same time increasing its influence at the local level. All three temporal dynamics indicate that speculation was central in this context and became an instrument for the state to navigate economic uncertainties (Zeiderman et al, 2015). Whether it was the speculative long-term waiting for the right investor at the right time, the stimulation of a range of speculative investments shortly after the official announcement of the project or the crafting of speculative narratives about grand futures of the region, speculation was not merely a by-product but was strategically utilized by the Thuringian state to manage uncertainty across various time scales. In doing so, state-level authorities acted contrary to national and European development agendas, advancing an in-depth subnational cooperation with Chinese corporations, or made significant concessions to the Chinese investor that were negotiated opaquely and enshrined in bilateral cooperation agreements before the project's public announcement.

Second, applying the lens of temporalities highlights that the prominent role of federal state-level actors in the project's deployment was rooted in the historical developments and sociopolitical context of the region. Emerging from the post-reunification restructuring of landownership and public institutions, the State Development Corporation of Thuringia, acting directly on behalf of the Thuringian Ministry of Economic Affairs, Science and Digital Society, strategically leveraged its position to shape the region's future trajectory, at the same time gradually marginalizing local municipal authorities and related planning, administration and policy professionals in decision-making processes and power networks (Kühn et al, 2017). Owning large plots of industrial land, they developed these areas to be fully equipped with transport and utility infrastructures, aiming to attract transnational investments, particularly focusing on the localization of large-scale industries of supraregional significance. While these efforts enhanced the region's transnational connectivity, they also entrenched a long-term development dependency on new transnational investments, which, since the mid-2000s, have repeatedly been required to counteract local economic crises and prevent job cuts as well as the under-utilization of on-site infrastructure.

Future research on the (trans)local urban effects of China's global infrastructure expansion, in relation to the BRI and beyond, should reconsider the role of host-state actors and the historically entrenched inequalities of locally situated sociopolitical contexts. This would prevent the biased perception of China's global activities being dominated by state-led initiatives of the Chinese government. Instead, as the analysis highlights, localization processes play out as a collaborative power project in which host-state actors become crucial driving forces (Lee, 2022). As I have sought to demonstrate in this contribution, focusing on time-infrastructure entanglements can deliberately expand our conventional understanding of infrastructures by effectively illuminating how global development dynamics and place-specific histories and power relations are mutually constitutive.

Appendix

All interviews were conducted by the author between March 2023 and June 2024. The interviews were semi-structured and conducted in person. They lasted an average of one hour and 30 minutes. Quotes from the interviews are presented in an anonymous and non-attributable form. Table A.1 provides an overview of the interviews.

References

Addie, J.P.D. (2024) Getting to work on time: the temporalities of urban infrastructure, in O. Coutard and D. Florentin (eds) *Handbook of Infrastructures and Cities*, Edward Elgar, pp 431–50.

Addie, J.P.D., Glass, M.R. and Nelles, J. (2020) Regionalizing the infrastructure turn: a research agenda, *Regional Studies, Regional Science*, 7(1), 10–26.

Addie, J.P.D., Glass, M.R. and Nelles, J. (2024) Infrastructural Times. *Temporality and the Making of Global Urban Worlds*, Bristol University Press.

Apostolopoulou, E. (2021) A novel geographical research agenda on Silk Road urbanisation, *The Geographical Journal*, 187(4), 386–93.

Table A.1: Interviewees

Code	Number of interviewees	Date	Interviewee position
AR01	1	2 March 2023	Local policy, representative
AR02	1	3 April 2023	Private planning company, division manager
AR03	1	4 April 2023	Private planning company, division manager
AR04	1	2 May 2023	Local policy, representative
AR05	1	3 May 2023	District administration, division manager
AR06	1	3 May 2023	District administration, division manager
AR07	1	14 June 2023	Federal state administration, staff
AR08	1	14 July 2023	Private transport company, logistics planner
AR09	1	14 July 2023	Private transport company, logistics planner
AR10-11	2	20 July 2023	District administration, division manager and staff
AR12	1	17 April 2024	Private construction company, lead engineer
AR13	1	19 April 2024	Private battery company, logistics planner
AR14	1	17 June 2024	Private planning company, division manager
AR15	1	27 June 2024	Private construction company, division manager

Apostolopoulou, E., Cheng, H., Silver, J. and Wiig, A. (2023) Cities on the new silk road: the global urban geographies of China's Belt and Road Initiative, *Urban Geography*, advance online publication. doi: 10.1080/02723638.2023.2247283

Auyero, J. (2012) *Patients of the State: The Politics of Waiting in Argentina*, Duke University Press.

Barak, O. (2013) *On Time: Technology and Temporality in Modern Egypt*, University of California Press.

Baumann, H. (2019) Disrupting movements, synchronising schedules: time as an infrastructure of control in East Jerusalem, *City*, 23(4–5), 589–605.

Besedovsky, N., Grafe, F.J., Hilbrandt, H. and Langguth, H. (2019) Time as infrastructure, *City*, 23(4–5), 580–8.

Biglieri, S. and Keil, R. (2024) Desynchronized infrastructures of care: suburban imaginaries re-examined, in J.P.D. Addie, M.R. Glass and J. Nelles (eds) *Infrastructural Times*, Bristol University Press, pp 227–48.

Bond, P. (2019) Contradictory time horizons of Durban energy piping in an era of looming climate chaos, *City*, 23(4–5), 631–45.

Brown, A. (2022) Net-zero Europe risks a heavy dependence on China, *MERICS*, 31 October. Available at: https://merics.org/en/comment/net-zero-europe-risks-heavy-dependence-china

Carse, A. and Kneas, D. (2019) Unbuilt and unfinished: the temporalities of infrastructure, *Environment and Society*, 10(1), 9–28.

Chien, S. and Woodworth, M.D. (2018) China's urban speed machine: the politics of speed and time in a period of rapid urban growth, *International Journal of Urban and Regional Research*, 42(4), 723–37.

Coutard, O. (2024) Shifting regimes of historicity and the control of urban futures through infrastructures: continuities, ambivalences, and tensions in the Anthropocene, in J.P.D. Addie, M.R. Glass and J. Nelles (eds) *Infrastructural Times*, Bristol University Press, pp 72–94.

DiCarlo, J. (2024) Speed, suspension, and stasis: waiting in the shadow of infrastructure, in J.P.D. Addie, M.R. Glass and J. Nelles (eds) *Infrastructural Times*, Bristol University Press, pp 207–26.

Dodson, J. (2017) The global infrastructure turn and urban practice, *Urban Policy and Research*, 35(1), 87–92.

Dunford, M., Lee, K.H., Liu, W. and Yeung, G. (2012) Geographical interdependence, international trade and economic dynamics: the Chinese and German solar energy industries, *European Urban and Regional Studies*, 20(1), 14–36.

Easterling, K. (2014) *Extrastatecraft: The Power of Infrastructure Space*, Verso.

Edwards, P.N. (2003) Infrastructure and modernity: force, time, and social organization in the history of sociotechnical systems, in T.J. Misa, P. Brey and A. Feenberg (eds) *Modernity and Technology*, MIT Press, pp 185–226.

Elias, N. (1992) *Time: An Essay*, Blackwell.

Elsner, I., Monstadt, J. and Raven, R. (2019) Decarbonising Rotterdam? Energy transitions and the alignment of urban and infrastructural temporalities, *City*, 23(4–5), 646–57.

Enright, T. (2022) The infrastructural imagination, *Journal of Urban Technology*, 29(1), 101–7.

Fabian, J. (2002) *Time and the Other: How Anthropology Makes Its Object*, Columbia University Press.

Giddens, A. (1987) Time and social organization, in *Social Theory and Modern Sociology*, Blackwell, pp 140–65.

Grafe, F.J. and Hilbrandt, H. (2019) The temporalities of financialization: infrastructures, dominations and openings in the Thames Tideway Tunnel, *City*, 23(4–5), 606–18.

Graham, S. (2010) *Disrupted Cities: When Infrastructure Fails*, Routledge.

Graham, S. and McFarlane, C. (2015) *Infrastructural Lives*, Routledge.

Huang, E. and Rathi, A. (2018) Beyond the Tesla bubble: the future of electric cars is being scripted in China, *Quartz Media*, 10 December. Available at: https://qz.com/1489228/beyond-the-tesla-bubble-the-future-of-electric-cars-is-being-scripted-in-china/

Immowelt (2025) Entwicklung der Immobilienpreise in Arnstadt. Available at: https://www.immowelt.de/immobilienpreise/arnstadt

Kratz, A., Zenglein, M.J., Sebastian, G. and Witzke, M. (2023) EV battery investments cushion drop to decade low: Chinese FDI in Europe 2022 update. Report by Rhodium Group and MERICS, *MERICS*, 9 May. Available at: https://merics.org/en/report/ev-battery-investments-cushion-drop-decade-low-chinese-fdi-europe-2022-update

Kühn, M., Bernt, M. and Colini, L. (2017) Power, politics and peripheralization: two Eastern German cities, *European Urban and Regional Studies*, 24(3), 258–73.

Lang, T. (2012) Shrinkage, metropolization and peripheralization in East Germany, *European Planning Studies*, 20(10), 1747–54.

Lawhon, M., Nilsson, D., Silver, J., Ernstson, H. and Lwasa, S. (2018) Thinking through heterogeneous infrastructure configurations, *Urban Studies*, 55(4), 720–32.

Lee, C.K. (2022) Global China at 20: why, how and so what? *The China Quarterly*, 250, 313–31.

Leitner, H. and Sheppard, E. (2023) Unleashing speculative urbanism: speculation and urban transformations, *Environment and Planning A: Economy and Space*, 55(2), 359–66.

Massey, D. (1992) Politics and space/time, *New Left Review*, 196, 65–84.

MDR (Mitteldeutscher Rundfunk) (2023) Doch kein 3. CATL Werk in Thüringen – Teil der Belegschafz in Urlaub geschickt, 8 December. Available at: www.mdr.de/nachrichten/thueringen/mitte-thueringen/arnstadt-ilmkreis/catl-batterie-strom-buergerinitiative-100.html

Nowotny, H. (1992) Time and social theory, *Time and Society*, 1(3), 421–54.

Oakes, T. (2021) The Belt & Road as method: geopolitics, technopolitics and power through an infrastructure lens, *Asia Pacific Viewpoint*, 62(3), 281–85.

Ogle, V. (2013) Whose time is it? The pluralization of time and the global condition, 1870s–1940s, *American Historical Review*, 118(5), 1376–402.

Raco, M., Durrant, D. and Livingstone, N. (2018) Slow cities, urban politics and the temporalities of planning: lessons from London, *Environment and Planning C: Politics and Space*, 36(7), 1176–94.

Rose, R. and Haerpfer, C. (1997) The impact of a ready-made state: East Germans in comparative perspective, *German Politics*, 6(1), 100–21.

Sawyer, L., Schmid, C., Streule, M. and Kallenberger, P. (2021) Bypass urbanism: Re-ordering center-periphery relations in Kolkata, Lagos and Mexico City, *Environment and Planning A*, 53(4), 675–703.

Schaal, S. (2019) BMW kauft Batteriezellen bei CATL und Samsung SDI im Milliardenwert, *Electrive*. Available at: www.electrive.net/2019/11/21/bmw-kauft-batteriezellen-bei-catl-und-samsung-sdi-im-milliardenwert/

Schindler, S. and Kanai, J.M. (2021) Getting the territory right: infrastructure-led development and the re-emergence of spatial planning strategies, *Regional Studies*, 55(1), 40–51.

Schindler, S., DiCarlo, J. and Paudel, D. (2022) The new cold war and the rise of the 21st-century infrastructure state, *Transactions of the Institute of British Geographers*, 47(2), 331–46.

Shatkin, G. (2022) Mega-urban politics: analyzing the infrastructure turn through the national state lens, *Environment and Planning A: Economy and Space*, 54(5), 845–66.

Shin, H.B., Zhao, Y. and Koh, S.Y. (2022) The urbanising dynamics of global China: speculation, articulation, and translation in global capitalism, *Urban Geography*, 43(10), 1457–68.

Silver, J. (2021) Decaying infrastructures in the post-industrial city: an urban political ecology of the US pipeline crisis, *Environment and Planning E: Nature and Space*, 4(3), 756–77.

Simone, A. (2004) People as infrastructure: intersecting fragments in Johannesburg, *Public Culture*, 16(3), 407–29.

Smith, M.L. (2016) Urban infrastructure as materialized consensus, *World Archaeology*, 48(1), 164–78.

TMIL (Thüringer Ministerium für Infrastruktur und Landwirtschaft) (2019) Baustart für CATL-Batteriewerk am Erfurter Kreuz, 12 October. Available at: https://wirtschaft.thueringen.de/ministerium/presseservice/detailseite/baustart-fuer-catl-batteriewerk-am-erfurter-kreuz/

TMWDG (Thüringer Ministerium für Wirtschaft, Wissenschaft und Digitale Gesellschaft) (2023) CATL startet Serienproduktion von Batteriezellen in Thüringen, 23 January. Available at: https://wirtschaft.thueringen.de/ministerium/presseservice/detailseite-1/catl-startet-serienproduktion-von-batteriezellen-in-thueringen

Waldersee, V. (2023) Politics aside, China's CATL ramps up cell production in Germany. Available at: www.reuters.com/technology/chinas-catl-german-plant-targets-six-battery-cell-production-lines-by-end-2023-2023-01-26/

Walker, G. (2021) *Energy and Rhythm: Rhythmanalysis for a Low Carbon Future*, Rowman & Littlefield.

Wiig, A. and Silver, J. (2019) Turbulent presents, precarious futures: urbanization and the deployment of global infrastructure, *Regional Studies*, 53(6), 912–23.

Young, D. and Keil, R. (2010) Reconnecting the disconnected: The politics of infrastructure in the in-between city, *Cities*, 27(2), 87–95.

Zeiderman, A., Kaker, S.A., Silver, J. and Wood, A. (2015) Uncertainty and urban life, *Public Culture*, 27(2), 281–304.

Zheng, H., Bouzarovski, S., Knuth, S., Pantheli, M., Schindler, S., Ward, K. and Williams, J. (2021) Interrogating China's global urban presence, *Geopolitics*, 28(1), 310–32.

6

Silk Road on Ice: Extractivism, Climate Change and Resistances

Ksenija Hanaček

Introduction

In the midst of the climate catastrophe, with ice in the Arctic rapidly diminishing, the Silk Road on Ice under construction is an ambitious development project for the Arctic as part of China's Belt and Road Initiative (BRI; Lim, 2018; Tillman et al, 2018). The BRI facilitates the Northern Sea Route development and encompasses infrastructure, scientific research, military activities and the extraction of gas, coal, oil and metals, with the aim of connecting Asian and European economies (Faury et al, 2021). In principle, China is open to all Arctic countries in the Arctic BRI plan. However, the collaborative efforts between Russia and China have led to the development of the Northern Sea Route being particularly focused on extractive activities across the Russian Far East (Lim, 2018).

In addition to the ideology of development, the rapid melting of ice due to global warming is used as both discourse and action to facilitate the expansion of the Northern corridor, enabling increased exploitation and year-round navigation. Moreover, the corridor offers a relatively short trade route, taking only 15 days between China and Europe (via Russia) compared to 40 days via the Suez Canal or the Strait of Malacca (Evseev et al, 2019; Hossain et al, 2019). However, Arctic Nations, including more than 40 different Indigenous Peoples, have long argued that such developments perpetuate colonialism through extractivism and exacerbate climate change (Stuhl, 2016). Thus, interrelated processes of extractivism, climate emergency and development of the corridor deserve an in-depth political ecology analysis. I do this by relating the Arctic commodity expansion frontier (Hanaček et al, 2022; 2024), the BRI expansion in the Arctic and climate colonialism (DeBoom, 2022; Sultana, 2022) to the Northern Sea corridor development. Yet, climate change, economic interests, extractivism and global trade along the Arctic corridor inevitably encounter resistance stemming from historical socio-environmental oppression rooted in colonialism and capitalism (Hanaček et al, 2022; Sultana, 2022).

Large-scale extraction began encroaching on Indigenous and non-Indigenous lands in the Arctic in the 16th century, awaking the resistance of Indigenous and local communities (Spangen et al, 2015; Kröger, 2016; Hanaček et al, 2022; Fjellheim, 2023). Today, Indigenous Arctic Nations are advocating for more active involvement in determining issues related to physical exploitation and climate change in the region (Nuttall, 2013; Dorough, 2014). These protests challenge extractive industries, Arctic colonial states and other economic interests like China's, which jeopardize anti-extractivist and anti-colonial struggles (Dwyer and Istomin, 2009; Naykanchina, 2012). It is precisely in this context that I explore the Silk Road on Ice, also known as the Polar Silk Road.

Much has been stated in the literature on geopolitical aspects of the Arctic, including international relations, global power dynamics and economic relations between East and West (Tillman et al, 2018; Woon, 2020; Nature Editorial, 2023). Although important for global concerns related to climate emergency, security, militarism and interest in Arctic resources (Malik and Ford, 2025), I diverge from this prevailing focus to centre my analysis on the political ecology of resistance to colonial extractivism and corridors, thereby situating it within the broader context of social inequality and uneven global developments (Apostolopoulou, 2021; Apostolopoulou and Pant, 2022). Amid the current historical conjuncture of global capitalism, climate change and socio-ecological crisis, I place human and other-than-human life defence in the centre of the analysis. By prioritizing local voices, the analysis allows for a holistic understanding of historical colonialism and mega-infrastructural BRI-related impacts (Ascensão et al, 2018). In what follows, local resistance against several megaprojects in the Russian Far East with BRI investments and economic trade are examined.

Arctic colonialism and expansion of the Belt and Road on Ice

From the 16th century onwards, land occupation, expeditions, resource frontiers and extractivism of Indigenous lands in the Arctic have underlined the colonial geography of the West and East (Muller-Wille, 1987; Stuhl, 2016). The Nordic countries as well as Russia, following the British settler colonialism in Alaska (the United States) and Northwest Territories in Canada, were driven by the fur and wood trade and, later on, by large-scale industrial extraction of the Arctic for gold, iron ore, nickel and oil (Foster, 2006; Avango et al, 2014). During the Soviet era, the Russian Arctic underwent heavy industrialization; today there is a persistent legacy of nickel, copper and cobalt-processing infrastructure (Venovcevs, 2021). In addition, the Northern Sea Route was used for extraction and military supply (Faury et al, 2021). The current wave of extractivism across the region, characterized by extensive and intensive commodity frontiers and corridors expansion, is now physically facilitated by climate change, which also serves to legitimize new pathways towards Arctic opening and exploitation (Bennett, 2016; Landrum and Holland, 2020; Kröger, 2023a; Hanaček et al, 2024). Setting such agendas aims to maintain patterns of colonial control over resources and domination over Indigenous peoples and their ancestral Arctic lands and waters (Cameron, 2012). Thus, infrastructure-led development projects and planning in the Arctic are driven by ideas of advanced technological progress, development, economic growth and climate change (Egerman et al, 2003).

Today, Arctic regions are integral parts of industrialized nation-states, with the exception of Greenland, a semi-autonomous territory within the Kingdom of Denmark (Muller-Wille, 1987; Nuttall, 2013). As a result, nation-states such as Canada, Denmark, Finland, Norway, Russia, Sweden and the United States, and also China as a 'near Arctic state', cater to particular economic sectors and corporations in various extractive industries across the region, easing their access to and exploitation of Arctic Indigenous territories. These interrelated processes sustain hegemonic colonial relations between both core and 'near core' economic powers and the Arctic 'periphery' (Hanaček et al, 2022). Existing corridors in the Arctic include the Northwest Passage stretching from Baffin Bay in Canada all the way to the Bering Strait between Alaska and Russia, creating a path from the North Atlantic to the North Pacific (NASA, 2007); the Northeast Passage connecting the Barents Sea north of Scandinavia to the Bering Strait between the Russian Far East and Alaska. The Northern Sea Route, which is my unit of analysis, constitutes a segment of the Northeast Passage. However, this route is under Russian jurisdiction (Moe, 2020) from the Novaya Zemlya Straits to the Kara Sea, Laptev Sea, East Siberian Sea and Chukchi Sea, all the way to Cape Zhelaniya on the Bering Strait between Alaska and Russia. Finally, the opening of the new Transpolar Sea Route, which would connect the Atlantic to the Pacific by traversing the middle of the Arctic Ocean, is dependent on ice-free conditions (Bennett et al, 2020).

Indeed, since 2017, the Arctic has become China's new frontier for extractivism and infrastructure development under the BRI through strong cooperation, mostly with Russia but also with European Nordic states (Hanaček et al, 2024). In theory, China aims to expand infrastructure necessary for resource extraction and trade while ostensibly maintaining a balance between exploitation and protection (Tillman et al, 2018). As indicated in the White Paper on the Arctic (The State Council, The People's Republic of China, 2018), China seeks 'to protect the Arctic by actively responding to climate change while enjoying the freedom or rights of scientific research, navigation, overflight, fishing, laying of submarine cables and pipelines, and resource exploration and exploitation in the high seas'. However, at least six megaprojects closely related to the Silk Road on Ice in the development of the Russian Arctic coast have faced significant opposition from local communities, Indigenous Peoples and in some instances international environmental organizations. These include the liquefied natural gas (LNG) project on Yamal peninsula (EJAtlas, 2023d) and the related Sabetta port project (EJAtlas, 2023b); the Vostok mega oil project under construction on the Taymyr Peninsula (EJAtlas, 2023c), which involves the development of approximately 15 towns for 400,000 industrial workers, a port, two airports and an extensive network of 800 km of pipelines elevated from permafrost grounds; the Dikson coal project,[1] which disrupts protected Arctic tundra and biodiversity hot spots; five floating nuclear power plants in Nagleyngyn on the Chukchi Sea, serving mining industries (EJAtlas, 2022); and the Akademik Lomonosov nuclear power plant at the Pevek harbour, providing electricity to the town and supporting the development of coastal infrastructure (EJAtlas, 2021). Additionally, a new LNG investment in the Gydan Peninsula is currently on hold due to Western sanctions against Russia's invasion of Ukraine. Overall, the development of the Polar Silk Road focuses particularly on advancements in Arctic Ocean maritime infrastructure and technology, including nuclear-powered icebreakers, deep-sea and ice-class vessels (as shown in Figure 6.1) and floating nuclear power plants.

Maritime-related extractivism refers to negative socio-environmental impacts of activities such as port infrastructure, oil drilling and mining, tourism and industrial fishing that bring harm to local communities and their lands, coastlines, waters and seas (Márquez Pérez, 2024). Along the Northern Sea Route, Yamal LNG is a joint project by Novatek (Russia), TotalEnergies (France), CNPC (China National Petroleum Corporation) and the Silk Road Fund, with an annual production of 16.5 million tons.[2] This is expected to increase by 40 per cent by 2030 (Llavero-Pasquina et al, 2024). The Gydan project (on hold) is also owned by Novatek (60 per cent), TotalEnergies (10 per cent), CNPC (10 per cent), CNOOC

Figure 6.1: Icebreaker *Xue Long* in the middle of the Arctic Ocean

Source: Photograph by Timo Palo. Licensed under the Creative Commons Attribution-Share Alike 3.0 Unported License. https://commons.wikimedia.org/wiki/File:Teadlased_ j%C3%A4%C3%A4l.jpg

(China National Offshore Oil Corporation; 10 per cent) and Japan Arctic LNG (10 per cent; EJAtlas, 2023a). These gas reserves are extracted from Indigenous Nenets territories and highly sensitive permafrost grounds that supply both Europe and China with what is called clean energy sources. For example, despite heavy extraction, TotalEnergies (2023) touts the Yamal project as the cleanest in the world (see also Reuters, 2022). In addition, LNG-powered vessels on the Route are promoted as 'the cleanest maritime fuel' by the company. The realization of the Yamal project marked the beginning of the Silk Road on Ice development, with CNPC stating: 'an important stronghold along the Ice Silk Road, Yamal LNG is now deemed as a model of international energy cooperation in the Arctic Region' (CNPC, nd). CNPC, thereby, becomes a frontrunner in the resource development in the Arctic. The President of Russia, Vladimir Putin, further highlighted: 'As [Akademik] Lomonosov once said, Russia will expand through Siberia. Now we can safely say that Russia will expand through the Arctic this and next century' (President of Russia, 2017).

Further along the Northern Sea Route, the massive Vostok oil and infrastructure project aims to produce up to 100 million tons of 'premium low sulfur oil' per year. The Vostok project is designed as a hydrocarbon cluster that will unite all oil and gas fields on the Taymyr Peninsula,

Indigenous Dolgan territories. While it was difficult to continue developing the project given the Western sanctions on Russian oil, Russia has turned to other Asian investors, developers and markets. Rosneft (Russia) holds a majority Vostok oil stake of 51 per cent, while ONGC Videsh, Oil India Limited, Indian Oil Corporation and Bharat Petroleum collectively hold 44 per cent, and Nord Axis, a Hong Kong-based entity, holds 5 per cent. Dikson coal, part of the Vostok project, is labelled as 'premium quality anthracite' with high carbon characteristics needed for steel and aluminium making, which will account for about 5 per cent of anthracite annual global production (Staalesen, 2017). The mega mine has been developing very close to a protected natural reserve boundary, the Bolshoi Arkticheskiy, or the Great Arctic State Nature Reserve. The irreversible socio-environmental consequences of nuclear-based floating plants and fuelled icebreakers along the Route have been raised as concerns in the academic literature (Bayraktar and Pamik, 2023) and by international environmental organizations (Haverkamp, 2018), as well as among Indigenous Peoples living with radioactive uncertainties and risks on their homelands.[3] Existing floating nuclear plants and several under construction at a shipyard in China (Nisen, 2022) serve ice-breaking and corridor expansion by nuclear power, controlling and facilitating the heavy extraction of northern oil, gas, coal, gold, copper and nickel.

Resistance to climate colonialism, extractivism and infrastructural 'off ice' necropolitics

Worryingly, the Arctic region is ground zero for climate change and is not unlikely to become 'ice-free' in less than a decade (Screen and Williamson, 2017). Arctic sea ice loss and permafrost thaw may endanger the Earth's whole climate system (Wang et al, 2019; Kröger, 2023b). To illustrate the alarming situation in the region, wildfires have increased drastically since 2019, destroying frozen and shallow peat-lands that regulate the global climate. Boreal forest (taiga), the Earth's northernmost forests, are vanishing under fire, as are slow-growing Arctic tundra ecosystems (Forbes et al, 2009). Additionally, 'zombie' fires, which burn at temperatures as low as −60 °C throughout the winter, are occurring more frequently due to hot summers with increased burning (Witze, 2020). Moreover, as the Arctic permafrost thaws, it releases methane emissions (Rößger et al, 2022). Extractivist endeavours and infrastructure-led development are not put in question although they contribute to climate change. This is another example of colonial envisioning of the Arctic.

As argued by political ecologists (DeBoom, 2022; Sultana, 2022), climate coloniality is linked to continuation of capitalism, extractivism and infrastructure, all of which exacerbate biophysical, atmospheric and socio-ecological dispossession and harm. Indeed, climate change is a result of colonial extractivism, and a deeper consideration of this connection is essential for understanding how extractivism not only contributes to such climate conditions, but also imposes the colonial perspectives and solutions of dominant powerful actors on the global climate emergency and development (Moore, 2016; Cameron et al, 2021; Bhambra and Newell, 2022). Osborne and Carlson (2023) suggest that climate emergency declarations and discourses without proper consideration of historical colonial and capitalist expansion contribute to climate coloniality, because they sustain state-corporate powers with inadequate 'solutions' or 'false solutions' to climate change. Across the Arctic, nuclear power and LNG are presented as 'transition energies', large wind parks are praised and mining of copper, nickel and palladium are presented as necessary in the battle against climate change (Dunlap, 2017; Fjellheim, 2022; Hanaček et al, 2024). In addition to conventional fossil fuel extractivism, green discourses and mining interventions purported to combat the global climate problem reproduce extractivism through technology, finance and economic modelling (DeBoom, 2022; Sultana, 2022). These ostensibly apolitical climate and 'green' growth agendas manage the climate crisis through adaptation and mitigation strategies that continue to displace historically oppressed peoples from their land and waters, disrupting plural ways of life and other-than-human life on Earth (Cameron, 2012). As such, climate coloniality underpins structural oppression and the suppression of collective climate action protests, causing social, environmental and atmospheric violence (DeBoom, 2022). Sámi activists discuss these structural colonial dynamics, further exacerbated by settler colonialism and extractivism, in the documentary by Suvi West (2021) titled *Our Silent Struggle*.

Climate coloniality thus persists through extractivism and infrastructure-led development, wherein disaster politics is perpetuated by a powerful colonial state-corporate nexus (Enns and Bersaglio, 2020; Apostolopoulou and Pant, 2022). As political theorists and political ecologists further explain, the current planetary socio-ecological breakdown and false climate solutions reinforce green sacrifice zones, epitomizing necropolitics (Mbembe, 2019; Truscello, 2020; Zografos and Robbins, 2020; Dunlap and Laratte, 2022). More precisely, expansion of infrastructure, extractivism and trade, alongside climate catastrophe, continue with permanent and irreversible harm and death to human and other-than-human natures globally (Truscello, 2020; Sultana, 2022; Kröger, 2023b; Lucatello and Fernández Carrill, 2023).

Therefore, the Arctic region is an important starting point for understanding resistance to extractivism schemes like the Polar Silk Road and colonial climate and ecological necropolitics that normalize climate disasters in the name of extractivism and corridor development. Indigenous peoples, leaders and local communities in the region (see Retter, 2021) have long contended that their lands were colonized and continue to be colonized by settlers, heavy industries and, more recently, climate change impacts and green colonialism (Normann, 2021; Fjellheim, 2022). The latter concept refers to addressing the climate crisis through land occupation and green discourses as a continuation of colonial extractivism and related infrastructure, whether low-carbon or otherwise, in the region. In this context, resistance movements in the Arctic, particularly those against Silk Road on Ice-related projects, continue to reshape anti-colonial ecologies (Hanaček et al, 2024). These movements articulate concerns about the continual invasion of territory, exploitation and industrial infrastructure, highlighting how infrastructural violence and harm fit into the larger narrative of colonial oppression (Bhambra and Newell, 2022; Kallianos et al, 2022).

Both old and new projected developments and infrastructures in the Arctic continue to be built on areas vital to reindeer herding, fishing and hunting, thereby erasing interrelated socio-ecological systems, human-nature bonds and ways of life (Kumpula et al, 2011; Kuokkanen, 2023). Another example, the proposal for the 'Arctic Railway' by Norway and Finland, which was to be financed by China, raised concerns about the central role of reindeer herding. Untenable tensions surfaced from on-the-ground struggles, as highlighted in a newspaper article titled 'Building a future … or destroying a culture?' (Quinn, 2019), where Sámi activists expressed fears that 'reindeer herding is always first to go' and that '[railway] infrastructure will not bring anything good, it will transport timber, mining products, oil and gas from the area'.

Similarly, projects closely related to the Belt and Road on Ice initiative – Vostok oil, coal, pipelines, floating nuclear power plants and so on – evoke long-standing worries and uncertainties regarding the livelihoods and survival of Arctic Nations, including the Nenets, Sámi, Nganasan and Dolgan peoples (Evseev et al, 2019). Their voices have been raised in forums such as the Global Landscape Forum of the Arctic Icescapes (Global Landscape Forum, 2019) and elsewhere (Monet, 2023). For example, they have emphasized that reindeer herding is more than just a local economic practice; it is a culture and identity intimately connected to survival, knowledge systems, climate and territorial management of Indigenous Peoples and local communities. In contrast, colonial discourses and development agendas underpinning the Belt and Road on Ice continue to portray the Arctic region as *Terra nullius* or a silent and empty polar space above 66° North, with the climate crisis as an opportunity to perpetuate extractive endeavours (Hanaček et al, 2024). This reflects another aspect of Arctic colonialism at work.

Resistance to projects related to the Polar corridor aim to deconstruct extractive erasure and the extinction of life on Earth stemming from past and present colonial actions (Sultana, 2021; DeBoom, 2022; Kröger, 2022). Resistances represent not only a global battle against the climate emergency (Temper and McKeon, 2016) but also anti-colonial necropolitical ecologies

(Dunlap and Laratte, 2022; Lucatello and Fernández Carrill, 2023). Resistance movements in the Arctic intersect in multiple ways with the colonial history of the region (Hanaček et al, 2024). As the climate crisis reaches a point of no return with consequences such as climate catastrophes, pandemics and wars (Kroger, 2023) as well as Polar amplification (Rantanen et al, 2022), initiatives like the Silk Road on Ice deepen the global climate disaster through extractivism and infrastructure-led development. More precisely, the Silk Road on Ice perpetuates a logic of land and resource extraction through both core colonial Arctic states and 'near Arctic states', with far-reaching global impacts. Currently, we are witnessing extractive expansions across the Arctic by China, Russia and the United States. For instance, as the Greenland Ice Sheet melts, critical minerals such as rare earth elements become accessible and of great interest to the imperial powers. Nevertheless, it is essential to transcend the dominant geopolitical focus in Arctic extractivisms and endorse initiatives that are at the forefront of socio-ecological necropolitics in the region.

Conclusion

This chapter has highlighted the issue of mega-infrastructure, extractivism and climate catastrophe in the Arctic in relation to Silk Road on Ice expansion and development projects on the Norther Sea Route. By examining these issues in the region and prioritizing Indigenous and local community voices, the chapter argues that processes of extractivism and infrastructure expansion are a consequence of historical colonial necropolitics perpetuated by Arctic nation-states (Dunlap and Laratte, 2022; Lucatello and Fernández Carrill, 2023; Hanaček et al, 2024). With the BRI, China, as a self-proclaimed near Arctic state, joins this process through investments and territorial control of the Arctic. Building on these points, the Silk Road on Ice continues to witness massive extraction of gas, oil and coal, metal mining, floating nuclear power plants and rare earth elements grab, resulting in the destruction of the atmospheric, biophysical and socio-ecological web of life (Li et al, 2022). Despite the prevalence of development discourses, these initiatives face opposition from Arctic Indigenous Peoples, local communities and international environmental organizations, leading to the emergence of resistance toward anti-colonial necropolitical ecologies amid a climate catastrophe. Though the BRI has garnered a lot of attention worldwide, sociocultural and ecological issues also link to the extractive and necropolitical realities that have long existed in the Arctic and are intensifying due to climate change (Apostolopoulou, 2020; DeBoom, 2022; Dunlap and Laratte, 2022; Hanaček et al, 2024). Indeed, climate coloniality is directly linked to exploitative and extractive colonial structures towards Artic peoples and nature, on which climate crisis is based (Osborne and

Carlson, 2023). Thus, socio-ecological breakdown is inseparable from climate issues, and the Silk Road on(off) Ice represents an infrastructural and extractivist expansion justified and implemented through climate and territorial colonialism (DeBoom, 2022; Hanaček et al, 2024). This chapter joins other political ecologist conversation on climate change, extractivism, colonialism and the BRI expansion (Truscello, 2020; Apostolopoulou and Pant, 2022; DeBoom, 2022; Kröger, 2023a; Osborne and Carlson, 2023; Sultana, 2022) by putting an emphasis on Arctic extractivism, which is inherently colonial and destructive. But there is resistance, alongside historical anti-colonial efforts for the Arctic.

Notes

1. EJAtlas: Dikson coal and Dundika port.
2. See the Yamal LNG website: http://yamallng.ru/en/
3. 'Rosatom started to build five floating NPPs in the Chukotka Peninsula to serve mining projects' (EJAtlas, 2022).

References

Apostolopoulou, E. (2020) Tracing the links between infrastructure-led development, Urban Transformation, and Inequality in China's Belt and Road Initiative, 53(3), 831–58.

Apostolopoulou, E. (2021) A novel geographical research agenda on Silk Road urbanisation, *The Geographical Journal*, 187(4), 386–93.

Apostolopoulou, E. and Pant, H. (2022) 'Silk Road here we come': infrastructural myths, post-disaster politics, and the shifting urban geographies of Nepal, *Political Geography*, 98, art 102704. doi: 10.1016/j.polgeo.2022.102704

Ascensão, F., Fahrig, L., Clevenger, A.P., Corlett, R.T., Jaeger, J.A.G., Laurance, W.F. and Pereira, H.M. (2018) Environmental challenges for the Belt and Road Initiative, *Nature Sustainability*, 1(5), 206–9.

Avango, D., Hacquebord, L. and Wråkberg, U. (2014) Industrial extraction of Arctic natural resources since the sixteenth century: technoscience and geo-economics in the history of northern whaling and mining, *Journal of Historical Geography*. doi: 10.1016/j.jhg.2014.01.001

Bayraktar, M. and Pamik, M. (2023) Nuclear power utilization as a future alternative energy on icebreakers, *Nuclear Engineering and Technology*, 55(2), 580–6.

Bennett, M.M. (2016) Discursive, material, vertical, and extensive dimensions of post-Cold War Arctic resource extraction, *Polar Geography*, 39(4), 258–73.

Bennett, M.M., Stephenson, S.R., Yang, K., Bravo, M.T. and De Jonghe, B. (2020) The opening of the Transpolar Sea Route: logistical, geopolitical, environmental, and socioeconomic impacts, *Marine Policy*, 121, art 104178. doi: 10.1016/j.marpol.2020.104178

Bhambra, G.K. and Newell, P. (2022) More than a metaphor: 'climate colonialism' in perspective, *Global Social Challenges Journal*. doi: 10.1332/EIEM6688

Cameron, E.S. (2012) Securing indigenous politics: a critique of the vulnerability and adaptation approach to the human dimensions of climate change in the Canadian arctic, *Global Environmental Change*, 22(1), 103–14.

Cameron, L., Courchene, D., Ijaz, S. and Mauro, I. (2021) 'A change of heart': Indigenous perspectives from the Onjisay Aki Summit on climate change, *Climatic Change*, 164(3–4), art 43. doi: 10.1007/s10584-021-03000-8

CNPC (China National Petroleum Corporation) (nd) Phase I of Yamal LNG project became operational. Available at: www.cnpc.com.cn/en/2014enbvfg/201807/2a1ed925047b4193b64bb71e056f4d24/files/1a74e3c91e2f4755945e9abfdf08baa3.pdf

DeBoom, M.J. (2022) Climate coloniality as atmospheric violence: from necropolitics toward planetary mutuality, *Political Geography*, 99, art 102786. doi: 10.1016/j.polgeo.2022.102786

Dorough, D.S. (2014) Declaration on the Rights of Indigenous Peoples, *11th Annual Conference on the Parliamentarias of the Arctic Region: Governance Models and Decision Making Process*.

Dunlap, A. (2017) Wind energy: toward a 'sustainable violence' in Oaxaca, *NACLA Report on the Americas*, 49(4), 483–88.

Dunlap, A. and Laratte, L. (2022) European Green Deal necropolitics: exploring 'green' energy transition, degrowth & infrastructural colonization, *Political Geography*, 97, art 102640. doi: 10.1016/j.polgeo.2022.102640

Dwyer, M.J. and Istomin, K.V. (2009) Komi reindeer herding: the effects of socialist and post-socialist change on mobility and land use, *Polar Research*, 28(2), 282–97. doi: 10.1111/j.1751-8369.2009.00108.x

Egerman, D.C., Nils, G., Haefele, M.H. and Latham, M. (eds) (2003) *Staging Growth: Modernization, Development, and the Global Cold War*, University of Massachusetts Press.

EJAtlas (2021) Floating nuclear power plant, Pevek, Arctic Russia. Available at: https://ejatlas.org/conflict/floating-nuclear-power-plant-pevek-arctic-russia

EJAtlas (2022a) Copper/gold mining, nuclear power in Nagleyngyn, Arctic Russia. Available at: https://ejatlas.org/print/five-new-nuclear-pp-in-nagleyngynthe-arctic-russia

EJAtlas (2022b) Coal mining in Arctic's natural reserve, Taymyr, Russia. Available at: https://ejatlas.org/conflict/coal-mine-for-exports-to-india-threatens-arctics-natural-reserve-taymyr-russia

EJAtlas (2023a) Liquefied natural gas project -LNG 2, Gydan peninsula, Arctic Russia. Available at: https://ejatlas.org/conflict/liquefied-natural-gas-project-lng-2-gydan-peninsula-arctic-russia

EJAtlas (2023b) Sabetta port, Yamal. Available at: https://ejatlas.org/print/sabetta-port-arctic-russia

EJAtlas (2023c) Vostok mega oil project, Taymyr, Arctic Russia. Available at: https://ejatlas.org/conflict/mega-oil-project-dudinka-taymyr-russian-arctic

EJAtlas (2023d) Yamal Mega natural gas project, Arctic Russia. Available at: https://ejatlas.org/conflict/mega-natural-gas-project-yamal-arctic-russia

Enns, C. and Bersaglio, B. (2020) On the coloniality of 'new' mega-infrastructure projects in East Africa, *Antipode*, 52(1), 101–23.

Evseev, A.V., Krasovskaya, T.M., Tikunov, V.S. and Tikunova, I.N. (2019) New look at territories of traditional nature use – traditional nature management lands at the coastal zone of the Ice Silk Road: a case study for the Russian Arctic, *International Journal of Digital Earth*, 12(8), 948–61.

Faury, O., Alix, Y. and Montier, N. (2021) From the USSR to the Polar Silk Road: the rise of the strategic Russian Arctic port range, *Post-Communist Economies*, 33(7), 842–61.

Fjellheim, E.M. (2022) Green Colonialism, Wind Energy, and Climate Justice in Sápmi. Available at: https://www.academia.edu/88827740/Green_colonialism_wind_energy_and_climate_justice_in_Sápmi

Fjellheim, E.M. (2023) 'You can kill us with dialogue': critical perspectives on wind energy development in a Nordic-Saami green colonial context, *Human Rights Review*, 24(1), 25–51.

Forbes, B.C., Stammler, F., Kumpula, T., Meschtyb, N., Pajunen, A. and Kaarlejärvi, E. (2009) High resilience in the Yamal-Nenets social-ecological system, West Siberian Arctic, Russia, *Proceedings of the National Academy of Sciences of the United States of America*, 6(52), 22041–8.

Foster, M. (2006) Understanding Alaska: People, Economy, and Resources, Institute of Social and Economic Research, University of Alaska Anchorage. Available at: https://doi.org/https://iseralaska.org/static/legacy_publication_links/UA_summ06.pdf

Global Landscape Forum (2019) Plenary - Voices of the Landscape GLF Bonn 2019 [video]. Available at: www.globallandscapesforum.org/video/plenary-voices-of-the-landscape-glf-bonn-2019/

Hanaček, K., Kröger, M., Scheidel, A., Rojas, F. and Martinez-Alier, J. (2022) On thin ice – the Arctic commodity extraction frontier and environmental conflicts, *Ecological Economics*, 191, art 107247. doi: 10.1016/j.ecolecon.2021.107247

Hanaček, K., Kröger, M. and Martínez-Alier, J. (2024) Green and climate colonialities: evidence on the Arctic extractivisms, *Journal of Political Ecology*, 30, 1–28.

Haverkamp, J. (2018) 5 reasons why a floating nuclear power plant in the Arctic is a terrible idea, *Greenpeace*, 2 May. Available at: www.greenpeace.org/international/story/16277/5-reasons-why-a-floating-nuclear-power-plant-in-the-arctic-is-a-terrible-idea/

Hossain, K., Xu, D.Y. and Lifan, P.L. (2019) China's BRI expansion and great power ambition: the Silk Road on the ice connecting the Arctic, *Cambridge Journal of Eurasian Studies*, 3, advance online publication. doi: 10.22261/CJES.F3OSGP

Kallianos, Y., Dunlap, A. and Dalakoglou, D. (2022) Introducing infrastructural harm: rethinking moral entanglements, spatio-temporal dynamics, and resistance(s), *Globalizations*, advance online publication. doi: 10.1080/14747731.2022.2153493

Kröger, M. (2016) Spatial causalities in resource rushes: notes from the Finnish mining boom. *Journal of Agrarian Change*, 16(4), 543–70.

Kröger, M. (2022) *Extractivisms, existences and extinctions: Monoculture plantations and Amazon deforestation*, Routledge.

Kröger, M. (2023a) Arctic resource extraction in the context of climate crises and ecological collapses, in A. Neef, C. Ngin, T. Moreda and S. Mollett (eds) *The Routledge Handbook on Global Land and Resource Grabbing*, Routledge, pp 223–33.

Kröger, M. (2023b) Socio-ecological crises and global climate tipping points as difficulties for expanding extractivisms: prognoses on the Arctic, *Globalizations*, 20(3), 465–81.

Kumpula, T., Pajunen, A., Kaarlejärvi, E., Forbes, B.C. and Stammler, F. (2011) Land use and land cover change in Arctic Russia: ecological and social implications of industrial development, *Global Environmental Change*, 21(2), 550–62.

Kuokkanen, R. (2023) Are reindeer the new buffalo? *Meridians*, 22(1), 11–33.

Landrum, L. and Holland, M.M. (2020) Extremes become routine in an emerging new Arctic, *Nature Climate Change*, 10, 1108–15.

Li, X.-M., Qiu, Y., Wang, Y., Huang, B., Lu, H., Chu, M. et al (2022) Light from space illuminating the Polar Silk Road, *International Journal of Digital Earth*, 15(1), 2028–46.

Lim, K.S. (2018) China's Arctic Policy and the Polar Silk Road vision, in L. Heininen and H. Exner-Pirot (eds) *Arctic Yearbook 2018*, Northern Research Forum, pp 420–32.

Llavero-Pasquina, M., Navas, G., Cantoni, R. and Martínez-Alier, J. (2024) The political ecology of oil and gas corporations: TotalEnergies and post-colonial exploitation to concentrate energy in industrial economies, *Energy Research & Social Science*, 109, art 103434. doi: 10.1016/j.erss.2024.103434

Lucatello, S. and Fernández Carrill, L.R. (2023) From necro-politics to necro-ecology: framing the current climate environmental politics in the Americas, *Qeios*, advance online publication. doi: 10.32388/BOLIMB

Malik, I.H. and Ford, J.D. (2025) Understanding the impacts of Arctic climate change through the lens of political ecology, *WIREs Climate Change*, 16(1), art e927. doi: 10.1002/wcc.927

Márquez Pérez, A.I. (2024) 'They are taking the sea from us' – maritime extractivism, dispossession and resistance in rural and ethnic communities of the Colombian Caribbean, *Latin American Perspectives*, 51(3), 111–30.

Mbembe, A. (2019) Necropolitics, *Public Culture*, 15(1), 11–40.

Moe, A. (2020) A new Russian policy for the Northern Sea Route? State interests, key stakeholders and economic opportunities in changing times, *The Polar Journal*, 10(2), 209–27.

Monet, J. (2023) 'Green colonialism': Indigenous world leaders warn over west's climate strategy, *The Guardian*, 23 April. Available at: www.theguardian.com/world/2023/apr/23/un-indigenous-peoples-forum-climate-strategy-warning

Moore, J.W. (2016) *Anthropocene or Capitalocene? Nature, History, and the Crisis of Capitalism*, PM Press/Kairos.

Muller-Wille, L. (1987) Indigenous peoples, land-use conflicts, and economic development in circumpolar lands, *Arctic & Alpine Research*, 19(4), 351–6.

NASA (2007) Northwest Passage open, 29 August. Available at: https://earthobservatory.nasa.gov/images/18962/northwest-passage-open

Nature Editorial (2023) China's Belt and Road Initiative is boosting science – the West must engage, not withdraw, *Nature*, 622(7984), 669–70.

Naykanchina, A. (2012) Indigenous Reindeer Husbandry, International Centre for Reindeer Husbandry. Available at: https://reindeerherding.org/images/projects/Nomadic_Herders/publications/UNPFII-2012-Reindeer-Husbandry_Final23Nov.pdf

Nilsen, T. (2022) Construction of second Arctic floating nuclear power plant is underway, *The Barents Observer*, 30 August. Available at: www.thebarentsobserver.com/nuclear-safety/construction-of-second-arctic-floating-nuclear-power-plant-is-underway/152261

Normann, S. (2021) Green colonialism in the Nordic context: exploring Southern Saami representations of wind energy development, *Journal of Community Psychology*, 49(1), 77–94.

Nuttall, M. (2013) Zero-tolerance, uranium and Greenland's mining future, *Polar Journal*, 3(2), 368–83.

Osborne, N. and Carlson, A. (2023) Against a nation state of emergency: how climate emergency politics can undermine climate justice, *Npj Climate Action*, 2(1), art 46. doi: 10.1038/s44168-023-00087-w

President of Russia (2017) Visit to Yamal LNG plant, 8 December [transcript]. Available at: www.en.special.kremlin.ru/events/president/transcripts/56337

Quinn, E. (2019) The Arctic railway: building a future … or destroying a culture? *CBC News*, 22 September. Available at: https://newsinteractives.cbc.ca/longform/the-arctic-railway/

Rantanen, M., Karpechko, A.Y., Lipponen, A., Nordling, K., Hyvärinen, O., Ruosteenoja, K. et al (2022) The Arctic has warmed nearly four times faster than the globe since 1979, *Communications Earth & Environment*, 3(1), art 168. doi: 0.1038/s43247-022-00498-3

Retter, G.-B. (2021) Indigenous cultures must not be forced to bear the brunt of global climate adaptation, *Arctic Today*, 25 November. Available at: www.arctictoday.com/indigenous-cultures-must-not-be-forced-to-bear-the-brunt-of-global-climate-adaptation/

Reuters (2022) TotalEnergies stays in Russia's Yamal LNG, 9 December. Available at: www.reuters.com/business/energy/totalenergies-stays-russias-yamal-lng-source-2022-12-09/

Rößger, N., Sachs, T., Wille, C., Boike, J. and Kutzbach, L. (2022) Seasonal increase of methane emissions linked to warming in Siberian tundra, *Nature Climate Change*, 12(11), 1031–6.

Screen, J.A. and Williamson, D. (2017) Ice-free Arctic at 1.5°C? *Nature Climate Change*, 7(4), 230–1.

Spangen, M., Salmi, A.-K., Aikas, T., Ojala, C.-G. and Nordin, J.M. (2015) Mining Sapmi: colonial histories, Sami archaeology, and the exploitation of natural resources in northern Sweden, *Arctic Anthropology*, 52(2), 6–21.

Staalesen, A. (2017) This dark shadow over the Russian Arctic comes from coal, *The Barents Observer*, 29 November. Available at: www.thebarentsobserver.com/arctic/this-dark-shadow-over-the-russian-arctic-comes-from-coal/105667

Stuhl, A. (2016) *Unfreezing the Arctic: Science, Colonialism, and the Transformation of Inuit Lands*, University of Chicago Press.

Sultana, F. (2021) Political ecology II: conjunctures, crises, and critical publics, *Progress in Human Geography*, 45(6), 1721–30.

Sultana, F. (2022) The unbearable heaviness of climate coloniality, *Political Geography*, art 102638. doi: 10.1016/j.polgeo.2022.102638

Temper, L. and McKeon, S. (2016) *Corridors of Resistance* [video], Environmental Justice Organizations, Liabilities, and Trade.

The State Council, The People's Republic of China (2018) China's Arctic Policy. Available at: https://english.www.gov.cn/archive/white_paper/2018/01/26/content_281476026660336.htm

Tillman, H., Yang, J. and Nielsson, E.T. (2018) The Polar Silk Road: China's new frontier of international cooperation, *China Quarterly of International Strategic Studies*, 4(3), 345–62.

TotalEnergies (2023) *More Energy, Less Emissions*. Available at: https://totalenergies.com/system/files/documents/2023-03/Sustainability_Climate_2023_Progress_Report_EN.pdf

Truscello, M. (2020) *Infrastructural Brutalism: Art and the Necropolitics of Infrastructure*, The MIT Press.

Venovcevs, A. (2021) Living with socialism: toward an archaeology of a post-soviet industrial town, *The Extractive Industries and Society*, 8(4), art 100835. doi: 10.1016/j.exis.2020.10.017

Wang, C., Wang, Z., Kong, Y., Zhang, F., Yang, K. and Zhang, T. (2019) Most of the Northern Hemisphere permafrost remains under climate change, *Scientific Reports*, 9(1), art 3295. doi: 10.1038/s41598-019-39942-4

West, S. (dir) (2021) *Eatnameamet – Our Silent Struggle* [documentary].

Witze, A. (2020) The Arctic is burning like never before – and that's bad news for climate change, *Nature*, 585(7825), 336–7.

Woon, C.Y. (2020) Framing the 'Polar Silk Road' (冰上丝绸之路): critical geopolitics, Chinese scholars and the (re)positionings of China's Arctic interests, *Political Geography*, 78, art 102141. doi: 10.1016/j.polgeo.2019.102141

Zografos, C. and Robbins, P. (2020) Green sacrifice zones, or why a green new deal cannot ignore the cost shifts of just transitions, *One Earth*, 3(5), 543–6.

7

Donor Competition, Local Agency and Contingency: Jakarta-Bandung High-Speed Railway in Indonesia

Caixia Mao

Introduction

Following the launch of the Belt and Road Initiative (BRI) by China in 2013, Japan, as a historical infrastructure provider, rebranded its international infrastructure initiatives under a single policy umbrella: Partnership for Quality Infrastructure in 2015. There has been increasing comparative analysis of the BRI and the Partnership for Quality Infrastructure, focusing on domestic economic drivers (Yoshimatsu, 2018), policy learning (Mao and Mueller, 2020), host-country engagement (Jain, 2019) and impacts for the host countries (Liao and Katada, 2020). This chapter takes a host-country-centric approach by discussing the agencies of different local actors in the case of China-Japan competition in the Jakarta-Bandung high-speed railway (HSR) in Indonesia. Infrastructure development has played a pivotal role in nation-building in Indonesia, aimed at creating a modern state following postcolonial independence and capitalist development interventions (Barker, 2005; Kusno, 2013). Under the administration of President Jokowi (2014–2024), known as the 'infrastructure president' (Iqbal and Asmara, 2019), infrastructure development has been framed as the core strategy for economic development and poverty alleviation. At the same time, Indonesia has historically relied on external actors' financial and technological resources for infrastructure development, particularly Japan and in recent years China.

Historically, Japan has been the major financial and material provider for Indonesia's infrastructure development. The provision started in 1951 as a part of Japan's war reparation to reconstruct the infrastructure Japan destroyed during World War II. Indonesia received JPY 288 billion in reparation and additional JPY 144 billion in economic cooperation (Nishihara, 1976). Later, economic cooperation continued with more loans and official development assistance (ODA) to Indonesia, beginning in 1968. Japan became Indonesia's main economic partner for foreign investments, trade and ODA. By 2016, Japanese support to Indonesia totalled USD 49 billion, making Japan Indonesia's largest bilateral aid provider and making Indonesia Japan's largest ODA recipient country (Japan International Cooperation Agency – JICA, 2018). Japanese-accumulated ODA support to Indonesia accounted for 45 per cent of all ODA Indonesia has received since the 1960s, 90 per cent of which were yen loans. In 1980, Japan began to support the Jakarta region as a business hub for Japanese companies and introduced railway modernization. Japan has been funding and constructing the first mass-rapid transit (MRT) in Jakarta since 2006. Due to its dominating position in infrastructure development support in Indonesia, the Jakarta MRT Phase 1 project was under the 'All-Japan' concept, which was to use only Japanese technology in the entire MRT system.

The initial ties between China and Indonesia were formed based on political ideologies of Communism rather than economic exchanges under the post-World War II Cold War context. The two countries shared their bond, based on anti-colonial and imperialist beliefs, at the Bandung Conference in 1955. Yet, the relations seriously deteriorated with the '30 September Event (G30P/PKI)' in 1965. In this event, it was alleged that the Indonesian Communist party, PKI, was responsible for the coup with the support of the Chinese government (He, 2000). As a result, the New Order government under Suharto froze its diplomatic ties with Beijing on 23 October 1967. It was not until 1999 that two countries resumed diplomatic ties, and from 2000 to 2017, Chinese development finance in Indonesia accumulated to USD 4.42 billion, making Indonesia the largest recipient of Chinese development finance in Southeast Asia (Malik et al, 2021). In 2013, during his visit to Indonesia, President Xi Jinping announced the 21st Century Maritime Silk Road initiative. In the following years, Chinese development finance has been tied to Jokowi's policy goals of developing the industrial capacity for minerals and expanding infrastructure. Chinese investment in Indonesia Morowali Industrial Park became the core partner under Jokowi's ambition to develop nickel processing capacity and ban unprocessed mineral exports. In 2015, after intense China-Japan competition in the project bidding for Indonesia's first HSR, the Indonesian government announced its acceptance of the Chinese proposal to build the Jakarta-Bandung HSR.

Recent studies on donor-recipient relations offer a nuanced approach to apply the concept of host countries' local agency to capture the contingent nature of decision-making process in infrastructure projects (Mohan, 2020). Although states are the key actor to launch infrastructure investment as donors, they adapt into 'contingent negotiated authority' to engage with actors in host countries (Gonzalez-Vicente, 2019, p 500). Thus, infrastructure donors often lack a coherent global vision, as their visions are 'swallowed up' in the complex local contexts in host countries and form their benefits and disbenefits in a contingent manner (Goodfellow and Huang, 2021). Often, among actors in host countries, governments of different levels leverage infrastructure projects to enhance their influences in domestic politics (Lim et al, 2021; Suhardiman et al, 2021). Moreover, with intensified donor competition (Yoshimatsu, 2018; Jiang, 2019; Liao and Katada, 2020), host countries are increasingly applying tactics such as hedging to balance security, geopolitical and economic interests (Liao and Dang, 2019; Schindler et al, 2021; Yan, 2023). Thus, infrastructure projects became the composition of assemblages with multiple levels of interactions between donor and host countries, and among actors within recipient countries.

In this context, I apply the concept of 'two-level games' (Putnam, 1988) to examine how projects alter donor-recipient relations, looking specifically at how local actors asserted self-interests in the negotiation and implementation process of the Jakarta-Bandung HSR project. By examining different Indonesian actors' agencies in different phases of the project development, I argue that local actors lack 'elite cohesion' and thus local agencies are formed on a contingent basis. The allegiances of local actors are developed based on the interaction with donors and other actors in a contingent manner. The chapter focuses on four types of actors: high-level politicians in central government; economic elites such, as state-owned enterprises (SOEs); political elites from regional governments; and the military. I conclude the chapter by suggesting that the exercise of local agency comes with multiple costs for Indonesia in terms of political risks for Jokowi in re-election and damaging ties with Japan. Most importantly, due to the huge cost overrun, the Indonesian government had to inject capital to SOEs to provide financial guarantee, despite the initial rhetoric offered by China of it being a 'business-to-business' deal without state budget. Lastly, I argue that the public-private partnership (PPP) mode of cooperation in infrastructure projects ultimately guarantees investment profits for the private sector at the expense of public interests.

Pragmatic neutrality and donor competition in Jakarta-Bandung HSR

Since Indonesia's independence, the international order envisioned by Mohammad Hatta has been based on 'sovereignty, sovereign equality, multilateralism, and non-alignment', and these remain the core principles today (Umar, 2023, p 1464). This conception in practice, as Hatta wished, allows Indonesia to engage with all countries and powers while also allowing it to develop its own autonomy to pursue its self-interests without interference from external actors (Umar, 2023). When Jokowi came into power, he reinforced this pragmatic interpretation of the neutrality principle to obtain material benefits for economic development. This sentiment is well-reflected by a government official quoting Jokowi's address to government officials in a meeting: 'we don't have any enemy, our only enemy is poverty' (personal communication, Jakarta, July 2023). This pragmatic neutrality became the principle when the Jokowi administration manoeuvred its negotiation with infrastructure development partners.

As 'Infrastructure President' (Iqbal and Asmara, 2019), Jokowi envisioned mobilizing state investment in SOEs as the driving force for economic development and expanding infrastructure, despite fiscal constraints and the failure to attract private capital (Kim, 2018). Jokowi was elected to office as the 'people's president' with the goal of growing the economy and enhancing the wellbeing of the people under the ambitious infrastructure plan, titled Rencana Pembanguan Jangka Menengah Nasional 2015–2019 (RPJMN 2015–2019). This plan included hundreds of infrastructure projects, estimated at USD 470 billion (Negara, 2016). The infrastructure expenditure from the state budget was set to increase by USD 10 billion annually from 2015 to 2019. In a key decision that set Jokowi apart from his predecessor, Susilo Bambang Yudhoyono, he reduced fuel subsidies to decrease fiscal expenditure and allow for increased infrastructure spending (Salim and Negara, 2018). Also, the government incorporated PPP to finance the infrastructure projects for RPJMN 2015–2019. To meet the infrastructure financing needs, in addition to 41.3 per cent from the government budget and 36.5 per cent from private sector investment, SOEs were expected to contribute 22.2 per cent (Salim and Negara, 2018). In short, infrastructure development was a key component in Jokowi's political rhetoric of measuring progress, to legitimize his rule, but he faced capital constraints. In this context, the contribution of foreign capital from China and Japan was vital in realizing Jokowi's infrastructure ambitions. With the China-Japan competition in Jakarta-Bandung HSR, Jokowi's administration was able to exercise its pragmatic neutrality in the donor negotiation in order to maximize material benefits in the cooperation conditions.

The Jakarta-Bandung HSR was first proposed by the Japanese government in 2007, and the intention was to use Japanese Shinkansen technology in Indonesia and Southeast Asia for the first time. The Japanese Ministry of Economy, Trade and Industry sponsored a feasibility study for a 730 km HSR from Jakarta to Surabaya, and proposed focusing on the 144 km stretch between Jakarta and Bandung, where passenger demand would be highest. In 2013, JICA conducted a more detailed feasibility study for the Jakarta-Bandung route, aiming to reduce the travel time from three hours to 45 minutes. In 2014, after Japan's long-term involvement in the project,

Jokowi expressed concern about the railway project due to its requirement for a large state budget, and this led to China entering the competition with Japan. Following Jokowi's launch in 2014 of the 'Global Maritime Fulcrum' to develop online and maritime infrastructure, Xi Jinping stated that the '21st Century Maritime Silk Road' under the BRI aligned with Indonesia's proposal to become a maritime power (Embassy of the People's Republic of China in the Republic of Indonesia, 2014). In March 2015, the Chinese National Development and Reform Commission and Indonesia's Ministry of State-Owned Enterprises signed a memorandum of understanding to cooperate on the Jakarta-Bandung HSR. In July 2015, facing pressure to compete with China, Japanese Prime Minister Shinzo Abe appointed special advisor Hiroto Izumi to offer a loan covering 75 per cent of the estimated USD 5 billion total cost, with an interest rate of 0.1 per cent over a 40-year payment period and with a 10-year grace period. Japan promised to start the test run in 2019 and complete it by 2021 (Sankei News, 2015; see Table 7.1). In August 2015, the Chinese government presented their feasibility study to Jokowi, improving their loan offer from USD 4 billion with a 25-year

Table 7.1: The final bidding proposals by China (KCIC) and Japan for the Jakarta-Bandung HSR

	China (KCIC)	Japan
Bidding value	USD 5.13 billion (includes land acquisition cost)	USD 6.2 billion (excludes land acquisition cost)
State guarantee	Not required	50%
Cooperation model	Business-to-business with Indonesian (60%) and Chinese (40%) SOEs bearing all the risks and liabilities	Government-to-government between Indonesian and Japanese governments, with the Japanese firms acting as regular contractors and the Indonesian government bearing all the risks and liabilities
Loan condition	25% equity by KCIC, 75% loan from CDB	75% loan from JICA, 25% Indonesian state budget
Loan terms	40 years with 10-year grace period	40 years with 10-year grace period
Currency	60% USD with 2% interest rate; 40% RMB with 3.46% interest rate	100% JPY with 0.1% interest rate
Local content	50.6%	40%
Technology transfer	A complete technology transfer and the possibility of opening a rolling stock plant in Purwakarta	No tangible technology transfer programme
Timeline	Operating in 2019	Operating in 2021

Source: Adapted from Yan (2023) and Salim and Negara (2016)

lending period and 2 per cent annual interest rate to USD 5.5 billion with a 50-year tenure, a 2 per cent interest rate and a 10-year grace period. The Chinese proposal comprised 60 per cent in US dollars and 40 per cent in renminbe, compared to the Japanese proposal which was 100 per cent yen-based (Salim and Negara, 2016). In the same month, special advisor Izumi proposed lowering the viability gap funding for the Indonesian government and enhancing the local procurement rate to contribute to the local economy, in an attempt to counter the Chinese approach of bringing resources and labour from China (Sankei News, 2015). However, on 3 September 2015, the Indonesian government unexpectedly announced the cancellation of the project due to cost and state guarantee concerns, saying that it intended to pursue lower-speed alternatives instead.

Following the announcement, China quickly revised its proposal to present the deal as a business-to-business agreement between SOEs in Indonesia and China, without state guarantee or budget. This was in contrast to the Japanese proposal, which required government funding for the viability gap. China also promised technology transfer to jointly produce railway cars in Indonesia, not only for the HSR but also for electric and light trains. These would be exported to other Asian countries, generating foreign exchange for Indonesia. Moreover, China agreed to construct an aluminium plant in Indonesia for railway car production (Jakarta Post, 2015). Furthermore, China planned to complete the construction in 2018 and begin operation in 2019, which coincided with Jokowi's re-election year. Despite Japan reducing its request for an Indonesian government guarantee from 100 per cent to 50 per cent, the proposal still expected part of the investment to come from the Indonesian state budget (Jakarta Post, 2015). The Chinese proposal, however, was flexible enough to accommodate Jokowi's preferences for not requiring government funding or debt guarantee and for adopting a business-to-business approach. The proposal also included the benefit of developing surrounding real estate and commercial facilities through the operation of the HSR (Globe Asahi Shimbun, 2018). In September 2015, the Indonesian government announced its acceptance of the Chinese proposal. This announcement came as a surprise to Japan, as the Indonesian government had previously explained to Japan that they would detail the projects and invite companies from various countries, including Japan, to participate in the bidding. Japan's chief cabinet secretary at the time, Yoshihide Suga, described the decision as 'incomprehensible and extremely regrettable' (Cabinet Office, 2015).

Local agency in the Jakarta-Bandung HSR

I apply Putnam's (1988) 'two-level game', a concept to describe the two levels of interaction in interstate negotiations: negotiation at the interstate-level

(level 1) – in this case. between the donor and host countries; and negotiation at the domestic level (level 2) – in this case, negotiation among domestic actors in host countries. This concept is applied to capture two levels of agency of Indonesian actors, particularly HSR supporters, in negotiations with China and Japan (level 1) and negotiations with different actors within Indonesia (level 2). Rather than the two processes occurring one after the other, I argue that they took place simultaneously, with the domestic Indonesian actors' negotiation and bargaining process affecting the Jokowi administration's interaction with donors. Moreover, single actors within Indonesia, such as those at the central ministry or members of the economic elite, can have conflicting views. The single actor needs to deal with donors and domestic actors at the same time. As well as having different views on whether to construct a HSR, local elites were also split on whether to choose the Chinese or Japanese proposals. By focusing on high-level political leadership, regional political elites, the military and economic elites, this section illustrates both how these actors interacted with the representatives from China and Japan and how they interacted with one another in relation to the Jakarta-Bandung HSR. Even though the donor competition enhanced the position of local agencies in negotiating with donors, Indonesian actors lacked a coherent view about the project and thus local agencies were formed on a contingent basis.

Among high-level political leadership, Jokowi and several ministers played leading roles in determining the launch of the project. As a single individual, Jokowi was perhaps the most powerful actor in pushing for the Jakarta-Bandung project. Despite Japan having proposed a HSR to the Indonesian government during the Yudhoyono administration, this was not listed in RPJMN 2015–2019 as a priority in the budget, due to the mixed financial viability assessment by JICA, and the Jakarta-Bandung route was considered an alternative option to the larger HSR plan to connect Jakarta and Surabaya (Liao and Katada, 2020). The project re-emerged at an opportune time for Jokowi's search for a 'quick fix' when his approval rating was dropping based on his radical policy to reduce fossil fuel subsidies to allow increased infrastructure spending (Salim and Negara, 2018; Liao and Katada, 2020). With strong ties with SOEs, Jokowi pursued 'projects with long maturities and/or positive externalities' to benefit his constituencies (Lim et al, 2021, p 8), as infrastructure projects were awarded to SOEs in Indonesia without a competitive bidding process (Salim and Negara, 2018). Also, geographically, the Jakarta-Bandung route served Jokowi's re-election strategy in 2019 in the West Java region, which would help him avoid another loss to his rival Prabowo Subianto, as happened 2014 with a huge vote margin of 4.6 million (Marzuki and Anindya, 2019). In other words, although Jokowi needed to justify the project to voters and negotiate with domestic actors, he had the power to determine whether to launch or cancel the project, rather than that being determined by a push by donors from either China or Japan.

Jokowi and several ministers welcomed the competition between China and Japan in order to get the best deal and manoeuvred within the process. In November 2014, right after starting his presidency, Jokowi visited Beijing to attend the Asia-Pacific Economic Cooperation Summit and signed a USD 50 billion loan for bilateral cooperation on infrastructure projects and a memorandum of understanding for the Jakarta-Bandung HSR. Even after signing the memorandum of understanding with China, Jokowi believed that continuously engaging with China and Japan could help him get better loan and cooperation conditions (Yan, 2023). He visited Tokyo in March 2015 and discussed the project with Abe, who proposed additional funding from JICA and a 50 per cent reduction in the state guarantee requirement (Liao and Katada, 2020). With eagerness from both China and Japan, Sofyan Djalil, former Minister of National Planning, and Luhut Pandjaitan, former Coordinating Minister of Maritime Affairs, both described the competition as a 'beauty contest' where Indonesia would pick the winner (Sihite and Mega SP, 2015; Tritto, 2020), instead of limiting itself to the conditions proposed by only one of the potential development partners.

As expected, both China and Japan made further revisions and presented more favourable conditions in July and August of 2015. However, the Indonesian government unexpectedly announced the cancellation of the project due to state guarantee concerns. It is not clear whether the cancellation was a response to the opposition voices to the project or a tactic to pressure both China and Japan for even better conditions. Regardless, China quickly revised its proposal and presented the deal as a business-to-business agreement between SOEs in the two countries, without state guarantee or budget, and included other favourable terms. By exploiting donor competition, Indonesia got a deal from China that dealt with the major opposition from other domestic actors as well as being more favourable in terms of fiscal responsibility. China promised a longer-term donor commitment and 'business-to-business' cooperation among the SOEs with technology transfer and without state budget and guarantee, whereas Japan lacked flexibility to make similar promises. After the launch of the project, to further reduce the risk for Indonesian SOEs from the project, Jokowi asked Coordinating Minister of Maritime Affairs Luhut Pandjaitan and Minister of SOEs Rini Soemarno to reduce the Indonesian SOEs' share in the project from the initial 60 per cent to 10 per cent, thereby increasing the Chinese side's risk in the project (Damuri et al, 2019). However, Jokowi eventually decided not to move ahead with this proposal due to the potential political risk of being seen as selling the project to China, with China having a majority of the share (personal communication, Bandung, July 2024). Additionally, when faced with project delays and cost overruns, Jokowi invited Japan to join the Indonesia-China consortium to extend the HSR into Surabaya, in order to improve economic viability. Japan declined the offer. Nevertheless, particularly at the time when he was seeking re-election, Jokowi had to respond to calls from domestic actors to reduce political costs and to form agencies on a contingent basis. Only with Jokowi's re-election in 2019 did the project move forward (Camba, 2020).

Nevertheless, the views among political leadership were divided on this project. Ignasius Jonan, former Minister of Transportation, and Andrinof Chaniago, former Minister of Planning, considered HSR not to be a priority. Jonan, especially, wished to develop infrastructure in rural areas and isolated islands and upgrade the existing railway systems (Yoshimatsu, 2018). He also favoured cooperation with Japan and lobbied Japanese companies to develop other infrastructure in the country instead of building a HSR (Lim et al, 2021). He expressed concern about the ability of China-Indonesia consortium Kereta Cepat Indonesia China (KCIC) to obtain all legal permits, comply with labour regulations and acquire all the land (Yan, 2023). He refused to issue a construction permit and delayed the project, and he was removed from his ministerial position by Jokowi (Negara and Suryadinata, 2018).

Post the New Order period, a series of rapid decentralization of policies on governance and resources was introduced under Law 22 and Law 25, both passed in 1999 (Ostwald et al, 2016). In this process, a range of new regional elites and institutions became powerful in the political power contestation (Bunte and Ufen, 2009). In the Jakarta-Bandung HSR project, the wealthy provinces like West Java, with great electoral power, felt entitled to take advantage of financial and political power to bargain for the interests of their own constituencies (Lim et al, 2021). Aa Umbara Sutisna, from West Bandung Regency, understanding the importance of attracting Chinese investment to fuel the economic growth in the region, took advantage of his position in relation to issuing the construction permits for the project (Lim et al, 2021). Withholding the issuing of construction permits, he demanded that the KCIC complete payment to the residents for the lands taken for the HSR construction in West Bandung Regency (Jakarta Post, 2019). He also demanded that the KCIC construct several additional facilities for the regency, including new roads and a new stadium, and expressed that the permit would not be issued without a written commitment on these points from the KCIC (Perdana and Gabrillin, 2019; Perdana and Ika, 2019). Such demands were outside the initial agreements among the SOEs in the KCIC and resulted in delays and cost overruns for the Jakarta-Bandung HSR.

Another key actor against the Chinese proposal was the military, who had been suspicious about China's intention in land grabs and concerned about a threat to national security (Lim et al, 2021). Since the tension between the military and Sukarno (Indonesia's first president), who had supported the Communist movement and the coup in 1965, the military had considered China as a threat to national interests and security. During the New Order regime, under the doctrine of Dwifungsi (dual function), the military ensured its role in national stability and economic development (Honna, 2009). After the New Order, while the military's power was weakened, it still expressed activism in politics by framing political discourses around 'Indonesian national unity' (Honna, 2009, p 238). The military perceived that the cooperation with China in the Jakarta-Bandung HSR meant China could have the capacity to intervene in Indonesia's domestic affairs, and framed this as a national security threat that it had a duty to safeguard against. The military propagated the idea that China may attempt to launch Communist revolutions through the HSR project (Priyandita, 2016). In Jokowi's second term, he co-opted Prabowo Subianto, who had strong military backing, as Minister of Defence to soften the opposition from the military (Lim et al, 2021). Also, the military's hostility towards China was rather reactive, responding to the Indonesian public's sensitivity towards Chinese influence. In 2019, when the KCIC acquired a large chunk of military land in Bandung, the General Commander asked the Director of Finance, who was from a Chinese SOE, to not attend the signing ceremony. When he was with a Chinese representative, the General Commander expressed concern that the Indonesian public would feel that the military was selling the land to China. Nevertheless, when the Indonesian media left the event, he invited the Chinese director to take photos together (personal communication, Jakarta, July 2024).

The economic elites, mostly SOEs, were generally in favour of the Jakarta-Bandung HSR and the Chinese 'business-to-business' proposal, as represented by the Minister of SOEs, but when the Indonesian government awarded the project to China, Japanese companies in Indonesia developed an alliance with civil society organizations to oppose the project. Japanese firms paid Indonesian civil society organizations to disrupt the project and delay it until the election in 2019, at which time the project could be cancelled if Jokowi lost in the re-election (Camba, 2020). To ease Japanese disappointment over the loss of the Jakarta-Bandung bid, the Jokowi administration invited Japan to upgrade the Jakarta-Surabaya medium speed railway through a non-competitive bidding process (Yuniar, 2019). Even so, some Japanese companies continued their protest against the project (Virgiawan, 2019). The state-owned railway company Kereta Api Indonesia, which traditionally had closer ties with Japan, did not support the project initially and some employees brought KCIC to court in an attempt to sabotage the project (personal communication, Jakarta, July 2024). This demonstrates that the interests of economic elites can be fragmented when there is large capital and social influence of foreign companies in Indonesia. From a donor perspective,

China and Japan recognized the non-monolithic nature of the Indonesian state and sought entry points through different spaces.

Lastly, it is worth mentioning that the agency of Indonesia in relation to donors not only pushed China and Japan to revise their loan conditions, with more favourable terms that met the interests of the Indonesian elites, but also changed how Japan provided its ODA. Following their loss, the Japanese government made several revisions to simplify its loan procedures. First, for the yen loan procedure, they limited government procedures to a maximum of one and a half years for important projects and two years for other projects. Second, they introduced a currency conversion option for ODA loans for upper-middle-income countries. Third, government guarantees for yen loans were exempted from sub-sovereign entities of recipient countries when certain conditions were met, such as conditions related to the recipient government's commitment and economic stability. Thus, due to the donor competition, the Indonesian government was able to apply pressure on the donors to provide more flexible cooperation terms, but they were also able to shape new norms in development cooperation with its historical ODA provider, Japan.

Conclusion

Chinese and Japanese competition in the Jakarta-Bandung HSR enhanced Indonesia's bargaining power and agency, allowing the Jokowi administration to get the best cooperation terms possible. Yet, local agencies in the Jakarta-Bandung HSR lacked the cohesion of the Indonesian elites. This phenomenon occurred in the context of a power vacuum in the post-New Order regime, which led to new actors gaining political power. With military power weakened, the decentralization led to the emergence of regional political elites who bargained with central government for regional interests. Moreover, once considered as an inferior actor in politics, business gained more direct political power, and this trend intensified under the Jokowi administration (Warburton, 2024). The SOEs' major role in infrastructure development under the strong state under the Suharto administration was transformed to include partnership with the private sector through PPPs under the guidance of international financial institutions (Larner, 2000). However, facing the challenge of attracting private capital for infrastructure development, Jokowi revitalized SOEs to finance non-bankable infrastructure projects and produce a form of PPP under the state-led development (Wijaya and Camba, 2021). The fragmentation of the new actors led to more policy bargaining around the Jakarta-Bandung HSR, and Jokowi managed to use the fractured nature of the decision-making process to achieve his goals.

Within the 'two-level games' (Putnam, 1988), the agency of different Indonesian actors played out in a contingent manner when interacting with donors and with different Indonesian elites. The Jokowi administration appears to have maximized its interests through manoeuvring in interactions with donors, meeting its need to construct the HSR to showcase Jokowi's infrastructure achievements. The Indonesian government managed to develop the HSR without a state budget and with guarantees under a 'business-to-business' deal with Chinese and Indonesian SOEs. China also promised technology transfer and completion of the HSR project in Jokowi's re-election year of 2019. Jokowi even renegotiated with Chinese SOEs so that they would take more ownership in the project, thereby reducing the risks for Indonesian SOEs. After the bidding loss, Japan revisited its modes of providing development cooperation, aiming to increase its flexibility towards host countries' needs. At a glance, the donor competition enabled Indonesia to move away from its reliance on its long-term development provider, Japan, and to establish its own norms of infrastructure development cooperation.

Yet, the exercise of local agency comes with multiple political, economic and social risks for Indonesian sides, including for Jokowi himself. Due to the lack of cohesion among Indonesian elites on this project, it faced opposition from several ministries, the military and Japanese firms, as well as the opportunist bargaining by West Bandung Regency. Such sabotage caused the delay in land acquisition and cost overruns for the project, with political risks for Jokowi. With the additional delays caused by the COVID-19 pandemic, the project failed to complete in 2019 and Jokowi was not able to showcase the completed project in his re-election year, as planned, but ironically he ended up showcasing the MRT, another infrastructure project, completed by Japan, as his major infrastructure achievement. With the opposing voices from multiple actors and project delays, it was only when Jokowi secured his second term that the continuity of the project was ensured and it could move forward (Camba, 2020). Moreover, the tactic to 'calm' its long-term major donor, Japan, by awarding the Jakarta-Surabaya MSR did not work in the end. The Japanese and Indonesian governments could not agree on the terms of cooperation for the project and it did not proceed (personal communication, Jakarta, June 2023). Indonesia's strategy of 'neutrality' in development cooperation ultimately did not work out in practice and, ultimately, damaged the relationship with Japan. This view is mirrored in a Japanese development cooperation expert's concern about whether 'Indonesian governments still want to work with us, or they don't need us anymore' (personal communication, Jakarta, June 2023). Lastly, the Indonesian public and even the elites held a bias that Japanese quality is superior. This led to a perception that the government had compromised quality to pursue cheaper Chinese products that would be of lower quality. This sentiment was observed in conversations with Indonesian policy makers and practitioners. Despite China building the longest HSR in the world domestically, it was still considered less experienced and less skilled compared to Japan. With multiple factors in Indonesia contributing to project cost overruns, as discussed here, it is hard to compare Japan's project costs under a hypothetical alternative scenario.

Most importantly, the rhetoric of a 'business-to-business' deal without state budget and guarantee was rather simplistic. Jokowi's main economic development strategy was to grow SOEs through infrastructure development. The government would need to intervene if the SOEs' assets, which were used as a guarantee for the projects, were seized due to project failure (Hickey, in Ray and Ing, 2016). The government had to provide a large budget to the SOEs, as they were too big to let them fail (Salim and Negara, 2018). According to Presidential Regulation 3/2016, the government still had the potential to guarantee the project financially (Ray and Ing, 2016). While the project deal seemed to be signed without a state budget and state guarantee, to mitigate potential public criticism over the project's high cost, in reality, the state's fiscal and guarantee burden was unavoidable, especially if the project were to fail. Ultimately, with Indonesian SOEs responsible for financing 60 per cent of the USD 1.25 billion cost overrun, Jokowi signed a Presidential Regulation in 2021 to allow SOEs to apply for funds under the Ministry of SOEs to cover the cost overruns and to provide a financial guarantee from the Ministry of Finance if the state capital was not sufficient. As a result, the Indonesian state had to intervene to provide state budgets and financial guarantees to cover the cost overruns. Even so, in August 2024, the former lead of the Indonesian side of the KCIC consortium, PT Wijaya Karya, went bankrupt and blamed the Jakarta-Bandung HSR project for overburdening the company's finances.

Due to the fiscal constraint for infrastructure projects in Indonesia, in rhetoric, PPP allows non-state capital and assets to alleviate state funding stress. But it also reinforces existing elite patronage ties and their vested interests, often at the expense of public interests (Davidson, 2015). Under the international scale of PPP, domestic oligarchies in the infrastructure sector partner with foreign companies and international financial institutions under the guise of introducing good governance for market functioning and developing regulatory frameworks for the state to provide support and share the risks of PPP projects (Wijaya and Camba, 2021). The inflow of private capital through PPP guarantees investment profits for the private sector while transferring the investment risks to the public. Mawdsley highlights how the development discourse on infrastructure development and economic growth promoted through PPP shifts costs and risks onto the public while channelling profits into private hands (2019). Under PPP, the role of the state is not only to act as a guarantor for the project but also to use its regulatory and executive power to simplify bureaucratic complexities. This is done by prioritizing projects and expediting environmental and social impact assessments, as well as state-led land clearance and expropriation for infrastructure projects in the name of public interests. Thus, the rhetoric of a 'business-to-business' deal without state budget and guarantee in the Jakarta-Bandung HSR guaranteed investment profits for the private sector at the expense of public interests.

Lastly, in contrast to the conventional portrayal in development studies of an unequal power balance between donor and recipient countries, this case tells a more nuanced story. It aligns with the claim of recent research that recipient countries have the agency to leverage donor competitions for their own interests. Indonesia's case adds the aspect that political and economic elites' agencies lack 'elite cohesion' and are formed on a contingent basis. Indonesia's search for autonomy and agency while depending on external finance and technology comes with large risks and costs for political and economic elites. Thus, the unintended consequences of the HSR project in Indonesia demonstrates the need for a more nuanced framing of local agency in development studies.

Funding statement

This work is supported by Grants-in-Aid for Scientific Research from the Japan Society for the Promotion of Science, JSPS KAKENHI Grant Number 19KK0038 and a Summer 2024 Sasakawa Young Leaders Fellowship Grant.

References

Barker, J. (2005) Engineers and political dreams: Indonesia in the satellite age, *Current Anthropology*, 46(5), 703–27.

Bunte, M., and Ufen, A. (2009) The New Order and its legacy: reflections on democratization in Indonesia, in M. Bunte and A. Ufen (eds) *Democratization in post-Suharto Indonesia*, Routledge, pp 3–30.

Cabinet Office (2015) Press Conference by the Chief Cabinet Secretary (Excerpt). Available at: http://japan.kantei.go.jp/tyoukanpress/201509/29_p.html

Camba, A. (2020) *Derailing Development: China's Railway Projects and Financing Coalitions in Indonesia, Malaysia, and the Philippines*, GCI Working Paper 008, Boston University Global Development Policy Center.

Damuri, Y., Perkasa, V., Atje, R. and Hirawan, F. (2019) *Perceptions and Readiness of Indonesia towards the Belt and Road Initiative*, CSIS Indonesia.

Davidson, J. (2015) *Indonesia's Changing Political Economy: Governing the Roads*, Cambridge University Press.

Embassy of the People's Republic of China in the Republic of Indonesia (2014) Xi Jinping Meets with President Joko Widodo of Indonesia. Available at: http://id.china-embassy.gov.cn/eng/gdxw/201411/t20141111_2047763.htm

Globe Asahi Shimbun (2018) Japan and China's railway competition: Indonesia's real dream (part 2).

Gonzalez-Vicente, R. (2019) Make development great again? Accumulation regimes, spaces of sovereign exception and the elite development paradigm of China's Belt and Road Initiative, *Business and Politics*, 21(4), 487–513.

Goodfellow, T. and Huang, Z. (2021) Contingent infrastructure and the dilution of 'Chineseness': reframing roads and rail in Kampala and Addis Ababa, *Environment & Planning A: Economy and Space*, 53(4), 655–74.

He, K. (2000) *Interpreting China-Indonesia Relations: 'Good-Neighbourliness', 'Mutual Trust' and 'All-Round Cooperation'*, Strategic and Defence Studies Centre Working Paper No 349, Strategic and Defence Studies Centre, Australian National University.

Honna, J. (2009) From *dwifungsi* to NKRI: regime change and political activism of the Indonesian military, in M. Bunte and A. Ufen (eds) *Democratization in post-Suharto Indonesia*, Routledge, pp 226–47.

Iqbal, M. and Asmara, C. (2019) 'Soeharto Bapak Pembangunan, Jokowi Bapak Infrastruktur', *CNBC Indonesia*. Available at: www.cnbcindonesia.com/news/20190208170515-4-54565/soeharto-bapak-pembangunan-jokowi-bapak-infrastruktur

Jain, P. (2019) *Japan's Foreign Aid and 'Quality' Infrastructure Projects: The Case of the Bullet Train in India*, JICA-RI Working Paper No 184, JICA Research Institute.

Jakarta Post (2019) West Bandung regent withholds permit for railway construction, 28 June. Available at: www.thejakartapost.com/news/2019/06/28/west-bandung-regent-withholds-permit-for-railway-construction.html

Jakarta Post (2015) RI may choose China bullet train. Available at: www.thejakartapost.com/news/2015/09/18/ri-may-choose-china-bullet-train.html

Jiang, Y. (2019) Competitive partners in development financing: China and Japan expanding overseas infrastructure investment, *Pacific Review*, 32, 778–808.

JICA (2018) *Japanese Cooperation Footprint to Indonesia*, Japan International Cooperation Agency.

Kim, K. (2018) Matchmaking: establishment of state-owned holding companies in Indonesia, *Asia & the Pacific Policy Studies*, 5(2), 313–30.

Kusno, A. (2013) *After the New Order: Space, Politics, and Jakarta*, University of Hawai'i Press.

Larner, W. (2000) Neo-liberalism: policy, ideology, governmentality, *Studies in Political Economy*, 63(1), 5–25.

Liao, J. and Dang, N. (2019) The nexus of security and economic hedging: Vietnam's strategic response to Japan-China infrastructure financing competition, *The Pacific Review*, 33(3–4), 669–96.

Liao, J.C. and Katada, S. (2020) Geoeconomics, easy money, and political opportunism: the perils under China and Japan's high-speed rail competition, *Contemporary Politics*, 27(1), 1–22.

Lim, G., Li, C. and Syailendra, E. (2021) Why is it so hard to push Chinese railway projects in Southeast Asia? The role of domestic politics in Malaysia and Indonesia, *World Development*, 138, art 105272. doi: 10.1016/j.worlddev.2020.105272

Malik, A., Parks, B., Russell, B., Lin, J., Walsh, K., Solomon, K. et al (2021) *Banking on the Belt and Road: Insights from a New Global Dataset of 13,247 Chinese Development Projects*, AidData.

Mao, C. and Mueller, L.M. (2020) *Learning from the Competition – China's, Japan's and the EU's Infrastructure Connectivity Rule Setting in Asia*, Occasional Paper No 45, Southeast Asian Studies at the University of Freiburg.

Marzuki, K. and Anindya, C. (2019) *West Java: Tough Fight in Key Battleground*, RSIS Commentary No 050, Nanyang Technological University.

Mawdsley, E. (2019) South–South Cooperation 3.0? Managing the consequences of success in the decade ahead, *Oxford Development Studies*, 47(3), 259–74.

Mohan, G. (2020) Below the belt? Territory and development in China's international rise, *Development and Change*, 51(3), 519–39.

Negara, S. (2016) Indonesia's infrastructure development under the Jokowi administration, *Southeast Asian Affairs*, 145–66.

Negara, S. and Suryadinata, L. (2018) *Jakarta-Bandung High Speed Rail Project: Little Progress, Many Challenges*, Perspective No 2, Yusof Ishak Institute.

Nishihara, M. (1976) *The Japanese and Sukarno's Indonesia-Tokyo-Jakarta Relations 1951-1966*, University Press of Hawaii.

Ostwald, K., Tajima, Y. and Samphantharak, K. (2016) Indonesia's decentralization experiment: motivations, success, and unintended consequences, *Journal of Southeast Asian Economies*, 33(2), 139–156.

Perdana, P. and Gabrillin, A. (2019) Bupati Bandung Barat: Saya Bukan Menolak Kereta Cepat, tetapi…, *Kompas.com*. Available at: https://regional.kompas.com/read/2019/07/09/16020061/bupati-bandung-barat-saya-bukan-menolak-kereta-cepat-tetapi#google_vignette

Perdana, P. and Ika, A. (2019) Bupati Bandung Barat: Saya Bukannya Merongrong, PT KCIC Saja yang Enggak Ngerti…, *Kompas.com*. Available at: https://regional.kompas.com/read/2019/07/09/16405871/bupati-bandung-barat-saya-bukannya-merongrong-pt-kcic-saja-yang-enggak

Priyandita, G. (2016) Behind Indonesia's Red Scare: why is the Indonesian military again warning of an imminent communist revolution? *The Diplomat*. Available at: https://thediplomat.com/2016/06/behind-indonesias-red-scare/

Putnam, R.D. (1988) Diplomacy and domestic politics: the logic of two-level games, *International Organizations*, 42(3), 427–60.

Ray, D. and Ing, L.Y. (2016) Addressing Indonesia's infrastructure deficit, *Bulletin of Indonesian Economic Studies*, 52(1), 1–25.

Salim, W. and Negara, S.D. (2016) Why is the high-speed railway project so important to Indonesia? *Perspective*, 16, Yusof Ishak Institute.

Salim, W. and Negara, S.D. (2018) Infrastructure development under the Jokowi administration: progress, challenges and policies, *Journal of Southeast Asian Economies*, 35(3), 386–401.

Sankei News (2015) Japan-China bidding competition closes to the end: Indonesia high speed railway.

Schindler, S., DiCarlo, J. and Paudel, D. (2021) *Transactions of the Institute of British Geographers*, 47(2), 331–46.

Sihite, E. and Mega, D., SP (2015) Indonesia plans 'beauty contest' between China and Japan for high-speed train, *Jakarta Globe*, 13 July. Available at: https://jakartaglobe.id/news/indonesia-plans-beauty-contest-china-japan-high-speed-train

Suhardiman, D., DiCarlo, J., Keovilignavong, O., Rigg, J. and Nicol, A. (2021) (Re)constructing state power and livelihoods through the Laos-China Railway project, *Geoforum*, 124, 79–88.

Tritto, A. (2020) Contentious embeddedness: Chinese state capital and the Belt and Road Initiative in Indonesia, *Made in China*, 6 May. Available at: https://madeinchinajournal.com/2020/05/06/contentious-embeddedness-chinese-state-capital-indonesia/

Umar, A. (2023) The rise of the Asian middle powers: Indonesia's conceptions of international order, *International Affairs*, 99(4), 1459–76.

Virgiawan, R. (2019) Warga Tanah Galian Tolak Pembebasan Lahan untuk Proyek Kereta Api Cepat Jakarta-Bandung, *Minews*, 17 July.

Warburton, E. (2024) Private power and public office: the rise of business politicians in Indonesia, *Critical Asian Studies*, 56(2), 184–206.

Wijaya, T. and Camba, A. (2021) The politics of public–private partnerships: state–capital relations and spatial fixes in Indonesia and the Philippines, *Territory, Politics, Governance*, 11(8), 1669–88.

Yan, K. (2023) Navigating between China and Japan: Indonesia and economic hedging, *The Pacific Review*, 36(4), 755–83.

Yoshimatsu, H. (2018) New dynamics in Sino-Japanese rivalry: sustaining infrastructure development in Asia, *Journal of Contemporary China*, 27, 719–34.

Yuniar, R. (2019) Indonesia set to choose Japan over China to get second rail mega-project on track, *South China Morning Post*, 13 September. Available at: www.scmp.com/week-asia/politics/article/3026962/indonesia-set-choose-japan-over-china-get-second-rail-mega

8

A Postcolonial Belt and Road Initiative? Dependency, Development and Geopolitics in China-Latin America Relations

Simone Vegliò

Introduction

The growing influence of China in Latin America can hardly be overstated. Whether in the form of deep concerns about the danger of a new geo-economic and geopolitical hegemony posed by an authoritarian regime (Ellis, 2022; Hairong and Sautman, 2023), or with the more hopeful idea of a departure from the United States' long-standing domination over the region (Harris, 2015; Suárez Torres, 2018), it is widely agreed that China has become a prominent protagonist in the Latin American landscape (Klinger and Narins, 2018; Wise and Chonn Ching, 2018). It is challenging to build a clear-cut evaluation of such an ample and constantly evolving situation; these polarized directions often correspond to divisions within national political spheres in the region and normally do not help critically explore such a complex, multifaceted and, at times, contradictory process. While delving into these themes, the chapter analyses the implementation of the Belt and Road Initiative (BRI) in Latin America, situating it within China's broader infrastructure strategy in the region. To do so, the discussion explores the evolution of China's engagement in Latin America over the past two decades, which has been delineated by a dramatic escalation of commercial and financial activities, transforming trade dynamics and investment flows and impacting geopolitical alliances. Conceptually, building on recent scholarship on the topic (Stallings, 2020; Chilcote and Salém Vasconcelos, 2022; Reis and de Oliveira, 2023), the chapter re-activates core insights from dependency theory, arguing that Latin America remains embedded in a substantial 'postcolonial' condition of dependency on a global scale. By bridging historical and contemporary perspectives, the discussion shows how structures of dependency have endured despite shifting geo-economic and geopolitical configurations.

Commercial relationships

The relationships between China and Latin America have expanded dramatically and deepened over the past two decades, a period in which a wide array of economic, political and cultural projects has solidified the ties between the Asian dragon and several Latin American countries. However, it is important to note that such a change did not occur abruptly. Since the 1950s, a wave of commercial agreements and political relations was already underway, albeit in a sporadic and fragmented manner. China and Latin America had been developing ties for decades before China's opening to the global market. Wise (2023) reconstructs this relationship, beginning with the post-1949 era, when the newborn People's Republic of China 'began a rich political and economic exchange between the leaders of the Chinese Communist Party (CCP) and civil society groups within various countries in Latin America'; she stresses that despite the 'multiple styles of governance and relationships' adopted by China in the region, the Asian country was systematically committed to principles of 'nonintervention and anti-imperialism' (Wise, 2023, p 2). This is particularly relevant in a region where the United States exerted a strong hegemony, frequently employing economic, political and even military aggression since the mid-19th century (starting with the Mexican-American War, when the US acquired around one third of Mexico's territory). Despite the different analyses and understandings of China's role and perception in the region, this element is crucial for understanding the development of contemporary China-Latin American relations.

China established formal and informal agreements with Chile in the early 1950s, Argentina in the 1960s and Brazil in the 1970s to obtain commodities such as copper and nitrogenous fertilizer from Chile, wheat from Argentina and iron ore from Brazil (Wise, 2023, p 6). This is a clear anticipation of the commercial relationships that would define the dawn of the 21st century. Since the early 2000s, China has become the top trading partner for many Latin American countries and, in almost every case, has achieved a prominent commercial position (Wise and Chonn Ching, 2018; Wise, 2023). Such a remarkable change began with the so-called 'commodity-boom', which started in 2002 when the global prices of raw materials and agricultural products suddenly exploded as a result of, among other factors, the rapid spike in demand for primary sector goods from Asian countries, and particularly

China. To give just a quick example, during the years following 2002, the price of copper, oil and iron tripled and that of soybeans and fish meals doubled (Wise, 2020). Of course, this was also a consequence of China joining the World Trade Organization in 2001, with the Asian country starting to widely operate in international markets.

While the commodity boom lasted intensely for a decade, it is worth noting that a significant political shift took place in Latin America during the same period. This period is commonly known as the 'pink tide', referring to a rapid sequence of Left-wing governments coming to power (Feierherd et al, 2023). Despite the significant differences that marked each case, these governments (particularly in Brazil, Argentina, Ecuador, Venezuela and Bolivia) used the favourable context of the commodity boom to expand the primary sector export markets and, with the outcomes of such operations, implemented social policies at the national level, which generally consisted of a substantial increase in public spending and an expansion of consumption circuits to social sectors that were previously marginalized (Clark and Rosales, 2023). This generated a remarkable reduction in income inequality, which is observable in several countries – a trend that clearly contrasts with the socioeconomic indicators emerging from previous and subsequent governments with different political orientation[s] (Feierherd et al, 2023). Moreover, another shared goal of pink-tide administrations was a radical shift away from the political influence of the United States, with China as a new alternative. When it comes to analysing the role and effects of the BRI in Latin America, it is essential to consider the elements and tensions shaping this 'triangle' of Latin America, China and the United States (Gallagher, 2016). Yet, at the same time, while the triangular vision helps understand many of the geo-economic and geopolitical tensions that have occurred in the region over the past two decades, this should not be viewed as an irreconcilable polarization in which China and the United States operate in complete opposition. Rather, it is possible to observe several economic overlaps and the coexistence of simultaneous interests on the ground, which vary in complexity depending on the case (Wise, 2023).

If the commodity boom saw a reduction of its formidable rise in prices after the 2008 economic crisis and came to a substantial end in 2013, trade between China and Latin America continued to thrive in the following decade (Stallings, 2020; Wise, 2023). Today, trade between the two regions continues to be characterized by the primary sector, and in particular by agricultural and extractive goods. The main commodities that determine current Latin America's exports to China are soybeans and cereals in agriculture and copper, lithium and crude oil in the extractive sector. To give one example, China today acquires over one third of the region's extractive products and one fifth of the agricultural ones (Albright et al, 2023; ECLAC, 2023). Within this picture, there has also been the rise of new subsectors, especially those regarding renewable energy; most significantly, the question of lithium has gained core importance given its fundamental role for the production of rechargeable batteries such as those used in mobile telephones. In Latin America, we find the so-called 'lithium triangle', which is made up of Argentina's north-west, Chile's north (especially in and around the Atacama Desert area) and Bolivia's south-west; the area contains more than 75 per cent of the world's entire lithium reserve (Ahmad, 2020; Valz Gris, 2023). While China is one of the key actors in the extraction of lithium in the triangle, the overall situation has brought about a number of social and environmental concerns – first and foremost, the severe issues related to water depletion which put at serious risk ecosystems and local populations (Bustos-Gallardo et al, 2021; Voskoboynik and Andreucci, 2022).

To sum up, while the reconfiguration of the commercial relationships between China and Latin America has moved the geo-economic axes of Latin America's trade toward Asia, the structure of Latin American national economies has not undergone substantial alterations, maintaining strong and nearly exclusive reliance on the primary sector. Such a situation has been identified as a process of 're-primarization' of national economies (Svampa, 2015), a project that thus reiterates the 'neo-extractive' architecture of the region (Gago and Mezzadra, 2017). As a consequence, this export-oriented structure, with China as a key recipient, requires an efficient infrastructure network that can support, expedite and possibly augment the circulation of commodities.

Financial relationships

In addition to commercial relationships, understanding the evolution of China-Latin America financial relations is essential when exploring China's infrastructure strategies and their effects. First and foremost, China's financialization has served as a fundamental vehicle fostering numerous mega-infrastructure projects across the Latin American region (The Dialogue, nd). From a broader perspective, 1999 was obviously a watershed moment: China announced its 'Going Out' strategy and rapidly opened its economic and financial frontiers. Since then, various financial initiatives and collaborations have flowed from China to other regions of the world, including Latin America (Ohashi, 2018).

It is possible to distinguish two forms of financial activities that China has pursued in Latin America: foreign direct investments (FDIs) and international loans. FDIs can be further divided into greenfield foreign direct investments (GFDIs), where capital is invested in new projects in the region, and mergers and acquisitions (M&As), where investments involve existing assets. As with the commodity boom, we can outline two cycles: the first from 2001 to 2013 and the second from 2013 to the present. As Stalling outlines, during the first period, the distribution of Chinese FDIs in the region was highly uneven, with 77 per cent concentrated in just three countries (Brazil, Argentina and Peru), Brazil alone accounting for 56 per cent of the total (Stalling, 2020, p 46). During the commodity boom, Chinese investments in the region were largely focused on the extractive sector, particularly copper mining (Wise, 2023). A significant shift occurred in the following decade, when infrastructure emerged as China's key investment strategy in the region (Albright et al, 2023). In the meantime, China strengthened institutional ties with Latin America by becoming a permanent observer at the Organization of American States in 2004, joining the Inter-American Development Bank (IDB) in 2008 and establishing the China-CELAC (Community of Latin American and Caribbean States) Forum in 2015 (Bernal-Meza and Xing, 2020).

After 2013, FDIs, especially in the form of M&As, involved infrastructure, frequently mobilizing funding through the China Development Bank (CHB) and the Export-Import Bank of the Republic of China (CHEXIM). Such a strategy was coupled with commercial needs, as it aimed to foster the acquisition of raw materials in the region and simultaneously develop foreign business opportunities for Chinese companies involved in infrastructure projects (Wise, 2020). More recently, Chinese GFDIs have focused on renewable energy, supporting the extraction and processing of raw materials, as well as manufacturing, such as lithium processing in Argentina and electric vehicle production in Brazil (Albright et al, 2023).

The other facet of China's financial strategy in Latin America, equally essential for the financialization of infrastructure projects in the region, centred on international loans. In this case, the above-mentioned Chinese banks (CHB and CHEXIM) played a crucial role in providing the loans. Between 2005 and 2013, the two banks loaned more money to the region than the World Bank and the IDB combined (Gallagher et al, 2012). Here again, the loans were concentrated in four countries, which received 92 per cent of the total; the largest share regarded Venezuela (60 per cent), followed by Argentina, Brazil and Ecuador in decreasing order (Stalling, 2020). The loans peaked in 2015, when they reached USD 21.3 billion, but then sharply declined to zero in 2020 due to the pandemic crisis. Loans from China to Latin America began to increase again in 2021, but their size was far below the mid-2010s peaks. For comparison, the total amount of Chinese loans to Latin America between 2019 and 2022 was just over USD 2.9 billion (Ray and Mayers, 2023). In more general terms, when considering the entire period of 2005–22, CHB and CHEXIM lent USB 136 billion to Latin America, with the biggest recipients being Argentina, Brazil, Ecuador and Venezuela. While 66 per cent of the total went to the extractive sector, almost 20 per cent was allocated to infrastructure projects (54 projects in total), particularly transportation and connectivity. These infrastructure investments were primarily directed to Argentina, Brazil and Ecuador until 2014, and later expanded to Mexico, Chile and Colombia (Myers and Gallagher, 2019; Ray and Mayers, 2023). In what follows, the discussion examines the multiple, and at times ambiguous, ways in which this relates to the arrival of the BRI in the region.

Infrastructure and the BRI in Latin America

As outlined in the chapter, the implementation of the BRI in Latin America should be understood within the specific and evolving context that shapes China's action in the region, rather than seeing the BRI as a linear and homogeneous global policy. In fact, some observers have already noted that the BRI consists of anything but a consistent and uniform strategy led by the Chinese government (Oliveira et al, 2020). In particular, although the role of the state in conceiving and promoting such an ambitious global infrastructure project is apparent, the BRI appears more problematic and imbued with contradictions when examined from the ground, something far from the government's typically centralized and allegedly uniform rhetoric (Ye, 2020). If we apply this aspect to the Latin American context, its ambiguity and fragmentation become even more pronounced. In other words, as a key point in this discussion, distinguishing the BRI from other Chinese infrastructure investments in the region is rather challenging – if not impossible.

Important institutions such as ECLAC (United Nations Economic Commission for Latin America and the Caribbean) outlined the substantial 'infrastructure gap' that characterizes most Latin American countries. Specifically, ECLAC suggested that these countries should spend around 6 per cent of their gross domestic product on infrastructure projects, while they were investing on average less than 3 per cent (ECLAC, 2014). And this is where the role of China came into play. Thanks to different financial formulas depending on each project, and using bilateral agreements as a principal method, China actively promoted mega-infrastructure operations across Latin America, providing the necessary capital to fully or partially finance new projects, as well as to renovate and expand existing ones. Between 2002 and 2018, China financed approximately 150 infrastructure projects in Latin America, 40 per cent of which specifically focused on transportation (Myers, 2018). Regarding transportation, Chinese investments in the sector increased significantly in the 2010s. Yet, the BRI began to be promoted in Latin America only in 2017, when Chinese president Xi Jinping, during the Belt and Road Forum in Beijing, iconically described the region as a 'natural extension' of the BRI (Xinhuanet, 2017), and several bilateral agreements were signed the following year (Jenkins, 2022; Teixeira and Azócar, 2023). Hence, Chinese infrastructure investments in the region have continued substantially since the early 2000s, with the BRI helping institutionalize and reinforce this trajectory. I will return to this point later.

Overall, the country that has received by far the most loans for infrastructure projects from China is Argentina (USD 13.6 billion), followed by Venezuela (USD 4.4 billion), Jamaica (USD 1.8 billion) and Brazil (USD 1.5 billion; Ray and Mayers, 2023). In addition to the two policy-banks, China's financial activities in Latin America have been conducted through commercial banks (ICBC, Bank of China, Agricultural Bank of China, China Construction Bank and Bank of Communications), as well as multilateral institutions such as the New Development Bank, the BRICS Bank and the Asian Infrastructure Investment Bank. As underscored by some scholars, instead of considering the development of these operations as something smoothly directed by China's state leadership, the context can be summarized as a 'highly varied, contingent, and tenuous emergence of the BRI in Latin America' that has involved 'relations among multiple actors, Chinese and non-Chinese alike' (Oliveira and Myers, 2021, p 482). As of January 2024, 22 countries in Latin America have officially signed a memorandum of understanding with China for the BRI (Wu, 2024); one of the latest was Argentina – the third-largest economy in the region – in February 2022 (Koop, 2022). Examining the overall infrastructure projects financed by China since the beginning of the century, there has been a significant rise in transportation infrastructure since 2015, operations that involved, among others, commercial ports, railway systems and airports (Dussel Peters, 2022). While these investments have not necessarily been framed within the official discourse of the BRI, it is undeniable that they have coincided with the progressive formalization of the BRI in the region. Among the numerous projects that have been proposed and at least partly realized over the past two decades, several are particularly noteworthy. These include the expansion of the Panama Canal, the creation of the Nicaragua Canal, the expansion of the railway network in Argentina's Northeast, the construction of hydroelectric dams in southern Argentina and, notably, the ambitious plan to implement a bi-oceanic railway and road corridor going from Brazil to Peru, which aims to create a shortcut for the commercial route from the Southern Cone's soybean and lithium territories to China (Myers, 2018; Dussel Peters, 2022; Jenkins, 2022). In this sense, the reshaping of Latin America's commercial routes according to new global geo-economic structures is clearly at play.

Dependency, development and postcolonial relationships

In light of this novel combination of commercial and financial relationships between China and Latin America, in which infrastructure investments have played a pivotal role both within and beyond the powerful albeit ambiguous framework of the BRI, analysts and observers have posed urgent questions about the political nature of this profoundly transformed relationship. As mentioned at the beginning of this chapter, the positions have frequently been divided into two camps: one denouncing the predatory dimension of China's action in the region, and the other arguing for more balanced 'South-South' relationships that have, at least in part, replaced the United States' aggressive presence. To engage with this question, the chapter mobilizes some concepts articulated by dependency theorists. In doing so, it proposes a 'postcolonial' reflection that examines the multifaceted reconfiguration of what I have elsewhere termed – within a similar effort to analyse socio-spatial and material transformations – the 'long colonial history' of the region (Vegliò, 2020, p 5).

From the late 1960s to the 1980s, dependency theory forged a conceptual framework aimed at accounting for the socioeconomic hardship that marked Latin American countries. As a reaction to development theory and other Western theories of modernization, *dependentistas* argued that socioeconomic growth in Latin America could not be achieved by merely implementing a pre-established set of economic and political measures. On the contrary, the weak internal socio-institutional structure was a legacy of the colonial period as well as the region's historically peripheral role in the international markets – mainly as an exporter of primary goods. This condition prevented Latin American countries from developing in a similar way to Western countries (Furtado, 1964; Cardoso and Faletto, 1979 [1969]; Prebisch, 1981). According to the prominent Marxist wing of dependency theorists, dependency was a condition for development; in other words, underdevelopment in the peripheries was the price to be paid for development in the centres (Marini, 1973; Bambirra, 1978; Frank, 2010 [1966]). Thus, by specifically bearing in mind this original version of Marxism, which highlighted the constitutive role of colonialism in shaping Latin America's space and which was elaborated *from* the world periphery, the chapter asks this question: How can we understand the implementation of the BRI in Latin America and the rearticulation of China-Latin America relations in light of dependency theory?

Before offering some tentative answers to the question, it is worth noting that dependency theory has recently experienced a resurgence, after undergoing a prolonged period of crisis (see Grosfoguel, 2000) – and critique – that began in the mid-1980s. Over the past few years, scholars have revisited dependency theory to comprehend the increased disparities produced by the international political economy, observing the persistence of socioeconomic disparities that have characterized the turn of the 21st century. Within these studies, Latin America has occupied centre stage, with the region analysed both in relation to its global geo-economic position and in its specific relationship with China (Giraudo, 2020; Stallings, 2020; Chilcote and Salém Vasconcelos, 2022; Martins, 2022; Rais and De Oliveira, 2023). To give just one example, in 2022, two entire issues of the journal *Latin American Perspectives* were exclusively dedicated to presenting readings of dependency theory. Overall, today's interest is the new manifestations of dependency (Treacy, 2022). As for the relationship with China, building on the concept of the 'Washington consensus', which indicated the United States' authoritative control in the region, some scholars have labelled the new bonds with China a 'Beijing consensus' (Svampa and Slipak, 2015). As argued in this chapter, the BRI in Latin America should be viewed in combination with China's commercial and financial relationships, and dependency can offer an important lens of analysis.

In terms of commercial aspects, despite the changes that have occurred over the past decade, China still represents a key partner for several Latin American economies, in a context in which the primary sector still heavily dominates the scene. This situation is very much akin to those defining dependency. The concentration of exports in a few primary goods necessarily signifies a substantial lack of diversification in national production, high vulnerability to fluctuations in global prices and minimal economic stability (Infante-Amate et al, 2022), such the case of soybean in Argentina demonstrates (Giraudo, 2020). In this sense, Latin America appears to simply reinforce its historical role global exporter of primary goods, a role it has played since the colonial period. With respect to financial relationships, it is interesting to note that, building on the work of iconic Marxist dependency theorists such as Vania Bambirra and Ruy Mauro Marini, scholars coined the term 'peripheral financialization' (Rais and De Oliveira, 2023), suggesting that 'financialized dependence' represents today's 'historical phase of dependency', the novelty of which consists of the predominant use of 'economic and social power of debt [...] for the reproduction of superexploitation' (Rais and De Oliveira, 2023, p 526). On the other hand, building on the more moderate and often referred to as *structuralist* wing of dependency theory, typically associated with Fernando Cardoso and Enzo Faletto, Stallings argued that Latin America's 'relations with China have undermined dependent development and done nothing to help promote inclusive development', hindering the growth of local industries and value-added exports (2020, p 68).

Evaluations of the BRI and China's infrastructure operations in Latin America should take into account this commercial and financial context marked by relationships of dependency. Two important aspects regarding infrastructure need to be emphasized. On the one hand, there is the absolute prominence of the natural resources flowing toward China and the consequent search for wider and faster circulation routes. On the other hand, it is crucial to consider Latin America's constant pursuit of financial support to bridge the infrastructure gap, which is conceived by various governments and institutions as a key element to trigger the region's socioeconomic growth. These two aspects are deeply interconnected. While China has undoubtedly contributed, within and beyond the frame of the BRI, to the overall increase in infrastructure in Latin America (Myers 2018; Stelling, 2020; Dussel Peters, 2022), existing and new projects have frequently focused on accelerating circulation from key areas of extraction, cultivation and processing of primary goods, thereby strengthening the export-oriented infrastructure network that has characterized the region since the colonial era. In a sense, to evoke Eduardo Galeano's (1971) famous expression, the *veins* of Latin America are still widely *open*.

And this is the meaning of the 'postcolonial' in this chapter. That is, a 'post' that, instead of indicating any radical interruption or cessation, sheds light on the elements of *continuity*, albeit differently articulated in specific spatio-historical configurations (Hart, 2016). Accordingly, when looking at the material trade flows, we find a clear case of 'ecologically unequal exchange' (Alonso-Fernández and Regueiro-Ferreira, 2022) in which natural resources are extracted in the world peripheries to be gathered in traditional and new central areas of production and exchange. Moreover, another essential point to take into consideration is that the environmental costs of this process are remarkable. Scholars have started to analyse the consequences of this neo-extractive architecture that combines the socio-ecological effects of the exploitation of the primary sector with the development of export infrastructure (for example, Arboleda, 2020; Hope and Arsel, 2022). Thus, there is an urgent need to expand the existing research on infrastructure operations in Latin America and consider their multifarious components. While the region is undergoing important geo-economic and geopolitical transformations, the role of infrastructure as a material component organizing and reinforcing extended power relations should not be underestimated; at the same time, episodes of resistance against recurrent systems of extraction and exploitation shed light on how infrastructure often exerts power and dominance over specific socio-natural environments, shaping the lives of those – human and non-human – who inhabit them (Gordillo, 2014; Arsel et al, 2016; Bebbington et al, 2018).

Conclusion

To sum up, the chapter has shown the large extent to which the structures of dependency still seem to be in place in Latin America. While observing infrastructure developments and the role of China, it is possible to identify well-defined geographies of global circulation in which the region clearly reiterates a peripheral function, the genealogy of which can be traced back to its long colonial history (Vegliò, 2020). Recalling one of the main notions of dependency theorists, it still seems evident that 'underdevelopment' in some areas of the planet is a necessary condition for 'development' in others (for example, Frank, 2010 [1966]). The arrival of the BRI in Latin America, as Jenkins (2022) has already noted, has not represented a noticeable change; instead, what can be distinguished is a substantial *continuation* of Latin America's relations with China. This suggests that the BRI in Latin America is primarily political in nature rather than a clear-cut and coordinated infrastructure programme, as a significant number of projects had already been established in the region. This, of course, does not diminish the critical importance of the BRI in strengthening and developing current bilateral and multilateral relationships with Latin American countries. China has certainly provided an important occasion for Latin America to find a new, formidable commercial and financial partner, a fact that, not least, has helped many countries respond to United States' hegemonic action. Yet, despite the opening of a massive new market full of potential, Latin America remains ensnared in a condition of dependency where its capacity to autonomously decide the structures of its socioeconomic future still figures as rather distant. An analysis of China's infrastructure development in the region seems to accurately reflect this 'postcolonial' picture.

References

Ahmad, S. (2020) The lithium triangle, *Harvard International Review*, 41(1), 51–3.

Albright, Z.C., Ray, R. and Yudong, L. (2023) *China-Latin America and the Caribbean Economic Bulletin: 2023 Edition*, Boston University Global Development Policy Center. Available at: www.bu.edu/gdp/files/2023/04/GCI-CH-LAC-Bulletin_2023-FIN.pdf

Alonso-Fernández, P. and Regueiro-Ferreira, R.M. (2022) Extractivism, ecologically unequal exchange and environmental impact in South America: a study using material flow analysis (1990–2017), *Ecological Economics*, 194, art 107351. doi: 10.1016/j.ecolecon.2022.107351

Arboleda, M. (2020) *Planetary Mine: Territories of Extraction Under Late Capitalism*, Verso.

Arsel, M., Hogenboom, B. and Pellegrini, L. (2016) The extractive imperative in Latin America, *The Extractive Industries and Society*, 3(4), 880–7.

Bambirra, V. (1978) *Teoría de la dependencia: una anticrítica*, Serie Popular Era.

Bebbington, D.H., Verdum, R., Gamboa, C. and Bebbington, A.J. (2018) The infrastructure-extractives-resource governance complex in the Pan-Amazon, *European Review of Latin American and Caribbean Studies*, 106, 183–208.

Bernal-Meza, R. and Xing, L. (eds) (2020) *China–Latin America Relations in the 21st Century: The Dual Complexities of Opportunities and Challenges*, Palgrave.

Bustos-Gallardo, B., Bridge, G. and Prieto, M. (2021) Harvesting lithium: water, brine and the industrial dynamics of production in the Salar de Atacama, *Geoforum*, 119, 177–89.

Cardoso, F.H. and Faletto, E. (1979 [1969]) *Dependency and Development in Latin America*, University of California Press.

Chilcote, R.H. and Salém Vasconcelos, J. (2022) Introduction: whither development theory? *Latin American Perspectives*, 49(1), 4–17.

Clark, P. and Rosales, A. (2023) Broadened embedded autonomy and Latin America's Pink Tide: towards the neo-developmental state, *Globalizations*, 20(1), 20–37.

Dussel Peters, E. (2022) *Monitor of Chinese Infrastructure in Latin America and the Caribbean 2022*, RED-ALC China.

ECLAC (Economic Commission for Latin America and the Caribbean) (2014) The economic infrastructure gap and investment in Latin America, *Bulletin FAL*, 332(4), 1–9.

ECLAC (Economic Commission for Latin America and the Caribbean) (2023) *International Trade Outlook for Latin America and the Caribbean 2023*, United Nations.

Ellis, R.E. (2022) *China Engages Latin America: Distorting Development and Democracy?* Palgrave Macmillan.

Feierherd, G., Larroulet, P., Long, W. and Lustig, N. (2023) The pink tide and income inequality in Latin America, *Latin American Politics and Society*, 65(2), 110–44.

Frank, A.G. (2010 [1966]) The development of underdevelopment, in C. Sing and P. Lauderdale (eds) *Theory and Methodology of World Development: The Writings of Andre Gunder Frank*, Palgrave Macmillan, pp 7–17.

Furtado, C. (1964) *Development and Underdevelopment*, University of California Press.

Gago, V. and Mezzadra, S. (2017) A critique of the extractive operations of capital: toward an expanded concept of extractivism, *Rethinking Marxism*, 29(4), 574–91.

Galeano, E. (1971) *Las venas abiertas de América Latina*, Siglo XXI Editores.

Gallagher, K. (2016) *The China Triangle: Latin America's China Boom and the Fate of the Washington Consensus*, Oxford University Press.

Gallagher, K., Irwin, A. and Koleski, K. (2012) *The New Banks in Town: Chinese Finance in Latin America*, The Inter-American Dialogue and Boston University Global Development Policy Center. Available at: www.thedialogue.org/analysis/the-new-banks-in-town-chinese-finance-in-latin-america/

Giraudo, M.E. (2020) Dependent development in South America: China and the soybean nexus, *Journal of Agrarian Change*, 20(1), 60–78.

Gordillo, G.R. (2014) *Rubble: The Afterlife of Destruction*, Duke University Press.

Grosfoguel, R. (2000) Developmentalism, modernity, and dependency theory in Latin America, *Nepantla*, 1(2), 347–74.

Hairong, Y. and Sautman, B. (2023) China, colonialism, neocolonialism and globalised modes of accumulation, *Area Development and Policy*, 8(4), 416–49.

Harris, R.L. (2015) China's relations with the Latin American and Caribbean countries: a peaceful panda bear instead of a roaring dragon, *Latin American Perspectives*, 42(6), 153–90.

Hart, G. (2016) Relational comparison revisited: Marxist postcolonial geographies in practice, *Progress in Human Geography*, 42(3), 371–94.

Hope, J. and Arsel, M. (2022) Infrastructure and Latin American environmental geographies: an introduction to our special issue, *Journal of Latin American Geography*, advance online publication. doi: 10.1353/lag.0.0192

Infante-Amate, J., Urrego-Mesa, A., Pinero, P. and Tello, E. (2022) The open veins of Latin America: long-term physical trade flows (1900–2016), *Global Environmental Change*, 76, art 102579. doi: 10.1016/j.gloenvcha.2022.102579

Jenkins, R. (2022) China's Belt and Road Initiative in Latin America: what has changed? *Journal of Current Chinese Affairs*, 51(1), 13–39.

Klinger, J.M. and Narins, T. (2018) New geographies of China and Latin America relations: introduction to the special issue, *Journal of Latin American Geography*, 17(2), 6–22.

Koop, F. (2022) Argentina joins China's Belt and Road Initiative, *Diálogo Chino*, 8 February. Available at: https://dialogochino.net/en/trade-investment/50966-argentina-joins-china-belt-and-road-initiative/

Marini, R.M. (1973) *Dialéctica de la dependencia*, Nueva Era.

Martins, C.E. (2022) The *longue durée* of the Marxist theory of dependency and the twenty-first century, *Latin American Perspectives*, 49(1), 18–35.

Myers, M. (2018) China's transport infrastructure investment in LAC: five things to know, *The Dialogue*, 13 November. Available at: www.thedialogue.org/blogs/2018/11/chinas-transport-infrastructure-investment-in-lac-five-things-to-know/

Meyers, M. and Gallagher, K. (2019) *Cautious Capital: Chinese Development Finance in LAC, 2018*, The Inter-American Dialogue and Boston University Global Development Policy Center. Available at: www.redalc-china.org/monitor/images/pais/ALC/investigacion/272_ALC_2019_Cautious_Capital.pdf

Myers, M. and Ray, R. (2023) *At a Crossroads: Chinese Development Finance to Latin America and the Caribbean, 2022*, The Inter-American Dialogue and Boston University Global Development Policy Center. Available at: www.bu.edu/gdp/files/2023/03/IAD-GDPC-CLLAC-Report-2023.pdf

Ohashi, H. (2018) The Belt and Road Initiative (BRI) in the context of China's opening-up policy, *Journal of Contemporary East Asia Studies*, 7(2), 85–103.

Oliveira, G.D.L. and Myers, M. (2021) The tenuous co-production of China's Belt and Road Initiative in Brazil and Latin America, *Journal of Contemporary China*, 30(129), 481–99.

Oliveira, G., Murton, G., Rippa, A., Harlan, T. and Yang, Y. (2020) China's Belt and Road Initiative: views from the ground, *Political Geography*, 82, art 102225. doi: 10.1016/j.polgeo.2020.102225

Prebisch, R. (1981) *Capitalismo periférico: crisis y transformación*, CEPAL.

Ray, R. and Mayers, M. (2023) *Chinese Loans to Latin America and the Caribbean Database*, Inter-American Dialogue.

Reis, N. and de Oliveira, F.A. (2023) Peripheral financialization and the transformation of dependency: a view from Latin America, *Review of International Political Economy*, 30(2), 511–34.

Stallings, B. (2020) *Dependency in the Twenty-First Century? The Political Economy of China-Latin America Relations*, Cambridge University Press.

Suárez Torres, A.P. (2018) China and Latin America, from neo-colonialism to interdependence? The case of Brazil, *Dimensión Empresarial*, 16(1), 185–94.

Svampa, M. (2015) Commodities consensus: neoextractivism and enclosure of the commons in Latin America, *South Atlantic Quarterly*, 114(1), 65–82.

Svampa, M. and Slipak, A.M. (2015) China en América Latina: del consenso de los commodities al consenso de Beijing, *Revista Ensambles*, 2(3), 44–6.

Teixeira, A.G. and Azócar, N. (2023) Infrastructure: The Belt and Road Initiative in Latin America, in A. Schneider and A.G. Teixeira (eds) *China, Latin America, and the Global Economy: Economic, Historical, and National Issues*, Springer International, pp 113–40.

The Dialogue (nd) China-Latin America Finance Databases. Available at: https://thedialogue.org/china-latin-america-finance-databases

Treacy, M. (2022) Dependency theory and the critique of neodevelopmentalism in Latin America, *Latin American Perspectives*, 49(1), 218–36.

Valz Gris, A. (2023) Beyond the boom: genealogies of corridor urbanism in the making of the lithium triangle, Argentina and Chile, *Geoforum*, 147, art 103913. doi: 10.1016/j.geoforum.2023.103913

Vegliò, S. (2020) *The Urban Enigma: Time, Autonomy, and Postcolonial Transformations in Latin America*, Rowman & Littlefield.

Voskoboynik, D.M. and Andreucci, D. (2022) Greening extractivism: environmental discourses and resource governance in the 'lithium triangle', *Environment and Planning E: Nature and Space*, 5(2), 787–809.

Wise, C. (2020) *Dragonomics: How Latin America Is Maximizing (or Missing Out on) China's International Development Strategy*, Yale University Press.

Wise, C. (2023) The past, present, and future of China–Latin America relations, in *Oxford Research Encyclopedia of International Studies*. Available at: https://oxfordre.com/internationalstudies/display/10.1093/acrefore/9780190846626.001.0001/acrefore-9780190846626-e-736

Wise, C. and Chonn Ching, V. (2018) Conceptualizing China–Latin America relations in the twenty-first century: the boom, the bust, and the aftermath, *The Pacific Review*, 31(5), 553–72.

Wu, L. (2024) Role constellations and foreign policy: Brazil and Chile's approaches towards the Belt and Road Initiative, *Canadian Foreign Policy Journal*, advance online publication. doi: 10.1080/11926422.2024.2311741

Xinuanet (2017) China, Argentina pledge to strengthen bilateral ties, 17 May. Available at: www.xinhuanet.com/english/2017-05/17/c_136292648.htm

Ye, M. (2020) *The Belt Road and Beyond: State-Mobilized Globalization in China: 1998–2018*, Cambridge University Press.

9

The Elusive Rainbow at the End of the Belt and Road: Chinese Investment, Finance and Trade Controversies in Southern Africa

Patrick Bond

Introduction

In Beijing, the Forum on China-Africa Cooperation (FOCAC) summit in 2024 followed the markedly unsuccessful Dakar FOCAC in 2021, at which Chinese investment commitments dropped radically, in turn following overhyped events in Beijing in 2018 and Johannesburg in 2015. To be sure, there are several current processes of importance, all deserving detailed analysis (beyond the scope of this chapter): the Nine Programs, the 2022–24 Dakar Action Plan, the China-Africa Cooperation Vision 2035, and the Declaration on China-Africa Cooperation on Combating Climate Change. But the main problem continues to arise and does not appear to be resolvable within FOCAC: the super-exploitative character of investment, finance and trade by Chinese capitalists in Africa, especially Southern Africa's extractive industries.

A USD 51 billion aggregate pledge was made by Beijing at the FOCAC 2024 summit for the period 2025–27, but of that, nearly 60 per cent will be in the form of loans. FOCAC's essential objective is to maintain the position that China has a positive role no matter its firms' fingerprints when it comes to Africa's ongoing deindustrialization, debt crises, resource looting, despotism and political instability (partly based on popular unrest such as had risen in Kenya and Nigeria in the weeks before the 2024 FOCAC). For example, Chinese state banks as well as commercial banks have a credit market share of just under 20 per cent of total sub-Saharan African loans and a far greater share than any other country of investments and trade. In the G20's (failed) Debt Service Suspension Initiative, run by the Bretton Woods Institutions, Chinese creditors reportedly accounted for 30 per cent of debt claims but contributed 63 per cent of debt service suspensions, rebutting the suggestion that Africa is caught in a specifically Chinese 'debt trap'.

Part of the problem associated with these capital flows is that the renminbi is essentially a hard currency – in terms of its value – even if Beijing retains capital controls, leaving it relatively non-convertible. The renminbi's rise against the dollar from the early 2000s – when it was nominally pegged at RMB 8.27/USD 1 – to 2014, when it hit RMB 6/USD 1, ended with the waning of China's locally directed industrialization and infrastructure boom, so it retreated to well over RMB 7/USD 1. The dollar was weak in the 2020–21 period due to Federal Reserve quantitative easing policies flooding the world with liquidity. But with the Fed raising interest rates starting in early 2022, the dollar's value strengthened. And in spite of persistent trade surpluses with nearly the entire world, China's authorities – while allowing some zigzagging – generally promoted a weaker renminbi, to the point where it exceeded RMB 7 to USD 1 for most of 2023–24. That fuelled accusations of currency manipulation (undervaluation) and, in turn, the new tariffs on Chinese exports, discussed later.

All of these trends, in turn, are confirmation that instead of a broad de-dollarization agenda and promotion of intra-BRICS+ (Brazil, Russia, India, China, South Africa+) economic connectivities, there are simply too many ways that the worst tendencies of international capitalism compel Chinese firms to become super-exploitative. There is enormous evidence of this process in Southern Africa, as discussed in later in the chapter, even if these problems were never flagged – much less contemplated in the depth deserved – in myriad FOCAC commentaries.

In the last decade, the context for FOCAC has changed markedly. A 'New Cold War' emerged in the mid-2010s (Pilger, 2016), spurred by Western economic and technological interests reacting to geopolitical and military pressure, largely as a backlash to China's expanding industrialization, exports, finance and direct investments, now spanning the globe. This trend was initiated by the US, evident from Barack Obama's strategic pivot of Pentagon resources to East Asia in the mid-2010s, followed by Donald Trump's protectionist policies from 2017 to 2021, and continued by Joe Biden's administration from 2021. By 2024, tensions had escalated further as Biden's foreign minister, Anthony Blinken, criticized Beijing's material support for Russia amid Western sanctions following the Ukraine invasion in 2022. In mid-2024, regions like the Taiwan Strait and the South China Sea experienced heightened tensions, particularly over disputed ocean territories claimed by the Philippines, which had previously seen conflicts with Vietnam. This added strain to existing disputes in the East China Sea over exclusive economic zone control with Japan and South Korea, as well as border tensions in the Himalayan mountains region with India and Bhutan. Additionally, the China-Pakistan Economic Corridor passing through contested Kashmir further exacerbated geopolitical tensions.

Long before the recent surge in tensions, which began with China's export economy in the early 1990s and intensified with the Belt and Road Initiative (BRI) in the early 2010s, geopolitical, economic and occasional military conflicts emerged. Even in Southern Africa, a region often overlooked in official BRI maps, which typically extend only as far south as Kenya, there have been revealing problems with Chinese investment, finance and trade. These relations are mainly characterized by underdevelopment and super-exploitation, stemming from Chinese capitalist crisis conditions. Viewing the BRI as a 'spatial fix' (see also Apostolopoulou, 2021) for 'overaccumulated capital' – that is, displacement of excess capacity in key industries through international geographical expansion, a process identified as early as 1913 by Rosa Luxemburg's *Accumulation of Capital* – helps explain some of the most extreme manifestations of global uneven development.

Indeed, Chinese economic involvement in the newly decolonizing Southern Africa economy was once characterized, particularly in the latter half of the 20th century after the 1949 Communist Revolution, mainly by South-South mutual aid. This included support for liberation movements, especially Zimbabwe's during the 1970s, as evidenced by Zhou Enlai's 'Principles for Collaboration', developed during his 1963–64 trip to various African countries. However, in the first decades of the 21st century, as Chinese business leaders shifted their focus from Third World solidarity to cutthroat capitalism following bursts of domestic productive overcapacity, and with the absence of Africans leaders with the stature and principles of the first-generation liberation leaders, the BRI offered new opportunities for business, *often at the expense of the public interest and environmental sustainability*.

Hence, it is fair to conclude that by the 2020s, the impacts of Chinese investment, trade and finance on Southern African society and natural environment had become mainly negative: severe local social disputes, extreme cases of corruption, so-called 'odious debt' (that ideally should not be repaid), deindustrialization and infrastructural bias towards a neocolonial mode of underdevelopment. These adverse impacts can be seen in at least 18 controversial Chinese investment and financing sites across the region – most of which were initiated under the rule of Xi Jinping since 2012. Despite tri-annual FOCAC meetings that initially raised hopes for positive outcomes, subsequent disappointments have overshadowed these expectations.

Although lessons from the broader region are touched on later, this chapter focuses primarily on six South African cases that, alongside trade-related deindustrialization, exemplify adverse economic relations. Archbishop Desmond Tutu's vision of South Africa as a 'Rainbow Nation', emerging as a multiracial democracy in 1994, epitomized the majority Black population's commitment to a 'non-racial' approach to reconciliation. This followed centuries of local and international solidarity struggles against successive manifestations of White power and Western capital. However, by the early 20th century, South Africa's integration into global capitalism brought about an extreme form of socioeconomic and ecological super-exploitation.

This was documented by Luxemburg as the 'metabolism between capitalist economy and those pre-capitalist methods of production without which it cannot go on and which, in this light, it corrodes and assimilates' (Luxemburg, 2003, p 327). In this context, British imperialists had, during the early 1900s, imported semi-colonized Chinese workers to Johannesburg because local labour had not yet mastered the deep mining techniques required to extract gold (Yap and Man, 1996, Accone, 2004). For those who remained in Johannesburg, a vibrant Chinatown prospered in the central area, before it moved to an eastern suburb in the early 1990s.

The Chinese workers were certainly exploited in the process. But when it comes to the depletion of South Africa's 'natural capital' – in the form of half the world's historic gold deposits – Johannesburg became the world's worst-ever case of uncompensated resource depletion (Bond, 2025b). British, US and South African capital drew out vast amounts of wealth, albeit leaving behind minerals whose value was still conservatively measured at USD 2.5 trillion by Citibank in 2012 (I-Net Bridge, 2012). However, through the 2010s, South Africa was considered by the World Bank (2021, p 204) as representing a major net loser of non-renewable resource wealth (even using a conservative measurement methodology; Bond, 2025b).

During 1948–94, the prevailing racial capitalism – that is, business drawing on both oppressed workers and mineral depletion to achieve the world's highest super-profits – entailed the imposition of apartheid laws by White Afrikaner ruling elites in Pretoria allied with local and global White English-speaking capital, which appreciated the inexpensive labour and electricity along with permission for generous mineral depletion (Saul and Bond, 2014). To be sure, during the 1970s – as a United Nations 'One China' policy came into effect and Henry Kissinger helped Richard Nixon reach out to Mao's Beijing – the apartheid regime was firmly supported by Taiwan. That entailed not only stronger trade but also a three-way collaboration between Pretoria, Taipei and Tel Aviv, sharing uranium and nuclear technologies (Miller, 1981). In addition, during the 1980s when economic decentralization occurred in an increasingly siege-economy South Africa, hundreds of Taiwanese factory owners took up the apartheid regime's invitation to super-exploit Bantustan labour (Hart, 2002). Ambassador H.K. Yang expressed their supposed common interests during late apartheid, stating, that South Africa and their country have been joined in the fight against communism and they were in favour of free enterprise, democracy and freedom (Pickle and Woods, 1989). But it was only in 1998 – after Taiwan did finally democratize, under pressure from organized labour – that Nelson Mandela cut official diplomatic relations with Taipei and recognized only Beijing as South Africa's Chinese partner.

Until the dawn of freedom in 1994, there was little to implicate the People's Republic of China in the looting of South African mineral resources and in unequal exchange through super-exploited labour. However, a disruptive, deindustrializing surge in trade with China emerged during the 1990s, followed by a period of major investments and financial ties that gained momentum when Chinese officials invited South African President Jacob Zuma (2009–18) to join the BRICS bloc in 2010.[1] Political power began to be wielded, such as when the Chinese embassy in Pretoria intervened on three occasions from 2009 to 2014 to prevent the Dalai Lama from receiving a visitor's visa. After the third visa rejection, Ambassador Lin Songtian bragged, 'We invest a lot of money in South Africa and we can't allow him to come and spoil the good relations' (in Mazibuko, 2015). Also in the sphere of political influence, in 2015, Zuma was reportedly pressured by Chinese financiers – who owned 20 per cent of the largest Johannesburg bank – to swiftly replace a controversial finance minister, Desmond van Rooyen, with someone more trusted by local business, namely Pravin Gordhan. This intervention, as reported by *Business Day* publisher Peter Bruce (2016), was widely welcomed by most South African business elites.

From early 2018, when Cyril Ramaphosa defeated Zuma in a palace coup and hosted that year's BRICS summit in Johannesburg, relations became more complex, in part because of escalating geopolitical tensions.[2] Despite subsequent interstate disturbances, BRI's political economy continued to unfold along a longer, deeper trajectory worth exploring in South Africa. The first manifestations are in aggregate terms: the way trade, followed by investment and finance, replicated and amplified neocolonial patterns. The next provides context, insofar as waves of overaccumulated capital washed into South Africa and the region. This is witnessed in the brief case studies in South Africa explored in this chapter. The conclusion assesses BRI as a spatial fix to overaccumulation, but one that has reached certain limits and barriers that appear profoundly debilitating in the mid-2020s.

BRI reaches South Africa

Since the 1990s, Chinese-South African trade has been controversial, largely due to the latter's import of manufactured goods and export of raw materials, and the resulting adverse impact on labour-intensive industries, plus the unequal ecological exchange associated with extractivism. Trade increased by an average of 16 per cent annually from 1994 to 2002, and by 2022 South African exports to China were valued at USD 23.4 billion, comprised in the majority of just three minerals: gold (USD 8.85 billion), diamonds (USD 3.36 billion) and platinum (USD 1.83 billion). Nearly all of these were dug from South African soil by multinational mining corporations with headquarters in London (hence, in racial terms, with largely White ownership). The USD 23.5 billion in South African imports from China included these top three categories: broadcasting equipment (USD 1.78 billion), computers (USD 1.04 billion) and electric batteries (USD 777 million). Such a neocolonial arrangement was devastating to South African manufacturing, which in 1990 reached nearly a quarter of gross domestic product (GDP). By 2022 that ratio had fallen to less than half that.

Moving to investment and finance, the role of China has attracted enormous criticism and social resistance. For instance, the South African government attempted to mimic Chinese special economic zones, offering low corporate taxes (15 per cent, just over half the national rate), state subsidies (especially in financing) and deregulated production conditions (Toussaint et al, 2019). Two prominent examples are the Musina-Makhado industrial zone near the Zimbabwe border and the Coega deep-sea port, which hosts two Chinese auto factories. These projects highlight the negative features of Chinese productive investment. Additionally, major transport and energy infrastructure deals in KwaZulu-Natal's coastal cities of Durban and Richards Bay have been plagued by corruption and neocolonial trade relations. Furthermore, the Mpumalanga coal region has faced challenges in electricity generation despite substantial foreign financing, including from the China Development Bank.

Most Southern African Development Community countries owe large debts to Chinese lenders, which carry high costs compared to the concessional debt from Germany and France. Additionally, direct Chinese investment in extractive industries explicitly underdevelops this vulnerable and highly unequal region. This is due to the global capitalist division of labour, where value chains continue to extract non-renewable resources and other raw materials from Africa without adequate compensation, a phenomenon termed unequal ecological exchange (Bond and Basu, 2021).

As Barry Sautman and Yan Hairong (2022), typically strong supporters of China's role in Africa, admitted in 2022:

> China is partly linked to the postcolonial capitalism in Africa that derives from the gross inequality and power asymmetry that was first created by colonialism. China as a trade driven industrial power is integrated into a world system ... [and] thus impacts Africa through its semi-neo-liberalism. It partly replicates the developed states' policies in Africa, of disadvantageous terms of trade, exploitation of natural resources, oppressive labor regimes and support for malign rulers.

That 'part replication' can even become an *amplification* under adverse conditions that prevail in so many Southern African settings (Bond, 2021). For instance, imports of Chinese consumer and capital goods destroyed capacity within many South African labour-intensive manufacturing sectors (such as clothing, textiles, footwear, appliances, electronics), leading to the collapse of what was once a large steel industry due to Chinese competition. While the rise of 'China mall' discounted wholesale and retail outlets has pleased South African consumers, the sector's menial workers, often low-paid migrant labourers from Zimbabwe and Malawi, face extreme systemic and flippant racism from Chinese shop owners. As ethnographer Mingwei Huang (2024) found, Johannesburg's 'China mall' retailers 'act within the global structural parameters of white supremacy, anti-Blackness, capitalism, and colonialism that they have not made but nevertheless inherited and further perpetuate', partly through cultural relations and exceptionally low wages, which are below the full reproduction cost of labour and, hence, super-exploitative (Bond, 2021).

Trade, finance and extractive industries are notorious for predatory practices. Even in South Africa's two main special economic sones, Coega and Musina-Makhado (MMSEZ), where Chinese manufacturing is present or planned, there have been profound problems. The BRI spatial fix is limited, as the severe overaccumulation of industrial capital at Chinese east coast production facilities undermines South Africa's efforts to develop its own manufacturing capacities in sectors like solar and wind infrastructure, batteries and electric vehicles (EVs). These industries are consistently undercut by the low prices of Chinese exports.

Trade, finance and extractive industries are notorious for predatory practices. Even in MMSEZ, where Chinese manufacturing production is present or planned, there have been profound problems. The limits to the BRI spatial fix can be blamed, as the severe overaccumulation of industrial capital at Chinese east coast production facilities undermines South Africa's efforts to develop its own manufacturing capacities in sectors like solar and wind infrastructure, batteries and EVs. These industries are consistently undercut by the low prices of Chinese exports.

China's persistent overaccumulation of capital and the BRI as a spatial fix

During their April 2024 trips to Beijing, US Treasury Secretary Janet Yellen and Secretary of State Tony Blinken, along with Ursula von der Leyen, during Xi Jinping's visit to Paris in May 2024, pointed out overcapacity in China's EV, solar panel and battery industries. However, this does not negate the reality: Chinese export-oriented factory overproduction is the contemporary ground zero of global capitalist crisis formation, as Marx predicted. It is important to acknowledge that two features are contested in 2024 debates among political economists, including some (politically) openly pro-Beijing scholars: the issue of excess capacity itself, and its implications for China's behaviour within global value chains, especially regarding mineral extraction (Bond, 2024).

Michael Roberts (2024) dismisses Yellen's concerns as 'nonsense', arguing that China has no problem selling its exports to eager global consumers and manufacturers. He criticizes the Western view that China is stuck in an outdated model of investment-led export manufacturing. Furthermore, Roberts contends that China 'cannot be considered even sub-imperialist, let alone imperialist', a stance supported by the Tricontinental Institute (2024), which argues that in the context of a 'hyper-imperialism' centred at the US Pentagon, 'there is no such thing as sub-imperialism or non-Western imperialist powers' and that such concepts obscure factual realities.

This narrative challenges a long-standing tradition in political economy initiated by Brazilian dependency theorist Ruy Mauro Marini (1972), further developed by David Harvey (2003), Sam Moyo and Paris Yeros (2011), and Samir Amin (2019). Amin, in his posthumously published autobiography, remarked that 'nothing has changed' in South Africa's post-apartheid economy, with its sub-imperialist role reinforced by the dominance of Anglo-American mining monopolies. By mid-2023, the integrated BRICS+ economies and regimes had gained even greater significance within the global corporate power structure, global value chains and Western-dominated multilateral institutions (Bond, 2024).

In 2024, eight out of the ten BRICS+ governments provided net-positive material support to Israel during the genocide of Palestinians, with only South Africa and Iran abstaining. Saudi Arabia pursued normalization processes following the lead of BRICS+ members Egypt and the United Arab Emirates. Sergei Lavrov remarked that the Netanyahu and Putin invasions of Gaza and Ukraine were 'nearly identical' in their pursuit of 'de-Nazification'. These geopolitical arrangements dampen optimism about BRICS+ opposition to Western imperialism. The April 2024 re-election of neoliberal economist Kristalina Georgieva as International Monetary Fund (IMF) managing director, with *unanimous BRICS+ support*, and the failure of the 'de-dollarization' initiative within the bloc's finance ministries, central banks and banks, further highlight their *sub-imperial*, rather than anti-imperial, stance (Bond, 2024).

Regarding the question of whether Chinese GDP is declining, Renmin University economist John Ross (2024) argues that 'the U.S. has launched a quite extraordinary propaganda campaign, including numerous straightforward factual falsifications, to attempt to conceal the real international economic facts'. According to Ross, these facts indicate that China's growth trajectory will result in an economy 60 per cent larger than the US economy by 2035, decisively overcoming the alleged 'middle-income trap' and, as stated in the 20th Party Congress, propelling China to the level of a 'medium-developed country'.

Critiques of Washington's conventional wisdom often overlook significant challenges, with crucial implications for the BRI and its impact on South Africa and Africa, major recipients of Chinese capital. Similar optimistic forecasts, like those made for Japan in the 1980s, preceded the massive financial crash of 1990 and subsequent stagnation of GDP. Indicators suggest a slowdown in Chinese capital accumulation, including declining profit rates in new-tech industries and concerning shifts of excess capital, such as banks redirecting lending from real estate to production. Using GDP as a primary measure of prosperity disregards critical factors like unpaid women's work in social reproduction, greenhouse gas emissions, local pollution and non-renewable resource depletion. While analysts like Ross, Roberts and the Tricontinental Institute staff led by Vijay Prashad offer valuable insights, their uncritical use of GDP and belief in China's socialism overlooks feminist-economic and ecological-economic perspectives, which are crucial given China's reliance on the *hukou* system and extractivism. Ho-fung Hung (2015) contends that China's capital accumulation follows the same logic and contradictions of capitalist development elsewhere, leading to an overaccumulation crisis evidenced by ghost towns and shuttered factories. By 2015, confirmed overcapacity levels exceeded 30 per cent in key sectors, contributing to a crash in raw materials prices.

Today, overproduction persists in heavy industrial sectors like steel, petrochemicals and cement, and in major construction projects such as coal-fired power plants. Chinese industry's utilization of 285,000 robots in 2022, compared to less than 50,000 in each of the next four most robot-populated countries (Japan, the US, South Korea and Germany), illustrates rising productive capacity and capital intensity (Statzon, 2023). To accommodate this investment surge, Chinese bank credit lines, once reserved for real estate developers, shifted urgently to manufacturing, resulting in a USD 700 billion increase in credit lines from 2022 to 2023. This production prowess contributed to China's trade surplus in manufactured goods rising from less than 0.3 per cent of world GDP before 2000 to over 1.5 per cent by 2022.

However, the higher-growth green economy did not absorb these production surpluses. By late 2023, Chinese excess capacity had reached exceptionally high levels in solar energy equipment, batteries and EVs. China's dominance in solar photovoltaic production components – modules (75 per cent), cells (85 per cent), wafers (97 per cent) and polysilicon (79 per cent) – far exceeds its consumption share of 36 per cent of world demand, and the location of the world's lithium-battery plants is revealing: 77 per cent are in China, followed by Poland and the US, then Germany and Hungary, *and nowhere else* (Statzon, 2023).

The extent of capital overaccumulation in EVs, solar and batteries is concerning, as these commodities ideally should serve as global public goods, ensuring unhindered demand as the world transitions to renewable energy. Multilateral agencies should prevent any demand constraints, with high-emitting countries – including many BRICS+ nations – providing solar, wind, non-invasive energy storage and electric transport at no cost as part of their climate debt repayment. This collective approach should prioritize commoning over unreliable, chaotic models like those of South Africa's Independent Power Producers.

Without this anti-capitalist approach, global capitalism will fail to achieve the necessary emissions reductions, endangering the survival of vulnerable Asian and African countries. The climate catastrophe hinted at by events like the rain bomb in Durban on 12 April 2022, which claimed 500 lives, underscores the urgency of systemic change. However, capitalism in the mid-2020s appears incapable of absorbing Chinese exports, even with significant subsidies from Beijing, as highlighted by Yellen and Blinken in their attempts to support US industries through the Inflation Reduction Act.

It appears inevitable that global effective demand for renewable energy and electric transport will continue to be severely constrained during a period, since early 2022, of rapidly rising interest rates, debt crises, financial chaos, productive sector stagnation, durable price inflation in some sectors, and worrying levels of geopolitical volatility that affect the economy (for example, the grain and energy price hikes following Red Sea shipping disruptions due to Yemenese solidarity with Palestine following Israel's genocide, or another potential Israel-Iran military flare-up).

Despite John Ross' (2024) optimism about China's rising GDP, the Chinese economy faces significant vulnerabilities. Foreign direct investment (FDI) into China plummeted to USD 33 billion in 2023, an 82 per cent decline from 2022 and the lowest level since 1993 (Bloomberg, 2024). By early 2024, China was grappling with a resurgence of productive sector overaccumulation, signalling the need for a viable international spatial fix after the apparent exhaustion of its local spatial fix, which had relied on massive infrastructure and housing expansion during the 2010s.

Importantly, the BRI encountered difficulties in displacing overaccumulated Chinese capital, exacerbated by financial crises emerging in various Asian and African countries. Despite a brief commodity price spike driven by the 2021–22 recovery from COVID-19 lockdowns, contradictions persisted along the BRI. Sovereign defaults and austerity programmes in some countries can be attributed to limits in the temporal fix, such as the US Federal Reserve's rapid interest rate increases in 2022–23 following loose quantitative easing practices worldwide in 2020–21.

The prior episode of overaccumulation in China during the 2010s provided valuable lessons. Some, including myself (Bond, 2019), believed that Beijing could effectively manage such overaccumulation. This could be achieved not only through displacement but also by actively devalorizing the overaccumulated capital through Beijing's centralized control and planning power. Examples of this approach included Beijing's directive to shut down high-carbon industries and coal-fired power plants in Hebei province ahead of schedule, in part to improve air quality. Another demonstration of Beijing's power to mothball polluting industries was observed during the Beijing Winter Olympic Games in 2022. Starting from late 2015, Beijing implemented 'supply-side structural reforms' aimed at guiding the economy towards a new normal. These reforms comprised five strategies: capacity reduction, housing inventory destocking, corporate deleveraging, reduction of corporate costs, and industrial upgrading with new infrastructure investment. The 'three cuts, one reduction, and one improvement' strategy was, the World Bank observed, a welcome departure from China's traditional demand-side stimulus policies (Chen et al, 2018).

In 2019, I posed a question regarding the potential for rising debt and the on-and-off trade war with the United States to turn China's managed process into capitalist anarchy, leading to worse overaccumulation (Bond, 2019). Xia Zhang (2017) provided a more realistic assessment, explaining China's capitalist externalization of uneven development as a geographical restructuring resulting from overaccumulation. This necessitates a 'spatial fix' on an unprecedented scale to sustain capital accumulation and expansion.

Throughout capitalist history, combating overaccumulation has involved two main strategies: a spatial fix involving trade, FDI and labour migration, and rising cross-border finance. However, Beijing faces a dilemma as Chinese banks overextended themselves, compounded by conflicts among the elite controlling the state sector, leading to capital flight and intensified struggles with foreign and private enterprises.

The IMF recognized the link between overaccumulation and Chinese firms' overseas mergers and acquisitions during the mid-2010s, attributing it to Beijing's subsidies to firms. This occurred amid slowing growth in China, declining capacity utilization and pressure on corporate profitability, prompting Chinese companies to seek new markets for capital relocation and expansion (Ding et al, 2021). Progressive Chinese activists criticized the BRI for exporting China's surplus capital, often at the expense of working people and the environment. And many of us in South Africa can testify to the reliance on accumulation by dispossession in Chinese displacement of overaccumulation.

All these insights are crucial for understanding how a genuine 'public goods' approach can emerge from the global (and Chinese) overcapacity crisis in solar, wind, energy storage and EVs, transforming them from commodities to decommodified contributions to planetary preservation.

Contradictions reflected in South Africa's Chinese-driven special economic zones

To begin a survey of the BRI at the tip of Africa, along South Africa's southern coastline, consider the Nelson Mandela Bay metropolitan area, where the Coega Special Economic Zone was initiated in the early 2000s. Two Chinese car factories were built there during the 2010s – First Auto Works (FAW) and Beijing Auto Industrial Corporation (BAIC) – and attracted widespread criticism for labour conflicts, for drawing down large South African state subsidies (and electricity supply), for their capital-intensive semi-knockdown kit status (instead of the anticipated integrated factories), for failing to produce EVs and for an exceptionally slow startup (eight years in BAIC's case). At FAW, the metalworkers union went on strike in 2021, because workers were 'paid R39 ($2.90) per hour, while their counterparts at other truck assemblers earn R99 ($6.60) per hour', according to the country's leading trade union (Chirume, 2021). In spite of promises to create 500 permanent jobs, there were only 190.

The much larger (USD 600 million) BAIC plant was co-financed in 2016 by the South African state's Industrial Development Corporation. In mid-2018, for an audience that included Xi and Ramaphosa, the first few semi-knockdown sport utility vehicles were rolled off the BAIC assembly line, just a day before the BRICS Summit was to start in Sandton. The experience led Lin Songtian to exclaim, 'I've been to many developing countries and industrial development zones and the Coega SEZ is by far the best of them all' (Toussaint et al, 2019). However, it would be nearly six years after the Xi and Ramaphosa unveiling of the BAIC's assembly line before the plant began producing its own cars, in March 2024.

Eric Toussaint et al (2019) offered other relevant critiques of various problems that arose, including inadequate Small, Medium and Micro Enterprise involvement, budget shortfalls for the start-up phase, differential labor laws, and delays in production. Journalists noted the high share of imported inputs, and the extensive work stoppages and language barriers encountered in the early stages. Even a partially Chinese-owned newspaper admitted in 2019 that 'serious doubts have been expressed in motor industry circles about the claims that the vehicle was manufactured in South Africa. [...] The local media reported that the construction had been moving at a snail's pace and all SMMEs had vacated the premises due to non-payment' (Cockayne, 2019).

Another industrial production site near the Zimbabwe border received even greater fanfare in 2018 at the Beijing FOCAC session co-chaired that year by Xi and Ramaphosa: the Musina-Makhado Special Economic Zone (Mokone, 2018; MMSEZ, 2020). If eventually built, it may become the single largest industrial megaproject in Africa, with a USD 10–40 billion estimated investment. However, like the BAIC plant, major delays are obvious, and perhaps fatal due to Xi's curtailing of BRI coal-fired power in 2021. In 2017, the MMSEZ operating licence was granted to entrepreneur Ning Yat Hoi's Shenzhen Hoi Mor investment firm even though he was on the Interpol red list for corporate fraud in Zimbabwe (at the country's largest gold mine, Freda) and Great Britain (Bond, 2025a).

The MMSEZ's main industrial ambitions are in an ecologically sensitive zone in the close vicinity of Ramaphosa's home village. But the USD 10 billion project requires not only piping in of vast water supplies (unavailable on site) but also finding an energy source which, until September 2021, was meant to be a 4,600 megawatt (MW) coal-fired power plant. Xi's speech to the United Nations General Assembly that month, in advance of the Glasgow United Nations climate summit, promised an end to such plants along Beijing's BRI, which soon compelled MMSEZ organizers to claim (dubiously) that the vast industrial facility could operate on local solar power supplies (Bond, 2025a).

The challenge of supplying energy to the MMSEZ is, in the 2020s, formidable given not only overconsumption by electricity-guzzling smelters elsewhere in South Africa, but also the desperate need to meet the power needs of labour-intensive industry, small businesses and households, especially where (patriarchy-determined) cooking chores based on hot plates are necessarily being replaced by dirty coal, wood and paraffin. And even without the thermal coal plant, Ning's other proposed MMSEZ industrial emitters – at 34 megatonnes annually, 8 per cent of South Africa's projected 2030 total – and their extensive local pollution were irrational. The irrationality is obvious for five key reasons:

- First, MMSEZ officials repeatedly deny the urgent need to decarbonize industry, or face the Carbon Adjustment Border Mechanism climate sanctions that will begin in Europe in 2026 and the UK in 2027.
- Second, Chinese-driven overproduction of most of the industrial metals proposed are already resulting in global gluts.
- Third, evidence of South Africa's global uncompetitiveness is seen in ongoing closures of other local steel mills (especially the Indian-owned ArcelorMittal mill and the Russian-owned Evraz Highveld mill).
- Fourth, by the 2020s, the national economy's annual steel output had halved from its 2005 peak of 8 million tonnes.
- Fifth, instead of replacing imports with MMSEZ-produced metals, displacement within the South African economy would result, since as one analyst remarked, 'the idea was that that instead of machinery and equipment being built in, say, Durban and shipped to a Southern African Development Community country, it could far more advantageously be done in the MMSEZ' (Ryan, 2019).

As noted earlier, global metals overcapacity created such pressure on South Africa that international steel giant ArcelorMittal continued its own radical downsizing of existing foundries, even while a major Chinese steel mill was being built in Manhize, central Zimbabwe, with potential capacity of 5.1 million tonnes/year. It's worth noticing here that South Africa's early 2020s national output had fallen to 4 million tonnes and was anticipated to drop further in coming years with more foundry closures.

Thousands of environmental impact assessment (EIA) complaints revealed that the MMSEZ would cause extensive local pollution and greenhouse gas emissions, severely harming Limpopo's fragile ecology. These emissions would far exceed the limits agreed to in South Africa's nationally determined contributions to cutting emissions, as mandated by the 2015 Paris Climate Agreement. Delta BEC (2021), the initial MMSEZ EIA practitioner, judged the coal-fired power plant indefensible without a working carbon capture system, which did not exist. Xi Jinping also rejected coal-fired plants for the BRI during a 2021 United Nations General Assembly speech, citing global climate responsibilities. Additionally, the MMSEZ power source debate arose as Eskom's load-shedding worsened. The promised 400 MW solar replacement would be insufficient given the high electricity demands of the planned MMSEZ smelters.

Furthermore, water supply for the MMSEZ was not immediately available. While vague options for a summer-time flood-overflow dam near Musina were suggested, it was more likely that the MMSEZ would rely on international transfers from aquifers in western Zimbabwe and eastern Botswana. Delta BEC (2021) acknowledged that by 2040, water demand for mining, industries and power generation would increase more than fivefold, from 45.0 million m^3/a to 249.1 million m^3/a. Much of this water would be used to wash thermal and coking coal near the MMSEZ for subsequent combustion, leading to further CO_2 emissions, which in turn would contribute to droughts and floods in a province and region set to be among Africa's worst affected by the climate crisis.

The overarching problem at the MMSEZ was whether a logic for regional economic development existed based on mining, beneficiation and intensive energy supply in Limpopo province and nearby countries and indeed whether such a logic has ever existed, especially considering that the returns on taxpayer investments of USD 5.2 billion in infrastructure were estimated to be only a cumulative USD 42 million over 20 years (Liebenberg, 2022). Moreover, and importantly, resistance to the MMSEZ grew from various environmental justice, conservationist and community movements (Thompson and Mbangula, 2021; Thompson et al, 2021).

Infrastructure corruption amid growing coal-export dependency

There have been warnings of such underdevelopment since the early 1990s, with trade-catalysed deindustrialization due to fast-rising South African imports from China and other East Asian economies, mainly through the

Durban port. Although higher capital intensity in surviving plants also played a role, imports from Asia have been the main contributor to the closure of South Africa's labour-intensive clothing, textile, footwear, appliance and electronic sectors. Moreover, the danger of corruption, particularly related to the MMSEZ's chosen management, is recognized due to visible financial and mercantile underdevelopment, notably in Beijing's relationship with the transport parastatal Transnet. For instance, the Durban port's seven new container cranes, purchased in 2011, were considered the world's most expensive because Shanghai Zhenhua Heavy Industries, along with the German-Swiss firm Liebherr, added millions of dollars in bribes to the notorious Gupta family empire when winning a USD 92 million tender.

In the other main infrastructure supply controversy, a 2013 order for Transnet's rail fleet involved hundreds of new locomotives from Beijing-based CRRC. Three problems arose: first, Pretoria tax authorities in 2022 found evidence of large scale corruption by CRRC as part of the Gupta 'state capture' of Transnet; second, tax fraud in excess of $200 million due to the world's largest rolling stock manufacturer substantially understating its tax liability and misrepresenting its interest earnings; and, third, a CRRC response to not only deny the evidence and refuse to pay its tax debt, but to also withhold vital locomotive parts during the early 2020s.

As a result, CRRC left more than 100 locomotives disabled, crippling Transnet's bulk exports and forcing mining houses to transition to rail-to-road transport using trucks. This caused severe ecological damage and dramatically lowered productivity. To pay CRRC for the locomotives, a high-profile USD 5 billion China Development Bank loan was granted to South Africa by Xi in 2013, coinciding with Durban hosting the BRICS summit. While not all of the loan was used and corruption was evident again via the Guptas, Beijing insisted on full repayment.

The financing of South African maldevelopment is also obvious in the continent's worst case of parastatal debt: energy generator Eskom's two new coal-fired power plants, Kusile and Medupi. Eskom received credits for Kusile from the China Development Bank (USD 2.5 billion in 2018) and for Medupi from the Shanghai-headquartered BRICS New Development Bank (USD 480 million in 2019). This occurred despite allegations that the World Bank and Western financiers had over the prior decade burdened South Africa with tens of billions of dollars' worth of odious debt due to Hitachi's bribery of the ruling African National Congress to secure the plants' main construction contracts in 2007.

The Tokyo firm was successfully prosecuted in 2015 in Washington (but not yet in Pretoria) under the US Foreign Corrupt Practices Act. But that did not stop Chinese lenders from contributing to South Africa's foreign debt, which had surpassed USD 180 billion at the time. Concurrently, Pretoria's state debt was declared 'junk' by two credit rating agencies in 2017, prompting taxpayers to take over the burden of repaying half of Eskom's loans. To repay the other half, Eskom residential customers have faced a 435 per cent rise in after-inflation prices for electricity from 2007 to 2024.

Meanwhile, neither Kusile nor Medupi were built to specifications, resulting in seven years of delays in construction and 7,000 cases of welding failure. This failure to supply the grid with the intended 4,800 MW each contributed to extreme electricity shortages. Additionally, the 35 million tonnes of CO_2 emissions from each power plant made this the worst-ever case of megaproject climate mismanagement in Africa. Just like their Western counterparts, the two China-based banks never forgave the repayment burden, so South African taxpayers and Eskom customers have continued to repay loans at what is the world's fourth-highest interest rate among the leading 40 countries issuing state bonds (Bond, 2024). And the worst damage, as leading South African environmentalist Makoma Lekalakala explained when organizing several protests against the BRICS New Development Bank, is that 'the projects they are funding are climate-destroying projects' (Bloom, 2019).

Likewise against the MMSEZ, visionary women's and community critique of extraction was generated by Lekalakala, a Goldman Environmental Prize winner who, according to Dineo Skosana and Jacklyn Cock (2023, p 87), is one of the 'black working-class women in mining-affected areas doing important eco-feminist work in four respects': social reproduction, meeting 'collective rather than individualised needs', a 'respect for nature that goes beyond the expansionist logic of capitalism' and 'taking responsibility for and caring for the sick' – for example, those in labour-sending as well as local-mining areas that are among the most victimized by COVID-19, tuberculosis or AIDS running rampant due to migrant-work conditions. The extractive industries' widespread despoliation of fresh water has led to further consideration about not only women's burdens during specific climate-catastrophic events (which Limpopo province is increasingly victimized by), but also the responsibility that patriarchy places on women to steward ecological inheritances, natural resources and life itself into future generations (Madhanagopal et al, 2022).

Conclusion

What lessons are to be drawn? Put simply, the exploitative relationships between the people and environment of Southern Africa, on one side, and the consumers of cheap labour in settler-colonial and Western corporate entities, on the other, are exacerbated by the neocolonial trade, investment and financing controversies evident in China–South African economic ties since the end of apartheid, at least those reviewed in this chapter.

Can these ties be reformed, or is it more appropriate to break the chains? Advocates of reform work within bilateral, FOCAC and BRICS+ networks, yet so far, the main advocacy groups, think-tanks and individual academics working within these circuits overlook the underlying contradictions. This reluctance, often observed among critical academics when it comes to China, may stem from concerns about the Communist Party's unforgiving perspective. For example, in early 2024, prominent South African BRI/BRICS scholar Bhaso Ndzendze dismissed claims of China exerting control over African infrastructure due to debt traps as 'fake news' (Ndzendre, 2024). He attributed such narratives to a lack of transparency in information sharing between African and Chinese governments or within the FOCAC process, which fosters speculation and exaggeration. This cautious approach, bordering on analytical timidity, must be overcome to pursue truth and justice. Otherwise, internal reform efforts will likely stall, as appears to be the case in early 2024.

In contrast, selective disengagement from the BRI by South African progressives, paralleling grievances against Western neocolonialism, could be inspired by two significant activist-driven processes: anti-apartheid sanctions from 1965–90 that were instrumental in weakening the repressive elites and then changing power relations to force the country's first free, democratic election in 1994, and the delinking of South Africa's economy from international pharmaceutical monopolies in 2004, which allowed local generic factories to supply the state, and seven million people living with HIV, with life-saving drugs and thus led to a rise in life expectancy (Saul and Bond, 2014).

The dilemmas for the BRI project appear to be as extreme in South and Southern Africa as in some of the other crisis-ridden sites in Asia and Africa, where Chinese capital has run up against what sometimes appear to be insurmountable barriers and setbacks. The potential for both analysis and activism is enormous, using the tools discussed here, even if refinement and sharpening are always needed.

Notes

[1] In early 2024, BRICS+ added new member states Egypt, Ethiopia, Iran and the United Arab Emirates, and in 2025, Indonesia was admitted as a full member. The October 2024 Kazan summit also added a half-dozen new 'partner' states.

[2] While Ramaphosa initially leaned towards Washington (Bond, 2018), and while at the BRICS Johannesburg summit in 2023 his leading economic allies in the Johannesburg financial sector (for example, Sim Tshabalala of Standard Bank) and the South African Reserve Bank and Treasury disdained Moscow bureaucrats' attempt to de-dollarize (Bond, 2023), turmoil in Pretoria-Washington relations suddenly emerged. Four incidents were widely remarked upon: Ramaphosa's Foreign Minister Naledi Pandor refused to work with Blinken against Moscow's invasion of Ukraine in 2022 (aside from one brief condemnatory statement shortly after the invasion); a Russian ship was forcefully alleged by the US Ambassador to Pretoria (without proof) to be importing South African military supplies in late 2022; the South African Navy hosted Chinese and Russian counterparts for (routine, BRICS-related) ocean war exercises in early 2023; and Pandor led the

International Court of Justice in early 2024 to declare a 'plausible genocide' by Israel against Palestine. In early 2025, the Trump administration further targeted South Africa with USD 450 million in (public health) aid cuts, due to its affirmative action policies and its Palestine solidarity.

References

Accone, D. (2004) *All Under Heaven: The Story of a Chinese Family in South Africa*, David Phillip.

Amin, S. (2019) *The Long Revolution of the Global South*, Monthly Review Press.

Apostolopoulou, E. (2021) Tracing the links between infrastructure-led development, urban transformation, and inequality in China's Belt and Road Initiative, *Antipode*, 53(3), 831–58.

Bloom, K. (2019) Medupi's R6.8bn New Development Bank injection and other BRICS climate crimes, *Daily Maverick*, 10 April. Available at: www.dailymaverick.co.za/article/2019-04-10-medupis-r6-8bn-new-development-bank-injection-and-other-brics-climate-crimes/

Bloomberg (2024) Foreign direct investment to China slumps to 30-year low, 18 February. Available at: www.bloomberg.com/news/articles/2024-02-18/foreign-direct-investment-into-china-slumps-to-worst-in-30-years

Bond, P. (2018) East-West/North-South or imperial-subimperial? *Human Geography*, 18(2), 1–18.

Bond, P. (2019) Degrowth, devaluation and uneven development from North to South, in E. Chertkovskaya, A. Paulsson and S. Barca (eds) *Towards a Political Economy of Degrowth*, Rowman and Littlefield, pp 157–76. Available at: https://rowman.com/ISBN/9781786608963/Towards-a-Political-Economy-of-Degrowth

Bond, P. (2021) Pros and cons of China's roles in Southern Africa, in A.M. Vasiliev, D.A. Degterev and T. Shaw (eds) *Africa and the Formation of the New System of International Relations: Rethinking Decolonization and Foreign Policy Concepts*, Springer Nature, pp 139–56. https://link.springer.com/chapter/10.1007/978-3-030-77336-6_10

Bond, P. (2023) BRICS+ emerge from Johannesburg, humbled as *sub-* (not anti- or inter-) imperialists, *ZNet*, 29 August. Available at: https://znetwork.org/znetarticle/brics-emerge-from-johannesburg-humbled-as-sub-not-anti-or-inter-imperialists/

Bond, P. (2024) *Extreme Uneven Development*, Palgrave Macmillan.

Bond, P. (2025a) Development or underdevelopment at South Africa's largest industrial mega-project? in M. Mdlalose, I. Khambule and E. Khalema (eds) *Contemporary South Africa and the Political Economy of Regional Development*, Routledge, pp 173–95.

Bond, P. (2025b) Pitfalls of resource-nationalist consciousness, *Review of African Political Economy*, 52(183), 104–14.

Bond, P. and Basu, R. (2021) Intergenerational equity and the geographical ebb and flow of resources, in M. Himley and E. Havice (eds) *Handbook of Critical Resource Geography*, Palgrave Macmillan, pp 260–73.

Bruce, P. (2016) Oops! Zuma, on slope, slips in snow, *Business Day*, 22 January. Available at: www.businesslive.co.za/bd/opinion/columnists/2016-01-22-thick-end-of-the-wedgeoops-zuma-on-slope-slips-in-snow/

Chen, L., Ding, D. and Mano, R. (2018) *China's Capacity Reduction Reform and Its Impact on Producer Prices*, International Monetary Fund. Available at: www.elibrary.imf.org/view/journals/001/2018/216/article-A001-en.xml

Chirume, J. (2021) Strike continues at Gqeberha automobile plant as union demands 100 per cent wage increase, *Ground Up*, 27 October. Available at: https://groundup.org.za/article/strike-continues-first-automobile-works-gqberha-plant-union-demands-100-wage-increase/

Cockayne, R. (2019) BAIC sets new timelines for projected SA vehicle, *Business Report*, 26 February. Available at: www.iol.co.za/mercury/business/baic-sets-new-timelines-for-projected-sa-vehicle-plant-19504827

Delta BEC (2021) *Environmental Impact Assessment, Musina Makhado Special Economic Zone*, Delta BEC.

Ding, D., Di Vittorio, F., Lariau, A. and Zhou, Y. (2021) *Chinese Investment in Latin America: Sectoral Complementarity and the Impact of China's Rebalancing*, IMF Working Paper, International Monetary Fund. Available at: www.imf.org/-/media/Files/Publications/WP/2021/English/wpiea2021160-print-pdf.ashx

Hart, G. (2002) *Disabling Globalization*, University of California Press.

Harvey, D. (2003) *The New Imperialism*, Oxford University Press.

Huang, M. (2024) *Reconfiguring Racial Capitalism*, Duke University Press.

Hung, H. (2015) China fantasies, *Jacobin*, 10 December. Available at: www.jacobinmag.com/2015/12/china-new-global-order-imperialism-communist-party-globalisation

I-Net Bridge (2012) SA failing to capitalise on its minerals wealth, *Sunday Times*, 6 February. Available at: www.timeslive.co.za/sunday-times/business/2012-02-06-sa-failing-to-capitalise-on-its-minerals-wealth/

Liebenberg, L. (2022) White elephant tender-fest trampling SA's impoverished far north, *Daily Maverick*, 28 November. Available at: www.dailymaverick.co.za/opinionista/2022-11-28-white-elephant-tender-fest-trampling-sas-impoverished-far-north/

Luxemburg, R. (2003 [1913]) *The Accumulation of Capital*, Routledge. Available at: www.marxists.org/archive/luxemburg/1913/accumulation-capital/ch29.htm

Madhanagopal, D., Bond, P. and Bayón, M. (2022) Eco-feminisms in theory and practice in the Global South: India, South Africa, and Ecuador, in D. Madhanagopal, C. Beer, B. Nikku and A. Pelser (eds) *Environment, Climate, and Social Justice: Perspectives and Practices from the Global South*, Springer Nature, pp 275–96.

Marini, R.M. (1972) Brazilian subimperialism, *Monthly Review*, 23(9), 14–24.

Mazibuko, P. (2015) Dalai Lama threat to China, SA. *Independent Online*, 28 December. Available at: www.iol.co.za/news/politics/dalai-lama-threat-to-china-sa-1964436

Miller, J. (1981) Three nations widening nuclear contacts, *The New York Times*, 28 June. Available at: www.nytimes.com/1981/06/28/world/3-nations-widening-nuclear-contacts.html

MMSEZ SOC (2020) *Strategic Plan, 2020-21 to 2024-25*. Available at: https://mmsez.co.za/wp-content/uploads/2021/03/South-African-Business-2021-MMSEZ-spreads.pdf

Mokone, T. (2018) Ramaphosa strikes deals in China to bring jobs, factories to Musina-Makhado corridor, *Times*, 3 September. Available at: www.timeslive.co.za/politics/2018-09-03-ramaphosa-strikes-deals-in-china-to-bring-jobs-factories-to-musina-makhado-corridor/

Moyo, S. and Yeros, P. (2011) Rethinking the theory of primitive accumulation, Paper presented to the Second International Initiative for Promoting Political Economy Conference, 20–22 May, Istanbul.

Ndzendze, B. (2024) Is China seizing African infrastructure? *bhasondzenze.co.za*, 29 March. Available at: https://bhasondzendze.co.za/2024/03/29/is-china-seizing-african-infrastructure/

Pickle, J. and Woods, J. (1989) Taiwanese investment in South Africa, *African Affairs*, 88(353), 515–22.

Pilger, J. (2016) The coming war on China. Available at: https://johnpilger.com/the-coming-war-on-china/

Roberts, M. (2024) China's unfair 'overcapacity', *The Next Recession*, 10 April. Available at: https://thenextrecession.wordpress.com/2024/04/10/chinas-unfair-overcapacity/

Ross, J. (2024) China's economy is still far out growing the U.S. – contrary to Western media 'fake news', *Monthly Review Online*, 27 February. Available at: https://mronline.org/2024/02/27/chinas-economy-is-still-far-out-growing-the-us-contrary-to-western-media-fake-news/

Ryan, E. (2019) Musina Makhado SEZ hosts packed investment conference to transform Limpopo's economy, *Mail & Guardian*, 6 December. Available at: www.pressreader.com/south-africa/mail-guardian/20191206/textview

Saul, J. and Bond, P. (2014) *South Africa*, James Currey.

Sautman, B. and Hairong, Y. (2022) Africa-China relations, *International Manifesto Group YouTube Channel*. Available at: www.youtube.com/watch?v=5p0T91Fnnj0&pp=ygUSY2hpbmEgYWZyaWNhIGJhcnJ5

Skosana, D. and Cock, J. 'Our existence is resistance': women challenging mining and the climate crisis in a time of Covid-19, in V. Satgar and R. Ntlokotse (eds) *Emancipatory Feminism in the Time of Covid-19: Transformative Resistance and Social Reproduction*, University of the Witwatersrand Press, pp 85–102. Available at: https://library.oapen.org/bitstream/id/88d3be70-9682-4c3c-bd0f-c9ae441dc24b/9781776148301.pdf

Statzon (2023) IFR World Robotics 2023 key takeaways, 13 October. Available at: https://statzon.com/insights/ifr-world-robotics-2023

Thompson, L. and Mbangula, M. (2021) Public participation is a farce in the Musina Makhado project, *Mail & Guardian*, 6 May. Available at: https://mg.co.za/opinion/2021-05-06-public-participation-is-a-farce-in-musina-makhado-project/

Thompson, L., Shirinda, H. and Mbangula, M. (2021) Musina Makhado metallurgical zone revision a back-peddle or a back-door? *Mail & Guardian*, 12 May. Available at: https://mg.co.za/thought-leader/opinion/2021-05-12-musina-makhado-metallurgical-zone-revision-a-back-peddle-or-a-back-door/

Toussaint, E., Mbangula, M., D'Sa, D., Thompson, L. and Bond, P. (2019) *Shifting Sands of the Global Economic Status Quo*, African Centre for Citizenship and Democracy Policy Paper No 2. Available at: https://southafrica.fes.de/event/accede-policy-working-paper-no2-shifting-sands-of-the-global-economic-status-quo-the-emergence-of-the-new-global-south-developmental-policy-narrative-and-south-africas-special-economic-zones

Tricontinental Institute (2024) *Hyper-Imperialism*, Studies on Contemporary Dilemmas No 4. Available at: https://thetricontinental.org/studies-on-contemporary-dilemmas-4-hyper-imperialism/

World Bank (2021) *The Changing Wealth of Nations 2021*. Available at: https://openknowledge.worldbank.org/entities/publication/e1399ed3-ebe2-51fb-b2bc-b18a7f1aaaed

Yap, M. and Man, D. (1996) *Colour, Confusion and Concessions: The History of the Chinese in South Africa*, Hong Kong University Press.

Zhang, X. (2017) Chinese capitalism and the Maritime Silk Road, *Geopolitics*, 22(2), 310–31.

10

Beyond the Logistical Monolith: Multiplicity and Differentiation Along the Adriatic Corridor

Francesca Governa, Leonardo Ramondetti, Astrid Safina, Angelo Sampieri and Alberto Valz Gris

Introduction

Several issues have contributed to the rapid development of intermodal transportation and the drastic increase in the volume of long-distance exchanges, especially by sea. These are: the delocalization and standardization of production, the reduction in transport costs and new information technologies. Logistical platforms, intermodal centres, integrated stations, interports, ports, dry ports, trans-shipments and roll-on/roll-off (RO-RO) have become part of a 'new urban vocabulary' and also part of the vocabulary of a 'global race' to infrastructurization (and investments in infrastructures; Schindler and Kanai, 2021). This situation is triggering deep-rooted changes, at lightning speed, in large areas of the world from North to South, including in Africa, Asia, Latin America and Europe.

By implementing the Belt and Road Initiative (BRI), China has become an excellent example of a 'globally oriented infrastructural State' (Scholvin, 2021; Turner, 2021). While the BRI questions the role of China as a global player in today's complex geo-economic and geopolitical redefinitions, not only does it spark profound material changes in places transformed and built by the interventions and 'occupied' by new forms of the logistical and infrastructural economy (Oliveira et al, 2020), but it also produces severe environmental, social and urban consequences in several geographical contexts (Wiig and Silver, 2019; Munir and Khayyam, 2020;

Ruwanpura et al, 2020; Apostolopoulou, 2021a; 2021b; Zheng et al, 2021; Apostolopoulou et al, 2023; Safina et al, 2023; Valz Gris, 2023).

In light of this, the focus of this chapter is to understand the relationships between global infrastructures and urbanization processes, and whether and how the *global infrastructure turn* (and the BRI in particular) can be 'part of, and can illuminate understanding of, extensive, uneven and fragmentary global urbanisation' (Kanai and Schindler, 2022, p 1599). With this in mind, the chapter concentrates on what happens on the ground in order to identify and detect the signs (and reasons) of the urban, the differentiations underway and the various processes and outcomes that are emerging in the global infrastructure race taking place in Southern Europe and, more specifically, in the ports of Trieste and Piraeus.

Although Piraeus and Trieste are located far from each other, they are also very close, united by the current reconfiguration of maritime trade linked to the increase in flows (of goods, services and people) along the Adriatic-Ionian macro-region as well as across the stretch of the Mediterranean that European policies call the 'Adriatic-Ionian Motorway of the Sea'. The latter was planned as a continuation of the Baltic-Adriatic Corridor, which, overland, connects the northern Adriatic region with northern Europe.[1] European Union documents use a simplified, abstract and a-spatial image to describe this maritime route where there are no conflicts, differences, friction or inequalities, but only exchanges, transport operations, logistics platforms, telecommunications, trade, flows, efficient and convenient relationships and links, an increase in investments, and opportunities to directly promote regional development and 'getting the territory right' (Schindler and Kanai, 2021).

To illuminate the 'dark side' of the corridor (Scholvin, 2021), we use the term 'Adriatic Corridor' critically in order to illustrate its composite and fragmentary configuration (Figure 10.1) and the complex and non-linear relationships established between global flows, political and economic factors of development, and the multiple forms of urbanization they generate. This enables us to also demolish a dual and only ostensibly contrary interpretation of infrastructure megaprojects when the latter 'alight' in specific contexts. On the one hand, this interpretation considers them as homogeneous and standardized spaces, marked by the reiteration of the set-ups and automation of uses (Easterling, 2014; LeCavalier, 2016; Lyster, 2016; Young, 2019) and, on the other, as fluid entities whose primary specificity is dynamism, material inconsistency and the absence of inertia, in other words a sort of amalgam redesigning 'the surface of the earth as a smooth, continuous matrix that effectively binds the increasingly disparate elements of our environment together' (Wall, 1999, p 247).

In both cases, when the focus is on the material nature of the spaces generated by global infrastructures – for example, ports and, more

Figure 10.1: Adriatic Corridor

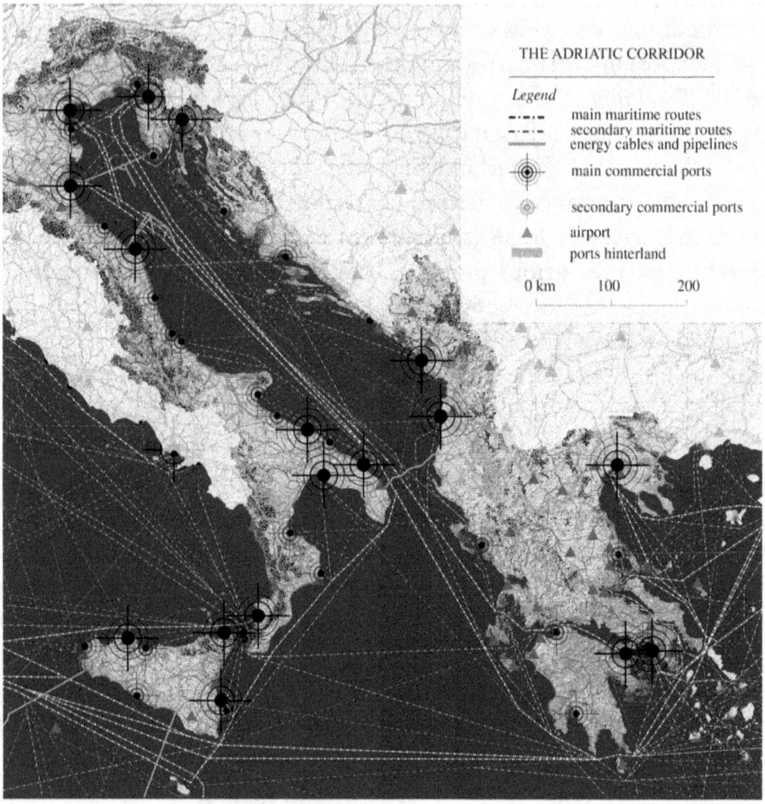

Source: Map elaborated by Leonardo Ramondetti

generally, logistics platforms – all the complex processes that have led to their construction appear to dissolve. On the contrary, along the Adriatic Corridor, and in particular coincident with the main ports of access to Central Europe – Athens, Rijeka, Trieste – these new international investments intersect the pre-existing trajectories of development; these spaces, policies and local and national socioeconomic dynamics have an enormous impact on the nature of change and profoundly influence the specific outcomes of the global turn to infrastructure. If we study this issue starting with the friction present in local contexts, we notice only part of the effects that are produced; above all, it does little to allow us to observe the transformations underway vis-à-vis broader, structuring infrastructural set-ups – that maelstrom of urbanization made up of 'supply zones, impact zones, sacrifice zones, and logistics corridors' (Brenner and Katsikis, 2018, p 24) that repositions and reconceptualizes the nature and status of the urban (Brenner and Schmidt, 2014; 2015).

Global China in Piraeus and Trieste

In the last fifteen years there has been an incremental increase in the presence of the state-owned enterprise China Ocean Shipping Company (COSCO) in Piraeus. The Chinese presence dates to 2009, the year in which its subsidiary Piraeus Container Terminal was awarded the management of the port container terminals operating on Pier II and the construction of the new Pier III as part of a 35-year concession agreement involving an investment of more than EUR 250 million (Psaraftis and Pallis, 2012). This led to a doubling of container traffic in the port to 6.2 million twenty-foot equivalent units (Piraeus Port Authority, 2021). Later on, due to the effects of the economic crisis in Greece and consequent bailout loan imposed by the European Commission, the European Central Bank and the International Monetary Fund, the Greek government decided to privatize state goods and services (Gialis and Herod, 2013), including the national railway system, the clean water supply, several energy sectors and big infrastructure nodes such as airports and ports. As regards the latter, it also included 51 per cent of the shares of the Piraeus Port Authority, which had been publicly owned. The privatization took place in 2016 after an open tender process in which only COSCO participated; its offer of EUR 280 million included the expansion of the port and a gradual increase in the participation of the Chinese company (Tsimonis et al, 2023). As a result, in 2021 COSCO invested another EUR 90 million, marking a gradual takeover of the Piraeus Port Authority, which is responsible for the management of the port's infrastructure. This made COSCO the biggest shareholder, with 67 per cent of the shares, but also the key player in the management and expansion of the port. Since then, COSCO has drafted several projects with respect to this commitment. At the time of writing, some have not been launched yet – for example, Container Pier IV – while others are being implemented – for example, a 60 ha cruise terminal that was approved in 2011 and backed by a EUR 120 million financing by the European Union, but has been indeterminately suspended due to a decision by the Greek Council of State regarding the lack of an environmental impact assessment and escalating protests by the local population. Overall, the takeover and increase in the direct control of the port by actors directly identifiable with China has meant that the port of Piraeus is perceived and promoted as the 'Dragon Head' (Brînză, 2016), referring to it being not only a hub for the European market, but also an outpost for the expansion of Chinese trade. It is worth noting, however, how this takeover occurred in the aftermath of the Greek debt crisis, highlighting how specific sociopolitical conditions may or may not lead to the entrance of foreign actors in strategic infrastructural assemblages such as ports.

The Port of Trieste is considered as being the main terminal regarding penetration into Europe by Chinese actors along the Adriatic Corridor. Nevertheless, unlike the Greek hub, Chinese protagonism is less obvious in this Italian port; this is the result of very difficult political and economic negotiations that are still ongoing at the time of writing. Since the mid-2000s, several Chinese companies have not only shown an interest in ports along the Adriatic, especially Taranto and Venice, but have also invested in them, without, however, there being any formal agreements (Canesi, 2019). In the memorandum of understanding between Italy and China (March 2019), Trieste is indicated by the government of the Asian country as a privileged hub. During that same period, a delegation of the China Communications Construction Company (CCCC) signed an agreement with the Trieste Port Authority involving Italian companies in pilot projects in the ports of Guangzhou and Jiangsu and the dry ports of Shanghai, Ningbo and Shenzen. The same Chinese company is also earmarked to build warehouses in the port of Trieste as well as modernize railway infrastructures, more specifically creating a link with the intermodal platform in Košiče in Slovakia, run by the CCCC as part of the Balkan supply route. Despite the initial enthusiasm, investments continued to languish, and two years had to pass before the CCCC made a small contribution of EUR 30 million to the construction of a railway link. In the meantime, the Port Authority launched a tender for the concession of a multipurpose terminal; the tender was awarded to the German company Hamburger Hafen und Logistik AG (HHLA). This outcome was so unexpected that it has been considered either an attempt by major European operators to stem Chinese expansionism in the Mediterranean or, conversely, as part of a strategy jointly planned with COSCO which, that same year, took over 35 per cent of the shares of the Container Terminal Tollerot in Hamburg, owned by the German terminal operator. While waiting for more massive investments by the Chinese, between 2019 and 2023 European authorities (through the Next Generation EU Plan), national governments (Italy and Hungary) and private companies (for example, British American Tobacco, Arvedi and HHLA; AdSP MAO, 2021) poured EUR 500 million into the Trieste hub. On the one hand, it is difficult to determine whether these investments come from funds or actors who are in some way linked to China or whether, on the contrary, they are an attempt by Western government agencies and European logistics operators to reclaim the biggest terminals that provide access to the continent, and are therefore 'actions to counter' the BRI. On the other hand, it is not easy to understand whether China is interested in investing in the port. In June 2022, the fourth China-Europe Land-Sea Express Line was inaugurated, connecting the port of Trieste to Velenje in Slovenia, where the general European headquarters of Hisense, a multinational Chinese company that manufactures household appliances, is located. In December 2023, however, the recently elected Italian government formally interrupted the country's participation in the BRI by not renewing the memorandum of understanding signed in March 2019. It is worth noting that Italy has been the first and only G7 member to sign a Belt and Road memorandum of understanding with China, and the decision to halt this agreement occurred in a moment of heightened geopolitical tension. If this is the case, then these factors would appear to preclude major Chinese investments in Europe and curb the Chinese protagonism that had characterized the season of Piraeus.

What we do notice regarding the development of the port of Trieste and the Italian political-economic context is that the BRI has worked in a more hushed and under-the-radar manner than it has done in Piraeus, where the takeover performed by COSCO has sought to establish full control over the port's infrastructures.

Actions performed in Trieste are a better example of a recent and different phase of Chinese foreign policy, resulting from alleged internal economic travails in the post-pandemic scenario and an international geopolitical situation which the West considers unfavourable to China (Schindler and Di Carlo, 2022). Geopolitical competition towards achieving network centrality in the context of the so-called Second Cold War sees energy and logistics infrastructure as a leading terrain of confrontation between the United States and China (Schindler et al, 2023). Given the network-based articulation of competition that differentiates the Cold War from the Second Cold War and the deep interconnectedness of these two economies, many countries will likely maintain infrastructural integration with both. This will likely occur in conjunction with the evolving sociopolitical conditions specific to each. In Trieste, the BRI is anything but non-existent, not only for its prominence in the press and public debate – and therefore in influencing political choices – but much more tangibly, albeit not within a precise institutional framework, due to the way in which it continuously appears and disappears in the implementation of specific projects. The multiple and uncertain occurrences of BRI-led investments and counter-investments in Trieste can be assumed to pertain to this attempt at obtaining, governing and maintaining centrality in global networks of production and circulation.

Port logistics

The more or less explicit presence of the BRI, and the heterogeneous nature of the actors and forms of investment, have modified the ports of the Adriatic Corridor and led to multiple logistics configurations. This is primarily due to the different roles that the ports of Piraeus and Trieste play as part of global trade and supply chains, for both their geographic position and their historical development trajectories: Piraeus, situated in the centre of the Mediterranean, close to the Suez Canal, is the last port of call for the unloading of containers from large ships arriving from the East to smaller feeder ships bound for European ports; Trieste, instead, is the hub between the maritime routes and the continental railway network (TEN-T).

The spatial transformations triggered by the BRI tend to intersect these trajectories and exacerbate this diversity. In Piraeus, Chinese funds were poured primarily into the construction of a platform specialized in transhipment operations. Between 2011 and 2014, COSCO renovated Pier II and built Pier III, creating an automated 40 ha infrastructure for moving containers. This expansion led to a 236 per cent increase in the volume of trade between 2011 and 2019, making Piraeus one of the most important container handling ports in the Mediterranean (Eurostat, 2022). Despite this significant expansion, the enormous increase in the volume of traffic bound for Europe means that this infrastructure is currently considered undersized. This is why in 2019 the Piraeus Port Authority proposed the construction of a fourth container pier, already envisaged in the port's master plan presented in 2011 and published in 2018. As mentioned earlier, this expansion is still very far off and impracticable due to its position in the port, marked by potential negative interactions with the environment and sociopolitical objections that in the past have emerged in this urban context. Nevertheless, several attempts to try and organize collaboration between the Greek administrations and Chinese companies are still ongoing as regards the construction of the Piraeus dry port and the enhancement of links with Europe through the Balkans (Shopov, 2022). This strategy hinges on the development of the railway link built in 2013 to connect the Neo Ikonio port area and its piers with the Thriasio Logistics Centre in the municipality of Aspropyrgos. The Thriasio Logistics Centre project dates to the early 2000s; it was built in stages in the next decade thanks to a EUR 180 million financing package by the European Union which envisaged that the platform could be managed by private companies (European Commission, 2017). Today, due to ineffectual concession agreements and multiple tenders that were declared null and void, most of the logistics centre remains unused. Speculation that COSCO may invest in the logistics area has been ongoing; however, to date there have been no concrete actions given the lack of an official statement of interest by the Chinese company. The piers in Piraeus and the Thriasio Logistics Centre are emblematic examples of a massive infrastructure intended to facilitate global flows thanks to the investment of huge capitals in the construction of specialized platforms.

In contrast, the numerous investments and multiple interests in the port of Trieste have reinforced its vocation as a composite hub that serves RO-RO, container traffic, and solid and liquid bulk cargo flows; it also hosts the Transalpine Pipeline Terminal, one of the most important European energy infrastructures for the handling of oil. However, terminal operators and freight forwarders share common interests, one of which is the efficiency

Figure 10.2: Trieste Port, Dock 5, May 2022

Source: Photograph by Leonardo Ramondetti

of the mobility system (Figure 10.2). The involvement of the CCCC has kickstarted a series of investments to boost the railway network, which is becoming increasingly widespread and far-reaching and re-activating disused rail links. Today, 56 per cent of container traffic and 29 per cent of the RO-RO traffic uses this network – in other words, roughly a hundred trains a week transporting goods to Central Europe (Assoporti, 2022). This enhancement continues in step with the modernization of logistics platforms, which takes place chiefly through forms of public-private partnership. The enlargement of Pier VII is emblematic. The project, already envisaged for 2014, laid stagnant until January 2021, when the consortium led by the German HHLA took over the wood yard and part of the reclaimed area of the former Servola steel mill; its aim was to build a new multipurpose terminal suitable for general cargo, containers and RO-RO. Similar interventions were performed on most of the wharfs. These include: the last stretch of the Navigable Canal, where a company controlled by the Hungarian government has reclaimed 32 ha and is building a new maritime terminal with a direct link to the railway; Pier V, where intermodal cranes have been installed to boost RO-RO traffic; the Pier VII container platform, which is being enlarged; and the quay belonging to the Arvedi steelworks, where new lifting equipment has been installed for the unloading of solid bulk cargo (AdSP MAO, 2021; see Figure 10.2). All this work has led to the construction of a mixed logistics platform that can be used by different kinds of traffic and is closely connected to the Central European logistic-production system.

New urbanizations

The spatial configurations of the ports of Trieste and Piraeus and the more or less strong presence of actors clearly traceable to China create different relationships with their local contexts, thus generating new and different urbanizations.

From 2012 to 2025, there have been several moments of friction with the community living in the urban space around Piraeus port (Tsimonis et al, 2023); this friction has often become public knowledge, not only due to numerous unions' demands, but also due to disputes against the enlargement of the terminals (Neilson, 2019). If we look beyond the boundaries of the port, we notice important implications caused by the logistics area in the plain of Aspropopyrgos, 12 km north of the hub. In recent years, many of the auxiliary functions of the port have been located here. Warehouses belonging to multinational companies such as Procter & Gamble, AstraZeneca and Estée Lauder have established offices in the northern part of the plain, while the central area is occupied by container storage sites and industrial buildings used by local entrepreneurs as production sites. These spaces have been characterized by irregularities and deregulation in the property market, unauthorized constructions and non-compliant uses of the land; this has led to the creation of a fragmented territory with empty spaces, unused areas and unsupervised zones (Mavrakis et al, 2015). The informal economies required to enable logistics to function flourish in these 'cracks', in particular: repair workshops, unauthorized spaces for the storage of containers and trucks, retail sales of spare parts and informal scrap metal landfills (Figure 10.3). Piraeus and Aspropyrgos are therefore two 'faces' complementary to the BRI: the first is emblematic of a massive and well-organized infrastructurization; the second is a complementary and 'delocalised' logistic environment governed by spontaneity, deregulation and improvisation (Safina, 2025).

Different kinds of changes are taking place in Trieste: the hub intends to capture global trade flows in order to activate the onsite processing of products in transit, thus slowing down the flow of goods and enhancing the emergence of manufacturing companies. To achieve this goal, the development of both the port area and dry port is implemented by grafting production activities onto the logistics platform, also thanks to fiscal aid. A perfect example is British American Tobacco, which has opened offices in the logistic-production area known as FREEeste. FREEeste was created in 2019 and is managed as a free point regime by the Interporto di Trieste spa, an investee of the Port Authority. This space (9,000 square metres) was previously occupied by the Wärtsilä marine engine factory, currently in crisis; British American Tobacco has now rented it as a storage area and place to produce pharmaceuticals. This transition reflects the industrial reconversion underway in Trieste, where traditional manufacturing companies are vacating

Figure 10.3: Container stocking in Aspropyrgos, June 2022

Source: Photograph by Astrid Safina

their premises, which are then being used for specialized processing as part of global chains. The Arvedi steelworks is another example of this trend. In 2017 the company dismantled its blast furnace and reconverted its steel activities into lower environmental impact productions that take advantage of the logistics support in order to be integrated into large-scale processing chains. The new British American Tobacco factory and the Arvedi steelworks are only two of the numerous examples reflecting the integrated logistics-manufacturing development currently underway in Trieste. This process has speeded up enormously since 2015, when the Port Authority took control of the organization that manages the industrial area next to the port, and it has been further facilitated by local government agencies which have created research institutes and technological centres to support the enterprises.

Piraeus and Trieste reflect the diverse relationships that the economies and transformations promoted by the BRI have established in the surrounding areas. Although different, they highlight aspects of 'logistics in action' (Chua et al, 2018) – in other words, the way in which smooth and rugged spaces, friction and facilitation, inefficiencies and hard work can influence territories, turning the latter into an integral part of global value chains.

Conclusion

Using the ports of Piraeus and Trieste to study the BRI allows us to identify at least three possible research topics with which to continue our considerations. First, it enables us to reflect on the persistence and the frequent deterioration of socio-spatial imbalances in local contexts where large international investments produce an impact – that is, investments which, through the BRI, claim to result in coherent, efficient and positive outcomes in terms of development and connectivity. Second, we can discuss the solidity and resistance of the mix between large-scale infrastructures and local contexts, a now 'classical' topic in urban studies, illustrating in particular to what extent the contradictions and aporiae of the infrastructural regime involve many different places. Finally, it is possible to observe the great variety of arrangements and initiatives that the BRI appears to assume and promote, and to theorize this variety as a feature that is neither haphazard nor instrumental, but functional to its global reach and intersecting with specific sociopolitical conditions and development trajectories. These different research trajectories schematically recall three issues: the urban role of the global infrastructure turn; the deflagration and partialization of development processes in incoherent trajectories (and as such not attributable to the effects of a single global initiative); the BRI as a 'revealing' construct capable of displaying multiplicity and variety by using a continuous interplay of references between the whole and the part, the general and the specific.

Piraeus and Trieste are both close and far; in many ways they function in a similar manner, but their configurations and uses are very different. The aim is not so much, or not only, to identify possible recurrent features or, on the contrary, highlight the many new phenomena and spaces that are generated, but to understand the incredible force and important implications of a transformation process which, by impacting on specific sites, displays its own inevitable differentiations and takes on an anything but monolithic character. The variety of forms and activities that make up the logistics machinery of the two ports does in fact give rise to a constellation that is anything but linear and unitary in its spaces and functions, conflicts and uses; it also sparks a gradual increase in the range of investments, complex management, unstable employment, and expansion towards the sea and hinterland, multiplying and diversifying environmental problems. Although the spaces in the ports are compact, well-defined and independent, designed to allow an efficient circulation of goods and people, in practice they sprawl beyond the 'enclosures' of the ports: their relationships, uses, functions, markets and economies – big and small, local and international, institutional and marginal, legal and illegal – belong to a new and different urban status. Considered from this viewpoint, the logistics machinery is itself part of a bigger 'urban machine' and transcalar process which, on the one hand, exhibits the socio-spatial imbalances in which ports find themselves and, on the other, helps to investigate the spatial complexity of value chains focused on the extraction of resources, integrated logistics and industrial production.

Apostolopoulou (2021a, p 832) writes: 'the BRI involves almost everything: from railways, airports, ports, pipelines, industrial parks, special economic zones (SEZs), real estate and commercial projects, to free trade agreements and treatise to boost foreign investment and market liberalisation'. 'From the ground', from Piraeus to Trieste – and probably in all the other places involved in the 'project of the century' – this 'almost anything' multiplies and diversifies further. The BRI is no longer a single initiative, but a plurality of routes, processes and projects that are varyingly complex depending on the many contexts in which they are implemented. Nevertheless, this variety and diversification is neither by chance nor unintentional, nor does it derive exclusively from the encounter/collision with the ground. As emphasized by Murton (2021, p 274), there is no official map of the BRI, but 'an array of maps depicting a usefully approximate but inexact network of roads, rails, sea lanes and other infrastructures'. Murton maintains that in this series of maps and visualizations, the issue at stake is obviously the role of the maps and the political 'silence' of the maps, as well as the variety of meanings of the BRI as a unitary project. At the same time, the BRI – better still, several projects linked to it – involve certain specific places, even though the latter are impossible to map and identify before something 'takes place' in them.

The BRI is neither a clearly defined plan nor a coherent strategy. It is a general idea, an offering, a sort of platform that varies depending on several agendas, ambitions and moments (at various spatial scales). The BRI is also a label useful to trigger infrastructure projects and development; it is used by several actors for different purposes. At the same time, it is a problematic label, as demonstrated by the port of Trieste and the few results officially obtained on the ground. The general features of the BRI are vague; they do not cope well with the unfolding of events or comparison with the material nature of transformations. This uncertainty and malleability of the BRI is its strong point; the BRI yields, hides, re-emerges and reveals processes which would otherwise be more implicit. If it involves a project, the BRI is a sort of 'deductive project' that does not exist beforehand and can be materially (as well as theoretically) pinpointed only when and where it takes place – perhaps even when there is no explicit reference to the BRI, but there was in the past, or vice versa. While the imagery and material manifestations of the BRI can be studied, they also involve urban processes – actors, interests, dynamics and so on – that go beyond and precede the BRI. Examining these situations that either move beyond or accompany the BRI can help us to not only reorient research on the BRI, quite apart from the role and the real or alleged exceptionality of China within the global infrastructure regime, but also concentrate on the problems that an infrastructure-led development regime poses to urban research (Kanai and Schindler, 2022).

The variegated urban geographies assembled by the Adriatic Corridor are a productive vantage point to observe the multiple registers of the BRI as it enters its second decade of development. In both Trieste and Piraeus, the BRI's 'spatial trilectics' – as discourse, materiality and experience – located by Cheng and Apostolopoulou (2023), demonstrate intermittent and dynamic overlays through both successful and failed attempts at adapting to local sociopolitical and spatial conditions. In Piraeus, the massive sell-out of publicly owned services during the post-2009 austerity era has been caught by COSCO as an opportunity for assuming almost total control of the port infrastructure. This has offered the chance to translate the BRI discourse into both a materialized infrastructure and a lived experience along these infrastructures. Quite the opposite happened in Trieste, where, despite the prominent discourse in the form of BRI memorandum of understanding, opportunities remained rather limited for CCCC, which, as a result, has searched for other ways and varied opportunities for gaining space in and around the port. At the same time, the materiality of COSCO's proxy presence in Trieste via its shares in Hamburg's Container Terminal Tollerot does not seem to require any discourse. Observed from the ground, the BRI's radical contingency seems to force its multiple registers to chase each other constantly.

Finally, the specific sociomaterial assemblages showcased by the Adriatic Corridor demands that urban geographic research on the BRI exceeds the BRI itself. Looking through the lens of Trieste in particular, and through the multiple international operators attempting to find their share of its port's infrastructures, the BRI appears as only one of the competing projects within a global infrastructure-led development regime. As we observe its presence as discourse, materiality and lived experience oscillating, sometimes in cooperation and sometimes in conflict with other global infrastructure projects, the BRI resembles a kaleidoscope rather than a monolith.

Note

[1] Within the framework of the Trans-European Networks in transport (TEN-T), energy (TEN-E) and telecommunications (eTEN), the term used in European Transport policy documents for maritime infrastructures is 'Motorways of the Sea', coined and used for the first time in the Treaty of Göteborg in 2001. As part of these policies, the Adriatic-Ionian Marine Motorway involves the countries present in this macro-region: Albania, Bosnia-Herzegovina, Croatia, Greece, Italy, Montenegro, Serbia and Slovenia.

References

Apostolopoulou, E. (2021a) A novel geographical research agenda on Silk Road urbanization, *The Geographical Journal*, 187(4), 386–93.

Apostolopoulou, E. (2021b) Tracing the links between infrastructure-led development, urban transformation, and inequality in China's Belt and Road Initiative, *Antipode*, 53(3), 831–58.

Apostolopoulou, E., Cheng, H., Silver, J. and Wiig, A. (2023) Cities on the New Silk Road: the global urban geographies of China's Belt and Road Initiative, *Urban Geography*, advance online publication. doi: 10.1080/02723638.2023.2247283

Assoporti (2022) Annual statistics. Available at: www.assoporti.it/it/autorita sistemaportuale/statistiche/statistiche-annuali-complessive

AdSP MAO (Autorità di Sistema Portuale del Mar Adriatico Orientale) (2021) Piano Operativo Triennale 2022-2024. Available at: https://trasparenza.porto.trieste.it/archivio19_regolamenti_0_4035.html

Brenner, N. and Schmidt, C. (2014) The 'urban age' in question, *International Journal of Urban and Regional Research*, 38(3), 731–55.

Brenner, N. and Schmidt, C. (2015) Towards a new epistemology of the urban? *City*, 19 (2–3), 151–82.

Brenner, N. and Katsikis, N. (2018) Operational landscapes: hinterlands of the capitalocene, *AD Architectural Design*, 90(1), 22–31.

Brînză, A. (2016) How a Greek port became a Chinese 'dragon head', *The Diplomat*. Available at: https://thediplomat.com/2016/04/how-a-greek-port-became-a-chinese-dragon-head/

Canesi, M. (2019) *Il Mezzogiorno e i suoi porti: la chiave di una nuova prospettiva di sviluppo*, FrancoAngeli.

Cheng, H. and Apostolopoulou, E. (2023) Locating the Belt and Road Initiative's spatial trilectics, *Geography Compass*, 17(4), art e12683. doi: 10.1111/gec3.12683

Chua, C., Danyluk, M., Cowen, D. and Khalili, L. (2018) Introduction: turbulent circulation: building a critical engagement with logistics, *Environment and Planning D: Society and Space*, 36(4), 617–29.

Easterling, K. (2014) *Extrastatecraft: The Power of Infrastructure Space*, Verso.

European Commission (2017) Thriasio Pedio freight complex to shift goods transport from road to rail, 20 December. Available at: https://ec.europa.eu/regional_policy/en/projects/greece/thriasio-pedio-freight-complex-to-shift-goods-transport-from-road-to-rail

Eurostat (2022) Top 20 ports – volume (in TEUs) of containers handled in each port, by loading status (main ports). Available at: http://data.europa.eu/88u/dataset/tGGldfQh9KVDwUOqRF30GA (accessed 5 June 2023).

Gialis, S.E. and Herod, A. (2013) Resisting austerity: the case of Greece: powerworkers and steelworkers, *Human Geography*, 6(2), 98–115.

Kanai, J.M. and Schindler, S. (2022) Infrastructure-led development and the peri-urban question: furthering crossover comparisons, *Urban Studies*, 59(8), 1597–617.

LeCavalier, J. (2016) *The Rule of Logistics: Walmart and the Architecture of Fulfillment*, University of Minnesota Press.

Lyster, C. (2016) *Learning from Logistics: How Networks Change Our Cities*, Birkhäuser.

Mavrakis, A., Papavasileiou, C. and Salvati, L. (2015) Towards (un)sustainable urban growth? Industrial development, land-use, soil depletion and climate aridity in a Greek agro-forest area, *Journal of Arid Environments*, 121, 1– 6.

Munir, R. and Khayam, U. (2020) Ecological corridors? The case of China-Pakistan economic corridor, *Geoforum*, 117, 281–84.

Murton, G. (2021) Power of blank spaces: a critical cartography of China's Belt and Road Initiative, *Asia Pacific Viewpoint*, 62(3), 274–80.

Neilson, B. (2019) Precarious in Piraeus: on the making of labour insecurity in a port concession, *Globalizations*, 16(4), 559–74.

Oliveira, G.L.T., Murton, G., Rippa, A., Harlan, T. and Yang, Y. (2020) China's Belt and Road Initiative: views from the ground, *Political Geography*, art 102225. doi: 10.1016/j.polgeo.2020.102225

Piraeus Port Authority (2021) Piraeus Port Annual Financial Report. Available at: www.annualreports.com/Company/piraeus-port-authority

Psaraftis, H.N. and Pallis, A.A. (2012) Concession of the Piraeus container terminal: turbulent times and the quest for competitiveness, *Maritime Policy & Management*, 39(1), 27–43.

Ruwanpura, K., Rowe, P. and Chan, L. (2020) Of bombs and belts: exploring potential ruptures within China's Belt and Road Initiative in Sri Lanka, *The Geographical Journal*, 186(3), 339–45.

Safina, A. (2025) The (in) visible face of global infrastructures: an exploration of logistics and informality from the ground up, *Environment and Planning D: Society and Space*, advance online publication. doi: 10.1177/02637758251319671

Safina, A., Ramondetti, L. and Governa, F. (2023) Rescaling the Belt and Road Initiative in urban China: the local complexities of a global project, *Area Development and Policy*, advance online publication. doi: 10.1080/23792949.2023.2174888

Schindler, S. and Kanai, J.M. (2021) Getting the territory right: infrastructure-led development and the re-emergence of spatial planning strategies, *Regional Studies*, 55(1), 40–51.

Schindler, S. and DiCarlo, J. (2022) Towards a critical geopolitics of China–US rivalry: pericentricity, regional conflicts and transnational connections, *Area*, 54(4), 638–45.

Schindler, S., Alami, I., DiCarlo, J., Jepson, N., Rolf, S., Bayırbağ, M.K. et al (2023) The Second Cold War: US-China Competition for Centrality in Infrastructure, Digital, Production, and Finance Networks, *Geopolitics*, advance online publication. doi: 10.1080/14650045.2023.2253432

Scholvin, S. (2021) Getting the territory wrong: the dark side of development corridors, *Area Development and Policy*, 6(4), 441–50.

Shopov, V. (2022) *Mapping China's Rise in the Western Balkans*, European Council on Foreign Relations. Available at: https://ecfr.eu/special/china-balkans/

Tsimonis, K., Giannoulou, A. and Frantzeskaki, A. (2023) Piraeus versos COSCO, *Global China Pulse*, 1(2), 96–103.

Turner, C. (2021) *The Infrastructured State: Territoriality and the National Infrastructure System*, Edward Elgar Publishing.

Valz Gris, A. (2023) Beyond the boom: genealogies of corridor urbanism in the making of the lithium triangle, Argentina and Chile, *Geoforum*, 147, art 103913. doi: 10.1016/j.geoforum.2023.103913

Wall, A. (1999) Programming the urban surface, in J. Corner (ed) *Recovering Landscapes*, Princeton Architectural Press, pp 232–49.

Wiig, A. and Silver, J. (2019) Turbulent presents, precarious futures: urbanization and the deployment of global infrastructure, *Regional Studies*, 53(6), 912–23.

Young, L. (2019) Neo-machine: architecture without people, *AD Architectural Design*, 89(1), 6–13.

Zheng, H.W., Bouzarovski, S., Knuth, S., Panteli, M., Schindler, S., Ward, K. and Williams, J. (2021) Interrogating China's global urban presence, *Geopolitics*, advance online publication. doi: 10.1080/14650045.2021.1901084

11

Capitalizing on the Logistical Future: Discounting Uncertainty in the Georgian Belt and Road Initiative

Evelina Gambino

It's September 2019 and my research assistant, Sopo, and I are in the village of Anaklia, West Georgia. We are walking along a large dirt path with houses and allotments on each side. Roughly 500 metres from the junction that links this path with the central part of the village, the sequence of houses is interrupted abruptly by a 4 metre tall wall of black sand, preceded by a metal fence. This is the edge of what used to be the building site for Anaklia Deep Sea Port. Commonly referred to as 'the project of the century' this port was set to become capable of hosting the biggest container ships in circulation and destined to turn Anaklia, and of course, Georgia, into a transit hub with global reach. Back in November 2018, the mass of dark sand was dredged from the sea to strengthen the existing soil, too damp to provide strong foundations for the future port, and left to rest there, waiting to be compacted into the ground, before moving on to the next phase of the works. This phase, however, never started. Today, the building site stands abandoned after the company in charge of its development failed to secure enough investment to proceed. This failure is looming over the village as a thick coat of uncertainty and doubt about the future of the development and the accomplishment of its promise of prosperity. Towards the end of the summer in 2019 strong winds arrived in the village, lifting the loose sand that lay on the top of the abandoned building site, and for days on end the houses rising in the proximity of the territory were inundated by this thick dust, infiltrating every corner and spoiling the immaculate bedding in private homes and hotels awaiting for tourists.[1]

Figure 11.1: Anaklia Port building site, 2018

Source: Photograph by the author

Between 2017 and 2019, I conducted ethnographic fieldwork in Anaklia, initially mapping the development of the port and its impact on the local community and, eventually, observing the demise of this project. This was followed by two shorter research visits in the spring and autumn of 2023. On 27 November 2024, Georgia's minister for economic development, Levan Davitashvili, announced that the port of Anaklia will be ready in 2029 (Agenda.ge, 2024). This announcement came four and a half years after Davitashvili's predecessor, a member of the same ruling party, announced the demise of the previous attempt to build Anaklia Deep Sea Port after a protracted crisis involving the government and the company in charge of the project, Anaklia Development Consortium (ADC). In the wake of a new wave of investment in Anaklia, this chapter builds on the fieldwork I undertook during the previous attempt to build the port in order to read the promise of logistical connectivity organizing Georgia's developmental horizon against its grain. In doing so, I take the port's failure as a standpoint. The project I studied, Anaklia Deep Sea Port, was understood to be vital for the country's transformation into a transit corridor and an element of the Belt and Road Initiative (BRI) that would forge new connections between Europe and Asia. Yet its success was never certain. Competition between different corridors is at the heart of the BRI (Wiig and Silver, 2019), and each physical infrastructure depends on a complex entanglement of (im)material infrastructures – concessions, contracts, synchronization of data and practices and so on – to become operative. Developmental promises attached to logistics are thus resting on shaky and often unpredictable grounds (Carse and Kneas, 2019). By tracing the events that led to the demise of the Anaklia Deep Sea Port project, I explore the gap between the futuristic visions attached to logistical developments in Georgia and their (im)material conditions of existence. In the wake of the port's failure, it is possible to observe the uneven ways in which the inevitable uncertainty of the future is discounted on different actors (Gambino, 2024).

A layering of projects

The village of Anaklia lies at the northwestern edge of the Republic of Georgia in the South Caucasus, only a few kilometres from Abkhazia, a de facto state and site of multiple conflicts since the collapse of the Soviet Union. This small settlement is set to become a transit node for goods and people, aimed at positioning Georgia as a key juncture among global logistics networks. Between 2015 and 2019, the infrastructural development of this site, was conducted through a public-private partnership between the Georgian government and the ADC, a multinational corporation composed of Georgia's largest private Bank – TBC – and the US company Conti Group. The corporation was awarded a 52-year concession to build and later operate the deep-sea port. Alongside this infrastructure, ADC was granted the freehold of 550 ha of land adjacent to the port territory to develop a special economic zone and a smart city (ADC, 2017). At the time of its attempted construction, it was understood that the port would become a key hub of the BRI's Middle Corridor; however, the recent developments in Anaklia exist in relation to a much longer history of Georgia's attempt to become a transit corridor.

The BRI in Georgia – like in many of the other countries tied together through its extensive networks – is *overwritten* onto the country's infrastructural history and translated through pre-existing developmental visions and geopolitical relations (Frederiksen, 2013; see also Akhter, 2018; Gambino, 2019). This overwriting is both discursive and material and needs to be taken in account when understanding its effects on specific locations (Rekhviashvili and Lang, 2024, p 6). In the wake of the Soviet Union's collapse, Eduard Shevardnadze, the second president of independent Georgia and former foreign minister of the USSR, set out to reposition Georgia within geometries of power emerging from the dismantling of Soviet territory. Shevardnadze's plan, in his own worlds, was to establish a land bridge between the easternmost parts of the former Union and Europe, a project that he themed the 'Great Silk Way' (Shevardnadze, 1999). Indeed, the idea of a Great Silk Way was first presented during his time as USSR minister of foreign affairs, in 1990 at Vladivostok International Conference (Gorshkov and Bagaturia, 2001). At the time, the Silk Road represented a vision of a new political horizon for countries that were shaking off the remains of the crumbling Soviet Union. Through rail connections, the enhancement of roads and maritime routes as well as the development of pipeline systems to effectively transport

Figure 11.2: Map of Georgia's key transit infrastructure

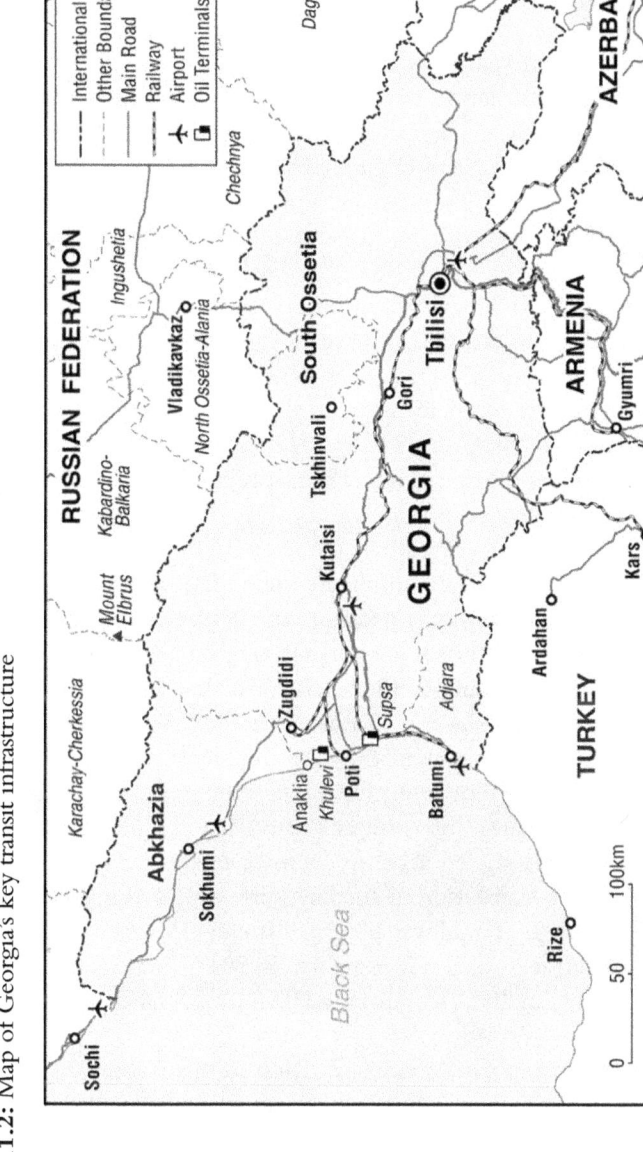

gas and oil from the Caucasian and Central Asian fields to Europe, the Great Silk Road provided a framework for economic as well as political cooperation between Eurasian countries. In 1993, this vision concretized into a transnational transport corridor sponsored by the European Union: the Transport Corridor Europe-Caucasus-Asia (TRACECA). The corridor, which includes 13 Commonwealth of Independent States countries, has since its inception secured funding from the World Bank and the European Bank for Reconstruction and Development, and it has provided a framework within which mega transnational projects, such as the development of the oil fields in Baku and the construction of the Baku-Supsa and Baku-Tbilisi-Ceyhan pipelines, has taken place. Three decades after Shevardnadze's vision was first outlined, and in the aftermath of an intensification of the conflict between Russia and the West, Xi Jinping's description of the BRI similarly stresses the ability of transit infrastructure to foster not just economic but social and cultural ties between East and West (National Development and Reform Commission, 2015). In June 2018, accords between the TRACECA and the BRI were stipulated to include the pre-existing framework of cooperation as part of the new politics of corridors set to shape BRI logistics.

The BRI places fair competition as the chief mechanism organising cargo mobilities across global space (Silver, 2021; see also World Bank, 2019). Envisaged as a series of multinational transit highways, logistical corridors are created as assemblages of public and private entities working together to streamline such competing flows (Arvis et al, 2014; Grappi, 2016, pp 178–82). Georgia had already nominally joined the BRI in 2015, but it is not included in any of the six corridors of the BRI. Instead, it aims to plug itself within these transnational networks through the Middle Corridor – a spin-off of the BRI's China-Central Asia-West Asia Economic Corridor. However, over the years, this corridor has struggled to establish itself (Nihjar, 2024). This is in part because of the bureaucratic hurdles attached to the synchronization of different countries' transit regimes and in part because of the lack of suitable transit infrastructure across the countries that compose it. In 2017, Georgia signed a comprehensive free trade agreement with China and began construction of Anaklia Port, which – together with the Baku-Tbilisi-Kars (BTK) railway passing through Georgia's south-western Samtske-Javakheti region, also inaugurated in 2017 – was set to address the country's infrastructural shortcomings and finally materialize its long-awaited transit future.

The recent history of Anaklia testifies to the accretive nature of Georgia's infrastructural regime and the twists and turns through which the relationship between the country and the BRI has taken shape. In its short life, Anaklia Deep Sea Port was commonly known as the 'project of the century', capable of catapulting the country into prosperity. In the aftermath of the port's failure, however, this *futurism* attached to the project (Pels, 2015) was transferred onto other infrastructures. Two highway developments have interchangeably been referred as projects of the century: the Rikoti highway in West Georgia and the North-South Corridor connecting Georgia with Russia (Ocakli and Ibele, 2023; Smolnik, 2023). Unlike the Anaklia project and the BTK, which aimed to attract Chinese investment after their completion, Chinese companies are in charge of construction of both highway projects, which count the Asian Infrastructure Investment Bank among their stakeholders (Rekhviashvili and Lang, 2024). Developed as public-private partnerships, these two developments thus mark an intensification of Chinese investment in Georgia. In July 2023, moreover, China and Georgia signed a strategic partnership agreement (Chinese Embassy in Georgia, 2023). The agreement, which comes in the aftermath of Putin's full-scale invasion of Ukraine in 2022, promises to strengthen the cooperation between the two countries beyond the economic realm. The document states that 'Georgia believes that Chinese modernization offers a new path and a new option for mankind to achieve modernization' (Chinese Embassy in Georgia, 2023, p 1), thus explicitly recasting Georgia's logistical developmental transformation within the framework of this cooperation. As the Russia's war in Ukraine complicated Europe-China trade connectivity through Russia, the so-called Middle Corridor has seen a remarkable increase in traffic. That has led the Georgian government to reclaim the Anaklia Port project once more in 2022, this time promising to keep a majority stake in the deep-sea project (Georgia Today, 2022). The call for tender was announced in summer 2023. In spring 2024, the ruling party Georgian Dream announced that a Chinese-Singaporean consortium led by China Communication Construction Company Limited had been awarded the contract, and the preliminary works for a new port started in the autumn of 2024. The announcement came after the signing of a memorandum especially addressing Chinese-Georgian cooperation on the Middle Corridor and is understood as marking Georgia's pivot towards China (Akhmedova and Gelashvili, 2024).

A layering of projects and projections makes up the recent history of Georgia's attempt to turn itself into a transit corridor for goods and resources (Barry and Gambino, 2024). Going through this developmental palimpsest, the 'project of the century' that I observed during my fieldwork appears as little more than a stitch in the larger tapestry of Georgia's developmental trajectory towards being a transit corridor. Yet, as new projects replace old ones and alliances are strengthened and contested, who is left to deal with the debris left behind by the seemingly endless trials and errors? Zooming into the story of Anaklia's failure allows us to see the labour that sustains accreted infrastructural projections and to make visible the uneven distribution of the damage that their failures inflict.

Figure 11.3: The abandoned port territory from Lela's window

Source: Photograph by the author

A materialized bet on the future

Staring at the sand mound marking the beginning of the abandoned port territory during my last visit to Anaklia in 2019, I remembered the words of one of the ADC managers; describing the ongoing works in October 2018, she said: 'We are making mountains!' Rather than terrestrial mountains, the tall plateaus were more reminiscent of lunar landscapes, smooth and lifeless. It is as if an inverted process of terraforming had taken place, remodelling the earth to look like an alien planet, rather than vice versa. Though apparently immovable, these extra-terrestrial mounds had been interacting with their surroundings, infiltrating their environment. That afternoon, we followed Lela, one of the inhabitants of this last stretch of the road, into her house. Peeking into every room of her sandy place, the dust appeared to me as an index of the deeper processes that have affected the life of the Anaklians since the beginning of the port's construction: pervasive, toxic and unexpected, the soot polluted newly built hotels and old structures alike, as a reminder of the unpredictability of the village's future, but also of the material impacts of each of the failed investments that have marked this place.

Not long before this visit to Lela's house, in the autumn of 2018, I was standing on top of that sand mound, led by ADC's deputy CEO on a tour of the port's building site. During this visit, beyond showing me the site, the deputy CEO explained to me the different state-of-the-art technologies that the firms employed by the Consortium were using and how these would be implemented across the nine phases of port construction. As our meeting drew to an end, he declared that when the port is built, 'logistics in Georgia will become faster, cheaper and more efficient for everyone, from the local winemaker from Kakheti[2] to large shipping companies. Everything will be accessible and streamlined … the sky is the limit!' This hyperbolic statement is indicative of the attitude I observed throughout my fieldwork in Anaklia when I sat through a variety of meetings chaired by the ADC to present their project to different publics – potential investors, affected communities, students, foreign diplomats, experts – and this was also evident in the promotional material published by the company that I collected and analysed. Across these events, Anaklia was presented by its developers and the government alike as the jewel of Georgia's infrastructural portfolio and a gateway to an infinite range of trade connections and opportunities, finally concretizing Georgia's century-long calling to become a corridor uniting East and West.

Yet, it is clear from its demise that the success of the port's developmental promise was never a certainty. Rather, as stipulated in the public-private partnership between the government and the ADC, the project's success was predicated on the consortium's ability to attract enough capital to pay for the construction of its infrastructure. In the context of ADC's attempted capitalization of their future infrastructure, therefore, the 'doability' of the project was inextricably connected with its projected ability to deliver profits over the medium term. Once developed, a large port is not dissimilar in its revenue model from a large real estate project, as the developers acquire their profits from different forms of rent. These vary from the 'route making' contracts that need to be stipulated with shipping companies (Khalili 2020) to the leases on berths, storage and office facilities, to a range of collateral activities that need to take place within the bounds of the port, such as ticket offices, insurance companies, food joints and others. A thriving port is a variegated enclave of lifeworlds, all of which need to slot into place in order to turn the space into a competitive hub amid the myriad of logistics routes that cross the neighbouring regions. Before proving to the nation its ability to transform the future, therefore, Anaklia port would need to demonstrate its 'investability'.

In his most recent work, Timothy Mitchell introduces his analysis of the notion of capitalization (Mitchell, in Abourahme and Jabary-Salamanca, 2016[3]; Mitchell, 2020). Capitalization is a common term in the financial world, but for Mitchell, it provides a way to address a particular relation to the future that he deems to be defining of contemporary financialized capitalism. Building on the work of political economists Jonathan Nitzan and Simon Bichler, Mitchell describes capitalization as a 'particular way of rendering the future available in the present' in order to extract profits from it (Mitchell, in Abourahme and Jabary-Salamanca, 2016, p 740; Nitzan and Bichler, 2009, p 212). Specifically, by building long-lasting structures, such as infrastructures, companies are able to tax their future use by selling future profits to present shareholders. Companies are, thus, able to operate by virtue of their promise to deliver profits to the investors that support them. The materiality of the infrastructures around which capitalization emerges is at the centre of Mitchell's account. The capacity of physical infrastructures to last in time allows contemporary investors to claim a degree of control over the future into which the infrastructure's durability is stretched – in other words, it allows them to harvest a time that does not yet exist to produce earnings for present investors. In its bid to capitalize Anaklia Port, ADC needed to prove it could build the material infrastructure *and* be able to turn it into a *durable structure of accumulation*.

How can a project that hasn't been built yet guarantee its ability to become a durable structure of accumulation while also competing against an infinite number of present and future projects? The answer we get from observing the development and failure of Anaklia port is simple: it can't. Projects like the one set up to transform Anaklia are thus always 'a materialised bet' on the future (Chua, 2021, p 78). This is because markets, especially when understood on a planetary scale, are a volatile and unpredictable realm, influenced by global geopolitical crises and environmental events and within which investors, rather than relying on competitiveness as a form of self-regulation, take all sorts of measures to shield themselves from the harsh consequences of a bad investment.

The labour of contracts

To manage and contain the inherent volatility of markets, beside relying on their material durability, large infrastructure projects, as Mitchell suggests, have historically relied on another type of durability: 'a form of political or legal guarantee' (Mitchell, 2020). Within the logic of free market competition that ostensibly organizes the logistical corridors part of the BRI, the risks for the investors can be very high. A deep-sea port on one of the possible routes of the New Silk Road does not just need to exist and be able to last in order to be used; it needs to be able to secure cargo traffic – through exclusive contracts with logistical operators and through clients to populate its berths – and to become a cog in a much bigger logistical network by establishing agreements with other infrastructures, governments and transnational institutions. Building a material infrastructure, in substance, is only one part of the labour of making it profitable; the rest depends on the establishment *of an infrastructure of a different kind*, one made of the agreements, regulations, quality certifications and diplomatic and corporate relations necessary to assemble logistical connectivity (Gambino, 2019). As Nitzan and Bichler insist, 'in society, the future contains an element of novelty, and novelty cannot be pre-assigned a probability: it is unique and therefore inherently *uncertain*' (2009, p 197). Therefore, it is necessary to not only construct a durable system of revenue through steel and iron, but also secure 'political control' over the infrastructure and its networks (Nitzan and Bichler, 2009, p 180; Mitchell, in Abourahme and Jabary-Salamanca 2016, p 742). To attract investors, therefore, the ADC needed to prove they had the capacity to politically, economically and *logistically* control the future, *even though that cannot be done.*

In January 2020, the Georgian government finally severed its contract with ADC, citing the company's inability to secure enough investment to complete the project. This was the culmination of a controversy that had started a year earlier, through which the Anaklia project became an element of a wider political situation (Barry, 2013). In August 2018, an inquiry into the co-founders of ADC, Mamuka Khazaradze and Badri Japaridze, was launched by the General Prosecutor Office of Georgia. The duo was accused of money laundering in 2008. As it progressed, Khazaradze's case was deemed by several observers to be a politically motivated attack at the hands of billionaire and former Prime Minister Bidzina Ivanishvili, who was also the chair of the ruling party, Georgian Dream. Months before the investigation, Ivanishvili, who had stepped down as prime minister in 2013, announced his return to politics. In June 2018, Kvirikashvili, then prime minister and fierce proponent of the Anaklia project, stepped down from his position, citing disagreements with Ivanishvili. In short, Anaklia had become entangled in the struggle of national political elites.

This sudden removal of political guarantees for Anaklia Port exposed the delicate balance of power between the nation-state and private corporations, which must be finessed to sustain a multinational project. The controversy over the port shows the work necessary to secure the financial stability of the port into the future (Gambino, 2021, pp 134–8). In 2019, the Georgian government made in public that the ADC had missed several deadlines to secure the necessary investments to fund the port construction and was, therefore, at risk of breaching its contract. In order to resolve the situation, potential investors, including the European Bank for Reconstruction and Development, AIB and the Overseas Private Investment Corporation, met with the consortium and the government to attempt to reach an agreement. After several meetings where no agreement was reached, then Minister of Infrastructure Maia Tskitishvili held a press conference to clarify the government's position. The investors had listed eight preconditions for their involvement, ranging from compliance with 'state of the art' environmental regulations to financial agreements. After prolonged negotiations, the government accepted most of these preconditions; however, a critical one remained unaddressed: the ADC and the banks demanded that the government would act as a guarantor of the infrastructure's profits in case of the port's inability to attract sufficient cargo flows. In other words, if market competition failed, state intervention would be required to protect the investors' profits. This demand, according to Tskitishvili, could not be met by the government, as it would imply that the entire risk of the project would fall on the state's shoulders: 'what is the point of private entrepreneurship if all the risk falls on the taxpayers?' Tskitishvili asked in a press conference (Civil.ge, 2019). In response to these statements, the ADC accused the state of boycotting Anaklia Port. The issue remained unresolved and led to the demise of ADC's project.

There is a 'modularity' to infrastructural projects (Appel, 2019, p 152). Observing this modularity from one place, we see the arteries of larger projects. Multiple accounts of transnational capitalist ventures have documented how political stability is pivotal to guarantee steady profits (Easterling, 2014; Appel, 2019). Crucially, the sudden removal of political guarantees from under Anaklia Port exposed the fragility of its projected capitalization. Predictions of competitiveness, which appeared to be paramount to Anaklia's success, were not enough to reassure potential investors, who instead demanded absolute certainty of future profits. This, rather than being an exception, is the norm. What is unusual was Tskitishvili's reaction. By vocally rejecting the unilateral discounting of risk demanded by the company and international banks, Maia Tskitishvili exposed the work that contracts do in guaranteeing and replicating investors profits *at all costs*.

Contracts, as many have pointed out, are the foundations on which contemporary capitalism rests, and the hinges between its different scales (Palan, 2006, p 85; Appel, 2019, p 150). As Hannah Appel details in *The Licit Life of Capitalism*, contracts are devised to shield international corporations from the risks of extracting value, and in their modular and repeatable form, they populate the distance between the unknowns of extractive frontiers and the offices of corporations, placing the state and its citizens as fodder for risk. As one of Appel's informants stated: 'In order to attract foreign investment, we had to really make things easy'. (Appel, 2019, p 157) It is for this reason that countries such as Equatorial Guinea, where Appel did her fieldwork, pride themselves on being *'the most flexible fiscal environment in the world'* (ibid, original emphasis) and Georgia's high ranking in the Ease of Doing Business index is elevated by its successive governments to the status of a development goal.

Contracts, as Appel suggests, are *aspirational*. They are instruments through which 'complex and unknowable' places like Georgia can aspire to forms of 'capitalism in their own image' (Appel, 2019, p 170). In the aftermath of the rescinding of the contract between the ADC and the Georgian government, the company declared its intention to take the matter to the international court. In an article titled: 'Arbitrations are not a good look for Georgia', a fellow of the Centre for European Policy Analysis in Washington stated that 'the Anaklia saga undermines Georgia's security by damaging its reputation as a safe place to invest' (Zallinger, 2020). Undoubtedly unbeknownst to the him, Zallinger's affirmation shines an unflattering light on the kind of development that projects such as Anaklia seek to materialize. The security that Zallinger is referring to – that throughout the article is referred to as 'Georgia's security' – is in fact not the physical and economic security of Georgia's populations, but the security of a future of guaranteed profits, a capitalized future (Mitchell, 2020). For international commentors like Zallinger, the Anaklia crisis is a clear sign that the Georgian government might not be able to guarantee the political control of the future necessary for international capital to thrive (Nitzan and Bichler, 2009, p 212). However, Zallinger's critique proves to be useful in revealing the *kind* of work that contracts do in discounting the risks connected to large developmental projects back onto the populations they allegedly seek to uplift (Rekhviashvili and Gambino, 2024).

When Anaklia port is described as 'the project of the century', one is tempted to forget that what is being described is an object that does not yet exist, and is likely to never exist (cf Günel, 2019, p 71). Unlike this futuristic denomination, the conditions stipulated by the contract show that developers and investors are well aware of the volatility of the future and sought to protect themselves from their consequences. In calling for an ethnography of infrastructure, Star once argued that infrastructures are systems that underwrite and sustain our worlds, yet

Figure 11.4: The abandoned port territory, April 2023

Source: Photograph by the author

they are invisible until they breakdown (Star, 1999; see also Harvey and Knox, 2012, p 529). It is beyond this chapter's remit to adjudicate the motives behind the Georgian government's rejection of the contract terms sustaining the Anaklia project. Before and after the rescinding of Anaklia's contract, the same government has been known to happily sponsor projects underwriting similar, if not worse, contractual conditions (Rekhviashvili, 2022), suggesting that rather than a rebellion against the geometries of power sanctioned by transnational capitalism, the Anaklia crisis might have its roots elsewhere. However, observing the demise of Anaklia shows us the work that immaterial infrastructures such as contracts do in sustaining the inequal power relations and forms of extraction that shape contemporary projects of accumulation. Despite being paper thin, contracts act as sturdy barriers, designed to shield investors and corporations from the mercurial workings of markets, effectively discounting the unpredictability of the future impacting on local populations and the environments they inhabit.

Conclusion

If capitalization is material, so are its failures. In the spring of 2023, I returned to Anaklia. Four years after I first observed the sand from the abandoned port territory seeping into the houses that surrounded it, I am told that despite several attempts, when the winds blows towards the village, it is impossible to fully protect those living closest to the port. In these years, however, people have had to adapt to living with the abandoned port. No longer an impenetrable expanse, now dirt roads allow cars to travel across it and cattle has started roaming on it. The wetland has reclaimed portions of the territory and some migratory birds visit it on their way to the nearby Kholketi National Park. But this slow transformation is abruptly interrupted by the new wave of development set to transform this territory. Neither the failure, nor the re-activation of the project to turn Anaklia into a transit hub are exceptional. Rather across the globe, megaprojects have been proven to be systematically 'over budget, over time, over and over again' (Flyvbjerg, 2011). As projects are abandoned and reassembled in quasi-cyclical ways, however, failures and their consequences often slide through the gap between new and old projections. In describing the thick black dust blowing from the abandoned port territory and depositing itself on the shiny surfaces of new hotels at the beginning of this chapter, I sought to bring failure into view, drawing from it questions to interrogate future projects. On whose shoulders – eyes, lungs – does failure rest? Following the demise of the Anaklia Deep Sea Port project, it appears that populations and environments were always meant to sustain potential risks on behalf of investors. The present eeriness of the abandoned port can thus be considered as an index of the unevenness that underwrites infrastructure-led development. While a new project is on its way, promising to finally materialize a future of logistical connectivity and prosperity, it is imperative to *stay with* previous failures, bringing to light those who have been left to pick up the pieces each time and why.

Notes

[1] In the following years, the sand kept plaguing Anaklia, carried by the strong seasonal winds and infiltrating buildings all over the town.
[2] This region in South-East Georgia is famous for its wineries.
[3] In this long interview with Abourahme and Jabary-Salamanca, Timothy Mitchell outlines his conceptualization of the relation between infrastructures and time mediated by capitalization (Abourahme and Jabary-Salamanca, 2016).

References

Abourahme, N. and Jabary-Salamanca, O. (2016) Thinking against the sovereignty of the concept, *City*, 20(5), 737–54.

ADC (Anaklia Development Consortium) (2017) The Anaklia Port Project, *Anaklia Development Consortium*. Available at: http://Anakliadevelopment.Com/Info/

Agenda.ge (2024) Georgian PM: gov't 'fully supports' One Belt One Road, Middle Corridor initiatives. Available at: https://agenda.ge/en/news/2023/3055#gsc.tab=0

Akhmedova, A. and Gelashvili, K. (2024) Impact of Chinese investment in Anaklia: strategic implications for Georgia and Europe, *China Observers in Central and Eastern Europe (CHOICE)*. Available at: https://chinaobservers.eu/impact-of-chinese-investment-in-anaklia-strategic-implications-for-georgia-and-europe/

Akhter, M. (2018) Geopolitics of the Belt and Road: space, state, and capital in China and Pakistan, *Logistical Asia: The Labour of Making a World Region*, 221–41.

Appel, H. (2019) *The Licit Life of Capitalism*, Duke University Press.

Arvis, J.F., Saslavsky, D., Ojala, L., Shepherd, B., Busch, C. and Raj, A. (2014) *Connecting to Compete 2014: Trade Logistics in the Global Economy: The Logistics Performance Index and Its Indicators*, The World Bank.

Barry, A. (2013) *Material Politics: Disputes along the Pipeline*, Wiley-Blackwell.

Barry, A. and Gambino, E. (2024) Projects of transition, *Economy and Society*, 53(3), 351–75.

Carse, A. and Kneas, D. (2019) Unbuilt and unfinished: the temporalities of infrastructure, *Environment and Society*, 10, 9–28.

Chinese Embassy in Georgia (2023) Full text: Joint Statement of the People's Republic of China and Georgia on Establishing a Strategic Partnership. Available at: http://ge.china-embassy.gov.cn/eng/xwdt/202308/t20230807_11123383.htm

Chua, C. (2021) Indurable monstrosities, in C. Benvegnú, N. Cuppini, M. Frapporti, E. Gambino, F. Millesi, I. Peano and M. Pirone (eds) *Gendering Logistics: Feminist Approaches for the Analysis of Supply-Chain Capitalism*, University of Bologna Press, pp 75–93.

Civil.ge (2019) Government, developer, investors meet on Anaklia Port Project financing, 23 May. Available at: https://civil.ge/archives/306472

Easterling, K. (2014) *Extrastatecraft: The Power of Infrastructure Space*, Verso.

Flyvbjerg, B. (2011) Over budget, over time, over and over again: managing major projects, in P.W.G. Morris, J. Pinto and J. Söderlund (eds) *The Oxford Handbook of Project Management*, Oxford University Press.

Frederiksen, M.D. (2013) *Young Men, Time and Boredom in the Republic of Georgia*, Temple University Press.

Gambino, E. (2019) The Georgian logistics revolution: questioning seamlessness across the New Silk Road, *Work Organisation, Labour & Globalisation*, 13(1), 190–206.

Gambino, E. (2021) *(Re)Producing the Logistical Future: Ethnography, Infrastructure and the Making of Georgia's Global Connections*, PhD Thesis, University of London.

Gambino, E. (2024) Domesticating logistical futures: a grounded account of failure, *Environment and Planning D: Society and Space*, 43(1), 181–204.

Georgia Today (2022) PM: Anaklia Port is to be built with co-participation of state, whereby 51% will be owned by state by our decision, *Georgia Today*, 13 December. Available at: https://georgiatoday.ge/pm-anaklia-port-is-to-be-built-with-co-participation-of-state-whereby-51-will-be-owned-by-state-by-our-decision/

Gorshkov, T. and Bagaturia, G. (2001) TRACECA—restoration of Silk Route, *Japan Railway and Transport Review*, 28, 50–5.

Grappi, G. (2016) *Logistica*, Ediesse Edizioni.

Günel, G. (2019) *Spaceship in the desert: Energy, Climate Change, and Urban Design in Abu Dhabi*, Duke University Press.

Harvey, P. and Knox, H. (2012) The enchantments of infrastructure, *Mobilities*, 7(4), 521–36.

Khalili, L. (2020) *Sinews of War and Trade*, Verso.

Mitchell, T. (2020) Infrastructures work on time, *Eflux*. Available at: www.e-flux.com/architecture/new-silk-roads/312596/infrastructures-work-on-time/

National Development and Reform Commission People's Republic of China (2015) Vision and actions on jointly building Silk Road Economic Belt and 21st-century Maritime Silk Road. Available at: http://En.Ndrc.Gov.Cn/Newsrelease/201503/T20150330_669367.Html

Nihjar, M. (2024) Challenges and considerations: a realistic look at the Middle Corridor's potential, *ODI*. Available at: https://odi.org/en/insights/challenges-and-considerations-a-realistic-look-at-the-middle-corridors-potential/

Nitzan, J. and Bichler, S. (2009) *Capital As Power: A Study of Order and Creorder*, Routledge.

Ocaklı, B. and Ibele, B. (2023) Georgia's modern (not so environmental) problems: the nature of road and energy infrastructures, in N. Mörner (ed) *Ecological Concerns in Transition: A Comparative Study on Responses to Waste and Environmental Destruction in the Region*, CBEES State of the Region Report, Södertörns högskola, pp 73–83.

Palan, R. (2006) *The Offshore World: Sovereign Markets, Virtual Places, and Nomad Millionaires*, Cornell University Press.

Pels, P. (2015) Modern times: Seven steps toward an anthropology of the future. *Current Anthropology*, 56(6), 779–96.

Rekhviashvili, L. (2022) *Struggle for Rioni Valley in between Civil and Political Society Terrains: Contested Infrastructures and Development Politics*, Heinrich Boell Foundation South Caucasus Regional Office. Available at: https://ge.boell.org/sites/default/files/2022-12/rioni_valley_struggle.pdf

Rekhviashvili, L. and Gambino, E. (2024) Failed infrastructure and the promise of development in Georgia, *Second Cold War Observatory*. Available at: www.secondcoldwarobservatory.com/dispatch-2024-4

Rekhviashvili, L. and Lang, T. (2024) Chinese investments as part of infrastructure-led development: multi-scalar contestations around Georgia's flagship infrastructure projects, *Eurasian Geography and Economics*. doi: 10.1080/15387216.2024.2311712

Shevardnadze, E. (1999) აბრეშუმის გზა: *TRACECA. PETRA. ევროპა–კავკასია–აზიის სატრანსპორტო დერეფანი. საერთო ბაზარი. პოლიტიკური და ეკონომიკური ასპექტები*. [Silk Road: TRACECA. PETRA. Europe-Caucasus-Asia Transport Corridor. Open Market. Political And Economic Aspects], National Library Archive.

Silver, J. (2021) Corridor urbanism, in M. Lancione and C. McFarlane (eds) *Global Urbanism*, Routledge, pp 251–8.

Smolnik, F. (2023) Dis/connectivity in the South Caucasus: Imaginaries, the Effects of Power, Ambivalences, SWP Research Paper No. 9/2023, Stiftung Wissenschaft und Politik.

Star, S.L. (1999) The ethnography of infrastructure, *American Behavioral Scientist*, 43(3), 377–91.

Wiig, A. and Silver, J. (2019) Turbulent presents, precarious futures: urbanization and the deployment of global infrastructure, *Regional Studies*, 53(6), 912–23.

World Bank (2019) *Belt and Road Economics: Opportunities and Risks of Transport Corridors*, The World Bank.

Zallinger, B. (2020) Arbitrations are not a good look for Georgia, *Eurasianet*, 10 August. Available at: https://eurasianet.org/perspectives-arbitrations-are-not-a-good-look-for-georgia

12

Infrastructure-Led Development, Urban Transformation and Inequality in China's Belt and Road Initiative: A Marxist Postcolonial Geographies Analysis

Elia Apostolopoulou

Introduction

In this chapter,[1] I aim to explore the intricate connections between infrastructure-led development, urban transformation and inequality within China's Belt and Road Initiative (BRI). By conceptualizing the BRI as primarily a spatial fix (Harvey, 2016) to the overaccumulation issues inherent in Chinese capitalism, I foreground urbanization as a critical process while considering the dialectical interplay between the territorial and capitalist logics of power (Gramsci, 1971; Harvey, 2005; Lee et al, 2018). Adopting the lens of Marxist postcolonial geographies (Hart, 2006; 2018; Apostolopoulou, 2021a), my goal is to provide a nuanced, relational analysis of diverse trajectories of socio-spatial urban change driven by BRI projects in different cities across the Global South and North with the goal being to understand how the New Silk Road is profoundly reconfiguring the urban geographies of the 21st century.

Examining how the BRI is poised to reshape the production of local urban space and the geographies of everyday life, this chapter aims to contribute to the burgeoning field of critical geographical scholarship on the urban aspects of the New Silk Road (see, for example, Wiig and Silver, 2019; Williams et al, 2020; Apostolopoulou, 2021a; 2021b; Smith, 2022; Zheng et al, 2023) while also engaging with broader research on post-crisis neoliberal urbanism

Figure 12.1: Piraeus port, Lipasmata redevelopment area, Athens, Greece

Source: Photograph by Elia Apostolopoulou

and the uneven production of urban space (Lefebvre, 1974; Castells, 1977; 2011; Massey, 1994; Smith, 2008; Christophers, 2011; Theodore et al, 2011; Harvey, 2012; Brenner, 2019). The empirical material that underpins my analysis is derived from extensive primary research, including both on-the-ground and virtual ethnography and numerous interviews with policy makers, workers involved in BRI projects and local activists, as well as document analysis of governmental reports and online sources focused on three cities: Athens (Greece), Colombo (Sri Lanka) and London (United Kingdom). These cities were selected for their strategic significance in the BRI's urban reconfiguration, encompassing new transport infrastructure, real estate projects and special economic zones, and because they show well how the BRI's infrastructural ambitions may (or may not) materialize both discursively and materially. Moreover, each city has a rich history of urban community activism, which has been sidelined to legitimize the reimagining of urban space. By analysing these dynamics, I hope to illuminate the socio-spatial and socio-environmental impacts of large-scale infrastructure initiatives like the BRI and the ways in which urban transformations are being shaped by global geo-economic/geopolitical imperatives, national political agendas and local resistances.

The central argument I aim to advance is that urban transformation driven by the BRI engenders both new urban formations and new urban politics that reconfigure urban space and transform the urban and social geographies of cities by creating, facilitating or exacerbating spatial fragmentation and social segregation. Despite the varied expressions across different contexts, the BRI-driven deepening of urban marginality and social inequality in diverse places across the Global South and North also opens the potential for new spatial resistances and local-global alliances. These dynamics generate novel possibilities for socio-spatial and socio-environmental change, challenging the hegemonic narratives of development and offering pathways towards more equitable urban futures.

Infrastructure-led development, urbanization and postcolonial geographies in the New Silk Road

The BRI was launched with the key goal of revitalizing economic growth by facilitating geographical restructuring and expansion. Over time, it has become an exemplary case of the near-global hegemony of infrastructure-led development, acting as a major spatial fix to capital's global overaccumulation crisis (Marx, 1887; Harvey, 2016; Summers, 2016; see also Bond's chapter in this volume). From the outset, urban development was accorded an upgraded role within the BRI, primarily due to its capacity to absorb surpluses that would otherwise be devalued (Lefebvre, 1974; Smith, 2008; Christophers, 2011; Harvey, 2018). This process usually involves a combination of surplus capital seeking productive investment, surplus commodities searching for buyers and surplus labour power looking for productive employment (Ekers and Prudham, 2017). Indeed, since 2013, China has invested billions in BRI projects to absorb capital and labour surpluses, redirecting its domestic overcapacity and capital towards infrastructure and urban development. The initiative facilitated the exportation of products such as steel, cement and aluminium to support the construction of overseas infrastructure, including railways, ports, highways, malls and housing. This strategy allowed Chinese goods and services to penetrate new overseas markets, aligning with the objectives outlined in the 13th Five-Year Plan (2016–20). Moreover, the BRI provided opportunities to improve trade relations with Southeast Asia, Central Asia and Europe. By channelling surplus resources into international infrastructure projects, the BRI aims not only to alleviate domestic economic pressures but also to extend China's influence through the construction of critical transport and trade networks that would support the integration of regional economies with China's, creating dependencies that reinforce China's centrality in global trade.

Cities have been attributed a central role in achieving the BRI's primary goal of reterritorialization through increased connectivity (Flint and Zhu, 2019; Apostolopoulou et al, 2023). The organization of the initiative around six main corridors illustrates this well, reflecting an effort to integrate subnational urban systems into transnational territories via networked infrastructure megaprojects (Schindler and Kanai, 2019). The 'Belt' component is designed to facilitate land-based integration of Central Asian, African and European techno-territorial constellations through newly constructed rail and road corridors. Meanwhile, the 'Road' component targets the maritime regions of Southeast and South Asia, the Middle East, East Africa and the Mediterranean by building or expanding ports to establish a maritime corridor. The key role of urban nodes is underscored by the BRI's Vision document, which emphasizes major cities within China, including port construction in coastal cities and international airports in Shanghai and Guangzhou. This focus on strategic urban investments supports a spatial paradigm that reproduces hegemonic capitalist developmental ideas (Summers, 2016). In essence, the aim of such initiatives – at least in theory – is to reconfigure urban spaces and socioeconomic landscapes by integrating local urban systems into a global network of trade and infrastructure. This strategy has the potential not only to enhance connectivity but also to reinforce the economic and political influence of participating regions within the broader framework of global capitalism. An emphasis on urban nodes highlights the dual role of cities as both hubs of connectivity and focal points of economic activity.

Nonetheless, acknowledging the BRI as a spatial fix should not lead to an underestimation of its territorial and geopolitical dimensions. The territorial and capitalist logics of power, though distinctive, are deeply intertwined (Harvey, 2005). While the BRI's primary drivers may be found in political economy, the revival of the Silk Road undoubtedly aims to advance China's regional and international influence, especially in the context of a polycrisis and US decline hegemony. Importantly, the BRI is not only a class-based development project enlisting Chinese capitalists across its route (Lee et al, 2018), but operates within the balance of class power in recipient countries (Olinga-Shannon et al, 2019). The geopolitical aspect of the BRI is thus mediated by local power dynamics and hegemonic politics along its corridors. The latter is evident in all the three cities that inspire the analysis in this chapter – Athens, Colombo, and London – along with the importance of social contestation against contentious infrastructural megaprojects.

These dynamics are crucial when examining how specific projects reconfigure urban geographies, recalibrate local economies and influence the (re)making of places, socionatures and the geographies of everyday life. In the next section, by employing a relational comparison (Hart, 2006), I aim to demonstrate how developments in different cities are the products of intertwined socio-spatial processes that exhibit both remarkable convergences and divergences. As Hart (2018) explains, relational comparison is grounded in Lefebvrian conceptions of the production of space, place and scale. Places are conceptualized as nodal points of connection within broader networks of socially produced space, embodying what Massey (1994) refers to as an extroverted sense of place. Urban spaces are thus viewed as articulated moments in intricate networks of social relations, socio-spatial trajectories, histories, experiences and understandings, many of which are constructed on scales that transcend the boundaries of each city (Massey, 1994). This approach is instrumental in dismantling methodological nationalism (Goswami, 2002) and aligns with both postcolonial comparative urbanism (Schmid et al, 2018) and countertopography (Katz, 2011). By invoking unexpected connections among disparate places, it facilitates the production of spatialized abstractions necessary for understanding the diverse ways the BRI reshapes urban space across the Global South and North. This analytical lens enables a nuanced understanding of how infrastructural investments are not merely economic or geopolitical undertakings but are deeply embedded in the political and social fabric of the cities they touch, highlighting how global initiatives like the BRI are locally manifested, producing interconnected yet unique urban experiences.

A tale of three cities

Albert Royal Docks: building a (Chinese) city within the City of London
'Silk Road freight train from China arrives in Barking' is the title of a BBC article published back in January 2017 to refer to the arrival of the first train from Yiwu, a trading centre in China's east coast, to London in 18 days to deliver Chinese goods. This is one of the longest distance freight rail routes from China to Europe and forms part of BRI's Eurasian Land Bridge. Three months later, within the context of escalating debate about the UK's post-Brexit future, the first UK-to-Yiwu export train departed from DP World London Gateway's terminal carrying UK products. The UK minister for trade policy characterized the new rail link as a boost for 'Global Britain' and a 'great step' for DP World's GBP 1.5 billion London Gateway Port, noting that following the ancient Silk Road trade route would carry British products around the world. The Chairman of Yiwu Timex Industrial Investment Co was also present at the inauguration to celebrate the Silk Road's restoration as a means by which China, North Europe and now the UK could exchange goods. The railway terminal has been a component of DP World London Gateway, a fully integrated logistics facility that opened in 2013. This comprises a deep-sea container terminal whose construction required the creation of artificial land extending 400 m beyond the shoreline, profoundly transforming Essex's coastline near Stanford-le-Hope by, inter alia, moving thousands of species 140 miles away in the biggest ever animal and habitat relocation project in the UK.

Even though the efficiency of these train routes remains a matter of controversy, it reveals a bigger story about Chinese investment in a 35 acre area at the Royal Albert Dock postindustrial site (ABP, 2017). The Albert Dock's regeneration has been supported by a major investment from Chinese developer ABP (Advanced Business Park) that aimed to transform the area into a new financial district and tech hub. The project has been discursively linked to the Yiwu-London train route and a number of transport upgrades whose importance had been repeatedly emphasized by ABP's owners, including an GBP 500 million investment in London City Airport and Crossrails' new terminals. The Albert Dock was framed as part of the wider transformation of the historical Docklands into a new 'boom town', including more than 4.7 million square feet of office, residential, retail and leisure space. The first phase of the GBP 1.7 billion development was completed in 2019 and entailed the creation of 460,000 square feet of office space across 21 new buildings. The second phase was supposed to include more offices, flats and a membership club, with the ABP hoping to create an 'Asian business port' transforming the area into London's third financial district.

As local community activists explained to me, the Royal Docks have a long history of grassroots activism against controversial regeneration plans. The dock's final closure to commercial traffic in 1981 led to massive unemployment, environmental degradation and rising social and economic inequality across East London. This marked the commencement of a regeneration programme that was met with major public opposition for ignoring social needs and local environmental conditions (Church, 1990). A significant moment in public resistance has been the formation of the People's Plan in 1983, which opposed the creation of STOLport (short take-off and landing airport; today London City Airport) while offering an alternative vision for the Docks (Brownill, 2018). The Plan expressed local communities' desire to gain democratic control over the area's future: it proposed the public ownership of land and community participation in urban planning. However, following concerns about the high proportion of public housing in the area and cuts to the housing programme under Thatcher's government, a shift towards prioritizing private sector investment gradually occurred. As involved officials stated back in 2005, looking 'too exclusively to the aspirations of the existing population' was a key problem for the area's regeneration, since investors would invest only if there was an availability of private housing. It was within this context that the London Docklands Development Corporation decided to appropriate public land and sell waterfront property to private developers, with the Toronto-based company Olympia and York taking a leading role (Henneke and Knowles, 2020) before its bankruptcy in 1993.

The ABP investment has been the latest stage in the process of market-led urban regeneration that since the 1980s mostly stood against people's demands to favour specific corporate interests. In 2013, a Development Agreement was signed between the Greater London Authority (GLA) and ABP, supported by the mayor at the time, Boris Johnson, who granted the company the tender to develop the 35-acre estate. This followed the transfer of public land to the GLAP, a commercial subsidiary of the GLA, under the Localism Act 2011. Despite the hegemonic rhetoric of transforming a 'wasteland' to a new 'global village', the agreement was criticised by grassroots groups, inter alia, due to the ABP's limited record as a real estate developer, concerns about its alleged involvement in forced evictions in Beijing and the absence of any meaningful public consultation. Local activists were critical about the company's vision to privatize and transform (public) derelict land into financial districts, smart eco-cities and elitist green enclaves. Indeed, since the agreement was signed, the area has become an enterprise and real estate zone that primarily targets leaders in high tech and wealthy investors, as the prices of available offices and nearby flats demonstrate. Importantly, the Royal Docks are one of London's opportunity areas and its only enterprise zone, formed as part of the 'war on rep tape' led by the 2011 Coalition government (Apostolopoulou and Adams, 2015). This means that it provides tax breaks and business incentives to attract foreign investment, including simplified planning procedures and business rate uplift retention for 25 years.

The regeneration project also promised to create seven new public squares and a waterfront walkway. The ABP has run several public workshops to discuss their development, but without making clear – at least when I was conducting fieldwork back in 2019–20 – who will manage these areas and which activities will be allowed. Despite the outcome of ongoing consultations, it has been obvious that Albert Dock was being transformed to a privatized public space welcoming to new enterprise communities and start-ups but hostile to public gatherings and non-commercial activities. The project, as its master planner explained, 'realises the dream of an unrivalled waterfront destination that places powerful international business alongside open public squares allowing space for relaxation and contemplation'. The new ABP development was claiming to reinvent an abandoned land by transforming it to '1,142 hectares of opportunity' for investors; its aspiration was not to simply modernize or improve a run-down area, as Hancox (2014) has aptly argued, but to wipe it out in a 'regeneration supernova'. This narrative of prosperity and employment opportunities had been powerful, especially as it was framed as the only alternative for the ethnically diverse East London, an area with one of the highest unemployment rates in the capital and which has been hit hard by austerity. It nonetheless neglected to mention that the area's regeneration was not only dispossessing the public from the potential of an open, accessible and welcoming urban space, but could also bring the displacement of low-income people, which has been a defining characteristic of gentrification processes within and beyond the Docklands. This does not only refer to physical relocation due to rising rents but also to urban marginality in an area where the collective imagination of its potential reappropriation for the people of London seems miles away from the current hegemonic regeneration narrative.

Importantly, in the summer of 2022, Mayor Sadiq Khan has removed the ABP from the development, with commentators talking about a 'wasted decade' (Donovan, 2022). At the time of writing, the plans for the Albert Royal Docks remain uncertain. A significant part of the land is already built on; however, the area resembles a 'ghost town' that can only offer a 'deserted film set for shooting the next zombie office-worker apocalypse' (Wainwright, 2022).

Piraeus port in Athens, Greece: the head of the dragon

Piraeus is the largest port in Greece. It is located around 10 km from the centre of Athens and has 37.7 km of quays and port facilities that cover four municipalities. Characterized as the 'head of the dragon' by the Chinese President Xi Jinping, Piraeus has been a key investment for China due to its strategic geographical position that renders it a gateway for Chinese products to enter Europe (Apostolopoulou, 2024). In 2008, COSCO (China Ocean Shipping Company), a Chinese state-owned shipping and logistics supplier company, obtained a 35-year concession from the Greek government to operate part of Piraeus' container terminal (Piers II and III) and established the Piraeus Container Terminal (PCT). The controversial decision to privatize Piraeus' most profitable sector was supported by major Greek shipowners who were expecting to gain favourable loan conditions from Chinese banks by agreeing to use Chinese shipyards. The concession contract included various terms that permitted COSCO to establish a hegemonic position in the market, with an indicative example being the agreement between the Piraeus Port Authority (PPA) and the PCT that no container terminal could be developed within an area of 200 km from the port without COSCO's permission. In 2016, COSCO signed an agreement with the Hellenic Republic Asset Development Fund (HRADF) to acquire the majority (67 per cent) of the PPA's shares, becoming the primary port operator. The deal was ferociously fought by trade unions and dock workers that have historically played an emblematic role in the Greek labour movement.

Similar to the Albert Dock, in response to escalating social contestation, both Greek and Chinese officials argued that transforming the port into a key BRI hub was a win-win deal that would bring jobs and prosperity, with HRADF's president stating that the day COSCO acquired the majority marked a turn of the Greek economy towards growth. What the privatization undoubtedly brought was a profound increase in the port's scale of operations: in 2017, annual throughput capacity exceeded four million twenty-foot equivalent units, an increase of over four times the capacity in 2010, making Piraeus the 36th biggest port globally and the 2nd in the Mediterranean, with media reports celebrating its 'renaissance' since its takeover from COSCO. In July 2017, during a visit of former Greek Prime Minister Alexis Tsipras to Beijing, China's president announced that Piraeus would become the largest container trans-shipment harbour in the Mediterranean, a landmark of sea-land transportation, an international logistic allocation centre and a key pivot of the BRI. Greece has been portrayed as a key communication bridge between China and the European Union and Piraeus as a 'home port' for Chinese tourists. COSCO's new plans reflected these aspirations, as described in its multimillion masterplan, which was approved by Greek authorities after a major debate with the affected communities in Piraeus. The port's new expansion, inter alia, includes an additional cruise-ship terminal, luxury hotels, a logistics centre and a shopping mall in a new artificial island that, if built, will transform the area profoundly. Importantly, Chinese investment is not limited to Piraeus; it has already transformed real estate in Athens, as evidenced in rising rents causing increasing housing insecurity for the city's low-income residents.

Despite the Chinese rhetoric of cooperation and Greek governments' reassurance that the agreement would be beneficial, empirical evidence, including my own fieldwork in the first half of the 2020s, has shown extensively that COSCO's concession has facilitated processes of accumulation, dispossession, and exploitation that extend far beyond the usual dynamics of terminal privatization (see also Neilson, 2019), exacerbating economic inequality, labour precarity and environmental injustice. It is indicative that when COSCO acquired the two Piers, at least 500 full-time workers lost their jobs through the imposition of an early retirement scheme. COSCO also used a combination of direct hiring (for 20 per cent of the workers) and subcontracting (for 80 per cent). But even the workers who are directly employed by COSCO have different employment contracts, benefits and wages than other workers in Piraeus, a common practice in work areas where collective bargaining agreements have been dismantled. Issues related to maximum working hours and health and safety regulations have also emerged, with dock workers being called to work 90 minutes before their shift and often being required to do overtime without being paid. These practices did not come as a surprise. They have been strategically used to curb trade unions' power in other cases of public asset privatization in the aftermath of the 2008 financial crash (Apostolopoulou and Adams, 2015). However, in the case of Piraeus, workers also have to deal with COSCO's top management, who are unreachable to collective demands. Piraeus' privatization has so far created a limited number of new jobs, with COSCO importing a significant part of the necessary technology from China while enjoying tax exceptions under Greek law and benefiting from Piraeus' operation as a European Commission Free Zone-Type II. Importantly, and relatedly, the environmental impacts of COSCO's operations, including a major increase in atmospheric and noise pollution that disproportionately affects the adjacent neighbourhoods, with people living in particular areas forced to tolerate 24-hour exposure to light and noise pollution, have never been seriously addressed. The expansion is further aggravating the situation and has been strongly resisted by grassroots groups for causing major accumulative environmental pressure in the area. Despite escalating opposition and amid calls from environmental NGOs that COSCO's operations are threatening Saronikos' marine ecosystems and fishing grounds as well as public health due to the release of hazardous waste in an area adjacent to primary schools, homes and playgrounds, in March 2020, despite the lockdown that had been imposed due to the COVID-19 pandemic, construction work for the new cruise terminal commenced without the approval of the Strategic Environmental Impact Assessment.

As with London's Docklands, Piraeus' history and social stratification is important for understanding what all this means for local people. The areas mostly affected – Keratsini, Drapetsona and Perama – are part of a former port-industrial zone whose emergence has been linked to an incoming wave of industrial workers and refugees in the 1930s and the expansion of poor-quality housing. Surrounding areas have been converted into working-class neighbourhoods with a record of radical community activism. Urban development eventually took the form of flat blocks due to Piraeus' transformation into an important shipping centre and the area's industrial development. However, the decline of the industrial and shipbuilding zone led to massive unemployment and abandonment. The financial crash of 2008 further hit industrial units and shipyards, causing a sharp rise in unemployment, leading many to economic despair and creating the ground for COSCO's promises to convince a part of the local community to accept the privatization. The Right-wing government promised several times that the port's expansion would be accompanied by regeneration plans, including a new international business centre and innovation hub in the municipality of Keratsini-Drapetsona, one of the five 'emblematic' projects that the new Prime Minister Kyriakos Mitsotakis announced back in 2019, echoing a type of urban regeneration similar to London's docklands that is relatively new for Greece. This consists of the creation of gentrified postindustrial enclaves in the outskirts of city centres with questionable social benefits and a high possibility to increase, instead of tackling, inequality. Regeneration promises have not so far convinced labour unions and grassroots groups, whose ongoing struggles have often been suppressed by the police. In one of my last meetings there, they reminded me that Piraeus never had suburbs desirable for the upper classes and has always been a symbol for the working class, adding that what they advocate for is social-environmental justice for one of the most emblematic areas in Athens where social and spatial inequality is inextricably linked to environmental injustice.

Colombo Port City: Sri Lanka's 'new Dubai'

Colombo Port City has been one of the most controversial infrastructure projects in Sri Lanka and was met from the beginning with local opposition. Even though the original proposal goes back to the 1990s, the project was launched in 2014 with President Rajapaksa stating in the inauguration ceremony, where the Chinese President was also present, that it is with the help from Chinese friends that the Sri Lanka people are able to make their dream come true. This followed the signing of a concession agreement between the Rajapaksa administration and China Harbour Engineering Company, a unit of the state-owned China Communications Construction Company (CCCC), which undertook the construction. Similar to Piraeus, it was agreed that Sri Lanka's government would not undertake competing infrastructure projects within a specific radius of the Port City (Gunawansa, 2018). CCCC was given the right to choose the contractor and no call for competitive bids occurred despite this being part of the official guidelines for public procurement projects (Gunawansa, 2018).

The new city is connected to Colombo Central Business District and is expected to become a key hub for the Maritime Silk Road. The expected overall investment reaches USD 15 billion, making it the largest single foreign direct investment in Sri Lanka's history. Colombo Port City, renamed the Colombo International Financial City (CIFC) by the new government at the time, has been based on a sea reclamation project that has profoundly affected Colombo's sea and landscape. This consists of five precincts: the central park, the financial district, the island living, the marina and the international island. The new city includes luxury hotels, shopping malls, high-end flats, beachfront villas, office towers, casinos, embassies and skyscrapers, with artistic impressions showing a cityscape comparable to Dubai or London's Canary Wharf. The project also includes an artificial beach and a yacht marina with water sports facilities. The city is supposed to also include public space but, as interviewees explained to me back in 2020, similar to the ABP development in London at the time of my fieldwork, there was no specific information on who would manage this space or have the right to access it, with the development's exclusive character creating concerns that access will be seriously restricted.

Foreign influence in shaping Colombo's urban future was evident before the Port City, with a primary example being the construction of luxury apartment complexes, such as the Astoria complex, a project by the Chinese state-owned Aviation Industry Corporation, located less than a mile from Colombo Port City. Astoria reflects a model of urbanism already prevalent in China: towers of luxury apartments with exclusive clubs, famous commercial brands, swimming pools and private gardens, and it is advertised as a smart investment for entering Colombo's real estate. Moreover, from 2005 to 2014, massive public investments in infrastructure, including roads, motorways, ports and airports, occurred in Sri Lanka funded by foreign loans, mostly from China. This included selling 80 per cent of Colombo's International Container Terminal, which is adjacent to the Port City, to a Chinese company. Similar to Piraeus, the privatization led to the sharp reduction of the workforce, with workers being hired from subcontractors at lower wages and with poorer labour rights. Importantly, as local activists told me, the exact details of the agreement have never been publicly available and the number of workers in the area remains unknown.

Chinese and broader foreign interest in the island nation of Sri Lanka relates to its strategic location in one of the busiest trade routes globally, offering a gateway between Southeast Asia and the Middle East, Africa and Europe. The City Port and Hambantota Port are of key importance for the BRI as major access points in the Indian Ocean. Colombo port was expected to become a maritime interchange for cargo and the CIFC an offshore financial centre operating under a British-style legal system with a new SEZ established to facilitate arbitration and settlement of international contracts, transforming the area to a financial, tourist and trade hub. Importantly, the Port City has not reflected only Chinese inspirations, but has been a key part of controversial urban regeneration plans by Sri Lanka's governments following the end of the 26-year civil war (in 2009), aiming to transform Sri Lanka into a liberalized economy open to foreign investors. These included the Western Region Megapolis and the City Beautification Program (Ruwanpura et al, 2020), whose implementation required the military's involvement and entailed mass evictions of the urban poor (Radicati, 2020), demolitions (Van Dort, 2016) and forceful slum clearance, continuing Sri Lanka's long history of displacements of low-income, multi-ethnic and multi-religious urban communities from city centres.

This context is important for understanding the opposition with which the City Port was met by grassroots groups, students, trade unionists, urban activists, fishing communities, clergy members and environmentalists from the very beginning. Despite differences among them, key issues were the environmental and social impacts of the new city with scientists and activists arguing that sand excavation would destroy Colombo's coastline, coral reefs and fishing breeding areas, posing threats of erosion and flooding to an area prone to natural disasters while also affecting the livelihoods of people living in Colombo's beaches and depending on fishing. There were also concerns about land grabbing and dispossession, inadequate compensation for lost income and housing damages, and criticism of the project's exclusive character that was expected to favour wealthy elites. Protesters also argued, as in Piraeus, that no comprehensive impact assessments had been conducted prior to the project's approval.

Amid increasing criticism, the project was temporarily suspended after the 2015 elections. The new Sirisena administration announced that the agreement would be scrutinized. However, in March 2016, within the context of a rising national external debt, a significant part of which was owed to China, and increasing recognition that reconsidering the agreement would not be financially feasible, the Sirisena administration gave permission for the project to resume citing its importance for Sri Lanka's economy and confirming that the CCCC's project was aligned with governmental aspirations (Gunawansa, 2018). Restarting the project did not remain unchallenged. An organization called the People's Movement against Port City, a coalition of fishing communities, religious leaders and civil society groups that had opposed the project from the beginning, organized several protests. In October 2016, fishing communities went on strike to protest the loss of houses and livelihoods, and in August 2017, women from fishing communities organized a protest under heavy police presence. Sri Lankan urban activists raised concerns about the CCCC's role as the 'landlord' of the Port City, and the former Urban Development Authority director stated in *The Guardian* that the Port City would be a separate entity where only a certain class of people will live (Safi, 2018). Moreover, there were increasing concerns about the impacts of the Port City on the iconic Galle Face Green, a 5 ha ocean-side urban park that is Colombo's largest open space and a popular destination for the working class.

As activists explained to me, despite major local opposition, the rhetoric of economic development managed to convince a part of the unprivileged working class that the Port City offers the possibility of a better future for their children. An agreement was thus made to move the dredgers farther offshore, with the CCCC promising to give LKR 500 million to the fishers' income support programme. In 2019, the project's first phase was completed, including the reclamation of 269 ha of land from the ocean. Even though the first compensations have been already given, gaining the consensus of some members of the local community, protesters have continued to argue that the project will lead to massive displacements and destroy Colombo. The Port City is projected to double Colombo's population and reflects a development model that ignores prior land uses, meaning that social needs and environmental risks are not considered, which creates a battleground between residents, investors, politicians and the working class. Its contested vision consists of a revived colonial view for making territories accessible, useful and visible within global production and trade networks (see also Enns and Bersaglio, 2020), mixed with neoliberal dreams of offshore financial hubs and low-tax havens designed to create exclusionary city enclaves targeting by definition only a particular economic and business elite.

In March 2024, after few years of severe crisis in Sri Lanka, a ceremony took place celebrating the Colombo Business Centre, which was expected to become operative by September 2024. Despite the major controversies, the Port City was still being advertised as a commercial and economic hub and a potential tax heaven that will transform Sri Lanka.

The emerging urban geographies of the New Silk Road

My work in Athens, Colombo and London, despite the striking divergences between the three cities, illuminates how BRI-driven urban transformation articulates with national, local and global processes to produce distinct urban geographies. Relational comparison allows us to see that different places/cities are fashioned by local social relations and power struggles while also conditioned by broader socio-spatial processes (Hart, 2018), including their repositioning within an increasingly interdependent and hierarchically organized global space-time (Goswami, 2002), novel infrastructural linkages and core-periphery relationships (Mayer and Zhang, 2020) due to their involvement with the New Silk Road. These dynamics lead to the emergence of new urban formations that show both the pivotal role of global infrastructure as a driver of contemporary urban transformation (Wiig and Silver, 2019) and the near-global prevalence of an urban-oriented regime of capital accumulation (Wu et al, 2016). These formations, in turn, bear distinct characteristics that signal the emergence of a new form of urbanism that is not only infrastructure-led and neoliberal but also increasingly authoritarian. This is supported at an unprecedented scale by novel urban growth coalitions that are both place-based and operate beyond specific places (Wachsmuth, 2017), creating particularly unfavourable conditions for urban dwellers. Even though this form of urbanism shares commonalities with similar processes stressed by other scholars (see Kuymulu, 2013; Bruff, 2014; Büdenbender and Zupan, 2017; Zhang, 2017; Tansel, 2019), it also differentiates from them because it is influenced by the BRI's entanglement with communities, places, socionatures, power and labour relations and the contingent ways the initiative engages with social and economic geographies, urban space and social relations (Lefebvre, 1974).

The first element that makes BRI-driven urban formations distinct is that they are the outcome of changing political-economic relations and dynamics of global capital accumulation and, particularly, a manifestation of China's rising hegemony and its attempt to render infrastructure a hallmark of its 'inclusive' globalization model (Chen, 2018). Even though China has invested 8–9 per cent of its gross domestic product in infrastructure, meeting a disproportionate part of the global infrastructure gap (Chen, 2018), and has promoted the BRI as a supporter of the United Nations Sustainable Development Goals and free trade, offering an alternative path to US protectionism under Trump, it has also benefited specific enterprises, with 90 per cent of contracts going to Chinese companies. This is evident in Athens, Colombo and London, where BRI projects embody the decisive role of foreign investment, predominantly from Chinese state-owned enterprises, as well as the transfer of strategic public infrastructure under Chinese ownership or/and management in the heartlands of capital cities. In that sense, we could argue that the BRI projects in Piraeus, London and Colombo are enabling the making of new bordered territories, generating 'structural holes' inside the tissue of national sovereign territory (Sassen, 2013, p 23). On the one hand, these local-global urban territories indicate a deeper integration of regions and countries across the Euro-Asian continent (Mayer and Zhang, 2020), placing China, and more broadly the Asian region, in a more competitive position vis-à-vis the United States, a tendency already identified from the early 2000s (Harvey, 2005). On the other hand, the interests involved in BRI projects unravel a more perplexing picture that illustrates the heightened role of multilateral agencies, corporate actors, transnational capital and infrastructure developers (Mayer and Zhang, 2020) and the realignment of diverse interests under the common goal of promoting their agenda in national and regional urban planning (Hilyard and Sol, 2017; Kanai and Schindler, 2019; Schindler and Kanai, 2019). The BRI's global outreach and convoluted local-global partnerships are evident both in its funding mechanism and the way BRI-related diplomatic discourse in Greece, the United Kingdom and Sri Lanka has accentuated the win-win outcomes of novel infrastructural corridors, trade relations and free capital movement. Even though the initiative's potential to benefit companies and governments beyond China highlights the complex dialectics between the territorial and the capitalist logics of power (Gramsci, 1971; Harvey, 2005), this should not create the illusion of a rosy picture that signals the end of intra-capitalist competition. Emerging alliances are mostly opportunistic, and in all the cities explored here, both Chinese and national political-economic elites struggle to turn BRI projects in their favour (Olinga-Shannon et al, 2019), and if their interests do not meet, conflicts will probably arise. The case of the ABP investment is indicative here and shows well the fragile nature of infrastructural fixes.

Second, and relatedly, these novel urban formations owe their existence first and foremost to their potential to act as spatial fixes. As such they are palpable expressions of the aggressive prioritization of private profits, corporate interests and multinational, cross-scale growth coalitions over the infrastructures of social reproduction (see also Apostolopoulou and Pant, 2022; Apostolopoulou and Pizarro, 2025). In all the three cities, BRI projects tried, albeit differently, to agglomerate (cheap) labour and capital and facilitate capital circulation through the combination of transportation with real estate and commercial projects. These projects have been concentrated in urban centres, confirming the transformation of cities to nodes of wealth, cosmopolitanism and entrepreneurship (Sassen, 2002; Jessop, 2019), which epitomises the departure from the spatial Keynesianism of the mid-20th century (Brenner, 2004). This did not of course come from parthenogenesis. Rendering urban space an arena for market-oriented growth and elite consumption practices has been at the core of framing the city as a growth machine (Logan et al, 2007) and a hallmark of the neoliberal urban regeneration of the last two decades (Peck and Tickell, 2007; Harvey, 2012; 2019; Apostolopoulou and Adams, 2015; Apostolopoulou, 2020). BRI interventions built on prior legacies, governmental agendas and hegemonic narratives and tend to exacerbate, in distinct and varied ways across different places, already unfolding uneven geographies of urban gentrification and displacement.

The third distinct characteristic of infrastructure-led, urban formations, which is a direct outcome of the previous two points, is that they engender a new stage of revanchist and authoritarian urban development that in most cases deepens spatial fragmentation, territorial stigmatization and social segregation. This not only intensifies existing regeneration and gentrification trends, as noted earlier, but often completely supersedes them by pursuing a remaking of cities that prioritizes capital accumulation above any other social and spatial planning consideration and, therefore, is deeply uneven, socially, environmentally and spatially. In cities of the Global North, like Athens and London, Chinese investment perceived an upgraded role within a context of prolonged crisis, privatizations, public disinvestment and austerity politics and, in collaboration with national governments and multinational investors, further fractured public infrastructures of social reproduction, entrenching urban marginality. Similar trends have been manifested in Colombo, where the Port City enhanced class-driven gentrification have aggravated the displacement and dispossession of Colombo's working class under the rhetoric of building a new city based on a neocolonial speculative imaginary for world-city investors and professionals (Goldman, 2011). This kind of city remaking – which is not of course limited to BRI projects but proliferates across the planet – by fetishizing consumption and disregarding both the urban commons and social needs, returns the places it touches to a year zero (see Hancox, 2014). Annulling prior legacies and people's histories is necessary to enable a spectacular re-inscription and reconfiguration of urban spaces as spatial products of homogenization, entrepreneurship and consumption, ideal to host newly emerging urban enterprise communities and re-invent the city for corporate investors. An exemplary example of the latter that extends beyond the BRI is unboundedly The Line.

Authoritarianism is manifested as economic coercion: infrastructure-led development reconfigures cities as nodes of wealth in broader transnational networks and as sites of capital accumulation, free trade, foreign investments and luxury (Sassen, 2002; Ong, 2006), escalating already identified trends of neoliberal urbanism (Theodore et al, 2011). But if capital, technology and elites benefit from easily flowing across metropolitan regions (Castells, 2011; Summers, 2016), the same cannot be said about labour: imposing positive exceptions for the capitalist class has been accompanied by unfavourable conditions for the working class, as evidenced in the dismantling of labour organization and workers' rights in Piraeus and Sri Lanka, the facilitation of the privatization and outsourcing of public infrastructures of social reproduction and urban space in London, and the replacement of collective rights (to the city) by contentious opportunities arising from bringing the urban poor close to wealth and luxury. Economic coercion finds its epitome in the way BRI projects have been linked in all cities explored here to the creation of lawless, special economic and financial zones that are creating neoliberal urban spaces of exception, graduated sovereignty, exploitation of nature (Tracy et al, 2017) and precarization of work (Ong, 2006; Hilyard and Sol, 2017). These zones have a long history in Greater Mekong Subregion, characterized by limited transparency, forceful displacements, labour exploitation and flawed environmental impact assessments (Thame, 2017).

The creation of new zones of exception within the ubiquitous life of the city means that authoritarianism also entails coercive and undemocratic urban politics. These differ across different cityscapes, as the tales and contested futures of BRI projects in Athens, London and Colombo show, but nonetheless are manifested in the increasing hegemony of the following four practices. The first is the negotiation of the direction of urban transformation through processes and forums that attribute privileged access to corporate elites and exclude social movements and grassroots organizations. The second is the devaluation of public consultation and collective bargaining and their replacement either with informal participation in workshops with no decision-making power – as in London, a city used to consensual politics – which is the result of the class victory of neoliberal forces (Massey, 2007), or with a tightly circumstanced participation, as in Piraeus. The third is the astonishing neglect of the public interest that is accompanied by the attempt to insulate BRI-related agreements from public protests. It is indicative that the Chinese government has clarified that it sees BRI developments as 'commercial cooperation projects between companies' and that issues related to their environmental and social impacts should be resolved through negotiation by 'relevant business partners'. The fourth is the (often violent) suppression of social struggles, which ranges from imposing a heavy police presence in demonstrations in Athens to forced evictions and violations of housing rights in Colombo (see Tansel, 2019, and Zhang, 2017, on similar trends in Turkey and Shanghai, respectively).

Importantly, in all the cities explored here, there is a narrative of prosperity that, combined with the Chinese rhetoric that overemphasizes the links with the ancient Silk Road – a historical network of trade routes started during the Han Dynasty – to support the benevolence of the contemporary Belt and Road (Mayer, 2018), aims to trap the working class and the urban poor into the imaginary of the elite. The monumental interests involved and the project lifetimes also sometimes make it hard for people to realize exactly how upcoming socio-spatial and socio-environmental change will affect their lives. Nonetheless, this type of urbanism is also a product of neoliberalism's decreasing legitimacy (Fraser, 2015; Harvey, 2019), as evidenced in the attempts to discipline resistance and insulate multibillion-dollar projects from social and political dissent (Bruff, 2014), to enforce exclusionary urban development models that contradict people's historical demands and current needs. But cities cannot be governed according to profitable investment portfolios. There is an inextricable link between urban planning and social movements (Castells, 1977) and between urban revolutions from above and urban revolutions from below (Sheppard et al, 2015). The current prevalence of the teleological imaginary of neoliberal urbanism, vividly expressed in the consensus that all governments –including a Left-wing and a Right-wing government in Greece with very different pre-electoral agendas – have shown to the materialization of BRI projects does not negate the fact that political struggle is internal to the formation of any spatial fix (Ekers and Prudham, 2017). New contradictions will arise because geographically immobilized forms of fixed capital, as new spaces of capital accumulation, will need to find ways to absorb the surpluses they generate through further geographical expansions (Smith, 2008). Spatio-temporal fixes are material and social relations and their evolving (re)configurations lead to conflicts and class struggles that ultimately determine how urban space is produced (Lefebvre, 1974; Harvey, 2012; Klinger, 2019).

Conclusion

BRI projects, as any contentious infrastructure project (Apostolopoulou, 2020), are thus exposed to struggle and contestation over their trajectory and legitimacy. Our relational spatial lens enables us to see that the deployment of global infrastructure in urban space materializes in contingent ways, and struggles against BRI projects are intertwining with local struggles around housing, employment, public health and social, spatial and environmental justice, which will intensify in the current context of a so-called polycrisis. These struggles show that there is no single space/spatiality; places are processes whose identities are multiple, shifting and potentially unbounded, and as such they are defined by conflict over both their present development and their future (Massey, 1994). It is through such struggles and conflicts that new forms of urban, collective solidarity may emerge to reclaim a radical re-appropriation and re-inscription of urban places by their citizens as spaces of protest, heterogeneity and differentiation (Lefebvre, 1974; Watson, 2006), opening up new pathways of transforming urban politics and engendering a new global sense of place (in the sense of Massey, 1994).

Note

1. This chapter is an edited version of the following paper: E. Apostolopoulou (2021) Tracing the links between infrastructure-led development, urban transformation, and inequality in China's Belt and Road Initiative, *Antipode*, 53(3), 831–58.

References

ABP (Advanced Business Park) (2017) ABP Royal Albert Dock London, *Quarterly Review*, 1 October. Available at: www.abp-london.co.uk/assets/

Apostolopoulou, E. (2020) *Nature Swapped and Nature Lost: Biodiversity Offsetting, Urbanization and Social Justice*, Springer Nature.

Apostolopoulou, E. (2021a) Tracing the links between infrastructure-led development, urban transformation, and inequality in China's Belt and Road Initiative, *Antipode*, 53(3), 831–58.

Apostolopoulou, E. (2021b) A novel geographical research agenda on Silk Road urbanisation, *The Geographical Journal*, 187(4), 386–93.

Apostolopoulou, E. (2024) The dragon's head or Athens' sacrifice zone? Spatiotemporal disjuncture, logistical disruptions, and urban infrastructural justice in Piraeus port, Greece, *Urban Geography*, advance online publication. doi: 10.1080/02723638.2024.2433968

Apostolopoulou, E. and Adams, W.M. (2015) Neoliberal capitalism and conservation in the post-crisis era: the dialectics of 'green' and 'un-green' grabbing in Greece and the UK, *Antipode*, 47(1), 15–35.

Apostolopoulou, E. and Pant, H. (2022) 'Silk Road here we come': infrastructural myths, post-disaster politics, and the shifting urban geographies of Nepal, *Political Geography*, 98, art 102704. doi: 10.1016/j.polgeo.2022.102704

Apostolopoulou, E. and Pizarro, A. (2025) Contesting the anticipated infrastructural city: a grounded analysis of Silk Road urbanisation in the multipurpose port terminal in Chancay, Peru, *Annals of the American Association of Geographers*, 115(1), 223–41.

Apostolopoulou, E., Cheng, H., Silver, J. and Wiig, A. (2023) Cities on the New Silk Road: the global urban geographies of China's Belt and Road Initiative, *Urban Geography*, advance online publication. doi: 10.1080/02723638.2023.2247283

Brenner, N. (2004) *New State Spaces: Urban Governance and the Rescaling of Statehood*, Oxford University Press.

Brenner, N. (2019) *New Urban Spaces: Urban Theory and the Scale Question*, Oxford University Press.

Brownill, S. (2018) The song remains the same: regeneration narratives in the Royal Docks, in A. Minton, A. Duman, M. James and D. Hancox (eds) *Regeneration Songs: Sounds of Investment and Loss in East London*, Watkins Media Limited.

Bruff, I. (2014) The rise of authoritarian neoliberalism, *Rethinking Marxism*, 26, 113–29.

Büdenbender, M. and Zupan, D. (2017) The evolution of neoliberal urbanism in Moscow, 1992–2015, *Antipode*, 49(2), 294–313.

Castells, M. (1977) *The Urban Question: A Marxist Approach*, Edward Arnold.

Castells, M. (2011) *The Rise of the Network Society*, John Wiley & Sons.

Chen, X. (2018) Globalisation redux: can China's inside-out strategy catalyze economic development and integration across its Asian borderlands and beyond? *Cambridge Journal of Regions, Economy and Society*, 11(1), 35–58.

Christophers, B. (2011) Revisiting the urbanization of capital, *Annals of the Association of American Geographers*, 101(6), 1347–64.

Church, A. (1990) Transport and urban regeneration in London Docklands: a victim of success or a failure to plan? *Cities*, 7(4), 289–303.

Donovan, T. (2022) Royal Docks: London mayor removes developer from £1bn project, *BBC*, 13 July. Available at: www.bbc.com/news/uk-england-london-62140112

Ekers, M. and Prudham, S. (2017) The metabolism of socioecological fixes: capital switching, spatial fixes, and the production of nature, *Annals of the American Association of Geographers*, 107, 1370–88.

Enns, C. and Bersaglio, B. (2020) On the coloniality of 'new' mega-infrastructure projects in East Africa, *Antipode*, 52, 101–23.

Flint, C. and Zhu, C. (2019) The geopolitics of connectivity, cooperation, and hegemonic competition: the Belt and Road Initiative, *Geoforum*, 99, 95–101.

Fraser, N. (2015) Legitimation crisis? On the political contradictions of financialized capitalism, *Critical Historical Studies*, 2(2), 157–89.

Goldman, M. (2011) Speculative urbanism and the making of the next world city, *International Journal of Urban and Regional Research*, 35(3), 555–81.

Goswami, M. (2002) Rethinking the modular nation form, *Comparative Studies in Society and History*, 44(4), 770–99.

Gramsci, A. (1971) *Selections from the Prison Notebooks*, in Q. Hoare and G.N. Smith (eds and trans), International Publishers.

Gunawansa, A. (2018) Creation of new urban land by reclaiming the sea in Colombo Port City, in K. Cashman and V. Quinlan (eds) *Strengthening Environmental Reviews in Urban Development*, United Nations Human Settlements Programme, pp 98–119.

Hancox, D. (2014) A 'regeneration supernova' is about to destroy East London as we know it, *Vice*, 22 April. Available at: www.vice.com/en_uk/article/nnq7q7/dan-hancox-regeneration-supernove

Hart, G. (2006) Denaturalizing dispossession: critical ethnography in the age of resurgent imperialism, *Antipode*, 38(5), 977–1004.

Hart, G. (2018) Relational comparison revisited: Marxist postcolonial geographies in practice, *Progress in Human Geography*, 42(3), 371–94.

Harvey, D. (2005) *The New Imperialism*, Oxford University Press.

Harvey, D. (2012) *Rebel Cities: From the Right to the City to the Urban Revolution*, Verso.

Harvey, D. (2016) *The Ways of the World*, Oxford University Press.

Harvey, D. (2018) *The Limits to Capital*, Verso.

Harvey, D. (2019) *The neoliberal project is alive but has lost its legitimacy*, The Wire. Available at: https://thewire.in/economy/david-harvey-marxist-scholar-neo-liberalism

Henneke, L. and Knowles, C. (2020) Conceptualising cities and migrant ethnicity: the lessons of Chinese London, in J. Solomos (ed) *Routledge International Handbook of Contemporary Racisms*, Routledge, pp 38–52.

Hildyard, N. and Sol, X. (2017) *How Infrastructure Is Shaping the World: A Critical Introduction to Infrastructure Mega-Corridors*, Counter Balance.

Jessop, B. (2019 [1997]) The entrepreneurial city, in: N. Jewson and S. MacGregor (eds) *Realising Cities: New Spatial Divisions and Social Transformation*, Routledge, pp 28–41.

Kanai, J.M. and Schindler, S. (2019) Peri-urban promises of connectivity: linking project-led polycentrism to the infrastructure scramble, *Environment and Planning A: Economy and Space*, 51, 302–22.

Katz, C. (2011) Accumulation, excess, childhood: toward a countertopography of risk and waste, *Documents d'anàlisi geogràfica*, 57, 47–60.

Klinger, J.M. (2019) Environment, development, and security politics in the production of Belt and Road spaces, *Territory, Politics, Governance*, 8, 657–75.

Kuymulu, M.B. (2013) Reclaiming the right to the city: reflections on the urban uprisings in Turkey, *City*, 17(3), 274–8.

Lee, S.O., Wainwright, J. and Glassman, J. (2018) Geopolitical economy and the production of territory, *Environment and Planning A: Economy and Space*, 50(2), 416–36.

Lefebvre, H. (1974) *La production de l'espace*, Anthropos.

Logan, J.R., Molotch, H.L. and Molotch, H. (2007) *Urban Fortunes: The Political Economy of Place*, University of California Press.

Marx, K. (1887) *Capital: A Critique of Political Economy*, Volume I, Progress Publishers.

Massey, D. (1994) *Space, Place and Gender*, University of Minnesota Press.

Massey, D. (2007) *World City*, Polity.

Mayer, M. (2018) China's historical statecraft and the return of history, *International Affairs*, 94, 1217–35.

Mayer, M. and Zhang, X. (2020) Theorizing China-world integration: sociospatial reconfigurations and the modern Silk Roads, *Review of International Political Economy*, advance online publication. doi: 10.1080/09692290.2020.1741424

Neilson, B. (2019) Precarious in Piraeus: on the making of labour insecurity in a port concession, *Globalizations*, 16, 559–74.

Olinga-Shannon, S., Barbesgaard, M. and Vervest, P. (2019) The Belt and Road Initiative (BRI): An AEPF Framing Paper, Asia Europe People's Forum.

Ong, A. (2006) *Neoliberalism as Exception: Mutations in Citizenship and Sovereignty*, Duke University Press.

Peck, J. and Tickell, A. (2007) Conceptualizing neoliberalism, thinking Thatcherism, in H. Leitner, J. Peck and E.S. Sheppard (eds) *Contesting Neoliberalism: Urban Frontiers*, Guilford Press, pp 26–50.

Radicati, A. (2020) The unstable coastline: navigating dispossession and belonging in Colombo, *Antipode*, 52(2), 542–61.

Ruwanpura, K.N., Brown, B. and Chan, L. (2020) (Dis)connecting Colombo: situating the megapolis in postwar Sri Lanka, *The Professional Geographer*, 72, 165–79.

Safi, M. (2018) Sri Lanka's 'new Dubai': will Chinese-built city suck the life out of Colombo? The Guardian, 2 August. Available at: www.theguardian.com/cities/2018/aug/02/sri-lanka-new-dubai-chinese-city-colombo

Sassen, S. (2002) Locating cities on global circuits, *Environment and Urbanization*, 14(1), 13–30.

Sassen, S. (2013) When territory deborders territoriality, *Territory, Politics, Governance*, 1(1), 21–45.

Schindler, S. and Kanai, J.M. (2019) Getting the territory right: infrastructure-led development and the re-emergence of spatial planning strategies, *Regional Studies*, advance online publication. doi: 10.1080/00343404.2019.1661984

Schmid, C., Karaman, O., Hanakata, N.C., Kallenberger, P., Kockelkorn, A., Sawyer, A. et al (2018) Towards a new vocabulary of urbanisation processes: a comparative approach, *Urban Studies*, 55, 19–52.

Sheppard, E., Gidwani, V., Goldman, M., Leitner, H., Roy, A. and Maringanti, A. (2015) Introduction: urban revolutions in the age of global urbanism, *Urban Studies*, 52, 1947–61.

Smith, N. (2008) *Uneven Development: Nature, Capital, and the Production of Space*, The University of Georgia Press.

Smith, N.R. (2022) Continental metropolitanization: Chongqing and the urban origins of China's Belt and Road Initiative, *Urban Geography*, 43(10), 1544–64.

Summers, T. (2016) China's 'New Silk Roads': sub-national regions and networks of global political economy, *Third World Quarterly*, 37(9), 1628–43.

Tansel, C.B. (2019) Reproducing authoritarian neoliberalism in Turkey: urban governance and state restructuring in the shadow of executive centralization, *Globalizations*, 16, 320–35.

Thame, C. (2017) *SEZs and Value Extraction from the Mekong*. Bangkok: Focus on the Global South.

Theodore, N., Peck, J. and Brenner, N. (2011) Neoliberal urbanism: cities and the rule of markets, in G. Bridge and S. Watson (eds) *The New Blackwell Companion to the City*, Wiley-Blackwell, pp 15–25.

Tracy, E.F., Shvarts, E., Simonov, E. and Babenko, M. (2017) China's new Eurasian ambitions: the environmental risks of the Silk Road Economic Belt, *Eurasian Geography and Economics*, 58, 56–88.

Van Dort, L.T. (2016) *Neoliberalism and Social Justice in the City: An Examination of Postwar Urban Development in Colombo, Sri Lanka*, Culminating Projects in Social Responsibility.

Wachsmuth, D. (2017) Infrastructure alliances: supply-chain expansion and multi-city growth coalitions, *Economic Geography*, 93, 44–65.

Wainwright, O. (2022) 'It's been a disaster': how Boris Johnson's docklands business hub turned into a ghost town, *The Guardian*, 20 July. Available at: www.theguardian.com/artanddesign/2022/jul/20/empty-promise-the-fantasy-city-within-a-city-that-turned-into-a-ghost-town

Watson, S. (2006) *City Publics: The (Dis)Enchantments of Urban Encounters*, Routledge.

Wiig, A. and Silver, J. (2019) Turbulent presents, precarious futures: urbanization and the deployment of global infrastructure, *Regional Studies*, 53(6), 912–23.

Williams, J., Robinson, C. and Bouzarovski, S. (2020) China's Belt and Road Initiative and the emerging geographies of global urbanisation, *The Geographical Journal*, 186(1), 128–40.

Wu, Y., Li, X. and Lin, G.C. (2016) Reproducing the city of the spectacle: mega-events, local debts, and infrastructure-led urbanization in China, *Cities*, 53, 51–60.

Zhang, Y. (2017) Family or money? The false dilemma in property dispossession in Shanghai, *International Journal of Urban and Regional Research*, 41(2), 194–212.

Zheng, H., Bouzarovski, S., Knuth, S., Panteli, M., Schindler, S., Ward, K. and Williams, J. (2023) Interrogating China's global urban presence, *Geopolitics*, 28(1), 310–32.

Afterword: The Material Futures of the Belt and Road Initiative

Elia Apostolopoulou, Han Cheng, Jonathan Silver and Alan Wiig

The contributions to this volume collectively underscore the intricate interplay of local and global political economies, geopolitics and social and environmental relations within the Belt and Road Initiative (BRI). They illuminate, among other themes, the persistence of extractivist patterns, the diverse disruptions produced by contentious megaprojects, the role of temporalities in shaping developmental trajectories, the complex interplay between BRI-driven urban transformation and legacies of regeneration, gentrification and austerity, and the importance of considering how changing patterns of global capital accumulation and emerging geopolitical balances intersect with these dynamics. Several chapters explore the contested agency of diverse local actors, the socioeconomic effects of BRI projects on local communities and the socio-spatial spaces of grassroots activism, emphasizing how local resistance and mobilization shape and are shaped by large-scale infrastructure projects. A critical examination of the environmental implications of BRI projects on people and natures also has a central role in the volume, revealing significant impacts on ecosystems and local livelihoods and highlighting the tensions between promised development goals and social-ecological sustainability and justice.

By bringing together cases from across the Global South and North, the volume illustrates the global and multifaceted nature of BRI-driven infrastructural and political ecological transformations. The cases explored in the chapters reveal the intricate dynamics at play, where power relations, historical-geographical contexts and socio-spatial configurations intersect to produce uneven development outcomes. By foregrounding these intersections, the volume provides a rich and grounded analysis of how BRI projects reconfigure the dialectics of social, spatial and environmental relations. The interplay of global ambitions and local realities generates both synergies and frictions, leading to contested outcomes that reflect broader patterns of geopolitical and economic restructuring. Therefore, the contributions collectively offer a nuanced understanding of the BRI as a catalyst for profound infrastructural and political ecological change, revealing the complex, often contradictory processes that shape 21st-century material geographies.

In what follows, we synthesize key concepts that emerged across the chapters, identifying points of commonality and divergence, as well as future directions for research on the material geographies of the BRI. This synthesis derives from the chapters in this volume, highlighting shared themes and diverse experiences, and shedding light on the BRI's global impact. Our aim is not to offer an all-encompassing theory that would link all the separate contributions, as such an endeavour would be both impossible and unnecessary, obscuring valuable variations. Instead, we hope to chart future research paths and emphasize the importance of combining an analysis of the 'context of context' (Brenner et al, 2010) – namely, the macro-spatial and economic landscapes within which the BRI is articulated – with a relational and grounded analysis of its unfolding in specific places (Katz, 2021). As noted in the introduction to this volume, and based on an 'extroverted' understanding of place (Massey, 1994), we argue that it is important for research on the BRI to explain how a Chinese-led strategy coalesces with diverse transnational, national and local, private and state interests, materializing within diverse contexts and producing homogeneity, unevenness and heterogeneity (Apostolopoulou, 2021).

Through this critical lens, the volume develops a nuanced and context-sensitive analysis of the BRI's far-reaching effects, with the aim of contributing a deeper understanding of its implications for global inequalities, environmental justice and the politics of infrastructure. It also calls for geographers, political ecologists and other critical scholars to engage with these emergent realities, advocating for inclusive and equitable approaches to development that foreground the voices and experiences of those most affected by these transformations.

Extractivist corridors

An important theme that is explored in the volume is the intricate interplay between debt, corruption and neocolonial pathways within BRI-funded projects, with the case of Sri Lanka serving as a poignant example. The country's debt crisis, compounded by support for corrupt regimes, underscores the enduring presence of colonial and neocolonial dynamics perpetuated by both international sovereign bonds creditors and Chinese lending. The ramifications of finance capitalism's neoliberal tenets, epitomized by projects like the Colombo Port City, necessitate a critical examination of capitalism's corruption and the imperative of commoning financial debt. Concepts such as 'debt to nature', 'debt to dispossessed communities' and 'debt to ecological systems' are particularly relevant here, shedding light on the multifaceted socio-environmental impacts of large-scale infrastructure projects. These concepts underscore the broader implications of BRI-funded developmentalism and the corrupt underbelly of financialized capitalism in the 21st century.

Similarly, the critical examination of the BRI's expansion in the Arctic exposes its complex entanglement with historical colonial necropolitics perpetuated by Arctic nation-states. This expansion acts as a conduit for extensive extractive activities, resulting in severe ecological degradation and socioeconomic disruptions. In this sense, the BRI's involvement in the Arctic signals infrastructural and extractivist expansion rationalized and perpetuated through climate and territorial colonialism. This has led to the emergence of anti-colonial movements aiming to mitigate exploitation and harm in the region.

The exacerbation of exploitative relations between people and the environment is also evident in Southern Africa. Here, neocolonial trade, investment and financing controversies, driven by settler-colonial and Western corporate entities' demand for cheap labour, are at the core of China–South African economic ties. In Argentina, the BRI perpetuates the historical role of the Latin American region as a global exporter of primary goods, reinforcing economic dependency and vulnerability to global market fluctuations. This extractive dynamic is reminiscent of dependency theory, which remains a useful framework for understanding the contemporary landscape of the BRI in Latin America. China's infrastructure projects in the region, while contributing to increased connectivity and economic growth, primarily serve the export-oriented infrastructure network that has characterized Latin America since the colonial era. This highlights the dual focus on natural resource extraction and the pursuit of financial support to bridge the infrastructure gap, seen as essential for socioeconomic development. However, these efforts often reinforce existing economic structures rather than transforming them.

From Sri Lanka to Argentina, from the Polar Silk Road to Southern Africa, the chapters in this volume highlight the reproduction of underdevelopment in new South–South relations facilitated by the BRI (Mawdsley, 2017; 2019). While much of the BRI's official narrative hinges on China's South–South cooperation rhetoric, drawing especially on the historical legacy from its revolutionary era, the material geographies of the BRI suggest that it has largely reinforced pre-existing social conditions in host countries. These conditions are strongly shaped by colonial and postcolonial relations as well as host countries' structurally disadvantaged positions in the global capitalist economy. Rather than championing progressive politics and non-capitalist futures, the BRI is firmly embedded in and exemplifies the prevailing logics and mechanisms of contemporary uneven development (Gonzalez-Vicente, 2019; 2022).

Socio-environmental conflicts and environmental justice

Many chapters in this volume focus on environmental justice and conflicts, articulating a nuanced understanding of the manifold and often detrimental localized impacts of the BRI. They underscore the varied and significant environmental justice issues arising from different projects, highlighting how these impacts unfold across diverse contexts globally. Collectively, they emphasize the importance of environmental justice in analysing the BRI's impacts, serving as a call for critical scholars to engage with the temporal, spatial and sociopolitical dimensions of these projects not only for understanding localized conflicts and injustices but also for situating them within the larger context of global infrastructure expansion and its role in perpetuating existing power dynamics and inequalities.

Within a focus on environmental justice, temporalities play a significant role in structuring the conditions for implementing large-scale BRI projects. For instance, the case of Thuringia, Germany, illustrates how the coexistence and interplay of multiple temporal registers enhance the region's transnational connectivity and economic centrality. However, this 'polychronism' also reinforces multi-scalar relations of dominance and dependence, particularly through the exclusion of local stakeholders from decision-making processes and power networks. This exclusion underscores the environmental justice conflicts inherent in BRI projects, where local voices are marginalized in favour of broader economic goals. Contrary to the perception of China's global activities as an orchestrated grand strategy of 'economic statecraft' (Leverett and Wu, 2017; Zhang and Keith, 2017), the host-state government in Thuringia has been instrumental in attracting and implementing the project. This highlights the importance of considering both the role of host-state actors and the structural deficiencies at the local level in future research on the effects of China's global infrastructure expansion. It reveals how local governments and their priorities can shape the implementation and outcomes of BRI projects, complicating the narrative of a unilateral Chinese agenda.

Additionally, as argued in the chapter about the coal-fired power plants (CFPPs) in Indonesia, the concept of 'embodied energy justice' (Healey et al, 2019) serves as a pivotal framework for understanding the transboundary and often hidden injustices associated with energy infrastructures. The impacts of CFPPs, as is the case with several projects of this scale, extend far beyond their immediate sites, affecting communities involved in coal mining, marine transport areas and river ecosystems. These socio-environmental conflicts highlight significant losses in traditional livelihoods and cultural values, which monetary compensation and corporate social responsibility initiatives often fail to adequately address. The rejection of financial remedies by some communities underscores the profound and irreplaceable nature of these losses. The framework of embodied energy justice helps capture the full spectrum of socio-environmental consequences, linking local struggles with broader national and global politics (see also Apostolopoulou and Cortes-Vazquez, 2018). Moreover, it highlights the importance of expanding the notion of justice to include a blue justice perspective to comprehend the ramifications of Chinese investment on marine socio-ecological systems and coastal livelihoods. This broader perspective ensures that justice concerns encompass both terrestrial and marine impacts, providing a more comprehensive understanding of the BRI's socio-environmental footprint.

Similarly, the imperative to adopt a broader perspective on justice becomes evident when considering the interconnected exploitation of workers, socionatures and communities residing along trade routes and freight corridors. This exploitation stems from the combined impacts of various factors, including increased pollution, ecosystem destruction, displacement, exploitative working conditions and disregard for social reproduction and housing (Mezzadra and Neilson, 2019; Apostolopoulou, 2021a; Danyluk, 2021). Expanding our understanding of justice to encompass these multifaceted dimensions is crucial for addressing the complex challenges posed by large-scale infrastructure projects like those within the BRI. By recognizing that environmental degradation, social injustices and economic exploitation are interconnected and mutually reinforcing, we can better understand the root causes of inequality and injustice along these corridors. Responding effectively to the produced inequalities, which disproportionately affect the most vulnerable communities, goes beyond addressing immediate issues such as pollution and displacement and requires tackling the underlying structural inequalities and power dynamics perpetuating injustice and confronting the systemic barriers that marginalize certain groups.

Uncertain futures

In Georgia, the envisioned logistical futures promised through mega-infrastructure projects tied to the BRI reflect both historical infrastructural legacies and aspirational futures that may or may not materialize. The BRI aims to transform logistical geographies fundamentally, driving material changes through a surge of plans, finance and construction activities. However, as the Georgian experience suggests, these grand plans do not always translate into tangible transformations. The discrepancy between planned and actual outcomes, also evident in the case of the Royal

Albert Dock in London, underscores once again the contingent nature of infrastructure development, where local contexts, political dynamics and economic realities shape the trajectory of these projects. Similar uncertainties are evident in the case of BRI's investments and plans to restructure the Adriatic Corridor. The territorial reordering envisioned by these projects is fraught with uncertainties that are as prominent as the plans and investments themselves. These uncertainties highlight the complex and unpredictable nature of infrastructure development, where the intended objectives may be disrupted or reshaped by various local and global factors.

In Indonesia, Chinese and Japanese actors need to navigate a complex web of interactions with a diverse array of local stakeholders, whose actions are deeply embedded in the sociopolitical and economic landscapes of their countries. These local actors, including governments at various levels, leverage infrastructure investments to bolster their political influence, often employing strategies such as hedging to balance competing security, geopolitical and economic interests. Infrastructure projects thus emerge as intricate assemblages characterized by multiple levels of interaction between external actors and host-country stakeholders, and among host-country actors. This multilayered dynamic includes not only state-to-state engagements but also significant involvement from subnational governments, which utilize the financial influx from these projects to enhance their domestic political clout. The attention to host-country local agency captures the dynamic, contingent and uncertain nature of making and remaking infrastructure projects.

As Zeidermann et al (2015, p 284) argue: 'These uncertainties can never entirely be overcome, nor is overcoming uncertainty always the objective, since uncertainty can be advantageous for some and disadvantageous for others, a problem at one scale and a solution at another.' This perspective is particularly relevant in the context of BRI projects, where uncertainty can serve different interests and outcomes across scales. For instance, local stakeholders may leverage uncertainties to negotiate better terms or to resist certain aspects of the projects, while international actors may find that these uncertainties complicate their strategic objectives.

Local agency, counter-movements and resistance corridors

A critical dimension of local agency is manifested in resistance movements against many BRI projects, which serve as pivotal examples of transformative change rooted in local sociopolitical contexts. In Indonesia, for example, despite challenges such as weak environmental governance and limited redress mechanisms, grassroots mobilizations persist, embodying a resilient form of 'self-governance' aimed at safeguarding cultural and ecological integrity.

These mobilizations highlight the disparity between the aspirational 'green BRI' vision and the harsh realities on the ground, exacerbated by insufficient environmental governance within host countries (Ascensão et al, 2018; Teo et al, 2019). The increasing entanglement between the extraction of transition minerals and the development of energy infrastructure further exacerbates this gap, with local communities often compelled to act in response to governance failures and environmental injustices. Their resistance underscores the profound agency and resilience of local populations in confronting these challenges.

In Thailand, grassroots movements demonstrate the ability to thrive and sustain themselves even under authoritarian regimes. Key factors enabling such activism include local state frictions driven by strong social ties and pressures, the formation of informal community bodies, and the deployment of counter-narratives to state propaganda. These movements often need to negotiate with authorities, balancing the promotion of democratic and inclusive development visions against the demands of state territorialization policies, such as those associated with special economic zones (SEZs). While such grassroots mobilizations can support more inclusive local development, further cross-case investigations are necessary to fully understand their limitations in resisting state territorialization under SEZ policies and countering authoritarian power on a larger scale.

The formation of global-local alliances is crucial for supporting opposition movements and exploring pathways to alternative futures. In some cases, these alliances bridge local concerns about livelihoods and environmental injustices with broader concerns, like the global climate crisis and concerns about fair energy transitions, and have proven indispensable for supporting local struggles against controversial large-scale infrastructure projects, navigating both domestic political constraints and the pervasive influence of global capital. For example, in the context of the Polar Silk Road, Arctic Indigenous Peoples, local communities and international environmental organizations have formed resistance corridors to counteract the exploitation and degradation of their lands by foreign actors driven by economic and geopolitical interests. These alliances exemplify the power of solidarity networks in challenging necropolitical ecologies and advocating for environmental and social justice amid an escalating climate crisis. Arctic Indigenous communities have raised their voices against industrial encroachment, forming potent coalitions with local and international allies to oppose the adverse impacts of large-scale projects and the exploitation and degradation of their ancestral lands and waters by foreign actors driven by economic and geopolitical interests, and to challenge the environmental and social injustices exacerbated by large-scale industrial projects. The importance of local-global alliances and new forms of spatial resistance is further emphasized in the analysis of diverse BRI projects in Greece,

Sri Lanka and the United Kingdom. Through case studies of urban marginality and social inequality across different contexts, it becomes evident that BRI-driven urban transformation generates novel possibilities for socio-spatial and socio-environmental change, challenging hegemonic development narratives.

Moreover, and relatedly, the inspiration from historical cases of activism, such as the anti-apartheid movement and efforts to delink from international pharmaceutical monopolies in South Africa, provides valuable strategies for addressing the complex challenges posed by China-South African economic ties. These historical examples highlight a significant reservoir of potential for both analytical and activist efforts in navigating the contemporary landscape of international infrastructure development and resistance. Overall, the examination of local agency and counter-movements in the context of BRI projects reveals the complex interplay of local and international actors, highlighting the potential for transformative change through grassroots mobilizations and global-local alliances. By understanding these dynamics, scholars and activists can better address the environmental and social injustices associated with large-scale infrastructure development and contribute to opening pathways toward more equitable futures.

A comparative and community-engaged research agenda

A research agenda on the BRI responds to long-standing postcolonial calls by shifting the focus of theory-making beyond the West (Robinson and Roy, 2016). The contributions in this volume offer valuable insights for developing a comparative methodology capable of theorizing this global, diverse phenomenon. Some chapters draw on postcolonial geographies, comparative urbanism, countertopography and comparative political ecologies (Katz, 2011; McFarlane and Robinson, 2012; Taylor and Hurley, 2016; Hart, 2018; Le Tran et al, 2020), showing the importance and potential of a relational comparison of diverse histories, socio-spatial and socio-environmental trajectories, and struggles.

By exploring a variety of projects – including the establishment of SEZs, industrial parks, coal-fired power plants, logistics centres, new cities, urban business districts, real estate developments and urban regeneration projects – across the Global South and North, the contributors in this volume demonstrate the need to understand the complex dialectics of heterogeneity and homogeneity in the geographical patterns of the BRI. Indeed, the unprecedented scale of the BRI and the extensive range of its interventions necessitates empirical research spanning across various continents and locations. This presents significant challenges for geographical and political ecology research, requiring, among other things, international collaborations and the establishment of novel, collaborative research networks. However, it also lies at the heart of a potentially innovative theory-building process. Relational comparison, grounded in Lefebvrian conceptions of the production of space, place and scale, emerges as pivotal in such an approach. By analysing the interconnections and interdependencies between different geographical locations and scales, relational comparison allows us to uncover underlying patterns, power dynamics and socio-spatial transformations, contributing to the development of a comparative methodology capable of theorizing a global, diverse phenomenon.

Several chapters also effectively demonstrate that the BRI is a highly contested process shaped by local social relations and power struggles. They shed light on social struggles and everyday practices of resistance, which have been overlooked in much of the relevant literature, suggesting the need for a reconceptualization of infrastructure-led development as the product of social and political struggle (Apostolopoulou, 2021b). By considering the particularities of place as crucial in the emergence of such struggles and by supporting community-engaged research, this approach can offer novel insights into the collective and individual strategies through which communities, including Indigenous peoples, reshape space, nature, social relations and everyday lives. This perspective allows for a deeper understanding of the materialization of infrastructure projects on the ground and can help us move beyond generic theorizations to offer a real-world

Figure A.1: Tangier, Morocco – a new waterfront development

Source: Photograph by Elia Apostolopoulou

analysis that acknowledges the centrality of people's struggles in shaping the material geographies of the 21st century.

To conclude, the chapters in this volume show well that the material transformations driven by BRI investments are not just about physical infrastructures but also about reconfiguring socio-spatial and environmental relations and power dynamics. These projects often intersect with local histories, politics and environmental considerations, making their outcomes highly contingent and contested. Understanding these dynamics requires a critical examination of the multiple scales at which BRI projects operate. This includes looking at how local actors, including governments, communities and grassroots movements, engage with and resist these projects, as well as how global actors navigate and exploit uncertainties to advance their agendas. The material transformations brought about by the BRI are marked by significant uncertainties, disruptions and contradictions. These projects, while ambitious and expansive, do not follow a linear path of development. Instead, they are characterized by contested territorial restructurings, where different actors and interests clash and negotiate outcomes. This complexity highlights the need for a nuanced approach to understanding how these projects are reshaping geographies and sociopolitical landscapes.

Focusing on the material transformations produced through the BRI, this volume sheds light on the uncertain futures and the often contradictory and contested ways in which territorial restructuring is proceeding. As the BRI enters its second decade, the need to develop further grounded analysis of this global initiative remains paramount for critical understandings of the transforming world around us.

References

Apostolopoulou, E. (2021a) Tracing the links between infrastructure-led development, urban transformation, and inequality in China's Belt and Road Initiative, *Antipode*, 53(3), 831–58.

Apostolopoulou, E. (2021b) A novel geographical research agenda on Silk Road urbanisation, *The Geographical Journal*, 187(4), 386–93.

Apostolopoulou, E. and Cortes-Vazquez, J.A. (eds) (2018) *The Right to Nature: Social Movements, Environmental Justice and Neoliberal Natures*, Routledge.

Ascensão, F., Fahrig, L., Clevenger, A.P., Corlett, R.T., Jaeger, J.A., Laurance, W.F. and Pereira, H.M. (2018) Environmental challenges for the Belt and Road Initiative, *Nature Sustainability*, 1(5), 206–9.

Brenner, N., Peck, J. and Theodore, N. (2010) Variegated neoliberalization: geographies, modalities, pathways, *Global Networks*, 10, 182–222.

Danyluk, M. (2021) Supply-chain urbanism: constructing and contesting the logistics city, *Annals of the American Association of Geographers*, 111(7), 2149–64.

Gonzalez-Vicente, R. (2019) Make development great again? Accumulation regimes, spaces of sovereign exception and the elite development paradigm of China's Belt and Road Initiative, *Business and Politics*, 21(4), 487–513.

Gonzalez-Vicente, R. (2022) In the name of the nation: authoritarian practices, capital accumulation, and the radical simplification of development in China's global vision, *Globalizations*, advance online publication. doi: 10.1080/14747731.2022.2121061

Hart, G. (2018) Relational comparison revisited: Marxist postcolonial geographies in practice, *Progress in Human Geography*, 42(3), 371–94.

Healy, N., Stephens, J.C. and Malin, S.A. (2019) Embodied energy injustices: unveiling and politicizing the transboundary harms of fossil fuel extractivism and fossil fuel supply chains, *Energy Research & Social Science*, 48, 219–34.

Katz, C. (2011) Accumulation, excess, childhood: toward a countertopography of risk and waste, *Documents d'anàlisi geogràfica*, 57, 47–60.

Katz, C. (2021) Splanetary urbanization, *International Journal of Urban and Regional Research*, 45(4), 597–611.

Le Tran, D., Martinez-Alier, J., Navas, G. and Mingorria, S. (2020) Gendered geographies of violence: a multiple case study analysis of murdered women environmental defenders, *Journal of Political Ecology*, 27(1), 1189–212.

Leverett, F. and Bingbing, W. (2017) The New Silk Road and China's evolving grand strategy, *The China Journal*, 77(1), 110–32.

Massey, D. (1994) *Space, Place and Gender*, University of Minnesota Press.

Mawdsley, E. (2017) Development geography 1: cooperation, competition and convergence between 'North' and 'South', *Progress in Human Geography*, 41(1), 108–17.

Mawdsley, E. (2019) South–South cooperation 3.0? Managing the consequences of success in the decade ahead, *Oxford Development Studies*, 47(3), 259–74.

McFarlane, C. and Robinson, J. (2012) Introduction: experiments in comparative urbanism, *Urban Geography*, 33(6), 765–73.

Mezzadra, S. and Neilson, B. (2019) *The Politics of Operations: Excavating Contemporary Capitalism*, Duke University Press.

Robinson, J. and Roy, A. (2016) Debate on global urbanisms and the nature of urban theory, *International Journal of Urban and Regional Research*, 40(1), 181–6.

Taylor, L. and Hurley, P.T. (eds) (2016) *A Comparative Political Ecology of Exurbia*, Springer.

Teo, H.C., Lechner, A.M., Walton, G.W., Chan, F.K.S., Cheshmehzangi, A., Tan-Mullins, M. et al (2019) Environmental impacts of infrastructure development under the Belt and Road Initiative, *Environments*, 6(6), art 72. doi: 10.3390/environments6060072

Zeiderman, A., Kaker, S.A., Silver, J. and Wood, A. (2015) Uncertainty and urban life, *Public Culture*, 27(2), 281–304.

Zhang, X. and Keith, J. (2017) From wealth to power: China's new economic statecraft, *The Washington Quarterly*, 40(1), 185–203.

Index

References to figures appear in *italic* type; those in **bold** type refer to tables.
References to endnotes show both the page number and the note number (194n1).

As 'BRI (Belt and Road Initiative)' and 'China' are the main topics, index entries for these are limited to general subjects only and readers are advised to search for more specific topics.

A

Abe, Shinzo 133, 136
ABP (Advanced Business Park) 218–19, 220–1, 224
acceleration temporal dynamic, EV (Electric Vehicle) battery production, Thuringia, Eastern Germany 95, 101, 103–5, 106, 107
'adaptive governance' 64
ADC (Anaklia Development Consortium) 199, 200, 205, 206, 207, 208–9
  see also Anaklia Deep Sea Port project, Georgia
Adriatic Corridor 16–17, 182–4, *184*, 242
  Piraeus, Greece *18*, 183, 185, 187–8, 190, *191*, 191–2, 193, 194, 215, *215*, 217, 227, 228, 230, 243
  Trieste, Italy 183, 184, 186–7, 188–9, *189*, 190–1, 192, 193, 194
'Adriatic-Ionian Motorway of the Sea' 183, 194n1
Advanced Business Park (ABP) 218–19, 220–1, 224
AEER 35, 36
African National Congress 175
Agricultural Bank of China 152
Ahmed, N. 11
AIB 207
Akademik Lomonosov nuclear power plant 116
Ake Jira Halmahera Community Alliance (Aliansi Masyarakat Ake Jira Halmahera) 37
Alaska, US 115
  see also Polar Silk Road
Albert Dock *see* Royal Albert Dock, London, UK

Aliansi Masyarakat Ake Jira Halmahera (Ake Jira Halmahera Community Alliance) 37
Aliansi Masyarakat Nusantara (Indigenous Peoples' Alliance of Nusantara) 37
All Ceylon Fisher Folk Trade Union of Sri Lanka 83, 84
Allama Iqbal Industrial City SEZ, Pakistan 2
ALMs (arable land minimums) 60, 67, 68
Amin, Samir 168
Anaklia Deep Sea Port project, Georgia 17, 198–200, *199*, *204*, *209*, 210–11, 241
  background and context 200, *201*, 202–3
  capitalization of future infrastructure 204–6
  role of contracts in 206–10
  see also ADC (Anaklia Development Consortium)
Apostolopoulou, E. 10, 193
Appel, Hannah 208
arable land minimums (ALMs) 60, 67, 68
ArcelorMittal 173–4
Arctic 15, 239
  Arctic tundra 118
  climate crisis 15, 113–15, 116, 118–22, 239
  see also Polar Silk Road
Arctic Nations 113
'Arctic Railway' 120
Argentina 147, 148, 150, 239
  China's international loans to 150, 151, 152
  lithium 148, 149, 150
Argueta, B. 86
Arnouts, R. 63
Arnstadt-Ichtershausen, Germany *see* Thuringia, Eastern Germany
Arts, B. 63
Arvedi steelworks 189, 191
ASEAN (Association of Southeast Asian Nations) Economic Community 44

249

Asian Development Bank 45
Asian Infrastructure Investment
  Bank 152, 202
Asia-Pacific Economic Cooperation
  Summit 136
Aspropyrgos logistics area 188, 190, *191*
authoritarian urban development 229–30
Aviation Industry Corporation 224
Ayeywady-Chao Phraya-Mekong Economic
  Cooperation Strategy 44

B

Baai island, Indonesia 32–3
BAIC (Beijing Auto Industrial
  Corporation) 172
Bakker, K. 62
Baku-Tblisi-Kars (BTK) railway 202
Bali, Indonesia
  Celukan Bawang power plant **32**, 33–5
  G20 Summit, 2022 33, 34
Bali Legal Aid Foundation 34
Baltic-Adriatic Corridor 183
Bambirra, Vania 154
Bandung Conference, 1955 130
Bangladesh-China-India-Myanmar
  Economic Corridor 4
Bank of China 152
Bank of Communications 152
Barbados 85
Battery Innovation and Technology
  Center 99
battery production
  Chinese overcapacity 167, 169, 170, 171
  Indonesia 36
  Thuringia, Eastern Germany 15, 93–6,
    97–101, *98*, *100*, 106–8
    acceleration temporal dynamic 95, 101,
      103–5, 106, 107
    stabilization temporal dynamic 95, 101,
      105–6, 107
    waiting temporal dynamic 95, 101–3,
      106, 107
Beazley, R. 9
Beijing Auto Industrial Corporation
  (BAIC) 172
'Beijing consensus' 154
Beijing Winter Olympics, 2022 171
Bengkulu, Indonesia, Teluk Sepang power
  plant 31–3, **32**, **34**
Bering Strait 115
Besedovsky, N. 96
Bharat Petroleum 118
Bhutan 163
Bichler, Simon 205, 207
Biden, Joe 162
Blinken, Anthony 162, 167, 170, 177n2
'blue bonds' 85
blue justice, Indonesia 38–40

Blue Sky Coalition (Koalisi Langit Biru) 33
BMW 98–9, 104
Bolivia 148, 149
Bolshoi Arkitecheskiy 118
Boreal forest (taiga) 118
Brazil 147, 148, 150, 151, 152
Brenner, N. 5, 184
BRI (Belt and Road Initiative) 182–3,
  193, 237–8
  'Belt' component 216–17
  competition between corridors 199
  critical research agenda 12–18, *18*, *19*, 20,
    20, 21–2
  environmental governance failures 61–4
  extractivist corridors 238–40
  future research agenda 244–6
  green BRI 30, 39, 64, 123
  Green Development Coalition 64
  grounded approach to 7–12
  infrastructure studies analyses 9–12
  introduction and overview 1–3, *2*
  Middle Corridor 202, 203
  political ecology analysis 8–9, 10–11, 12
  'Road' component 217
  scale and scope of 3
  as a 'spatial fix' for China's capital
    overaccumulation crisis 1–2, 16, 163,
    165, 167–71, 214, 216, 217, 228–9
  as territorial restructuring 3–7, *6*
BRICS Bank 152
BRICS (Brazil, Russia, India, China,
  South Africa) 165
BRICS+ (Brazil, Russia, India, China,
  South Africa+) 162, 168, 177n1
BRICS New Development Bank 175, 176
Bridgetown Initiative 86
British America Tobacco 190–1
Bruce, Peter 165
BRWCG (Bun Rueang Wetland
  Conservation Group) 52–3
BTK (Baku-Tblisi-Kars) railway 202
Bun Rueang wetland protection, Chaing Rai
  province, Thailand 45, 46–7, *47*, 52–4

C

Cameron, David 82
Canada, Arctic/Polar region 115
capital overaccumulation crisis, China,
  BRI as a 'spatial fix' for 1–2, 16, 163,
  165, 167–71, 214, 216, 217, 228–9
capitalization 205–6, 210
captive CFPPs (coal-fired power plants) 30,
  31, **32**, 36–7
Carbon Adjustment Border Mechanism 173
Cardoso, Fernando 154
Caribbean 4
Carlson, A. 119
Carrai, M.A. 64

250

INDEX

CATL (Contemporary Amperex Technology Co Limited) 98–9, 101, 102–4, 105, 106
CCCC (China Communications Construction Company) 79, 80–1, 83, 224, 226
  Anaklia Port project, Georgia 203
  Trieste, Italy 186, 189, 194
Celukan Bawang power plant, Bali **32**, 33–5
Centre for Environmental Justice 83
CFPPs (coal-fired power plants) 29–31, 169
  South Africa 173, 174, 175–6
  see also Indonesia, CFPPs (coal-fired power plants)
Chaiya community forest dispossession, Nongkai SEZ, Thailand 45, 47–9, *48*, 50–1, 53, 54
Chan, L. 78
Chancay, Peru 10, *20*
Chaniago, Andrinof 137
CHB (China Development Bank) 149, 150
CHEC (China Harbour Engineering Company) 79, 82, 224
Cheng, H. 194
CHEXIM (Export-Import Bank of the Republic of China) 149, 150
Chiang Khong Intermodal Facility, Thailand 46
Chiang Khong SEZ, Chaing Rai province, Thailand (Bun Rueang wetland protection) 45, 46–7, 47, 52–4
Chiang Saen, Thailand 46
Chile 147, 148, 149, 151
China
  13th Five-Year Plan (2016–20) 216
  car manufacturers 98
  construction boom 1
  debt-for-nature swaps 85
  East China Sea disputes 163
  'ecocivilization' environmental ideology 59–60, 67
  GDP decline 168–9
  and geopolitics 2
China Communications Construction Company (CCCC) *see* CCCC (China Communications Construction Company)
China Construction Bank 152
China Development Bank (CHB) 149, 150, 175
China Harbour Engineering Company (CHEC) 79, 82, 224
China Huadian 35
China Huadian Corporation 36
China Huadian Engineering 33
'China mall' retailing, South Africa 167
China National Offshore Oil Corporation (CNOOC) 116–17
China National Petroleum Corporation (CNPC) 116, 117

China Ocean Shipping Company (COSCO) *see* COSCO (China Ocean Shipping Company)
China Railway Construction Corporation 70
China Railway Engineering Group 70
China Railway Eryuan Engineering Group 66
China Railway Group 69
China Railway Kunming Group 61, 66
China Road and Bridge Corporation 5
China State Railway Group 61, 66
China-Africa Cooperation Vision 2035 161
China-ASEAN Free Trade Area 44, 47
China-CELAC (Community of Latin American and Caribbean States) Forum, 2015 150
China-Central Asia-Western Asia Economic Corridor 4, 202
China-Europe Land-Sea Express Line 186
China-Indochina Peninsula Economic Corridor 4, 47
China-Laos Railway 14, 59, *60*, 60–1
  Yuxi-Mohan railway (YMR) 14, 61, 65–6, *66*, 70–1
  land occupation issues 61, 63, 67–8
  water shortage issues 61, 63, 68–70
China-Mongolia-Russia Economic Corridor 4
China-Myanmar Economic Corridor 4
China-Pakistan Economic Corridor (CPEC) 4, 163
Chongqing, China 4
Chongqing-Xinjiang-EU transcontinental railway corridor 4
Choyr, Mongolia 4
Chukchi Sea nuclear power plants 116
CIFC (Colombo International Financial City), Sri Lanka 224, 225
City Beautification Program, Sri Lanka 225
climate crisis 97, 243
  Arctic/Polar region 15, 113–15, 116, 118–22, 239
  Indonesia 29, 34, 39
  Southern Africa 161, 170, 173, 174, 176
  Sri Lanka 78, 85–6
CNOOC (China National Offshore Oil Corporation) 116–17
CNPC (China National Petroleum Corporation) 116, 117
coal-fired power plants (CFPPs) *see* CFPPs (coal-fired power plants)
cobalt 115
Cock, Jacklyn 176
Cockayne, R. 172
Coega SEZ, South Africa 166, 167, 172
Colombia 151
Colombo International Financial City (CIFC), Sri Lanka 224, 225

251

Colombo, Sri Lanka
  Colombo Business Centre 226–7
  see also Port City Colombo, Sri Lanka
colonialism
  Arctic/Polar region 114–22, *117*
commodity-boom 147–8, 150
community resistance see
  resistance movements
Contemporary Amperex Technology
  Co Limited (CATL) 98–9, 101, 102–4, 105, 106
Contemporary Amperex Technology
  Thuringia GmbH 96
Conti Group 200
contracts, role of in infrastructure
  developments 206–10
copper
  Arctic/Polar region 115, 119
  Latin American exports to China 148
corporate violence 11
COSCO (China Ocean Shipping
  Company) *19*, *22*, 186
  Piraeus, Athens *18*, 185, 187, 188, 194, 221–3
COVID-19 pandemic 93
  Sri Lanka 81, 82
CPEC (China-Pakistan Economic
  Corridor) 4, 163
Crossrail 219
CRRC 175

D

Dakar Action Plan 2022–24 161
Dalai Lama 165
Darkah, Mongolia 4
Datta, A. 11
Davitashvili, Levan 199
DB Cargo 99, 104
De Oliviera, F.A. 154
debt
  'other debts' 82
  see also Sri Lanka, debt crisis and nature
Debt Service Suspension Initiative, G20 162
Declaration on China-Africa Cooperation on
  Combating Climate Change 161
Delta BEC 174
Denmark 115
Department of Coast Conservation and
  Coastal Resource Management, Sri Lanka 83
dependency theory 168, 239
  Latin America international relations 147, 153–4, 156
Development Corporation Thuringia 100–1
diamonds, South Africa 166
Digital Silk Road 5
Dikson coal project 116, 118
Djalil, Sofyan 136

dockland regeneration, London see Royal
  Albert Dock, London, UK
Dolgan peoples 118, 120
Dongfeng 98
donor-recipient relations 130–1
  see also Jakarta-Bandung High-Speed
    Railway (HRS), Indonesia
DP World London Gateway 218
Duisburg, Germany 4
Durban, South Africa 166

E

Ease of Doing Business index rating,
  Georgia 208
East Africa, LAPSSET (Lamu Port-South
  Sudan-Ethiopia Transport Corridor) 5
East China Sea, ocean territory
  disputes 162–3
Eastern Germany
  socioeconomic development 99–100, 105–6
  see also Thuringia, Eastern Germany
ECLAC (United Nations Economic
  Commission for Latin America and the
  Caribbean) 151
ecological economics, languages of
  valuation 30, 39
ECRLs (eco-environmental redlines) 60, 67
Ecuador 85, 148, 150, 151
Egypt 168
Ehfurter-Kreuz industrial park see Thuringia,
  Eastern Germany
EJAtlas (Global Atlas of Environmental
  Justice) 13, 30, 31, **32**
Eksom 175–6
embodied energy justice, Indonesia 38–40, 240–1
environmental flows, metabolism of 8, 9
environmental governance failures 61–4
environmental issues 12, 240–1
  embodied energy justice, Indonesia 38–40, 240–1
  Piraeus, Greece 222–3
  see also resistance movements
Equatorial Guinea 208
Ethiopia-Djibouti Railway 64
Eurasian Land Bridge 218
European Bank for Reconstruction and
  Development 202, 207
European Central Bank 185
European Commission 185
European Commission Free Zone-Type II 222
European Union (EU) 185
  Baltic-Adriatic Corridor 183
  car manufacturers 98–9
  European Union Global Gateway 13
  green transition 15, 93–4
  Next Generation EU Plan 186

INDEX

TRACECA (Transport Corridor Europe-Caucasus-Asia) 202
EV (Electric Vehicle) production
  Brazil 150
  Chinese overcapacity 167, 169, 170, 171
  see also battery production
Export-Import Bank of China 5, 36
  Kenya railway infrastructure development 21
Export-Import Bank of the Republic of China (CHEXIM) 149, 150
extractivism
  Arctic/Polar region 113–14, 115, 116–22, 239
  extractivist corridors 237, 238–40
  Southern Africa 165, 169, 239

F

Faletto, Enzo 154
FAW (First Auto Works) 98, 172
FDIs 171
  into China 170
  Chinese investment in Latin America 149, 150
'financialized dependence' 154
Finland 115, 120
FOCAC (Forum on China-Africa Cooperation) 161, 162, 163, 176, 177
Foreign Corrupt Practices Act, US 175
Fraunhofer Institute for Ceramic Technologies and Systems 99

G

G20, Debt Service Suspension Initiative 162
Galeano, Eduardo 155
Gaza 168
gentrification
  Colombo, Sri Lanka 229
  Royal Albert Dock, London 220
Georgia
  Ease of Doing Business index rating 208
  see also Anaklia Deep Sea Port project, Georgia
Georgieva, Kristalina 168
GLA (Greater London Authority) 219
Global Atlas of Environmental Justice (EJAtlas) 13, 30, 31, **32**
global financial crisis 2008 1, 148, 222
global 'infrastructure turn' 59, 93–4, 183, 192
Global Landscape Forum of the Arctic Landscapes 120
'Global Maritime Fulcrum,' Indonesia 133
GMS (Greater Mekong Subregion) 44, 230
  Greater Mekong Subregion Economic Cooperation Programme 44, 45
  North-South Economic Corridor 46, 47

'Going Out' Strategy, China 29, 148, 149
gold, South Africa 166
Gordhan, Pravin 165
governance failures 61–4
  China-Laos Railway 14, 59
Great Arctic State Nature Reserve 118
'Great Silk Way,' Georgia 200, 202
Great Western Development, China 1
Greater London Authority (GLA) 219
Greater Mekong Subregion (GMS) *see* GMS (Greater Mekong Subregion)
Greece
  debt crisis and bailout 185
  see also Piraeus Port, Athens, Greece
green BRI 30, 39, 64, 123, 243
Green Canopy (Kanopi Hijau) 33
'green development' 8–9
Greenland 115
Greenpeace, Bali 34–5
greenwashing 86
  CATL (Contemporary Amperex Technology Co Limited) 106
Guangzhou, China 186, 217
Gupta family business empire 175
Gwasar, Baluchistan 4
Gydan Peninsula LNG project 116–17

H

Hairong, Yan 166
Hambantoto International Port, Sri Lanka 76, 78, 79
Hamburger Hafen und Logistik AG (HHLA) 186, 189, 194
Hancox, D. 220
Harlan, T. 8–9
Hart, G. 217
Harvey, David 168
Hatta, Mohammad 131–2
Healy, N. 38
Hellenic Republic Asset Development Fund (HRADF) 221
HHLA (Hamburger Hafen und Logistik AG) 186, 189, 194
hinterland areas, logistical network expansion in 4–5
Hisense 186
Hitachi 175
Howlett, M. 62
HRADF (Hellenic Republic Asset Development Fund) 221
Huang, Mingwei 167
Huayou Group 36
Hung, Ho-fung 169
Hyundai 98

I

IBCB 152
Ichterhausen *see* Thuringia, Eastern Germany

IDB (Inter-American Development
    Bank) 150
IMF (International Monetary Fund) 77,
    85–6, 168, 171, 185
Independent Power Producers, South
    Africa 170
India 163
India-Middle East-Europe Economic
    Corridor 13
Indian Ocean
    China's access to 4, 225
    LAPSSET (Lamu Port-South
    Sudan-Ethiopia Transport Corridor) 5
Indian Oil Corporation 118
Indigenous peoples 245
    Arctic Nations 113, 114, 116, 117, 118–22
Indonesia, resistance to CFPPs (coal-fired
    power plants) 36–7
Indigenous Peoples' Alliance of Nusantara
    (Aliansi Masyarakat Nusantara) 37
Indonesia
    CFPPs (coal-fired power plants) 13, 240–1
    Celukan Bawang power plant,
        Bali **32**, 33–5
    community resistance 30, 32–3, 34–7,
        38–40
    context and overview 29–31
    embodied energy justice and blue
        justice 38–40, 240–1
    IWIP (Indonesia Weda Bay Industrial
        Park), North Maluku **32**, 36–7, 39
    Sumsel-8 (Bangko Tengah) power plant,
        South Sumatra **32**, 35–6
    Teluk Sepang power plant, Bengkulu
        31–3, **32**, **34**
    and China 130
    and Japan 129–30
    Just Energy Transition Partnership 33
    see also Jakarta-Bandung High-Speed
        Railway (HSR), Indonesia
Indonesia Morawali Industrial Park 130
Indonesia Weda Bay Industrial Park (IWIP),
    North Maluku, Indonesia **32**, 36–7, 39
Industrial Development Corporation, South
    Africa 172
inequality issues 11–12
    and infrastructure-led development 17,
        214–18, 231–2
    Colombo Port City, Sri Lanka 215, 217,
        224–7, 228, 229, 230
    Piraeus Port, Athens, Greece 215, *215*,
        217, 221–3, 227, 228, 230
    Royal Albert Dock, London, UK 215,
        217, 218–21, 223, 224, 227,
        228, 230
    urban geographies 227–31
Inflation Reduction Act, US 170
infrastructural violence 11–12

infrastructure projects
    'modularity' of 208
    role of contracts in 206–10
'infrastructure turn' 59, 93–4, 183, 192
infrastructure-led development, postcolonial
    geographies analysis 17, 214–18, 231–2
    Colombo Port City, Sri Lanka 215, 217,
        224–7, 228, 229, 230
    Piraeus Port, Athens, Greece 215, *215*,
        217, 221–3, 227, 228, 230
    Royal Albert Dock, London, UK 24, 215,
        217, 218–21, 223, 227, 228, 230
    urban geographies 227–31
Intel 105
Inter-American Development Bank (IDB) 150
international loans
    China-Latin America 149, 150
    China-sub-Saharan Africa 161–2
International Monetary Fund (IMF) 77,
    85–6, 168, 171, 185
international sovereign bonds (ISBs) 77, 87
Iran 168
ISBs (international sovereign bonds) 77, 87
Isiolo, Kenya 6
Israel 168, 170
Ivanishvili, Bidzina 207
IWIP (Indonesia Weda Bay Industrial Park),
    North Maluku, Indonesia **32**, 36–7, 39
Izumi, Hiroto 133

J

Jakarta-Bandung High-Speed Railway
    (HRS), Indonesia 131–4, **133**, 139–42,
    242
    donor competition 15, 129–30
    economic elites/SOEs (state-owned
        enterprises) 131, 138–9, 140, 141
    high-level politicians 131, 135–7
    local agency 134–9, 140
    military 131, 137–8, 139, 140
    PPPs (public-private
        partnerships) 131, 141–2
    regional government political elites 131,
        134–5, 137, 138
Jamaica 3, 152
Japan
    East China Sea disputes 163
    infrastructure investment, Indonesia
        129–30, 139, 140
    Jakarta-Bandung High-Speed Railway
        (HRS), Indonesia 129, 132–3, **133**,
        134, 136–7, 138, 139, 140
    Jakarta-Surabaya MSR (medium-speed
        railway) 15, 132, 137, 138, 140
Japan Arctic LNG 117
Japaridze, Badri 207
Jenkins, R. 156
Jiangsu, China 186

INDEX

JICA 132
Johannesburg, South Africa 164
Johnson, Boris 219
Jokowi *see* Widodo, Joko (Jokowi)
Jonan, Indasius 137
Joniak-Lüthi, A. 9
Just Energy Transition Partnership, Indonesia 33

K

Kamardeen, Naazima 84
Kanai, J.M. 183
Kanopi Hijau (Green Canopy) 33
Kashmir 163
Katsikis, N. 184
Kazakhstan 3
KCIC (Kereta Cepat Indonesia China) 137, 138, 141
Kenya 3
  Kenyan Vision 2030 Plan 6
  LAPSSET (Lamu Port-South Sudan-Ethiopia Transport Corridor) 5, 6, 7, 9
  Northern Corridor *19*
  railway infrastructure development 9, *21*
Kereta Api Indonesia 138
Kereta Cepat Indonesia China (KCIC) 137, 138, 141
Khan, Sadiq 220–1
Khazaradze, Mamuka 207
Kissinger, Henry 164
Koalisi Langit Biru (Blue Sky Coalition) 33
Koster, Wayan 35
Kunming, Yunnan province *60*, 60–1
  see also China-Laos Railway
Kusile CFPP, South Africa 175–6
Kvirikashvili, Giorgi 207

L

labour force issues 7–8, 230, 241
  Colombo, Sri Lanka 225
  Piraeus, Greece 222
  see also resistance movements
Lahore, Pakistan 9, *19*
land dispossession, Thailand 49–51
land occupation issues, Yuxi-Mohan railway (YMR) 61, 63, 67–8
languages of valuation 30, 39
Lao PDR
  Economic Quadrangle 45–6
  and Thailand's SEZs 14, 45, 48, 49
  see also China-Laos Railway
LAPSSET (Lamu Port-South Sudan-Ethiopia Transport Corridor) 5, 6, 7, 9
Lassoie, J.P. 9
Latin America 4, 16, 146–7, 155–6, 239
  commercial relationships 147–9
  dependency, development and postcolonial relationships 152–5
  financial relationships 149–51
  infrastructure and the BRI 151–2
Lavrov, Sergei 168
Lee, C.K. 64
Lekalakala, Makoma 176
Lemos, M.C. 62
Lesutis, G. 9
LG Chem, South Korea 98
Liebherr 175
Lin Songtian 165, 172
lithium 148, 149, 150, 169
Liu, L. 66
LNG, as a 'transition energy' 119
Localism Act 2011, UK 219
logistical network expansion 4–5
London City Airport 219
London Docklands Development Corporation 219
Luxemburg, Rosa 163, 164

M

Mai Sai, Thailand 46
Mandela, Nelson 165
Mao Zedong 164
marine conservation
  debt-for-nature swaps 85–6
  see also Port City Colombo, Sri Lanka
Marini, Ruy Mauro 154, 168
Maritime Silk Road 5, 130, 133
Marxism 153, 154
M&As (mergers and acquisitions)
  Chinese investment in Latin America 149, 150
Massey, D. 94, 217
Mawdsley, E. 141
Medupi CFPP, South Africa 175–6
Mercedes-Benz Group 98
Merryline International Pte Ltd 33–4
Mexican-American War 147
Mexico 151
Middle Corridor, BRI 202, 203
mine-mouth CFPPs (coal-fired power plants) 30, 31, **32**, 35–6
Ministry of Ecology and Environment, China 67
Ministry of Land Resources (MLR), China 67
Ministry of Natural Resources, China 67
Ministry of Railways, China 69–70
Mitchell, Tony 205–6
Mitsotakis, Kyriakos 223
MLR (Ministry of Land Resources), China 67
MMSEZ (Musina-Makhado SEZ), South Africa 166, 167, 172–4, 175, 176
Mongolia *see* China-Mongolia-Russia Economic Corridor
Moramudali, U. 77

'Motorways of the Sea' 194n1
Mottley, Mia Amor 86
Moyo, Sam 168
Mpumalanga coal region, South Africa 166
Murton, G. 193
Muse Border Economic Zone, Myanmar 4
Musina-Makhado SEZ (MMSEZ), South Africa 166, 167, 172–4, 175, 176
Myanmar 65
  Economic Quadrangle 45–6
Myers, M. 152

N

Nagleyngyn nuclear power plants 116
narratives and counter-narratives, grassroots resistance to SEZs, Thailand 53–4, 55
'Naya Nepal' 11
NCPO (National Council for Peace and Order) no 3/2559, Thailand 48
NCPO (National Council for Peace and Order) no 17/2558, Thailand 48
Ndzendzem, Bhaso 177
necropolitics 119
Nenet peoples 117, 120
Nepal 3, 9, 11
Netanyahu, B. 168
New Development Bank 152
New Eurasian Land Bridge Economic Corridor 4
New Silk Road *see* BRI (Belt and Road Initiative)
Next Generation EU Plan 186
Neyra, R. 30
Nganasan peoples 120
Nicholas, B. 77
Nicholas, H. 77
nickel
  Arctic/Polar region 115, 119
  Indonesia 36–7, 39, 130
Nine Programs 161
Ning Yat Hoi 173
Ningbo, China 186
Nitzan, Jonathan 205, 207
Nixon, Richard 164
Nongkai SEZ, Thailand (Chaiya community forest dispossession) 45, 47–9, *48*, 50–1, 53, 54
Nord Axis 118
Nordic countries 115, 116
North Maluku, Indonesia, IWIP (Indonesia Weda Bay Industrial Park) **32**, 36–7, 39
Northeast Area Revitalization, China 1
Northeast Passage 115
Northern Sea corridor 114
Northern Sea Route 113, 115, 116
North-South Corridor, Georgia 202
Northwest passage 115
Northwest Territories, Canada 115

Norway 115, 120
Novatek 116
Nowotny, H. 96
nuclear power
  Arctic/Polar region 116, 118
  as a 'transition energy' 119

O

O Haongana Manyawa (Tobelo Dalam; 'forest people') 37
Obama, Barack 162
Oil India Limited 118
oil pipelines, Georgia 202
Oliviera, G.D.L. 152
Olympia and York 219
'One China' policy, United Nations 164
O'Neill, B. 11
ONGC Videsh 118
Orange Line metro, Lahore, Pakistan 9, *19*
Organization of American States 150
Osborne, N. 119
Our Silent Struggle (West) 119
Overseas Private Investment Corporation 207

P

Palestinians 168, 170
palladium 119
Pandjaitan, Luhut 136
Pandor, Naledi 177n2
Panduwawala, T. 77
Pant, H. 11
Paris Climate Agreement, 2015 174
Partnership for Global Infrastructure and Development 13
Partnership for Quality Infrastructure (PQI) policy 15, 129
PCT (Piraeus Container Terminal) 187, 221
  see also Piraeus, Athens, Greece
People's Movement Against the Port City 84
People's Plan 1983, London, UK 219
'peripheral financialization' 154
Perlus Technology 36
permafrost 118
Peru 147, 150
Peters, B.G. 62
Pevek Harbour nuclear power plant 116
Philippines 162
'pink tide' 148
Piraeus, Athens, Greece *18*, 183, 185, 187–8, 190, *191*, 191–2, 193, 194, 215, *215*, 217, 221–3, 227, 228, 230, 243
Piraeus Container Terminal (PCT) 187, 221
Piraeus Port Authority (PPA) 185, 188, 221
Pizarro, A. 10
platinum 166
'pluritemporalism' 96
Polar Corridor 15, 120

INDEX

Polar Silk Road 5, 15, 113–14, 121–2, 239
  Arctic colonialism and BRI extension 114–18, *117*
  resistance to 114, 116, 118–21, 122, 243
political guarantees, role of in infrastructure developments 206–8
polychronism 95, 107, 240
  see also temporality, in infrastructure development
Port City Colombo, Sri Lanka 78, *78*, 79–82, 215, 217, 224–7, 228, 229, 230, 238, 244
  Colombo Port City Economic Commission Bill 81–2
  EIA (environmental impact assessment) 83, 84
  SEIA (supplementary environmental impact assessment) 81, 83–4
  social and environmental debts 82–5
postcolonial dependency
  China-Latin America relations 147
  Latin American international relations 153, 155
postcolonial geographies analysis 17, 214–18, 231–2
  Colombo Port City, Sri Lanka 215, 217, 224–7, 228, 229, 230
  Piraeus Port, Athens, Greece 215, *215*, 217, 221–3, 227, 228, 230
  Royal Albert Dock, London, UK 215, 217, 218–21, 223, 224, 227, 228, 230
  urban geographies 227–31
PowerChina (Power Construction Corporation of China) 32
PPA (Piraeus Port Authority) 185, 188, 221
  see also Piraeus, Athens, Greece
PPPs (public-private partnerships)
  Georgia 203 (*see also* Anaklia Deep Sea Port project, Georgia)
  Indonesia 131, 132, 139
  Jakarta-Bandung High-Speed Railway (HRS), Indonesia 131, 141–2
PQI (Partnership for Quality Infrastructure) policy 15, 129
Prashad, Vijay 169
'pre-approval land use' (*xianxing yongdi*) 67
Project Company, Port City Colombo, Sri Lanka 81, 84
PSA Peugeot Citroën 98
PT General Energy Bali 33–4
PT General Energy Indonesia 34
PT HBAB (PT Huadian Bukit Asam Power) 35
PT Intraco Penta 32
PT PLN, Indonesia 31, 32
PT SBP (PT Sawindo Bumi Permai) 35–6
PT Tenaga Listrik Bengkulu 32
PT Weda Bay Nickel 37
PT Wijaya Karya 141
PTBA (PT Bukit Asam Tbk) 35
Putin, Vladimir 117, 168
Putnam, R.D. 134

R

Radicati, A. 78
Rail Logistics Center, Thuringia 99, 103–4
Rais, N. 154
Rajapaksa, Gotabaya 76, 81, 224
Rajapaksa, Mahinda 79, 80, 81
Ramaphosa, Cyril 165, 172, 173
Ranawana, A.M. 78
rare earth minerals 121
redlining, China 60, 67, 68
Rencana Pembanguan Kangka Nasional (RPJMN) 2015–2019 143
renminbi, as a hard currency 162
resistance movements 230, 242–4, 245
  CFPPs (coal-fired power plants), Indonesia 30, 32–3, 34–7, 38–40, 242–3
  Colombo, Sri Lanka 225, 226
  Piraeus, Greece 222–3
  Polar Silk Road 113, 114, 116, 117, 118–21, 122, 243
  Royal Albert Dock regeneration, London, UK 220
  SEZs, Thailand 53–4, 55
Richards Bay, South Africa 166
Rikoti highway, West Georgia 202
Roberts, Michael 168, 169
robots, China 169
Rodgers, D. 11
Rogelja, I. 38
Rosneft 118
Ross, John 168–9, 170
Royal Albert Dock, London, UK 215, 217, 218–21, 223, 224, 227, 228, 230, 241–2, 244
RPJMN (Rencana Pembanguan Kangka Nasional) 2015–2019 143
Ruili, China 4
Russia
  Arctic/Polar region 115, 116, 121
  and China 113
  Russian Far East 113
  war against Ukraine 162, 168, 177n2, 203
  see also China-Mongolia-Russia Economic Corridor

S

Sabetta port project 116
Sámi peoples 119, 120
Samsung C&T 106
Samsung SDI 98
Sarvananthan, M. 77
Saudi Arabia 168
Sautman, Barry 166

257

scale, in environmental governance
  failures 63–4
Schindler, S. 183
Second Cold War 187
Seychelles 85
SEZ Policy Committee Announcement no 2/2558, Thailand 48
SEZs (special economic zones) 44
  Allama Iqbal Industrial City SEZ, Pakistan 2
  South Africa
    Coega SEZ 166, 167, 172
    MMSEZ (Musina-Makhado SEZ) 166, 167, 172–4, 175, 176
  Thailand 13–14, 44–5, 54–5, 243
    Chiang Khong SEZ, Chaing Rai province (Bun Rueang wetland protection) 45, 46–7, 47, 52–4
    development context 45–9, 47, *48*
    grassroots movements against 45, 47, 52–5
    Nongkai SEZ (Chaiya community forest dispossession) 45, 47–9, *48*, 50–1, 53, 54
  state-making through SEZ territorialization 49–51
Shanghai, China 186, 217
Shanghai Zhenhua Heavy Industries 175
Shenzen, China 186
Shevardnadze, Eduard 200, 202
Silk Road Fund 116
Silk Road on Ice *see* Polar Silk Road
Silver, J. 104–5
Sino-Inner Asia borderlands 9
Sirisena, Maithripala 80, 81, 226
Sivaram, K. 80
Skosana, Dineo 176
'social time' 96
Soemarno, Rini 136
SOEs (state-owned enterprises), Indonesia 131, 132, 133, 135, 136, 138–9
solar energy equipment, Chinese overcapacity in 167, 169, 170, 171
South Africa
  apartheid regime 164–5, 244
  carbon emissions 174
  'China mall' retailing 167
  Chinese investment and the BRI 16, 165–7, 169
  colonialism 164
  deindustrialization 174–5
  infrastructure corruption and coal-export dependency 174–5
  and Israel 168
  'Rainbow Nation' vision 163–4
  SEZs (special economic zones) 166, 167, 172–4, 175, 176
  see also Southern Africa
South China Sea 162

South Korea 163
South Sumatra, Indonesia
  Sumsel-8 (Bangko Tengah) power plant **32**, 35–6
Southern Africa 16, 161–2, 163
  see also South Africa
Southern African Development Community 166, 173
South-South relations 153, 163, 239–40
Space Silk Road 5
Sri Lanka 244
  debt crisis and nature 14–15, 76–8, *78*, 82–5, 86–7, 238–9
  debt-for-nature swaps 78, 85–6, 239
  political economy 79–82
  see also Port City Colombo, Sri Lanka
Sri Lanka Ports Authority 79, 83
stabilization temporal dynamic, EV (Electric Vehicle) battery production, Thuringia, Eastern Germany 95, 101, 105–6, 107
Stallings, B. 149–50, 154
Standing, A. 87
Star, S.L. 209–10
State Development Corporation of Thuringia 99, 101, 102–3, 107–8
steel industry, overcapacity in 173–4
Subianto, Prabowo 135, 138
Suga, Yoshihide 129, 132, 134
Sumsel-8 (Bangko Tengah) power plant, South Sumatra, Indonesia **32**, 35–6
SungEel HiTec 106
Sutusna, Aa Umbara 137
Sweden 115

T

Taiwan 164–5
Taiwan Strait 162
Tangier, Morocco 21, *245*
Tanjung Agung Bersatu Community Forum 35–6
Taymyr Peninsula 116, 117–18
TBC 200
Teluk Sepang power plant, Bengkulu, Indonesia 31–3, **32**, **34**
temporality, in infrastructure
  development 94, 96–7, 240
  EV (Electric Vehicle) battery production, Thuringia, Eastern Germany 94–5, 106–8
  acceleration temporal dynamic 95, 101, 103–5, 106, 107
  stabilization temporal dynamic 95, 101, 105–6, 107
  waiting temporal dynamic 95, 101–3, 106, 107
TEN-T (continental railway network) 188, 194n1
territorial restructuring, BRI (Belt and Road Initiative) as 3–7, *6*

INDEX

Thailand
  Economic Quadrangle 45–6
  SEZs (special economic zones) 13–14, 44–5, 54–5, 243
    Chiang Khong SEZ, Chaing Rai province (Bun Rueang wetland protection) 45, 46–7, *47*, 52–4
    development context 45–9, *47*, *48*
    grassroots movements against 45, 47, 52–5, 243
    Nongkai SEZ (Chaiya community forest dispossession) 45, 47–9, *48*, 50–1, 53, 54
    state-making through SEZ territorialization 49–51
Thriasio Logistics Centre 188
Thuringia, Eastern Germany
  EV (Electric Vehicle) battery production 15, 93–6, 97–101, *98*, *100*, 106–8, 240
  acceleration temporal dynamic 95, 101, 103–5, 106, 107
  stabilization temporal dynamic 95, 101, 105–6, 107
  waiting temporal dynamic 95, 101–3, 106, 107
  property prices 104
  tourism development 104
Thuringian state government 100–1, 107
  Thuringian Ministry of Economic Affairs, Science and Digital Society 99, 107
Tianjin, China 4
Tiefensee, Wolfgang 105
Tobelo Dalam; 'forest people' (O Haongana Manyawa) 37
TotalEnergies 116, 117
Toussaint, Eric 172
Town Planning Act BE 2518 (1975), Thailand 48
Toyota 98
TRACECA (Transport Corridor Europe-Caucasus-Asia), EU 202
Transalpine Pipeline Terminal 188
Transnet 175
Transpolar Sea Route 115
Tricontinental Institute 168, 169
Trieste, Italy 183, 184, 186–7, 188–9, *189*, 190–1, 192, 193, 194
Trump, Donald 162, 227
Tsingshan Group 36
Tsipras, Alexis 221
Tskitishvili, Maia 207, 208
Tutu, Desmond 163–4
'two-level games,' Jakarta-Bandung High-Speed Railway (HRS), Indonesia 131, 134–5, 139–40

U

Ukraine, Russia's war against 162, 168, 177n2, 203
UK-Yiwu rail link 218
Ulan-Ude, Russia 4
ulayat (community-owned) land, Indonesia 35–6
United Arab Emirates 168
United Nations
  Glasgow climate summit 173
  'One China' policy 164
  Sustainable Development Goals 227
United Nations Economic Commission for Latin America and the Caribbean (ECLAC) 151
United Nations General Assembly 29, 173, 174
United States
  Arctic/Polar region 115, 121
  and China 2, 187
  declining hegemony of 217
  Foreign Corrupt Practices Act 175
  Inflation Reduction Act 170
  interest rate increases, 2022–23 170
  international relations policy 162
  and Latin America 147, 148, 153, 156
  protectionist policies 227
  US dollar, as a currency 162
  'Washington consensus' 154
University of Moratuwa 83
urban growth boundaries 60
urban transformation, postcolonial geographies analysis 17, 214–18, 231–2
  Colombo Port City, Sri Lanka 215, 217, 224–7, 228, 229, 230
  Piraeus Port, Athens, Greece 215, *215*, 217, 221–3, 227, 228, 230
  Royal Albert Dock, London, UK 215, 217, 218–21, 223, 224, 227, 228, 230
  urban geographies 227–31

V

Valencia port, Spain *21*
valuation, languages of 30, 39
van Rooyen, Desmond 165
Velenje, Slovenia 186
Venezuela 148, 150, 152
Ventiane Industrial and Trade Area 49
Ventiane, Lao PDR *60*, 60–1
  see also China-Laos Railway
Vietnam 162
Volkswagen 98, 99
von der Leyen, Ursula 167
Vostok mega oil project 116, 117–18
vulnerable groups 7, 9–10

W

Wainwright, O. 221
waiting temporal dynamic, EV (Electric Vehicle) battery production, Thuringia, Eastern Germany 95, 101–3, 106, 107
WALHI 33
Wall, A. 183

'Washington consensus' 154
water shortage issues, Yuxi-Mohan railway
    (YMR) 61, 63, 68–70
Watson, C. 86
West Bandung Regency, Indonesia
    137, 140
West Java, Indonesia 137
West, Suvi 119
Western Region Megapolis,
    Sri Lanka 79, 225
Western time 96
wetlands, Bun Rueang wetland protection,
    Chaing Rai province, Thailand 45, 46–7,
    47, 52–4
Wickremesinghe, Ranil 80
Widodo, Joko (Jokowi) 31, 32–3
  Jakarta-Bandung High-Speed Railway
    (HRS), Indonesia 129, 132, 134, 135–7,
    138, 139–40, 141
Wiig, A. 104–5
*Wijana Surfarlan, Astava & Greenpeace
    Indonesia v Governor of
    Bali* 34–5
Wise, C. 147
Woods, O. 78
Wooley, A. 76
World Bank 44, 164, 202
World Trade Organization 148

X

Xi Jinping 1, 29, 80, 130, 133, 151, 163,
    167, 172, 173, 174, 175, 202, 221–2
xianxing yongdi ('pre-approval land use') 67
Xinjiang, China 4

Y

Yamal peninsula, LPG project 116, 117
Yang, H.K. 164
Yellen, Janet 167, 168, 169, 170
Yeros, Paris 168
Yiwu Timex Industrial Investment Co 218
Yudhoyono, Susilo Bambang 31, 132, 135
Yunnan province, China
  Economic Quadrangle 45–6
  GMS North-South Economic Corridor 46, 47
  see also China-Laos Railway
Yuxi-Mohan Railway (YMR) *see*
    China-Laos Railway

Z

Zallinger, B. 209
Zeidermann, A. 242
Zhang, Xia 171
Zhenshi Group 36
Zhou Enlia 163
Zimbabwe 163
Zuma, Jocob 165

www.ingramcontent.com/pod-product-compliance
Lightning Source LLC
Chambersburg PA
CBHW051532020426
42333CB00016B/1895